Issues In Christian Thought

Issues In Christian Thought

JOHN B. HARRINGTON
Professor of Philosophy
Lewis and Clark College

MCGRAW-HILL
BOOK COMPANY
NEW YORK
ST. LOUIS
SAN FRANCISCO
TORONTO
LONDON
SYDNEY

Issues In Christian Thought

Library of Congress Catalog Card Number 68-13515

26746

1234567890   MAMM   7432106987

The issues presented in this book are contemporary, and yet they are among man's perennial concerns. The readings reflect twentieth-century thought, but again, the various writers make connection with the continuing Judeo-Christian heritage. These selections begin with "The Lost Dimension in Religion" in today's world and end with the challenge to traditional beliefs posed by the "death of God" theologians. Between the first and last pages, the student is invited to think through problems about God, man and the language we use to express the divine-human relationship.

A distinctive feature of this book is that two kinds of material are included: the text portion by the author and twenty-four carefully selected readings by contemporary writers (with the one exception of Søren Kierkegaard, who really belongs to our twentieth century insofar as influence is concerned). Each reading has been chosen to speak to the particular issue under discussion; taken together, the readings form a coherent sequence and feed into each other. The various chapters of the text are designed not to give an exposition of the readings but rather to focus on the problems with which the readings deal. Thus the student is encouraged to use both the author's text and the readings as a stimulus to his own thinking. In some instances, the reader will want to turn to the reading selection immediately and then go back to the text chapter related to it. Each reader will find his own way. Most important, the Suggested Reading list at the end of the book will aid further exploration of topics of special interest.

Three kinds of concern, with materials appropriate to each, are involved in this textbook: historical, theological and philosophical. This suggests that the book may be found useful in different kinds of college courses. Thus a course offered by a department of religion could concentrate on the historical and/or doctrinal materials. And a philosophy of religion course, offered by either a department of philosophy or a department of religion, would find the philosophical portions helpful. Or a course in contemporary religious thought might well center on today's theological issues. In each instance, supplementary readings would fill in more specific content. This text is frankly oriented in the Western, Judeo-Christian tradition, but it might well serve as an integral part of total curricula in the history of religions in which the Judeo-Christian heritage is contrasted and compared with non-Western religions.

Part I of the book, "The Judeo-Christian Faith," in particular, centers on the historical background of the Judeo-Christian tradition and yet includes theological problems and philosophical inquiry about the religious and theological uses of language. This first part, although it may seem traditional, provides background essential for contemporary religious thought. Part II, "Can the Christian Theist Justify His Central Claim?" moves more directly to discussion of the relations of religion and theology to philosophy. The analysis of religious and theological uses of language comes to focus in this part. Then the student is encouraged to stand with contemporary philosophers and take a new look at the so-called arguments for the existence of God. Part III, "Challenges to Contemporary Man," continues this philosophical concern about how we can possibly "verify" the theist's claims. But, then, the final two chapters involve the student in the thinking of Existentialists and the new, radical theologians. Where do we go from here? The issues are not settled. The questions are open-ended. Religious thought is now in flux. A new generation perhaps needs to learn how to think in these areas more than it needs settled answers. The last chapter and readings ask: Are we living in a post-Christian age, theologically and culturally? If so, how shall today's men and women meet the challenge? I hope this book will make some contribution to this end.

I wish to express appreciation to Georgiana Bertholf, Emma Jahnke, Sheila Johnson and my wife, Carolyn, for invaluable assistance in preparing the manuscript and the details of correspondence.

John B. Harrington

Contents

Issues In Christian Thought

Introduction: The Religious Dimension

Critical study of the article by Paul Tillich, "The Lost Dimension in Religion," raises some basic questions. We begin with this reading selection primarily because it sharpens our understanding of the predicament of man in our time. Also this theologian, who is among the most outstanding contemporary scholars, anticipates so many of the important questions which form the content of our whole study of religion. We may not settle all these questions at the outset, but it is essential to see what tasks challenge modern man with urgency and insistence.

Religion and the Religious

Tillich's article raises questions and issues like the following: May a distinction be made between the noun *religion* and the adjective *religious*? Is religion nothing but the beliefs, symbols and practices of specific historical traditions? Or is "religion in its innermost nature" more adequately characterized by the phrase "the religious dimension of depth"? Words and phrases like "depth" and "dimension of depth" are spatial metaphors. It requires imagination to catch the nonliteral, symbolic use of such terms.

Religion may thus be both narrowly and broadly interpreted. We speak of specific religions as against the more general designation, "the religious dimension." This distinction is an aid to understanding, but it also poses a serious dilemma. Who are the religious? One view is to say that only those who embrace a particular form of faith, such as Protestant Christianity, are religious. Others say that everyone who lives in the dimension of depth is to be accounted religious. Many who never darken the door of any established church are possessed of an ultimate concern. Are these persons then religious, in the broader sense of the term?

Consider the student in a state of rebellion against the particular beliefs and practices of his own religious tradition. Perhaps his rebellion is itself a form of serious quest, of ultimate concern, of living in a dimension of depth. But surely this student is not religious in the same sense

1

as his classmate who consciously avows his allegiance, for example, to one of the communions of Christianity and, through its specific forms of practice and belief, expresses his commitment of the whole person to his God. Is it then possible to be *religious* without embracing *a religion*? This is the practical thrust which this dilemma takes for many a thoughtful student.

Forms of the Religious Dilemma

The religious dilemma then may be defined in this way: Is it possible to be religious in the broader sense of this term without embracing a particular religion? This dilemma, posed by Tillich's contrast between religion and the religious, takes different forms. But, in all of these, the thoughtful reader will see that there is a tension inherent in man's religious situation itself.

First, mature religious expression does entail the formulation of ordered beliefs, systems of theology and modes of worship and conduct. Yet forms become cold and impersonal. Firsthand religion is personal; it involves the whole beings of men and women. The religious has to do with the way men and women orient all their energies toward a single and total allegiance.

A second form of dilemma is involved here. The religious dimension does not afford means of escape from the joys and responsibilities of *this* world, but neither is it identical with any of the specialized functions which men carry out in their individual and social lives. Yet, on the other hand, religion has to do with the way in which men and women focus all these everyday concerns into a central unity of purpose. Religion cannot be pinned down in a specialized area of human life. It is not one more department added to all the rest, as if religion were alongside economics, politics, business, science, art, as is the formal study of "religion" in the university curriculum. For, as Tillich writes elsewhere of firsthand religion: "It is at home everywhere, namely, in the depth of all functions of man's spiritual life. Religion is the dimension of depth in all of them. Religion is the aspect of depth in the totality of the human spirit."[1]

A third aspect of our study involves the meanings of the terms "religion," "religious," "religious dimension of depth," "depth" and "ultimate concern." For the dilemma of the religious life strikes us in

---

[1] Paul Tillich, "Religion as a Dimension in Man's Spiritual Life," *Theology of Culture,* ed. by Robert C. Kimball, Oxford University Press, Fair Lawn, N.J., 1959, p. 6.

another form. The problem is not simply that of tension between the formal and the personal or between religion as a special activity and as a way of focusing all human activities into a central purpose. The urgent question is this: Is everyone who undertakes a serious quest religious? Some men never find that for which they seek. Is it the asking that is all-important? Are there no answers? Yet, for Tillich, it is the concern that matters—an "ultimate concern." Everybody seems then to have an ultimate concern. There is a difference between an ultimate concern and all the essential particular concerns we have for food, shelter, work, recreation, the fulfillment of human love and the like. But the question returns. What of those who have never found a satisfying form of religious faith? Can men live without answers? Is the seeking enough? Tillich seems to suggest that it is possible to live with ultimate concern without finding concrete expression through the beliefs and practices of a particular historic religious community. This is the paradoxical situation in which many thoughtful students are practically involved. Is it possible to be religious without a religion?

Pointing toward a Definition

It is difficult to define the term "religion" in contrast to "religious." Positively speaking, we find it helpful to use the adjective *religious* rather than the noun *religion*. For, in a sense, religion is nothing in itself. It is not a thing or an entity. The religious involves the whole personality of men and women. It is a functional word used to describe what happens to people when they come into vital relationship with an object of supreme and total devotion. John Hutchison speaks of religion as "total life-orientation." Its function is not to explain or to inform as the sciences do. Rather religion relates whole persons to what for them is of highest value. There are consequences of orienting one's entire life with singleness of direction and purpose. In view of this total life-orientation a man enters into distinctive relationships with the world of nature, history and other persons around him. He focuses *all* that he lives for into a single concern in terms of which everything else finally makes sense.

I have recorded elsewhere[2] the story of David Livingstone, the courageous Christian missionary, as he received an honorary degree from one of

[2] John B. Harrington, *Essentials in Christian Faith*, Harper & Row, Publishers, Incorporated, New York, 1958, pp. 94–95. I have been unable to trace the source of this incident.

the Scottish universities. On such occasions the students sat in the balcony and called out all sorts of names and raucous remarks. One wonders what they did when Livingstone stood there with injured arm hanging limp at one side and his face like leather. What did the students do in the presence of a person like this? They rose as one man and stood in absolute silence.

This response is not to abstract moral codes nor to systems of theological creed nor to universal philosophical principles. Youth and age alike rather respond to a vibrant person who has committed his whole being to that which he holds to be the source and center of meaning for human existence. For this is the dynamic quality of the religious dimension which, in the case of a man like David Livingstone, had taken him to the edge of civilization and back again to fulfill his all-consuming purpose. Paul Tillich uses the term "ultimate concern" to express this characteristic religious response. In his *Systematic Theology*, he says:

> Ultimate concern is the abstract translation of the great commandment: "The Lord, our God, the Lord is one; you shall love the Lord your God with all your heart, and with all your soul and with all your mind, and with all your strength" [Mark 12:29, Revised Standard Version]. The religious concern is ultimate; it excludes all other concerns from ultimate significance; it makes them preliminary. The ultimate is unconditional, independent of any condition of character, desire or circumstance. The unconditional concern is total; no part of ourselves or of our world is excluded from it; there is no "place" to flee from it [Psalm 139]. The total concern is infinite: no moment of relaxation and rest is possible in the face of a religious concern which is ultimate, unconditional, total and infinite.[3]

Religion is thus, in one perspective, the *quest* for the ground and goal of human existence, the search for some unifying purpose, the desire for personal relationship with some final object of utter loyalty. To embark on this quest is to live in the religious dimension. But we record a critical comment. If we take Tillich seriously, we would agree that every person is at least capable of asking these serious questions. But it is not appropriate to say that everyone has found an answer, expressed in specific forms of worship, practice and belief. It is essential, therefore, to distinguish the religious as quest from religion as answer. Seeking with serious concern is different from settled commitment. Not all who seek succeed in finding.

[3] By permission. From Paul Tillich, *Systematic Theology*, The University of Chicago Press, Chicago, 1951, vol. I, pp. 11–12.

Modern Man's Predicament

In the selected reading, Tillich claims that the contemporary religious situation is characterized by the loss of ultimate or infinite concern and the loss of the dimension of depth. As we have suggested, "depth" is a spatial metaphor. It requires imagination to catch the nonliteral, symbolic use of words like these. What ails modern man? "Immorality . . . impiety," some voices thunder from pulpits, judges' benches, college convocation platforms. But, says Tillich: "Modern man is neither more pious nor more impious than man in any other period." The loss of the dimension of depth is due to man's relation to himself and his world. He is busy using science and technology to bring nature under control. Goals of "bigger and better" and "more and more" drive him on and on. Man extends his conquests even out into the far reaches of interplantary space. He wants to know and transform his universe. This is, metaphorically speaking, the "horizontal dimension" replacing the "dimension of depth," in which we all are involved.

But we are reminded not to disparage this kind of drive and way of speaking, for man must have confidence in his ability to bring the forces of nature under scientific understanding and technical control. Nonetheless, we would ask what man is doing and seeking on the horizontal dimension. It is not enough to say that he is merely intoxicated with sheer movement, for, in surging ahead, man is transforming his world and thereby himself. He is engaged in changing everything into a tool and therefore himself into a tool. "But if he asks, a tool for what, there is no answer."

This situation is modern man's predicament. He fills each moment with pressing demands. Tillich asks each man to stop and become aware of himself, not caring what comes next in the push of practical affairs, silencing the voices of the many immediate demands and listening to ". . . the voice of the ultimate concern." Loss of this kind of sensitivity is ". . . the loss of religion in its basic and universal meaning."

The Religious Use of Language

Every religion uses language of word, act and sacred object to point beyond itself to the ultimate. Religious expression employs symbols in a way that differs from the methods of the sciences or commonsense experience. To confuse these uses of language creates serious misunderstanding. We shall be concerned with the more precise functions of religious language in later chapters and readings. Meanwhile, the Tillich selection opens up this central issue for us.

Defenders of religion sometimes treat religious utterances as if they were of the same order as the factual statements of the scientists or the informative statements of everyday affairs. Critics of religion often make the same mistake as its defenders, that of confusing language uses and appropriate categories. The result is frequently a senseless argument that ought never to have started.

Scientific hypotheses require experimental verification, in precise terms, usually expressed in mathematical correlations. Here the end to be achieved is description, explanation, prediction and control of phenomena in nature. Religious utterances do not serve the same purpose. If statements of religious faith fail to meet the test required of scientific explanatory hypotheses, we need to ask what distinctive role they do serve. There is no scientific *evidence* for believing such statements as the following: "In the beginning God created the heavens and the earth." "God is love." "God so loved the world that He gave His only begotten Son." Tests of experiment and observation applied to these utterances render them false or apparently senseless. Thus the sciences and the religious appear to enter the arena and, standing on the same ground with equal footing, proceed to battle it out to the finish. But such a conflict is a false rivalry based on a grave misunderstanding. This mistake in the uses of language, for Tillich, is a root cause of the disappearance of the "great symbols" of the religions of our Western world and hence also of the loss of the dimension of depth. He states:

> The first step toward the non-religion of the Western world was made by religion itself. When it defended its great symbols, not as symbols, but as literal stories, it had already lost the battle. In doing so the theologians (and today many religious laymen) helped to transfer the powerful expressions of the dimension of depth into objects or happenings on the horizontal plane. There the symbols lose their power and meaning and become an easy prey to physical, biological and historical attack.

We need to consider the religious significance of such biblical accounts as those of creation, the fall of man and the coming of a Savior of the world, as well as the idea of God and symbols like goodness, greatness, power, infinity and love which we apply to Him. And we inquire concerning various views of the nature of man himself, his being and destiny: Are these to be treated as items demanding proof for which evidence is sought and none found? It is a serious question as to whether

God is a being among others whose existence or nonexistence we can argue on the basis of evidence. In every one of these cases, we are liable to make a mistake about the language level on which we choose to move. Mistakenly to use religious symbols as if they were verifiable scientific statements is to shift from the dimension of depth to the horizontal plane.

Awareness of Loss

Is Tillich's conclusion then valid? For he states that when man loses the dimension of depth and the symbols which express it, he himself ". . . becomes a part of the horizontal plane." What does it mean to say that man thus ". . . loses his self and becomes a thing among things"? It is obvious that these modes of expression are themselves couched in metaphors. Tillich seeks to illuminate modern man's situation: "But man has not ceased to be man. He resists this fate [of becoming himself an object or a machine in the processes of production and consumption] anxiously, desperately, courageously. He asks the question for what? And he realizes there is no answer." Man then becomes aware of an emptiness which he only tries to cover over with his many activities. He does not quite know what has happened to him but only that he has lost the "meaning of life." It is on this level and out of this awareness that the religious has any significance and is accepted or rejected.

It is strange therefore that this awareness of the predicament of Western man should find most poignant expression not in the sanctuary of formal religion but in the art, literature and, to some extent, the philosophy of our time. But note that it is the religious question and not necessarily any strong affirmation of religious commitment that is expressed. "This art, literature, philosophy is not religious in the narrower sense of the word; but it asks the religious question more radically and more profoundly than most directly religious expressions of our time."

Is There an Answer?

The concluding paragraphs of the Tillich reading refer to our need today for sincere self-searching. "Is there an answer?" he asks. "There is always an answer, but the answer may not be available to us. We may be too deeply steeped in the predicament out of which the question arises to be able to answer it."

He refers to answers given by popular leaders of mass resurgence of faith and piety, and he states that these men are not dealing with the religious question but simply intensifying the problem to which they claim to bring solutions. As for increase in church attendance and interest in religious activities, this also ". . . does not mean much more than the religious consecration of a state of things in which the religious dimension has been lost." Is it correct to say that many people join churches for social approval and a sense of security? "This is not necessarily bad," Tillich states, "but it certainly is not an answer to the religious question of our period."

Martin E. Marty, in *The New Shape of American Religion,* describes the recent religious revival. He states that what we are witnessing is a broad resurgence of interest in religion but an interest accompanied by an increase in secular ways of thinking and living. In the 1940s, mechanical computers suddenly recorded increasing church attendance and membership statistics. Pollsters armed with questions concerning belief in God reported that almost everyone stated that he held some such belief. Best sellers, popular box-office attractions, businessmen's prayer rooms, popular music with a Gospel beat, the church-building industry, strong emphasis on "sincerity" in belief (no matter in what), all were taken as signs of a religious upsurge. Marty believes that this popular increase in religious interest has seriously affected our views of God and of man:

America has tended to package God, to make Him more marketable. He has been useful to boxers who fervently prayed as they entered the ring intent on severing their opponents' heads from their bodies. He has ridden— they said so!—with daredevils and racers. He has bided time with and guided the fortunes of motion picture actresses of questionable repute— they said He did. He helped rearrange affairs toward the positive prosperity of men.[4]

Here, for the asking, is a religion that can be used to achieve desirable practical ends. Men in our society are already manipulated and used. "There is a danger that religion under the auspices of a revival such as that of the 1950's could conspire in this manipulation." Furthermore, says Marty:

The churches often found themselves riding the band wagon of sanctified manipulation of men. They were in a position to patternize men by *ersatz*

---

[4] From *The New Shape of American Religion,* p. 18, Copyright © Martin E. Marty. Reprinted with the permission of Harper & Row, Publishers, Inc., New York.

versions of Christian fellowship in the use of group dynamics as means toward institutional ends. They could contribute to the passivity of men by preaching the old-time individualist compulsions in a day when individuals could not begin to carry them out. They could, through borrowed techniques of persuasion and projection, further confine already closed-in-upon men. In a time of quest for authentic personhood, the world around the Church was asking but one question of the spokesmen: not, Is what they are saying true? but, Are they sincere? Or, to borrow Hollywood's blurb for the Peter Marshall film, Are they "God's kind of guys"?[5]

Answers That Are No Answers

What shall we think about this movement toward mass religious revival in our time? Back in the eighteenth century, the evangelist tried to ". . . *awaken* a lethargic community to find itself in God." The response was a renewal of the relationship already established between God and the whole community. This relationship was conceived in terms of a covenant or agreement between God and the total community. The eighteenth-century evangelist said to the people in effect: "You were bapitized in this Church, and if you will now come before the body and 'own' the covenant, then your children can in turn be baptized." Marty remarks that this was ". . . the last time in American history that Protestant Christian evangelists could with some plausibility address the community gathered in the church in the spirit of a line from Christopher Fry's play, *A Sleep of Prisoners:* 'You were born here [in church], chum. It's the same for all of us.' "[6]

But in the nineteenth century the evangelist attempted to revive individual Christians and ". . . to ask them to reform the society which was cutting itself off from God." Here the response was that of ". . . personal conversion followed by the organization of reforming institutions." By contrast, at the beginning of the twentieth century, the evangelist ". . . *crusaded* against a mass that was somehow estranged and had cut itself off from the will of God, from which individuals must be separated and saved." Now the ". . . characteristic response was personal decision for Christ."

By the middle of the twentieth century, Marty states, ". . . a completely different presupposition about the environment of mass evangelism existed in the mind of the *evangelist* than existed in the *public's*."[7] No

[5] *Ibid.*, p. 20.
[6] *Ibid.*, p. 23.
[7] *Ibid.*, pp. 22–23. Italics mine.

longer does the total community accept the eighteenth-century assumption that a covenant relationship—a covenant into which men were born—holds between itself and God. Now the crusader charges: "Because we [Americans] are out of the will of God we have lost the will to do right." Marty reminds us that it is a long path from "You were born here" to "You are out of the will of God." The rootage of the eighteenth century is now cut off. But, despite the changed situation, the present-day evangelist still holds to the older assumptions about mass evangelism. A few folk within the nation are of course attracted by the nostalgic appeal of "old-time religion." It is said that the speaker told his hearers that ". . . they were *damned! damned! damned!* This charmed them."[8]

Marty asks: How could this possibly be? How can people listen to a preacher thundering that they were lost only to be "charmed"? "Because *few very seriously read themselves into the pattern of denunciation. . . .* 'You are out of the will of God,' then, was taken to mean somebody else."[9]

A kind of "religion in general," a vague "faith in faith," convenient and useful, has caught on in America. Many, of course, have long since disavowed traditional relationship with any of the existing churches. But these same folk are not ready to read themselves out of the community of religion in general. They may occasionally hear preaching about a God of righteousness and judgment, but they do not feel judged. The result seems to be that even the recent religious revival itself, now virtually spent, moved (in Tillich's terms) on the horizontal dimension and failed to reach modern men where they live in the dimension of depth. Thus the religious "question" remains unanswered.

Toward Genuine Answers

Is there any answer? Tillich says in conclusion:

> There is always an answer, but the answer may not be available to us. We may be too deeply steeped in the predicament out of which the question arises to be able to answer it. To acknowledge this is certainly a better way toward a real answer than to bar the way to it by deceptive answers. And it may be that in this attitude the real answer (within available limits) is given.

[8] *Ibid.,* p. 25.
[9] *Ibid.,* pp. 25–26. Italics mine.

Two sides of religion's expression must be held in balance. Only in this way will it be possible for modern men and women to cope with the dilemma of religious life. To summarize, the dilemma is this: Is it possible to be *religious* without embracing *a religion*? For Tillich reminds us that ". . . the real answer to the question of how to regain the dimension of depth" is not to be found exclusively in increased church membership or attendance. The answer will be discovered by the ". . . awareness that we have lost the decisive dimension of life, the dimension of depth, and that there is no easy way of getting it back."

The point, then, on which this view expressed by Tillich turns is this: that such awareness of our loss is in itself ". . . a state of being grasped by that which is symbolized in the term, dimension of depth." Why is this so? The person who realizes that he is ". . . separated from the ultimate source of meaning shows by this realization that he is not only separated but also reunited."

This, therefore, is the one side of the total situation, that awareness of the religious predicament is essential for churched and unchurched alike. Neither conventional observance of rites nor lip service to traditional words and forms will capture the "creative power" of religion for our culture.

But the other side of the dilemma of the religious situation must also be held in balance. Is it possible to live with ultimate concern without finding specific and concrete expression through the beliefs and practices of a particular historic religious community? The final paragraph of Tillich's article leaves us with a serious question as to what modern-minded men and women intend to do with traditional religious symbols. Some believe they should be dismissed, for they have lost their meaning as interpreted literally. But understood as bearers of an answer to man's perennial religious quest, they become ". . . powerful, revealing and saving symbols." Is such a new understanding of the expressions of religion possible in our day?

1

PAUL TILLICH | *The Lost Dimension*
*in Religion**

Every observer of our Western civilization is aware of the fact that
something has happened to religion. It especially strikes the observer
of the American scene. Everywhere he finds symptoms of what one has
called religious revival, or more modestly, the revival of interest in religion. He finds them in the churches with their rapidly increasing membership. He finds them in the mushroomlike growth of sects. He finds
them on college campuses and in the theological faculties of universities.
Most conspicuously, he finds them in the tremendous success of men like
Billy Graham and Norman Vincent Peale, who attract masses of people
Sunday after Sunday, meeting after meeting. The facts cannot be denied,
but how should they be interpreted? It is my intention to show that these
facts must be seen as expressions of the predicament of Western man in
the second half of the twentieth century. But I would even go a step
further. I believe that the predicament of man in our period gives us also
an important insight into the predicament of man generally—at all times
and in all parts of the earth.

There are many analyses of man and society in our time. Most of them
show important traits in the picture, but few of them succeed in giving a
general key to our present situation. Although it is not easy to find such
a key, I shall attempt it and, in so doing, will make an assertion which
may be somewhat mystifying at first hearing. The decisive element in
the predicament of Western man in our period is his loss of the dimension of depth. Of course, "dimension of depth" is a metaphor. It is taken
from the spatial realm and applied to man's spiritual life. What does it
mean?

It means that man has lost an answer to the question: What is the
meaning of life? Where do we come from, where do we go to? What shall

* By permission. From Paul Tillich, "The Lost Dimension in Religion," *Saturday
Evening Post*, June 14, 1958, p. 29.

we do, what should we become in the short stretch between birth and death? Such questions are not answered or even asked if the "dimension of depth" is lost. And this is precisely what has happened to man in our period of history. He has lost the courage to ask such questions with an infinite seriousness—as former generations did—and he has lost the courage to receive answers to these questions, wherever they may come from.

I suggest that we call the dimension of depth the religious dimension in man's nature. Being religious means asking passionately the question of the meaning of our existence and being willing to receive answers, even if the answers hurt. Such an idea of religion makes religion universally human, but it certainly differs from what is usually called religion. It does not describe religion as the belief in the existence of gods or one God, and as a set of activities and institutions for the sake of relating oneself to these beings in thought, devotion and obedience. No one can deny that the religions which have appeared in history are religions in this sense. Nevertheless, religion in its innermost nature is more than religion in this narrower sense. It is the state of being concerned about one's own being and being universally.

There are many people who are ultimately concerned in this way who feel far removed, however, from religion in the narrower sense, and therefore from every historical religion. It often happens that such people take the question of the meaning of their life infinitely seriously and reject any historical religion just for this reason. They feel that the concrete religions fail to express their profound concern adequately. They are religious while rejecting the religions. It is this experience which forces us to distinguish the meaning of religion as living in the dimension of depth from particular expressions of one's ultimate concern in the symbols and institutions of a concrete religion. If we now turn to the concrete analysis of the religious situation of our time, it is obvious that our key must be the basic meaning of religion and not any particular religion, not even Christianity. What does this key disclose about the predicament of man in our period?

If we define religion as the state of being grasped by an infinite concern we must say: Man in our time has lost such infinite concern. And the resurgence of religion is nothing but a desperate and mostly futile attempt to regain what has been lost.

How did the dimension of depth become lost? Like any important event, it has many causes, but certainly not the one which one hears often mentioned from ministers' pulpits and evangelists' platforms, namely, that a widespread impiety of modern man is responsible. Modern man is neither more pious nor more impious than man in any other period. The loss of the dimension of depth is caused by the relation of man to his world and to himself in our period, the period in which nature is being subjected scientifically and technically to the control of man. In this period, life in the dimension of depth is replaced by life in the horizontal dimension. The driving forces of the industrial society of which we are a part go ahead horizontally and not vertically. In popular terms this is expressed in phrases like "better and better," "bigger and bigger," "more and more." One should not disparage the feeling which lies behind such speech. Man is right in feeling that he is able to know and transform the world he encounters without a foreseeable limit. He can go ahead in all directions without a definite boundary.

A most expressive symbol of this attitude of going ahead in the horizontal dimension is the breaking through of the space which is controlled by the gravitational power of the earth into the world-space. It is interesting that one calls this world-space simply "space" and speaks, for instance, of space travel, as if every trip were not travel into space. Perhaps one feels that the true nature of space has been discovered only through our entering into indefinite world-space. In any case, the predominance of the horizontal dimension over the dimension of depth has been immensely increased by the opening up of the space beyond the space of the earth.

If we now ask what does man do and seek if he goes ahead in the horizontal dimension, the answer is difficult. Sometimes one is inclined to say that the mere movement ahead without an end, the intoxication with speeding forward without limits, is what satisfies him. But this answer is by no means sufficient. For on his way into space and time man changes the world he encounters. And the changes made by him change himself. He transforms everything he encounters into a tool; and in doing so he himself becomes a tool. But if he asks, a tool for what, there is no answer.

One does not need to look far beyond everyone's daily experience in order to find examples to describe this predicament. Indeed our daily life in office and home, in cars and airplanes, at parties and conferences, while reading magazines and watching television, while looking at advertisements and hearing radio, are in themselves continuous examples of a life which has lost the dimension of depth. It runs ahead; every moment is filled with something which must be done or seen or said or planned. But no one can experience depth without stopping and becoming aware of himself. Only if he has moments in which he does not care about what comes next can he experience the meaning of this moment here and now and ask himself about the meaning of his life. As long as the preliminary, transitory concerns are not silenced, no matter how interesting and valuable and important they may be, the voice of the ultimate concern cannot be heard. This is the deepest root of the loss of the dimension of depth in our period—the loss of religion in its basic and universal meaning.

If the dimension of depth is lost, the symbols in which life in this dimension has expressed itself must also disappear. I am speaking of the great symbols of the historical religions in our Western world, of Judaism and Christianity. The reason that the religious symbols become lost is not primarily scientific criticism, but it is a complete misunderstanding of their meaning; and only because of this misunderstanding was scientific critique able, and even justified, in attacking them. The first step toward the non-religion of the Western world was made by religion itself. When it defended its great symbols, not as symbols, but as literal stories, it had already lost the battle. In doing so the theologians (and today many religious laymen) helped to transfer the powerful expressions of the dimension of depth into objects or happenings on the horizontal plane. There the symbols lose their power and meaning and become an easy prey to physical, biological and historical attack.

If the symbol of creation which points to the divine ground of everything is transferred to the horizontal plane, it becomes a story of events in a removed past for which there is no evidence, but which contradicts every piece of scientific evidence. If the symbol of the Fall of Man, which points to the tragic estrangement of man and his world from their true being is transferred to the horizontal plane, it becomes a story of a human couple a few thousand years ago in what is now present-day Iraq. One of the most profound psychological descriptions of the general human predicament becomes an absurdity on the horizontal plane. If the symbols of the Saviour and the salvation through Him which point to the healing power in history and personal life are transferred to the horizontal plane, they become stories of a half-divine being coming from a heavenly place and returning to it. Obviously, in this form, they have no meaning whatsoever for people whose view of the universe is determined by scientific astronomy.

If the idea of God (and the symbols applied to Him) which expresses man's ultimate concern is transferred to the horizontal plane, God becomes a being among others whose existence or non-existence is a matter of inquiry. Nothing, perhaps, is more symptomatic of the loss of the dimension of depth than the permanent discussion about the existence or nonexistence of God—a discussion in which both sides are equally wrong, because the discussion itself is wrong and possible only after the loss of the dimension of depth.

When in this way man has deprived himself of the dimension of depth and the symbols expressing it, he then becomes a part of the horizontal plane. He loses his self and becomes a thing among things. He becomes an element in the process of manipulated production and manipulated consumption. This is now a matter of public knowledge. We have become aware of the degree to which everyone in our social structure is managed, even if one knows it and even if one belongs himself to the managing group. The influence of the gang mentality on adolescents, of the corporation's demands on the executives, of the conditioning of everyone by public communication, by propaganda and advertising under the guidance of motivation research, et cetera, have all been described in many books and articles.

Under these pressures, man can hardly escape the fate of becoming a thing among the things he produces, a bundle of conditioned reflexes without a free, deciding and responsible self. The immense mechanism, set up by man to produce objects for his use, transforms man himself into an object used by the same mechanism of production and consumption.

But man has not ceased to be man. He resists this fate anxiously, desperately, courageously. He asks the question, for what? And he realizes that there is no answer. He becomes aware of the emptiness which is covered by the continuous movement ahead and the production of means for ends which become means again without an ultimate end. Without knowing what has happened to him, he feels that he has lost the meaning of life, the dimension of depth.

Out of this awareness the religious question arises and religious answers are received or rejected. Therefore, in order to describe the contemporary attitude toward religion, we must first point to the places where the awareness of the predicament of Western man in our period is most sharply expressed. These places are the great art, literature and, partly at least, the philosophy of our time. It is both the subject matter and the style of these creations which show the passionate and often tragic struggle about the meaning of life in a period in which man has lost the dimension of depth. This art, literature, philosophy is not religious in the narrower sense of the word; but it asks the religious question more radically and more profoundly than most directly religious expressions of our time.

It is the religious question which is asked when the novelist describes a man who tries in vain to reach the only place which could solve the problem of his life, or a man who disintegrates under the memory of a guilt which persecutes him, or a man who never had a real self and is pushed by his fate without resistance to death, or a man who experiences a profound disgust of everything he encounters.

It is the religious question which is asked when the poet opens up the horror and the fascination of the demonic regions of his soul, or if he leads us into the deserts and empty places of our being, or if he shows the physical and moral mud under the surface of life, or if he sings the song of transitoriness, giving words to the ever-present anxiety of our hearts.

It is the religious question which is asked when the playwright shows the illusion of a life in a ridiculous symbol, or if he lets the emptiness of a life's work end in self-destruction, or if he confronts us with the inescapable bondage to mutual hate and guilt, or if he leads us into the dark cellar of lost hopes and slow disintegration.

It is the religious question which is asked when the painter breaks the visible surface into pieces, then reunites them into a great picture which has little similarity with the world at which we normally look, but which expresses our anxiety and our courage to face reality.

It is the religious question which is asked when the architect, in creating office buildings or churches, removes the trimmings taken over from past styles because they cannot be considered an honest expression of our own period. He prefers the seeming poverty of a purpose-determined style to the deceptive richness of imitated styles of the past. He knows that he gives no final answer, but he does give an honest answer.

The philosophy of our time shows the same hiddenly religious traits. It is divided into two main schools of thought, the analytic and the existentialist. The former tries to analyze logical and linguistic forms which are always used and which underlie all scientific research. One may compare them with the painters who dissolve the natural forms of bodies into cubes, planes and lines; or with those architects who want the structural "bones" of their buildings to be conspicuously visible and not hidden by covering features. This self-restriction produces the almost monastic poverty and seriousness of this philosophy. It is religious—without any contact with religion in its method—by exercising the humility of "learned ignorance."

In contrast to this school the existentialist philosophers have much to say about the problems of human existence. They bring into rational concepts what the writers and poets, the painters and architects, are expressing in their particular material. What they express is the human predicament in time and space, in anxiety and guilt and the feeling of meaninglessness. From Pascal in the seventeenth century to Heidegger and Sartre in our time, philosophers have emphasized the contrast between human dignity and human misery. And by doing so, they have raised the religious question. Some have tried to answer the question they have asked. But if they did so, they turned back to past traditions and offered to our time that which does not fit our time. Is it possible for our time to receive answers which are born out of our time?

Answers given today are in danger of strengthening the present situation and with it the questions to which they are supposed to be the answers. This refers to some of the previously mentioned major representatives of the so-called resurgence of religion, as for instance the evangelist Billy Graham and the counseling and healing minister, Norman Vincent Peale. Against the validity of the answers given by the former, one must say that, in spite of his personal integrity, his propagandistic methods and his primitive theological fundamentalism fall short of what is needed to give an answer to the religious question of our period. In spite of all his seriousness, he does not take the radical questions of our period seriously.

The effect that Norman Peale has on large groups of people is rooted in the fact that he confirms the situation which he is supposed to help overcome. He heals people with the purpose of making them fit again for the demands of the competitive and conformist society in which we are living. He helps them to become adapted to the situation which is characterized by the loss of the dimension of depth. Therefore, his advice is valid on this level; but it is the validity of this level that is the true religious question of our time. And this question he neither raises nor answers.

In many cases the increase of church membership and interest in religious activities does not mean much more than the religious consecration of a state of things in which the religious dimension has been lost. It is the desire to participate in activities which are socially strongly approved and give internal and a certain amount of external security. This is not necessarily bad, but it certainly is not an answer to the religious question of our period.

Is there an answer? There is always an answer, but the answer may not be available to us. We may be too deeply steeped in the predicament out of which the question arises to be able to answer it. To acknowledge this is certainly a better way toward a real answer than to bar the way to it by deceptive answers. And it may be that in this attitude the real answer (within available limits) is given. The real answer to the question of how to regain the dimension of depth is not given by increased church membership or church attendance, nor by conversion or healing experiences. But it is given by the awareness that we have lost the decisive dimension of life, the dimension of depth, and that there is no easy way of getting it back. Such awareness is in itself a state of being grasped by that which is symbolized in the term, dimension of depth. He who realizes that he is separated from the ultimate source of meaning shows by this realization that he is not only separated but also reunited. And this is just our situation. What we need above all—and partly have—is the radical realization of our predicament, without trying to cover it up by secular or religious ideologies. The revival of religious interest would be a creative power in our culture if it would develop into a movement of search for the lost dimension of depth.

This does not mean that the traditional religious symbols should be dismissed. They certainly have lost their meaning in the literalistic form into which they have been distorted, thus producing the critical reaction against them. But they have not lost their genuine meaning, namely, of answering the question which is implied in man's very existence in powerful, revealing and saving symbols. If the resurgence of religion would produce a new understanding of the symbols of the past and their relevance for our situation, instead of premature and deceptive answers, it would become a creative factor in our culture and a saving factor for many who live in estrangement, anxiety and despair. The religious answer has always the character of "in spite of." In spite of the loss of dimension of depth, its power is present, and most present in those who are aware of the loss and are striving to regain it with ultimate seriousness.

Part I | The Judeo-Christian Faith

If twentieth-century seekers wish to understand the Bible, they must, in a sense, *participate* in the events of which these writings are the record. As critical events of long ago are remembered, men of today may become dynamically involved, in new and momentous ways, in contemporary events and issues. Thus God may disclose Himself and call men to act responsibly in our modern world just as He did in the ancient world. This point of view is basic to grasping the significance of the Bible.

Those who open the Bible, perhaps at first out of idle curiosity, may be caught up in a venture which involves risk and courage. Men and women are confronted not with a matter of merely casual interest but rather with one of choice between ultimate loyalties. For the final issue of this process of decision involves the direction and push of whole persons in relation to God and the world. In the Judeo-Christian view, this is the same God who lives and moves in events of history and experiences of men and women today as He did long ago.

The Biblical View of History

H. H. Rowley writes that, despite the diversities within the Bible, there is ". . . a more profoundly significant unity running through it all."[1] This, he says, is a ". . . dynamic unity and not a static unity." There is *development* throughout the Bible, especially from the Old Testament to the New. Yet, in Rowley's words,

> . . . it is not to be supposed that development was brought about by the unfolding of the human spirit through the mere passage of time. There is no automatic spiritual growth of mankind, and the Bible nowhere tells the story of such a growth. It records how men of God, acting under a direction which they believed to be of God, mediated ideas and principles to

---

[1] From *The Unity of the Bible,* by H. H. Rowley. Published in the U.S.A. by The Westminster Press, 1955. Used by permission. Reprinted also with the permission of Lutterworth Press, London.

2 3

men. It does not tell how men by the exercise of their minds wrested the secrets of life and the universe from a reluctant Unknown, but how God laid hold of them and revealed Himself through them. If there is any truth in this, then a unity of the Bible is to be expected. If God was revealing Himself, then there should be some unity about the revelation, since it was the same Being Who was being revealed. There is still room for diversity, since God was revealing Himself to men of limited spiritual capacity and could only reveal to each what He was capable of receiving.[2]

The following recurring words belong to each other within the life of biblical religion: *faith, encounter, response, history, event, sign, revelation.* Here and now, within the immediate happenings of everyday, God discloses or reveals Himself. It is persons who respond. But we Western individualists tend to forget that, for the biblical view, it was to the whole community that God disclosed Himself and that it was the whole community that made response. There were no isolated individuals outside the community. It is within this community relationship of encounter and response that revelation takes place even today.

Both Judaism and Christianity take history seriously. Christianity is called a historical religion and biblical faith a historical faith. It is difficult for modern-minded students to grasp the special significance of this term "historical." The Judeo-Christian tradition has a history. All religions of the world do. The historian attempts to study the origins of these various religions, the biographies of founders, the teachings of prophets, the rites and ceremonies, systems of belief and social effects. But biblical faith is itself a series of events. It therefore does not simply *have* a history: it *is* a history. "Biblical faith is *faith enacted as history,* or it is nothing at all."[3]

Events Lived and Interpreted

The Hebrews lived at the southwestern end of that arch of land called the Fertile Crescent. Peacetime traders and wartime armies traveled through Palestine on roads connecting Egypt to Asia Minor and the Mesopotamian kingdoms. As H. H. Rowley says:

> It has never been the centre of a great empire or the home of a culture whose influence has spread throughout any large area. At no time has its

---

[2] *Ibid.*, pp. 7–8.

[3] Will Herberg, "Biblical Faith as *Heilsgeschichte*," *Christian Scholar*, vol. 39, p. 25, March, 1956.

language been used widely beyond its own borders. Yet it has exercised an influence on the world that is unique, and the adherents of three great religions count it holy. Here monotheism was born, to become the heritage not alone of Judaism but of Christianity and Islam.[4]

Yet, as important as its religious and moral influences have been, this little land never achieved political unity within its own borders or freedom to live its life unmolested. Egypt, Assyria, Babylonia, Persia, Greece and Rome moved across the land of the Hebrews in successive waves of political and military conquest. In spite of indignity, exile and poverty, however, the Hebrews became a community in a distinctive sense. In the midst of external pressures and in response to grave hardships, these wandering folk expressed their faith in terms of obedience to God. They believed that, as a people with a unique destiny, they were linked to God through a distinctive covenant relationship. A covenant is an agreement of pledged loyalty and devotion. In terms of this relationship, the Hebrews lived and interpreted all significant events of their history. For the covenant was linked to that central event called the Exodus, through which they believed God had acted to deliver them from slavery in Egypt and to lead them into the Promised Land.

The narratives found in Exodus 15:22–19:2 relate how Moses led the people of Israel through the wilderness to the region of Mount Sinai. Throughout the years of hardship and near loss of faith, God guided the people through barren wastes, provided daily sustenance, empowered them in battle against their enemies and brought them into the oasis of Sinai. Here the wanderers found time to consider the meaning of their experiences and the distinctive character of their community. For it was at Sinai that there was established, in definite form, the covenant relationship which gave to this community its center of meaning.

In a study of the covenant conception, George E. Mendenhall[5] indicates that in the case of international treaties of biblical times two kinds of covenants, parity and suzerainty covenants, were employed. In a parity covenant, parties equal in status to each other come to a reciprocal agreement in which obligations are binding on both. A suzerainty covenant is one in which a king binds his vassal. Here the ruler in authority grants the covenant privilege and guarantees security and protection, and in

---

[4] H. H. Rowley, *The Modern Reader's Bible Atlas*, Association Press, New York, 1961, p. 1.

[5] George E. Mendenhall, "Law and Covenant in Israel and the Ancient Near East," *Biblical Colloquium*, 1955; reprinted from *Biblical Archaeologist*, May, 1954, pp. 26–46; September, 1954, pp. 49–76.

return the vassal, being inferior in social status, is obligated to obey the rules and commands of the one in authority. But what motivates obedience is gratitude for deeds of benevolence and expressions of personal relationship.

It is the suzerainty covenant which Israel took as the closest model of her own relationship with God. "Clearly, Israel's covenant was not a parity covenant, a bargain or commercial contract between equals. Rather it was a covenant given by God, a relationship conferred upon the people by the Sovereign. Hence it was a covenant that required obedience."[6]

The precise terms of the covenant are set forth in the Book of Exodus (Chapter 20), starting with the familiar Ten Commandments. God addressed His people in direct, person-to-person terms: "I am the Lord, thy God, who brought thee up out of the Land of Egypt, thou shalt have no other gods before me." Two dimensions are involved in the people's pledged obedience to God's will under the terms of the covenant: absolute and exclusive allegiance to God Himself and loving and just concern for their fellowmen within the covenanted community.

But the covenant has no meaning apart from God's act in the Exodus, for it is Yahweh who has taken the initiative all along. It is He who has called the people of Israel to a special vocation—has, in fact, been calling them through the years, gathering, freeing, guiding them through the wilderness wanderings. By the power of His love and concern, He has pointed the direction of their journeying, given them food, helped them to ward off dangers and enemies. Have they no gratitude now? Is there no response? No decision on their part? For all these things Yahweh has done are signs pointing beyond themselves to Himself as the Author of their very existence. A new task awaits them now and at every turn of their history down into the future, in constant renewal of their response to Yahweh's call. Thus God commissioned Moses to announce to the community the nature of the covenant He offered them:

> Thus shall you say to the House of Jacob, and tell the people of Israel: You have seen what I did to the Egyptians, and how I bore you on eagles' wings and brought you to myself. Now therefore, if you will obey my voice and keep my covenant, you shall be my own possession among all peoples; for the earth is mine, and you shall be to me a kingdom of priests and a holy nation.[7]

"If you will obey my voice and keep my covenant"—that is the condi-

---

[6] Bernhard Anderson, *Christian Scholar*, vol. 39, p. 68, March, 1956.
[7] Exodus 19:3–6.

tion. Then the God of all creation will make these folk His own possession and give them not just a privilege but a task, that of becoming a community of those who serve God among the nations.

Looking Back to Origins

The actual origin of the Hebrews is difficult to trace. Their real history began under Moses with deliverance out of Egypt and establishment of the covenant (1290–1250 B.C.). Thus this creative act of God and His choosing of Israel to be His covenanted people became the focus of interpretation for prophets and psalmists. In terms of this divine act and relationship, the prophets and psalmists called Israel to remembrance of her past, her mission in the present and her destiny for the future. Here event and interpretation are inseparably bound together.

Only through such historical vision as Moses initiated could the Hebrews understand the meaning of the Exodus and covenant relationship. But also, through the same historical perspective, they grasped their origins as a people during the earlier time called the patriarchal period. For the account of events recorded in the Book of Exodus is preceded by a prologue found in Chapters 12 to 50 of the Book of Genesis. Earlier and later periods were linked in historical and religious continuity. At the time of his call to leadership, a voice said to Moses: "I am the God of your father, the God of Abraham, the God of Isaac, the God of Jacob" [Exodus 3:6]. Thus it was Abraham (Genesis 11:31) who became the founder of Israel. He migrated with his family into Canaan, as Palestine was called in earlier times. Abraham was followed by his son Isaac and Isaac by his son Jacob. The twelve sons of Jacob bore the names of the twelve tribes of Israel.

As to the religion of the patriarchal period, it is difficult to be accurate because these earlier accounts of Genesis have been interpreted in the light of the later central event of the Exodus and covenant. But evidence points to nature religions of the Fertile Crescent as the source of religious life and practice. Abraham called his God El Shaddai, meaning "the One of the Mountains," a mountain god or storm god called Baal ("lord") by the Canaanites. But profound differences were to take place between these conceptions of nature deities and the God of the Hebrews. The God of the Hebrews, Yahweh, was worshiped and served first and foremost not as a God of nature but as a God of historical destiny and peoplehood. Bernhard Anderson states that the

. . . patriarchal religion was infused with a historical sense that is characteristically Semitic or Hebraic. Unlike the settled Canaanites, who were more concerned with adjusting to the cycles of nature and preserving the social equilibrium, the unsettled Hebrews were more prone to express their faith in the dynamic language of history. They were wanderers and adventurers who, in response to a divine summons, left their homeland and went into the unknown and the uncertain—toward a land their God would show them in due time. They lived by a venture of faith, trusting that the future was in the hand of their God. To be sure, the story of Abraham's migration from Mesopotamia, in response to God's call, is colored by later theological reflection. Yet some dim apprehension of God's activity in history must have provided the background of the account in the Book of Exodus which relates that Moses was addressed by the God of the fathers.[8]

The Bible as a Record of History

The first five books of the Old Testament, called the Pentateuch, are the product of several literary sources blended into a composite work. These materials exhibit varieties of style and interpretation. For writing and editing took place across several centuries (950–400 B.C.), and behind the earliest writing lay a long period of oral transmission. But despite the reliving and reworking of these materials, the common themes center on the Exodus and the covenant faith. The main themes of this faith are promise to the patriarchs, God's deliverance of Israel from Egypt, His guidance through the wilderness, giving of law and covenant and reaching the Promised Land.

After the Exodus and wilderness wanderings (1290–1250 B.C.), these covenanted people undertook the slow and difficult conquest of the land of Canaan (ca. 1200–1020 B.C.). During this time there reigned the so-called judges. These leaders procured the right of the people by military action or arbitration of legal disputes. Yet their authority was acknowledged because they were possessed of divine charisma, or the spirit of their God, Yahweh.

About 1020 B.C. a new unifying political-religious force emerged in the person of Saul, and there was established a monarchy. Together with his son Jonathan, Saul waged successful war against the Philistines. After a period of intense struggle, military, political and spiritual, David became king and centered his strong rule in Jerusalem. The basic character of

[8] By permission. From Bernhard Anderson, *Understanding the Old Testament*, Prentice-Hall, Inc., Englewood Cliffs, N.J., 1957, p. 24. See Genesis 15.

Israel now changed. The people had been bound together exclusively in a covenant loyalty under Yahweh. Now they also became citizens of a state bound together politically. Thus Israel stood in danger of losing her genius as a religious community. For the people tried now to play the power game among the emerging empires of the Near East.

Sometime about 950 B.C., the first of the literary artists contributed distinctive materials to those that make up the Pentateuch. Scholars designate this unknown writer by the letter J because he uses the name Yahweh for God (Y and J are indistinguishable in Hebrew). The monarchy had brought about a radical change in the social structure of Israel. The old twelve-tribe confederacy had given way to unified control centered in the royal city of Jerusalem. Up to this time the people had remembered and retold, in stories, hymns and prophetic oracles, the sacred events of their experienced history. The stories expressed the faith and loyalties of the various tribes. But with the establishment of the monarchy and the royal sanctuary at Jerusalem, the oral recitations, acts of worship and shrines seemed to conservative religious folk to be doomed.

The J, or Yahwist, writer met this social and religious crisis. He took these older materials of the oral tradition and pulled them together into a literary epic of events from the creation of the world to the entrance into Canaan. Of course, a central theme of the covenant relation binding on all Israel had been taking shape. Although we speak of approximate dates when the various writers did their work, many materials actually assumed distinctive form much earlier. The Yahwist did not start from scratch. Rather, he drew together stories and cycles of stories, changing them very little but giving these traditional materials a new literary and theological perspective. He let old forms of expression stand but set them in the context of the whole of Israel's history. From remembrance of the Exodus, the covenant and the conquest of Canaan, his epic reached back to embrace creation, the Garden of Eden and the patriarchal period. He wrote the epic backward, so to speak. For he began with the historical events of Israel and then affirmed, through the accounts of creation of the world and man, faith in Yahweh, who is the God not only of history but of the whole of nature as well.

This approach of the Yahwist became the basic method adopted by subsequent writers. It is that of relating the events of the past to their own current situation, all under the guidance of their God. More than a century later (ca. 750 B.C.) there was added another document written in, and reflecting the interests of, the northern kingdom. The writer's source materials are called E (God is Elohim in Hebrew). E begins with Abraham and reaches its climax in the account of Joseph in Egypt. The

Elohist writer lacks the comprehensive sweep of J, but his account is dependent on J and at some points is interfused with it to form JE. This drawing together of the E materials took place after the northern kingdom had fallen in 722 B.C.

About the middle of the seventh century, still another strand, this time a code of law used for purposes of reform by King Josiah in Judah in 621 B.C., was composed. This account is called D and forms the nucleus of the Book of Deuteronomy.

This literary activity was carried on within the context of critical historical events in which these covenanted people were involved. For, meanwhile, the brief unity enjoyed under the monarchy had been broken. The northern and southern kingdoms went their separate ways. Each succeeding century brought more serious crises in their relations with foreign powers. In the eighth century, during the period of the prophetic activity of Amos, Hosea, Micah and Isaiah, Assyria (722 B.C.) took the northern kingdom, Israel, into captivity. The southern kingdom, Judah, managed to hold onto some semblance of independence until 586 B.C., when the Babylonians conquered it and carried segments of the population into exile. After the Judeans' return to Jerusalem, they rebuilt their walls and Temple. Through new stress on ceremonial worship and observance of the Law, they attempted to preserve purity of practice in the midst of a turbulent world of political and military pressures.

About 500 B.C., the priestly writings called P took shape. These comprise large blocks of material found in the Pentateuch, particularly in Genesis, Exodus, Leviticus and Numbers. As Bernhard Anderson points out:

> There was a time when it was believed that the priestly material was the oldest part of the Pentateuch, and that all other literary sources were built on it. But this view has been abandoned, for it is evident that in style and theological outlook P in its final form best fits the exilic and post-exilic community. And yet the first impression of scholars was partially right. In the first place, P does preserve many ancient traditions. This does not mean that everything in P is as old as the Mosaic period, for clearly one of the motives of the writer was to authorize the views and practices of Jerusalem priests by showing that they had their origin at Sinai. Still, a good deal of the old tradition, which developed out of the cultic practice of the time of Moses and the Tribal Confederacy, has been preserved in P by the Jerusalem priesthood. Remember that the date of literary composition does not necessarily provide an index to the age of the material itself [sic!]. No longer do we think of the Pentateuch being made up of sources that followed one another in chronological succession—J in about 950 B.C., E in

750 B.C. or earlier, D in 650–600 B.C., and finally P in the period of the Exile. Rather, those are *parallel* traditions stemming from ancient times. . . .[9]

Finally, about 400 B.C., this document P was blended with JE and D to bring the Pentateuch to completion. Thus the priestly editor began with the historical epic of Israel (JE) and introduced at certain points the priestly interpretation centered in the Temple at Jerusalem. This procedure means that the priestly material has a unified theme of its own, but it leans on the JE epic for dramatic movement. Then the Book of Deuteronomy was inserted into the priestly edition of JE just before the account of Moses' death (Deuteronomy 34).[10]

Space does not permit discussion of how the other materials (the Prophets and Writings) were composed and became Scripture. But devotion to the Torah (the books of the Law contained in the Pentateuch) remained the center of unity throughout Jewish history. The Jews believed they were God's chosen people, living in the light of God-given law, God-controlled history, pure worship, mutual relations within the covenant among their brothers and neighbors.

What Is the Miracle That Occurred?

Some modern-minded men and women would dismiss the biblical accounts of "miracles" as the mistaken utterances of a prescientific age. For, from the point of view of modern science, miracles, as unpredictable intervention in the natural order, simply do not happen. We would progress more rapidly in an enlightened grasp of things, we are told, if we ignored the "miraculous" stories written by men who could not have known better and concentrated on the "spiritual truths" they contain.

But this approach misunderstands the way the biblical writers came to grips with the world. As Howard Clark Kee states:

Contrary to the common definition of miracle as a deviation from the laws of nature, the biblical writers do not regard the universe as operating by laws at all. There is no such thing as "nature," in the sense of a force, immanent in the world, by which its function is empowered and guided. Rather, the universe was created by God, is sustained by God, and its destiny is determined by God's will. His will is not perceived as a blueprint,

[9] *Ibid.*, p. 382. See chart on p. 383 of Anderson's book.
[10] *Ibid.*, pp. 382–383.

which, once it has been drawn up, cannot be deviated from. On the other hand, the will of God is not capricious, but orderly. The writer of Genesis (8:22) is confident that the world will continue its pattern of daily, seasonal and vegetal cycles. But the cycles are not the result of regulations built into the universe; they are indications of and expressions of the loving care of God for his creation.[11]

Recall, by way of summary, the series of events that took place as parts of the whole act of Yahweh in delivering His people: the saving of the infant Moses, plagues in Egypt, crossing the Marsh Sea, the pillar of cloud and fire, the manna and quails, the rock producing water, the defeat of Amalek. We must keep in mind the motive for recording these incidents, indeed many years after their occurrence. They are not presented as objective, exact, photographic reports of what took place down to the last detail. They are events as experienced within the community of faith and thus interpreted and relived in terms of that faith. For Israel, they became *signs* which *signified* or pointed beyond themselves to the God who is their Author.

But these accounts are not simply falsehoods or fictions. That kind of conclusion is possible only if scientific, empirical tests are applied: this occurred; that happened because of these conditions and with these results! Such an investigation is legitimate for the scientist or the objective historian. However, the results, pro and con, of that sort of investigation have no bearing on the religious question. As persons of religious concern, we do more than observe, calculate and draw conclusions: we ask about men's relation to the ultimate. The religious question has to do with overcoming the disruption and separation between ourselves, our fellow-men and God and finding a centered self in God. It concerns living in a total history which illuminates all the rest. In fact, as participants, we become involved in the concrete situations and actual crises of human existence: theirs! ours! every man's! These are the areas of religious search and of God's action in reconciling men to Himself and with each other. Critical events thus become signs, and signs are concrete, visible indicators of the presence and purpose of God. As we shall see later, such signs are not conclusive objective evidence or self-evident proof of God's existence. Why this is so we shall have to investigate. Whether or not these incidents actually happened is a problem for empirical investigation. But their significance for men of faith is that God is creatively at work then as now.

[11] By permission. From Howard Clark Kee, "The Biblical Understanding of Miracle," *Christian Scholar*, vol. 39, pp. 50–51, March, 1956.

What Then Is Revelation?

Bringing this discussion to summary conclusion, we would emphasize that the Bible is the *record* of the unique signs and revelatory events through which men of responsive faith are brought into dynamic relationship with the living God. As we today read that record, conditions are created under which the same kind of encounter and response may occur in and through ourselves.

Revelation is not identical with the literal words of language. It does not provide us with verifiable statements informing us of "divine" truths. By the same token, faith is not simply assent to sets of propositions in an order of "right" belief. Nor is the Word of God identical with the *words* of the Bible. Rather God's "Word" is a term borrowed by analogy from the sphere of person-to-person human relationships. Just as you and I communicate to others who we are and what we are, so does God disclose Himself. The Bible is the medium of that self-disclosure. Thus revelation is God's disclosure of Himself in and through specific climactic events in human history. These revelatory events are recorded, remembered, re-lived. Men today may participate in the same events and respond to God's love and justice. Thus, through the medium of life here and now, God may utter a new Word for our times to which men may make decisive response.

The Bible, as the record of revelatory events, is then inspired, but in a distinctive sense. For as Alan Richardson writes:

> When we speak of the inspiration of the Scriptures we ought primarily to mean the inspiration of the men who wrote them, if it is men who are inspired and not books or words, except in a figurative sense. In this way a new theory of inspiration was reached. . . . One might speak about the inspiration of the Bible only because the Bible was the record of the religious experience of inspired men. Its power to evoke a similar experience in us was the pragmatic test of its inspiration, and when judged by this test it was found to be authoritative and normative; it stood in a class by itself amongst the religious literature of the world. . . . The degree of inspiration of the Bible . . . was to be measured by the level of truth which it contained and by its power to awaken in us a genuine experience of God.[12]

H. Richard Niebuhr, in *The Meaning of Revelation*, distinguishes "history as lived" from "history as seen." He illustrates this contrast by

[12] By permission. From Alan Richardson, *A Preface to Bible Study*, The Westminster Press, Philadelphia, 1944, pp. 34–35.

comparing the abstract, external, matter-of-fact account as found in the *Cambridge Modern History* with the same event as viewed by a participant in a living tradition. The first begins:

> On July 4, 1776, Congress passed the resolution which made the colonies independent communities, issuing at the same time the well-known Declaration of Independence. If we regard the Declaration as an assertion of an abstract political theory, criticism and condemnation are easy. It sets out with a general proposition so vague as to be practically useless. The doctrine of the equality of men, unless it be qualified and conditioned by reference to special circumstances, is either a barren truism or a delusion.

But Lincoln's Gettysburg Address speaks the convictions of one who lives and relives the same event:

> Fourscore and seven years ago our fathers brought forth upon this continent a new nation, conceived in liberty and dedicated to the proposition that all men are created free and equal.[13]

This distinction between history as lived and history as seen then leads to a clear definition of revelation. Niebuhr writes:

> Revelation means that part of our inner history which illuminates the rest of it and which is itself intelligible. Sometimes when we read a difficult book, seeking to follow a complicated argument, we come across a luminous sentence from which we can go forward and backward and so attain some understanding of the whole. Revelation is like that. In his *Religion in the Making*, Professor Whitehead has written such illuminating sentences and one of them is this: "Rational religion appeals to the direct intuition of special occasions and to the elucidatory power of its concepts for all occasions." The special occasion to which we appeal in the Christian Church is called Jesus Christ, in whom we see the righteousness of God, His power and wisdom. But from that special occasion we also derive the concepts which make possible the elucidation of all the events in our history. Revelation means this intelligible event which makes all other events intelligible.[14]

To conclude, then, if revelation is to take place, an *I* and a *Thou* must be joined in creative interrelationship. God discloses, and man receives and responds. The medium through which this reciprocal process takes

---

[13] By permission. From H. Richard Niebuhr, *The Meaning of Revelation*, The Macmillan Company, New York, 1941, p. 60.

[14] *Ibid.*, p. 93.

place consists of events and experiences, of which the Bible is the record. H. H. Rowley states:

> In all this there is nothing to suggest that every experience is sent by God or reflects His will. . . . Not all human experience is the medium of divine revelation. It is when God chooses to make it the medium of revelation that it may become so, and before it can become so there is needed a man of sensitive spirit to receive the revelation.[15]

But such events are interpreted, seen from the inside. Again Rowley writes that there are

> . . . personal and impersonal factors woven together in what the Hebrews believed to be God's manifestation of Himself. The medium of revelation here is not to be found in the separate factors, but in their combination into a single complex.[16]

Herberg suggests important clues to two contemporary concerns: first, the meaning of faith in relation to revelation in the Judeo-Christian tradition; and second, practical hints as to how to read the Bible today. Faith is this personal history. It is not the abstract knowledge of "eternal truths" or "loyalty to eternal values" but ". . . personal acceptance . . . of what God has done, is doing, and will do. . . ." Thus as we use the Bible today, we do not simply look on a record of events as ". . . a recital that we hear and understand. It is also a demand upon us, for out of it comes the voice of God. Faith is responding to the call of God that comes to us from out of the midst of redemptive history."

[15] H. H. Rowley, *The Faith of Israel,* The Westminster Press, Philadelphia, 1956, p. 34.
[16] *Ibid.,* p. 45.

2

WILL HERBERG | *Biblical Faith as Heilsgeschichte**

The uniqueness—the "scandal"—of biblical faith is revealed in its radically historical character. Biblical faith is historical not merely because it has a history, or deals with historical events; there is nothing particularly novel in that. Biblical faith is historical in the much more profound sense that it is itself essentially a history. The message biblical faith proclaims, the judgments it pronounces, the salvation it promises, the teachings it communicates, are all defined historically and understood as historical realities, rather than as timeless structures of ideas or values. The historicity of biblical faith has long been a source of embarrassment to philosopher and mystic, yet it cannot be eliminated without virtually eliminating the faith itself. Dehistoricizing biblical faith is like paraphrasing poetry; something called an "idea content" remains, but everything that gave power and significance to the original is gone. Biblical faith is *faith enacted as history*, or it is nothing at all.

I

How shall we understand this radically historical character of biblical faith? Is it merely a cultural trait of the "Hebraic mind", or does it reflect something deeper, something in the very grain of reality, particularly human reality?

There are, fundamentally, three ways in which man has attempted to understand himself, to establish his being, and to relate himself to what is ultimate. One of these, culturally perhaps the oldest, is the way of heathenism. Heathen man sees reality as *nature;* nature—divine since it is the locus of all ultimate sanctities, that beyond which there is nothing—is the

* By permission. From Will Herberg, "Biblical Faith as *Heilsgeschichte,*" *Christian Scholar,* vol. 39, pp. 25–31, March, 1956.

context in which heathen man strives to understand himself and establish the meaning of his existence. The reality of his being is the "nature" in him, and rightness is to be achieved by engulfing himself in nature and its cyclical rhythms as an organic part of it. This is heathen man's way of realizing his humanness; heathen man feels wrong, and (if I may so put it) not truly himself, to the degree that he stands out of nature as an incommensurable element. Heathenism is thus at bottom total immanence, a primal unity of the divine, nature, and man.

Heathenism in this sense is obviously not something confined to primitive peoples remote in time and place. On the contrary, the heathen way of understanding man in his relation to ultimate reality seems to enter into the spirituality of men at all times and places, including our own. It emerges in the nature-pantheism of so many spiritually minded people of our time, as well as in the "hard-boiled" scientistic naturalism that holds nature to be ultimate and sees man as nothing more than a biological organism adjusting to its environment.

Standing in a kind of polar opposition to the heathen outlook is the outlook characteristic of the tradition of Greek philosophy and Oriental mysticism. Here it is not nature which is held to be ultimate and really real—though it is often spoken of as in some sense divine—but the *timelessly eternal* behind nature. A sharp dualism of appearance and reality is basic to this view: appearance is material and empirical, multiple, mutable, temporal, engrossed in flux; reality is one, immutable, timeless, eternal, spiritual. This ontological dualism of appearance and reality, the temporal and the eternal, is mirored in a body-soul dualism in terms of which the human being is analyzed. The real self is the soul, and human self-realization becomes essentially the extrication of the self from nature and time (the body) and its elevation to the timeless realm of spirit. It is surely unnecessary to document the pervasiveness of this type of outlook, with its spiritualistic emphasis and its disparagement of time and history, among the religious people of our time. It is perhaps necessary to remind ourselves that however highminded and spiritual it may appear, this outlook, like the heathenism it replaces, is utterly alien to biblical faith, which understands human existence and ultimate reality in very different categories.

II

Biblical faith defines a view of reality and human existence that marks a sharp break with the presuppositions of both heathenism and Greek-

Oriental spirituality. In biblical faith, nature is real and time no illusion, since they are the creation of God: this is the biblical witness against the spiritualistic devaluation of the natural and the temporal. Yet though real, they are not self-subsistent or ultimate, since they look to God as their creator: here biblical faith takes its stand against heathen immanentism. In exactly the same way, biblical faith refuses to dissolve man into nature, as does heathenism, or into timeless spirit, as is the effort of so much of philosophy and mysticism. In biblical faith, man is understood as (to use a modern and perhaps inexact term) a psychophysical unit, really and truly part of nature, yet transcending it by virtue of his "spirit", his freedom, his self-awareness, his capacity to get beyond and outside of himself, by virtue of the "image of God" in which he is made.

This complex, multidimensional conception makes it possible, for the first time, to understand man as a genuinely personal and historical being. Heathen naturalism assimilates man's time (history) to nature's time, and feels the uniqueness of the self—insofar as that emerges—as a threat to the oneness with nature which is blessedness. Greek-Oriental eternalism necessarily devaluates history as pure temporality and finds no place for the self, with its uniqueness and multiplicity, in the realm of the really real. It is in biblical faith that the self and history come into their own, for in biblical faith it is man's "essential dignity" that he is a self and ". . . can have a history."[1] Indeed, the two are really one; in biblical faith, human history is intrinsically personal, and the self is an historical structure.

Here we come close to the heart of the matter. Biblical faith understands human existence and human destiny in irreducibly historical terms. If the question is asked what is the real reality of man, what is it the actualization of which constitutes the fullness of his being, the heathen (turned philosopher) would say nature; the Greek metaphysician and the Oriental mystic would say that which is timeless and eternal in him; but the biblical thinker would say his *history*. History is the very stuff out of which human being is made: human existence is potential or implicit history; history is explicit or actualized existence. And it is not very different on the corporate level. In attempting to explain to someone who really does not know what it means to be an American, it would be futile to try to contrive some conceptual definition of "Americanness." Would it not prove more appropriate to tell the story of America and rely upon that story to communicate the fullness of what it means to be an American? "The human person and man's society," Reinhold Niebuhr

[1] Søren Kierkegaard, *Either/Or* (Princeton, 1946). Vol. II, p. 209.

has profoundly observed, "are *by nature historical* . . . [and] the ultimate truth about life must be mediated historically"[2] (emphasis, added).

This is the biblical understanding of man as an historical being. On the basis of this understanding, biblical faith insists that man can realize himself only in and through his life in history. It is in and through history, that God calls to man; it is in and through history, human action in history, that man responds; and it is in and through history that God judges. Heathen man pursues his life in nature below the level of history; Greek-Oriental man aspires to escape from history into the realm of timeless eternity. Biblical man, on the contrary, seeing human existence as essentially historical, strives to redeem history, though realizing that it is not in his time or by his hand that the work can be completed.

It is in this context that the biblical notion of *Heilsgeschichte* (redemptive history, "sacred history") emerges and becomes intelligible. Lessing, in his inaugural address at Jena, protested that ". . . particular facts of history cannot establish eternal truths," least of all the truths of religion; and Fichte reiterated that ". . . the metaphysical only and not the historical can give blessedness." They were both repeating Celsus' outraged remonstrance against the "scandal of particularity," which is the "scandal" of history. But he who understands the reality of human being in biblical terms will find no difficulty in understanding that the ultimate truth about human life and destiny, about man's plight and man's hope alike, is truly and inexpugnably historical, and can be expressed in no other way. (Hence the Bible is composed so largely of stories, recitals, histories.) The structure of faith is an historical structure, because being, living, and acting are, in the biblical conviction, radically historical in character.

III

Once we come to understand our existence in terms of history, and to analyze the human situation in historical terms, we begin to grasp what it means to think of faith as *Heilsgeschichte*. Examining the structure of our existence, we see that each of us has—or rather *is*—many partial histories, reflecting the many concerns and interests of life. We are Americans, members of a particular family and ethnic group, intimately associated with particular social institutions and movements. Each of these concerns, allegiances, and associations has its own special history

---

[2] Reinhold Niebuhr, "Religion and Education", *Religious Education*, November–December, 1953.

through which it is expressed and made explicit. But most of these histories, we ourselves realize, are merely partial histories; they define only fragments of our being and do not tell us who we "really" are. Underlying and including the partial histories of life, there must be some "total" history, in some way fundamental and comprehensive, some really ultimate history. Such a history, the history which one affirms in a total and ultimate manner, is one's *redemptive history* (*Heilsgeschichte*), for it is the history in terms of which the final meaning of life is established and the self redeemed from the powers of meaninglessness and non-being. This is the history that defines, and is defined by, one's faith; it is, indeed, the history that *is* one's faith. "To be a self," H. Richard Niebuhr has said, "is to have a god; to have a god is to have a history."³ If we reverse this—"To have a history is to have a god; to have a god is to be a self"— we get a glimpse of the full significance of the relation of faith and history.

Whatever history I take to tell me who I "really" am may thus be taken to define my actual faith. If I take my American history to define not merely the American aspect of my life, but also the fullness and ultimacy of my being as a person, I make "Americanism" (the American Way of Life) my faith and the nation my god. A moment's thought will show us how real this faith is in the lives of most of us today, and how clearly it is expressed as *Heilsgeschichte*. It has its symbols, liturgy, and ceremony, its holy days and cultic observances; it has its "sacred history" and its sense of messianic vocation.⁴ Marxism, the great rival of Americanism in the conflict of secular religions, is as thoroughly historical in

³ H. Richard Niebuhr, *The Meaning of Revelation* (Macmillan, 1941), p. 80.

⁴ In this country, more than anywhere else in the world perhaps, the old Christian church year has been all but replaced in law and in fact by a round of holidays (Columbus Day, Washington's Birthday, Independence Day, Memorial Day, Armistice [or Veterans] Day, etc., etc.) that mark great events in our national history; these are the days that Americans, insofar as they celebrate anything, celebrate as the "holy days" that really count. (Christmas and Easter are virtually all that remain of the old church calendar for the mass of Americans, and even these holidays have been largely voided of their religious content.) Perhaps even more revealing is the response of a group of outstanding Americans to the request that they rate the hundred most significant events in universal history. First place was given to Columbus' discovery of America, while Christ, either his birth or crucifixion, came fourteenth, tied with the Wright brothers' first plane flight (see the report in *Time*, May 24, 1954). This order of priority, so shocking in terms of Christian faith, becomes quite intelligible, even inevitable, once it is realized that the framework of faith in which it is made is the faith of "Americanism". This faith is defined by American history taken as ultimate and redemptive; it is only natural that those who hold this faith and this redemptive history should see Columbus' discovery of America (or alternatively, the American War of Independence) as the most important event in the annals of mankind. See also Will Herberg, *Protestant-Catholic-Jew: An Essay in American Religious Sociology* (Doubleday, 1955), chap. V.

structure, and even more obviously the reflection of the absolutization of a partial history. Marxism takes the partial history defined by the modern worker's being a proletarian as the ultimate and "total" history, and this history it proclaims as redemptive. From this standpoint, Marxism is, fundamentally, a secularized version—and therefore perversion—of biblical "sacred history", in which God is replaced by the Dialectic, the "chosen people" by the proletariat, the "faithful remnant" and even the Messiah by the Party, while the "beginning" and "end" of history, the "original rightness" lost and the "restored rightness" to come, are robbed of their transcendence and made points *within* the historical process. That Marxism is essentially a faith—an idolatrous faith—enacted as history, and therefore a *Heilsgeschichte*, is now almost a commonplace.

And so generally. Idolatrous faiths (particularly those emerging in the history-conscious West) are faiths defined by, and defining, partial histories made ultimate. They bear witness to gods that are idolatrous, in the sense that they are gods who are something of this world—some idea, institution, movement, power, or community—divinized and turned into absolutes. The idolatrous god thus has his idolatrous "sacred history"; very frequently, it is the idolatrous "sacred history" that is more vivid in men's minds than the god to whom it points.

Biblical faith, because it is faith in the living God, the God who is "beyond the gods" of the world, expresses itself in a redemptive history in which this God is central and the "holy people of God" the crucial historical community. And just as faith in the living God is the only alternative to idolatrous faiths, so, in the last analysis, the definition of life in terms of the "sacred history" of God's dealings with men given in biblical tradition is the only alternative to the idolatrous "totalization" of one or another of the partial histories which make up our lives. The ultimate existential decision is a choice between "sacred histories" as it is a choice between gods.

IV

Biblical faith, understood as history, presents us with a grand and stirring drama of human existence and destiny. It is not my purpose to describe this cosmic drama, since that has been done and magnificently done in a number of recent works on biblical religion. In its essentials, it defines a three-phase pattern in which the present "wrong" and contradictory existence of man and society is seen as a falling away from the original "rightness" of God's creation, and as destined for restoration and rectification in the final fulfillment of the kingdom of God. Within this vast orbit, it traces the history of the "people of God," God's instrument for the redemption of mankind. All human history falls under its range and sweep, since its purpose is universal, though its center—the crucial revelatory, community-creating event (Exodus-Sinai in Judaism, Calvary-Easter in Christianity)—is particular. But no attempt is made to impose a final "philosophy of history" upon the historical material, which is drawn from legend, saga, oral tradition, and written documents. Every understanding of history is felt to be partial and fragmentary; in the end, everything is swallowed up in the mystery of divine providence. Yet, however limited and uncertain our grasp of it may be, it is the "sacred history" that tells us who we are, where we stand, and what we hope for—that, in short, gives meaning to existence.

It has been repeatedly pointed out in recent years, and not by theologians alone, that this understanding of history tends to make for a creative realism that escapes utopianism on the one side and despair on the other. It is, in fact, the only real alternative to the many historical idolatries of our time, which are now seen to be distortions, often demonic distortions, of the historical faith and hope of the Bible.

Yet even with this understanding we have not penetrated to the heart of biblical faith as *Heilsgeschichte*. For we are still, as it were, on the outside looking in. Biblical "sacred history" possesses a double inwardness. It is, first of all, an interpretation through the eyes of faith of acts and events that, from another standpoint, might well be interpreted in an altogether different way: to Thucydides, the victorious Assyrian would hardly have appeared as the rod of God's anger against a wayward Israel. But it is inward also in another and perhaps deeper sense, in the sense that, as the history of God's redemptive work, it can become actually redemptive *for me*, redemptive existentially, only if I appropriate it in faith as *my personal history*, the history of my own life. "Faith in the New Testament sense," writes Oscar Cullmann, "is the way by which the past phase of redemptive history becomes effective for me. . . . Faith in the New Testament sense means to be convinced that this entire happening takes place for me."[5] Remembrance and expectation are the two foci of existence in faith. "He who does not himself remember that God led him out of Egypt, he who does not himself await the Messiah," says Martin Buber, "is no longer a true Jew."[6] Religion is thus not the apprehension of eternal truths or loyalty to eternal values; it is rather the personal acceptance, through commitment and action, of what God has

[5] Oscar Cullman, *Christ and Time* (Westminster, 1949), p. 219.

[6] Martin Buber, "Der Preis", *Der Jude*, October, 1917.

done, is doing, and will do for the redemption of mankind, in the first place of oneself.[7] From this angle, the act of faith is double: the existential affirmation of a history as one's redemptive history and the existential appropriation of this redemptive history as one's personal background history, and therefore in a real sense the foundation of one's personal existence. "In the history of Israel," to quote Buber once more, "we see the prehistory of our own life, each of us the prehistory of his own life."[8]

But this means that redemptive history is not merely a recital that we hear and understand. It is also a demand upon us, for out of it comes the voice of God. Faith is responding to the call of God that comes to us from out of the midst of redemptive history. It is (to borrow from Kierkegaard) as though we sat witnessing some tremendous epic drama being performed on a vast stage, when suddenly the chief character of the drama, who is also its director, steps forward to the front of the stage, fixes his eye upon us, points his finger at us, and calls out: "You, you're wanted. Come up here. Take your part!" This is the call of faith coming from out of "sacred history", the call to cease to be a spectator and come forward to be an actor in the great drama of redemption. We are none of us comfortable with this call; we much prefer the anonymity and irresponsibility of being spectators, and we resent the demand that we come forward, assume responsibility, and become actors. But precisely this is the demand of biblical faith as redemptive history. Unless we receive this call and respond to it, the redemptive history that we apprehend is not redemptive. It does not really tell us who we are, where we stand, and what we may hope for; it does not really give meaning to existence. The history which redeems is a history in which one is both object and subject, both spectator and actor; but paradoxically, it is a history in which one is not object unless he is subject, one is not spectator unless he is actor, for unless one is really actor and subject, the "sacred history" ceases to be personal history and loses all religious significance. Redemptive history, to be truly redemptive, must be existential, appropriated in inwardness in personal existence as a demand and a responsibility. This is the meaning of biblical faith as *Heilsgeschichte*.

[7] In other words, redemption in the biblical sense is history, though history is not, as the Marxists or liberal utopians think, redemptive.

[8] Martin Buber, "Hasidism in Religion", *Hasidism* (Philosophical Library, 1948), p. 199. This is true for both Jew and Christian, though the Christian, of course, extends the "old Israel" into the "new Israel" of the Church.

3

BERNHARD ANDERSON | *How the Past Speaks to Us**

Several conclusions are evident from this critical study of the Old Testament. In the first place, we are dealing with documents which are considerably removed, in point of time, from the period of the events described. The traditions about the beginnings of Israel were passed down orally for centuries before they were first reduced to writing by J and E. The situation would be comparable if we had no early records concerning the migration of the Pilgrims to America, but had to rely solely upon traditions (poems, legends, anecdotes, and so on) passed down orally to the historian of the twentieth century. Even when we consider the remarkable power of memory of the ancient Semites, we must make due allowance for the fact that the traditions come to us through folk channels in which the interest was in the telling of the story, not the communication of accurate factual information. In this connection, scholars often point out that narratives written down by an eyewitness of the events, like the account of David's domestic affairs in II Samuel 9–20, usually give a comparatively straightforward and unadorned presentation, while narratives that are dependent upon an oral tradition are replete with miracle tales, as in the case of the Elijah-Elisha cycle of stories. This does not mean that we should dismiss the miracle faith as an invention of the popular imagination, but it does mean that we should study it in terms of the folk mind in which it took shape and evolved.

Again, we must be clear about the attitude toward the past reflected in these documents. We may be sure that J and E, the earliest historians, did not write down the traditions of Israel because of a curiosity about what actually happened "back there" in the days of long ago. We can hardly imagine these writers, after the manner of modern historians, carefully

* By permission. From Bernhard Anderson, *Rediscovering the Bible*, Association Press, New York, 1951, pp. 48–63.

checking all the available sources and objectively weighing the evidence in order that the past might be reconstructed accurately. This was not the Hebrew way of writing history. For these writers the past was not so much "back there" as it was a present reality in the memory of a people, giving meaning to daily events and casting its light ahead into the future. In other words, we are dealing with what Nels Ferré whimsically described in a university chapel sermon as "the is-ness of the was," the presentness of the past in the life of a historical community. Each of us knows how within himself he bears his own past. This past is not written down in a diary, or represented by photograph albums containing pictures of what actually took place. Rather, it is held in the remembrance of the present, thereby giving each of us a unique outlook upon the actions of the day and the aspirations for tomorrow. Likewise in the case of Israel we are dealing primarily with *remembered* events. The traditions of the past were preserved in the oral memory and eventually written down in various documents, not because of historical curiosity but because the meaning of these events was a vital part of the life of each generation. Through the remembrance of the past God continued to speak in the present (see Amos 2:9–16; Jeremiah 2:1–19). So, for instance, the annual observance of the ancient rite of the Passover kept alive and fresh the memory of the Exodus.

The fact that the past is not treated in textbook fashion helps to explain something which bewilders us about the composition of the Pentateuch. What led the editors to piece together various documents in disregard of plagiarizing others' work and forging Moses' name, and above all in seeming unawareness of the inconsistencies resulting from such a "scissors-and-paste" method? The answer is that writing under a pseudonym was a widespread and respectable practice in antiquity, and "authorship rights" was hardly a consideration when authors and editors were unconcerned about their personal autograph. While the editors of the Pentateuch were probably aware of inconsistencies resulting from their work, their governing consideration was not logical consistency but the preservation of the tradition in all its richness. These writings, in other words, must be understood primarily as a continuing proclamation of Israel's faith. And since all generations were linked together in the chain of witnesses, the voices of the past were summoned to testify in the present as the traditions were subjected to a fresh editorial revision. The incorporation of J, E, D, and P into a single work is perhaphs analogous to our hymnbooks in which hymns of different ages are conserved and used, despite differences among them, as witness of a common faith.

Finally, all these sources are unanimous in their emphasis upon miracle.

Obviously there are real differences between the various writings of the Pentateuch. J and E seem to reflect the prophetic viewpoint of the ninth and eighth centuries B.C., D seems to represent an alliance of prophets and priests, and P definitely views the past through the eyes of priests. J and P begin with the Creation, E starts with Abraham, and D is concerned primarily with the Mosaic period. Each writing reflects different historical circumstances that prevailed at the time of its composition and employs a characteristic style, vocabulary, and theological language. But despite these and other differences all the sources agree that miracle stories are indispensable in the proclamation of Israel's faith.

Moreover, if we were to pursue our investigation beyond the *written* sources of the Pentateuch back into the period of the *oral* transmission of the faith, we would discover that the experience of miracle lies at the very heart of the tradition. In recent years a great deal of light has been thrown on this point by a school of study known as "Form Criticism."[1] Accepting the basic outline of the Documentary Hypothesis, these scholars have attempted to study the preliterary forms into which the tradition was cast and the life situations of the community in which the small fragments were remembered, long before they were incorporated into the literary cycles of J and E. They have isolated certain units, now embedded in the literary strata of the Pentateuch, and have found after careful analysis that they bear the marks of being heirlooms handed down from an ancient time, shortly after the period of the Exodus. As an example we may cite the confession of faith which, according to Deuteronomy 26:5–10 (cf. 6:20–24), the worshiper makes at the sanctuary in connection with his offering of the first fruits:

> A nomad Aramean was my father; he went down to Egypt to reside there, with a small company, and there he became a nation, great, mighty, and numerous; the Egyptians treated us harshly, oppressed us, and imposed hard servitude upon us; but we cried to the Lord, the God of our fathers, and the Lord heard our cry, and seeing our affliction, our toil and our oppression, *the Lord brought us out of Egypt with a strong hand and an outstretched arm, with great terrors, signs, and portents;* and bringing us to this place, he gave us this land, a land flowing with milk and honey. And now see, I have brought the first of the produce of the soil, which thou, O Lord, hast given me.

---

[1] See chapter 7 [of *Rediscovering the Bible*] for the application of this method to the New Testament. This approach was first used in Old Testament study and was known as *Gattungkritik*, the study of the *Gattung* or unit as to its "form" and history.

This ancient cultic confession is really a recitation of the "mighty acts" of God which brought the Israelite community into being and which were remembered by succeeding generations as the basis of the community's ongoing life. A narrative like J is actually only an elaboration of the theme of *Heilsgeschichte* or the Drama of God's Redemptive Acts—a theme that was a part of the oral tradition from an early time.

Of course, this study of the folk mind of Israel, aided by the comparative examination of other folk traditions, has helped us to understand how the tradition was embellished as the years went by. It would be rash, however, to assert that miracle stories were foreign to the authentic tradition of Israel or that they were mere inventions of popular imagination. On the contrary, both a literary examination of the Pentateuch and a form-critical study of the oral transmission of Israel's faith lead to the conclusion that the experience of miracle was native to Israel's faith.

THE SIGNIFICANCE OF THE EXODUS

We have attempted to prepare for the consideration of our question by recognizing that the Pentateuch does not provide us with an on-the-scene report of events, and that the motive for remembering and eventually writing these stories was not the historian's desire to produce an accurate textbook of history. Now we must face the central issue: what is the nature of the miracle faith which was stated anew as each generation retold the stories, and as various editors gave the tradition fresh statement by reworking the literary sources?

The book of Genesis gives us the impression that God's special action in history began with his calling Abraham to leave Mesopotamia and to go out by faith into the Land of Promise (Genesis 12:1; cf. Hebrews 11:8). Thus the God who called Israel out of Egypt is, as the documents of the Pentateuch testify, "the God of the fathers": Abraham, Isaac, and Jacob. In a sense this is profoundly true. God's deliverance of the Israelites from Egypt was preceded by his providential guidance of their ancestors in the past. This claim, however, was made *in retrospect*, just as one who is called into Christian service looks back from the standpoint of faith and sees that in his earlier years God was guiding and preparing him for his vocation. Therefore the prevailing interpretation of the book of Genesis, including the "call" of Abraham, is probably a projection backward of the meaning discerned in later events of Israel's history, especially the Exodus. We can understand how the ancient traditions have been treated if we imagine American historians beginning with an interpretation of American history derived, say, from the Revolutionary War and, by backward projection, viewing everything from Columbus' discovery of America on as preparation for the signing of the Declaration of Independence.

The stories of the patriarchal age are folk stories which were preserved, in the first instance, for their enthralling interest, not for their historical value. Admittedly, they contain a measure of historical accuracy, as archaeologists are now pointing out. Excavations at Ur, Abraham's native city, and other places in the Near East have enabled us to see the patriarchal narratives against the background of ancient civilization and the movement of population across the coveted arc of land which has been called the "Fertile Crescent."[2] Abraham's migration from Ur to Haran and from Haran into Palestine was undoubtedly a phase of a great movement of population which occurred sometime between 2000 and 1700 B.C. The discovery of the names Abram and Jacob in the records of these peoples clearly indicates that Semitic elements were involved. But the question as to what actually motivated Abraham to go into Palestine cannot be answered merely by reading the story in Genesis 12. We must remember that the patriarchal traditions of Genesis are governed by a religious view which, properly speaking, came from the period of Moses and later. The light of God's revelation to Moses and the prophets shone backward into the period of the patriarchs and even into the mythological period of "prehistory" (Genesis 1–11). Thus J projects the worship of God under the special name "Yahweh" back to the time of Adam's grandson (Genesis 4:26), contrary to E and P, which emphasize the special revelation in the Mosaic period (see Exodus 3:14–15 [E]; 6:3 [P]).[3]

Turning to the period of the Exodus, immediately the question arises: why should the Exodus have this pivotal significance in Israel's faith? Viewed by itself the flight of a handful of slave-laborers from the borderland of Egypt is nothing extraordinary. To be sure, the book of Exodus in its present form gives us the impression that the presence of Hebrews in Egypt constituted a real political threat to the country and that their petition to leave caused reverberations throughout the land. Again we must remember, however, that these events are described in documents of a much later period, and from an Israelite point of view. Unquestion-

[2] The "Fertile Crescent" is J. H. Breasted's designation of the fertile strip of land which skirts the Mediterranean coast (Palestine-Syria) and bends around, following the valley of the Tigris-Euphrates down to the Persian Gulf.

[3] The J source employs the word "Yahweh" throughout the book of Genesis, while E and P refrain from using the special name until the time of Moses. This alternation in the use of divine names was one of the chief clues which led to the unraveling of the sources of the Pentateuch.

ably the historical situation was considerably magnified in the folk tradition owing to the profound significance of the Exodus in Israel's faith. In Egyptian records of the period the event is passed over in complete silence. We learn from Egyptian sources that it was customary for Egyptian officials to admit Asiatics into the Delta region (Goshen) especially during a time of famine, and moreover we are told that pharaohs like Rameses II used *Habiru* (evidently the Egyptian equivalent of "Hebrews") to do hard labor on public projects. But the flight of this particular group of Hebrews was, from the Egyptian standpoint, an event of such minor significance that it did not even receive official mention, so far as we know. This is no argument against the historicity of the Exodus. It is only an indication of the different standpoints from which the event was viewed. To Egyptians this was only a minor border incident; to the Hebrews involved it was a "mighty act" of Yahweh.

This difference in standpoint should warn us immediately against assuming that the extraordinary wonders and signs attending the Exodus were proofs which compelled people to acknowledge the power of Yahweh. Today many people suppose that the performance of miracles in the biblical period is an argument which should convince all rational people of the truth of the Bible. How could these marvelous things have occurred, it is asked, without the supernatural intervention of God? If, however, a modern skeptic had been on hand at the time, he would not necessarily have seen what the Israelites saw, and certainly he would not have found proofs that compelled his reason to acknowledge the redemptive activity of God in history. The miracle of the Red Sea was no proof to hostile Egyptians or to ficklehearted Israelites who longed for the "fleshpots" of Egypt. But to those who saw *in faith*, it was the assurance that God was with them, fighting for them against impossible odds. This is the conviction expressed in an ancient scrap of poetry which scholars believe was composed by one who witnessed the cataclysm of the Red Sea:

> Sing ye to the Lord, for he hath triumphed gloriously,
> The horse and his rider hath he thrown into the sea!
> —Exodus 15:21

Here we are up against the tantalizing problem of election, the mystery that some men see the action of God while other rational men, beholding the same outward manifestations of his sovereignty, are spiritually blind. We cannot properly discuss the question of what happened at the Red Sea until we have grappled with this more basic issue, for it is commonplace knowledge that one's attitude makes all the difference in what he sees. Israel's election consisted in the gift of spiritual sight which enabled this people to trace the working of God's hand in human affairs. Why *they* saw God's action in history, when others about them did not, can be explained only by saying that God caused them to see—which, of course, is no explanation at all. But apart from this spiritual discernment of the chosen people we are at a loss to understand why Israelites saw the hand of God everywhere, even in things we would regard as commonplace or capable of some scientific explanation.

Consider, for instance, the miracle of the Red Sea. For many people the biblical story has lost its glamour because scholars have pointed out that: (a) the body of water referred to is not the Red Sea but the shallow "sea of reeds" or Marsh Sea further north; (b) the miracle occurred during a violent storm when the wind reached such a velocity that the shallow waters were temporarily held back, as the J narrative suggests ("a strong east wind," Exodus 14:21); and (c) this "natural event" has been witnessed in more recent times in this area. This very plausible theory fails to explain the perfect timing: the strange coincidence of the natural phenomenon with the emergency of the fugitive Hebrews. (Compare the modern exodus from Dunkirk!) But even if it could be proved beyond a shadow of doubt that such a natural phenomenon actually underlies the biblical tradition we would not necessarily arrive at an understanding of the biblical meaning of the event. Suppose, says the skeptic, the Hebrews *were* lucky enough to get across the Marsh Sea during a windstorm. So what? After all, nature is full of freakish things, as any modern scientist knows. So after discussing what might or might not have happened we come again to the stubborn fact that what to one person may be a sign of God's providence to another may be interpreted quite differently, depending on his sight, his perspective upon history. This leads one scholar to state that ". . . there is no Miracle except to the eye that perceives it: we might add that to the eye which perceives it, it ceases in one sense to be a 'Miracle' at all," for all things are touched by the hand of God.[4]

THE ROLE OF MOSES

In any discussion of the Exodus, and the extraordinary signs and wonders that accompanied it, we must begin with the supreme miracle of Israel's election and the unique outlook of this people upon history. Moreover, we must give due attention to the role of Moses, whose call is inseparably

---

[4] W. J. Phythian-Adams, *The Call of Israel* (Oxford, 1934), p. 177.

related to the call of Israel. To the historian Moses presents a tremendous problem, a problem greater than the much discussed issue of the "historical Jesus." Anything said about Moses must be qualified by the caveat that his career antedates the earliest written documents of the Old Testament by at least four centuries, and that he is known to us only in the framework of the faith of the Israelite community.

The account of Moses' call is given in the vivid narrative found in Exodus 3. Moses was tending the flocks of his Midianite father-in-law, so the story goes, when he came to the slopes of Horeb, otherwise known as Sinai. There, while he was brooding over the plight of his fellow men in Egypt, "the Angel of the Lord" appeared to him in a flame of fire out of the midst of a bush. Knowing that we are dealing with a story which in its written form is much later than Moses' time, and knowing furthermore that in the Old Testament faith finds expression in the rich imagery of oriental symbolism, we should not fall into the error of rationalizing this as a portrayal of something which took place objectively, as though the burning bush could have been pictured with a movie camera or the Voice recorded by a phonograph had someone been around with those modern instruments. To ask the question "Did this happen just as it is described?" betrays our inability to understand the Hebraic mode of thinking, which makes no sharp distinction between what we would call the inner and the outer, the subjective and the objective, the world of imagination and the realm of hard fact. To us of the West these are two separate dimensions; to the oriental mind, however, they blend together as one. Therefore, literalism kills the meaning of the story. Of course God did not actually reveal himself in fire; but how could the truth be stated more vividly that God, though hidden from mortal sight, makes known his glory in commonplace situations? Likewise, God did not literally carry on a conversation with Moses; but is it not profoundly true that this dialogue has been repeated again and again when men have encountered God? Just as the poet addresses himself to the poet within us, so the narrative of Exodus 3 speaks from faith to faith.

It is important to recognize that God's word came to Moses in a moment when he was acutely conscious of the historical situation of his people in Egypt. We cannot properly consider Moses as a mystic who had a private experience of God's presence out in the silence and solitude of the desert. In Moses' case, as indeed with all the prophets, our attention fastens first upon the historical situation in Egypt which was integrally related to what was taking place in the ancient world during the second millennium before Christ. Moses' role was not that of telling his countrymen about a private religious experience; it was, rather, that of mediating to them the meaning of a specific historical crisis in which they were all involved. He was, of course, the leader who took the initiative in setting his people free; but, like the prophets, he was also the divine spokesman who interpreted the signs of the times. In this sense Hosea is correct in saying: "By a prophet the Lord brought Israel out of Egypt" (12:13).

God's revelation to Moses, then, came as the interpretation of a historical situation: Israel's bondage in Egypt. One conviction dominates all the narratives of the Pentateuch: the completely wonderful outgoing of God's love toward Israel, his stooping down mercifully to rescue his "son" from the house of bondage (Exodus 4:22). "And the Lord said, I have surely seen the affliction of my people which are in Egypt, and have heard their cry by reason of their taskmasters; for I know their sorrows, and I am come down to deliver them . . ." (Exodus 3:7–8). What made the Exodus crucial for Israel was not the bare events, like the escape from Egypt or the crossing of the Marsh Sea, but the meaning revealed in those events. To the outsider the Exodus was only a phase of the continual shifting of population in the ancient world; to Israel, however, this was the event which revealed God as Lord and Redeemer. Looking out from this standpoint of faith, miracles were seen on every hand, giving assurance of his mercy, his protection, his guidance, and his faithfulness.

DID THE MIRACLES HAPPEN?

Up to this point we have said that the supreme miracle was wrought by God in history: his creation of a people to be his own in a special sense.

> I will take you as my own people, and I will be your God, and you shall know that it is I, the Lord your God, who shall free you from the burdens of the Egyptians.
>
> —Exodus 6:7

It is wrong to detach a miracle story from this context of faith and study it in isolation. The miracle stories, collectively and individually, must be viewed in the light of the central affirmation of faith: God's call of Israel. The deliverance of the infant Moses from the pharaoh's massacre, the plagues in Egypt, the crossing of the Marsh Sea, the pillar of cloud and fire, the sending of the manna and quails, the striking of the rock to obtain water, the defeat of Amalek—each one of these incidents, viewed from the standpoint of faith, was an assurance or sign of the saving activity of God in the history of his people, Israel. We could go so far as to say that even though any one of these stories could be shown on historical grounds to be an inaccurate or legendary account of the actual situation, the truth of the miracle tradition as a whole would not be affected in the slightest. For it is precisely the central element of the tradition, namely the call of Israel, which lies beyond the scope of historical or scientific inquiry. Israel's faith did not rest merely upon the Exodus and accompanying incidents, which are open to historical or archaeological study; rather, Israel's faith rested upon the experience that the Exodus was *God's redemptive act.* A people had been created by God's sovereign activity in history! This was the miracle that "happened."

We insist, however, upon pressing the question as to whether a particular episode, which illustrates this central truth, actually took place. This is a matter for discussion in terms of historical criticism. For instance, the story about the infant Moses floating down the Nile in a basket is so obviously based on familiar legends that we may conclude that here the tradition has been embellished by a folk motif.[5] Even so, the folk story in this case expresses the religious truth that God's redemptive purpose was at work even before Moses' later awareness of it. In the providence of God the evil design of the pharaoh actually became the means whereby Egyptians trained the future leader of the Hebrews! Similarly, the stories concerning Moses' wonder-working rod (for example, Exodus 7:10–13) betray the interests of the folk mind. But in every case these popular superstitions not only add vividness to the story but also imaginatively express the truth of God's sovereignty over the priestly wizardry of Egypt and over all powers that would oppose the accomplishment of his purpose in history.

Other stories may be imaginative exaggerations of natural occurrences which attended the Exodus, the wilderness wandering, and the invasion of Canaan. Some scholars believe that most of the plagues can be explained on the basis of a natural catastrophe: the inundation of the Nile River. We have already noticed that some explain the crossing of the Red Sea in terms of a violent windstorm which occurred at the critical moment; others theorize that a volcanic explosion caused the sea-bottom to be raised up and produced other extraordinary phenomena, such as the pillar of cloud and fire.[6] The quails in the wilderness present no great

[5] The birth story of Moses strikingly resembles the legend of the famous Sargon, king of Akkad. See G. A. Barton, *Archaeology and the Bible,* 7th ed. (American Sunday School Union), p. 375.

[6] On the assumption that Sinai at this time was an active volcano, W. J. Phythian-Adams (*op. cit.,* pp. 137–172) rather fancifully accounts for the plagues, the cataclysm of the Red Sea, the pillar of cloud and fire, and the awe-inspiring phenomena experienced at the sacred mountain.

problem, for we are told that during the course of their migration north-ward in the spring they are numerous in the area and, when exhausted, can easily be caught. Similarly the "manna" from heaven may have been a honeylike substance from a kind of tamarisk tree that grows in the region (Arab still call it *mun*). And so on. These "explanations" should be taken with a critical grain of salt. Historical criticism impresses us with the difficulty of reaching back through the haze of the oral tradition and reconstructing what actually happened. It also warns us of the im-possibility of sharply separating fact from interpretation in a literature concerned primarily with proclaiming Israel's faith.

Whatever natural events accompanied the Exodus we may be sure of this: the book of Exodus is not concerned primarily with telling about freakish natural events which took place in seeming disruption of what we would call "natural law." These stories were remembered not because men were interested in nature as such, but because nature also manifested the glory of the God of history. We find it difficult to understand the Bible on this matter because today nature is something we look at "out there," something we control by means of our science, something which is in-different to the history in which men are involved. According to the Bible, however, nature is involved in history because God is Lord of both nature and history. Nature is, as it were, a mirror which reflects the meaning of man's life in history. This is the case in the book of Exodus. Stories which to us seem to describe abnormal natural events are really manifes-tations of the supreme miracle: God's saving activity in the history of his people, Israel. God is described as fighting for Israel by using the forces of nature to protect and sustain his people (Exodus 14:25). Here is an interpretation of history which recognizes that the course of events is affected by something more than natural or human factors.

Is this miracle faith true? Did God speak to Moses and did he lead Israel out of Egypt "with a strong hand"? This question, as we have said, lies beyond the boundaries of natural science and historical inquiry. It can be answered only by the decision of faith. As Alan Richardson re-minds us, however, any denial of the miracle faith of the Bible will be made from the standpoint of a rival interpretation of the meaning of man's life, and that interpretation itself will be based on faith, not on an impartial and neutral study of the facts.[7] Historical criticism has clarified our problem by liberating us from the false notion that the Bible is an accurate and infallible record of the past, and by helping us to understand what the men of the Bible were saying when they used the language of

[7] *Christian Apologetics* (Harper, 1947), p. 173.

miracle. It is no longer necessary to choose between either the Bible or the assured conclusions of the natural sciences. The alternative is the biblical understanding of man's history or some other view. Christianity takes its stand upon the conviction that God manifested his love and purpose in that unique series of historical events which began with the Exodus and culminated in the coming of Jesus Christ. This is the miracle which "happened"; and this is the abiding experience of the miracle stories. For in so far as, by faith, we look out upon history from this biblical standpoint, our eyes are opened to behold the mystery and majesty of God's redemptive love. The miracle stories then occasion no difficulty; in fact, they express the faith of one who sees all of life touched by divine miracle. As Elizabeth Barrett Browning writes:

> Earth's crammed with heaven,
> And every common bush afire with God;
> But only he who sees takes off his shoes.

Chapter 2 | God, Creation and the World

The Bible opens with the words "In the beginning God created . . ." [Genesis 1:1] and closes with "The grace of the Lord Jesus be with all the saints. Amen" [Revelation 22:21]. Between the front and back covers moves a cosmic drama. According to Judeo-Christian conviction, it is God who acts in human history. God enters this world to *create*, to *redeem*, to bring into being a unique *community*. The God of the Bible is no remote, static, impersonal idea. The biblical writers employ not nouns but verbs to speak of the character of Yahweh: what He has done, is doing and will do.

From History to Creation

The focus of the biblical drama is not what we moderns call external nature but human history. While the Old Testament starts with God's creation of the world of nature, this is clearly not the point at which its writers began to tell the story. Their commencement was, as we have stressed, that pivotal event on which they believed their nation's whole destiny turned: God's act of deliverance from slavery in Egypt, the formulation of a special community, the establishment of the covenant relationship, the call to a sacred task among the nations. As Bernhard Anderson points out, this is Act I of the biblical drama.[1] As the curtain falls on this act, we witness the military power of the Babylonians carrying out Yahweh's judgment on a rebellious Israel. Act II depicts the tragic years of the Babylonian exile, as the background of God's assurance that He is mindful of the people's plight. Then the scene shifts back to Palestine, where the covenanted people becomes a "holy Jewish Community."

With the beginning of Act III, the New Testament portrays John the

---

[1] By permission. From Bernhard Anderson, *Rediscovering the Bible,* Association Press, New York, 1951, p. 236.

Baptist calling Jews, who have settled down into a self-righteous legalism, to renewal and repentance. He announces the coming of the long-expected Messiah. For Christian faith, the biblical drama reaches its climax in that event, of which the person of Jesus Christ is the center, including His life, teaching and God's raising His Son from the dead. Empowered by Christ's continuing presence, the disciples now believe in a way distinctively different from that which has held them in loyalty even before His death. As this third act closes, they become a faithful community of a new covenant relationship with the Father of their Lord, Jesus, the Christ. This new community is then empowered by God with a message to proclaim to the world.[2]

But this biblical drama of God's redemptive acts in human history also has a *prologue* and an *epilogue*. The prologue begins with the creation of the world and the fall of man. The epilogue paints a vivid and imaginative picture of final judgment and a new creation. The beginning and the end, creation and consummation, belong together. They form the farthest reaches of the time span within which God moves. For the biblical writers, the creation is also an act of history. The Creator is the same God whom they had known first in and through the revelatory events of their life as a people. The creation, the end and also the covenant (both old and new) are involved. For the biblical writers held to the conviction that history is purposive; it is not illusory but actual, not circular but linear. At its center are here-and-now events through which God discloses Himself. His purpose is to reconcile man, whom He has created, to Himself and to establish and sustain His people, who are chosen for a special task among the nations. "The covenant is the goal of creation, creation is the way to the covenant. . . ."[3] Or, in the words of Edmond Jacob, ". . . creation is secondary to that of the covenant, of which it is both the condition and the consequence. . . . But the covenant is only possible within the framework of creation."[4] "Why had God created the world? The Old Testament would answer: He has created it for the covenant, that is to say because of his plan of love and salvation for humanity by means of Israel."

Thus this picture of a purposive history is incomplete without a beginning and an end. The creation, then, is an affirmation of man's utter dependence upon God. Everything that *is*, the world of nature, history and man's personal existence (individual and communal), has its ground in Him.

[2] *Ibid.*, pp. 236–237.

[3] Karl Barth, *Dogmatic III*, i, p. 106.

[4] Edmond Jacob, *Theology of the Old Testament*, trans. by Arthur W. Heathcote and Philip J. Allcock, Harper & Row, Publishers, Incorporated, New York, 1958, p. 136.

Myths of Creation in the Biblical Tradition

For moderns, this seems like a strange world view. For example, Henry A. Murray, professor of psychology at Harvard University, pleads with us to leave behind the old ". . . mythologies of dependent and compliant childhood, . . . the father-son mythology of the religion we inherited. . . ." In place of the biblical Testaments, he would write *his* "new testament." "This testament would differ radically from the Bible inasmuch as its mythology would be consonant with contemporary science: its personifications would all refer to forces and functions *within* nature, human nature."[5]

But this view misunderstands the significance of the biblical Testaments. It does so in two ways: first, as to the relevance of the *sciences;* and second, concerning the biblical use of *myth.* First, sign-events, "miracles" of the "natural" order, the occurrences of the Exodus point beyond themselves to the God who acted to deliver and establish His chosen community. "Nature" as some sort of force operating by "laws" within the world is a modern conception. Our contemporary approach would have made no sense to the biblical writers. They viewed the universe as created and sustained by God's will and loving care. In fact, they evidenced ". . . no primary interest in nature as such, except as it revealed God's creative power and as it was used by him to further his purposes in history."[6] It is fruitless, therefore, to try to reconcile the biblical accounts of creation with the findings of the modern sciences.

There are two stories of the beginning. The account of man, Paradise and the fall, which appears second in our Bible (Genesis 2:4b–3:24), is the work of J and therefore the older as to date of writing. We shall discuss this account in Chapter 3, "The Nature of Man."

Genesis 1:1–2:4a is the work of the later writer P, who takes his stance within the worshiping community which had been brought into being at the Exodus. From this perspective he looks back to the creation. His account is not a scientific statement describing *how* the world came into existence. "The issue lies, properly speaking, beyond the domain of science and is independent of any cosmology, whether ancient or modern. The purpose of the chapter is to declare that everything is dependent for its existence and meaning upon the sovereign God."[7]

---

[5] Henry A. Murray, "Beyond Yesterday's Idealism," address before the Harvard chapter of Phi Beta Kappa, 1959. See Crane Brinton, *The Fate of Man,* George Braziller, Inc., New York, 1961, p. 16.

[6] *The Interpreter's Bible,* Abingdon Press, Nashville, Tenn., 1952, vol. I, p. 359.

[7] Bernhard Anderson, *Understanding the Old Testament,* Prentice-Hall, Inc., Englewood Cliffs, N.J., 1957, p. 385.

Second, we moderns have difficulty in grasping the biblical use of mythological materials of the ancient world. This issue is closely connected with the first problem of the relevance of the sciences to the stories of creation, for the biblical writers adopted the cosmology or picture of the universe prevalent among nearby peoples of their time. The religions of their neighbors were "natural religions," and thus their neighbors' gods were "nature gods." The perspective of these people was the precise opposite of Israel's. Instead of seeing the role of nature in terms of history, they understood the problems of human life over against the forces of nature. These natural forces were divine forces. Or, contrariwise, the deities were the personifications of the powers of nature. The realm of the gods and the realm of nature were identical. Within this order of nature man and society found the locus of human existence. In particular, the gods represented the recurring processes of fertility and productivity. To these cycles of nature men had to adjust themselves if they were to survive, for their very lives depended on these cosmic rhythms. In Babylon men believed themselves to be slaves of the gods and to be bound completely to the burdens of irrigating the soil, planting the seeds and harvesting the crops. This kind of polytheism (worship of many gods) is no revolutionary religion but a religion of the *status quo,* the existing order of things. The good man adapted himself to the hierarchy of established authority, both human and divine. The bad man asserted his own will against the orders of authority, for sin was seen as disruption of the recurring rhythms of the cosmos.

The Judeo-Christian view, on the other hand, is based upon an entirely different conception of God in relation to His created world. The term "creation myth," for the biblical writers, has a distinctive meaning.

Meanings of "Myth"

As to the various usages of the term "myth" itself, there is much disagreement among scholars. When we say the word *myth,* we tend to think of fictions, legends, fairy stories which cannot possibly be true. Or we become analysts of contemporary social classes or groups and distinguish biased, stereotyped generalizations, or "myths," from the "facts." Obviously, some say, enlightened men and women will abandon myths which falsely portray the characteristics of a given group or class and, instead, seek and express the truth about them.

But in the context of religious language, the word *myth* has a different meaning. Here men seek to express, somehow in symbol of word and act, their relationship to the ultimate. The richly imagic language of the *beginning* and the *end* of all things speaks in tones utterly different from, and yet not contradictory to, those of sciences and philosophies. Mythic utterance begins with the images of our everyday world. Imagination works freely on these images, interpreting, moving out from them into all sorts of envisioned possibilities. Of course, new insights, in the sciences, the arts, literature and philosophies, have their source in creative imagination. But there are significant differences between these rational or critical uses of imagination and those of religion. John Hutchison distinguishes these in this way:

> Rational or critical thought consists in bringing images into responsible relation to facts. Thus, for example, once a new idea comes into being in science, it is deliberately tested on facts. The measure of its truth is its adequacy to the facts. This is true, in varying ways and measures, in all thinking; the life of reason is a quest for adequacy.
>
> The mode of religious or mythical thinking consists in the occurrence in the mind of the religious person of compelling or authoritative images. Where in art the mind contemplatively enjoys images evoked by the work of art, in religion these images possess authority or force over a person's whole life. Indeed the essence of religious experience is just such an image. Religion is thus poetry by which men live. The reference to action makes clear why religion entails morality and poetry does not.[8]

But scholars make a distinction between varying uses of mythic utterance. The approach of the biblical writers differs from that employed in either the mystical tradition or the nature religions of Babylonia and Canaan. Some contemporary scholars would abandon the term "myth" altogether as inappropriate to biblical writing. Others retain the word but make it clear that they are using it in a unique way. The mystical approach denies the reality of this world of space and time, for mystics seek to escape the actual world of history and achieve union with a transtemporal Reality. But biblical myths, as we have emphasized in all our discussion, express the actuality of time and history. On the other hand, nature religions use myths, couched in the fanciful language of poetic metaphor, to speak of man's relations to cosmic, natural forces. They speak of the origins of the gods themselves and the conflict of universal powers. The biblical writers refer rather to "a whole plan of action," showing us that ". . . God's plan in history has creation as its starting point."

---

[8] By permission. From John Hutchison, *Faith, Reason, and Existence*, Oxford University Press, Fair Lawn, N.J., 1956, pp. 56–57.

The Old Testament does reflect several creation myths from Babylonian and Canaanite traditions.[9] But Edmond Jacob, for instance, takes the position that these traces of mythical materials can be discerned less clearly in the Genesis narratives than in other passages.[10] Therefore these biblical accounts are ". . . a history of creation and not a myth of creation; the features characteristic of myth are absent from it."

According to this view, then, a myth proper belongs to the context of nature religion. The nature myth employs ritualistic repetition to celebrate periodically the origins of the gods themselves and their struggles with the forces of darkness. These are characteristics of the religions of surrounding cultures but not of Israel itself. To be sure, there are chaos and darkness in the biblical account. But God, who through the generations has been Israel's Guide and Sustainer, could use these forces of evil for His creative purpose. Over whatever is a vast waste and void in the universe, His spirit moves. Karl Barth asserts that "saga" rather than "myth" is the appropriate term to use in connection with the biblical account. He writes:

> It is assuredly a basic error to speak of creation myths. At best a myth may be a parallel to exact science; that is, a myth has to do with viewing what has always existed and will exist. A myth has to do with the mighty problem that at all times propounds itself to man and therefore is timeless, the problem of life and death, of sleep and wakening, of birth and dying, of morning and evening, of day and night, and so on. These are the themes of myth. Myth considers the world as it were from its frontier, but always the world which already exists. There is no creation myth because creation as such is simply not accessible to myth. Thus in the case of the Babylonian myth of creation, for example, it is quite clear that we are concerned with a myth of growth and decay which fundamentally cannot be brought into connexion with Genesis 1 and 2. At most we can say that certain mythical elements are to be found there. But what the Bible makes of that has no parallel in myth. If we are to give the biblical narrative a name, or put it in a category, then let it be that of *saga*. The Bible speaks in Genesis 1 and 2 of events which lie outside of our historical knowledge. But it speaks upon the basis of knowledge, which is related to history. In fact, the wonderful thing about the biblical creation narratives is that they stand in

[9] Jacob, *op. cit.*, p. 138.

[10] *Ibid.* See passages in the Old Testament such as Job 7:21ff, 26:10–13, 38:8–11; Psalms 74, 89:11ff; Isaiah 51:9ff. In these passages, we can trace the themes of the ancient myths from Canaanite and Babylonian sources: divine struggle with rival powers, with sea monsters such as Rahab and Leviathan, the victory in the Babylonian tradition of Marduk, the national god, over Tiamat (the deep), and, in the Canaanite tradition, the struggles of Baal, the supreme god, against the sea. See Jacob, *op. cit.*, pp. 56–58.

strict connexion with the history of Israel and so with the story of God's action in the covenant with man. The first and second creation accounts alike stand plainly in connexion with the theme of the Old Testament: the first shows the covenant in the institution of the Sabbath as the *goal*, the second account as the *continuation* of the work of Creation.[11]

We are faced, thus, with alternatives as to how to employ the term "myth," whether to abandon its use in connection with the Bible or to retain it. If we decide on the latter alternative, we shall consider how to distinguish its meaning in the biblical tradition from that in other religious traditions.

[11] By permission. From Karl Barth, *Dogmatics in Outline*, trans. by G. T. Thompson, Harper Torchbooks/The Cloister Library, Harper & Row, Publishers, New York, 1959, pp. 51–52. I have put the word *saga* in italics for emphasis.

4

JULES LAURENCE MOREAU | *The Mythic Stance of*
*the Old Testament**

It is a commonplace of modern Biblical study to speak of certain aspects of the Biblical narrative as myth and to characterize the expression in these parts of the Bible as mythic. A recent writer has indicated that one of the typical problems involved in analyzing religious language is that of distinguishing between factual propositions and figurative statements.[1] The process of distinguishing is not complete, however, until some steps have been taken to discover what the mythic statements mean.

As a term used to designate a particular type of narrative and the thinking involved in the production of such narrative, "myth" does not mean the same thing to all who employ the term as scholars. R. G. Collingwood contends that ". . . myth proper has always the character of *theogony*."[2] This notion of myth arises from Collingwood's having used the Babylonian *Poem on Creation* as a type of myth. He does distinguish the Hebrew use of myth on the grounds that ". . . it replaces theogony by ethnogony."[3] If Hebrew myth replaces the story of the origin of the gods by a story of the origin of the nation, it would appear to lack the distinct character of "myth proper"; hence, it is hard to see precisely what Collingwood understands myth to be. In terms almost diametrically opposed to those of Collingwood, Susanne Langer states, "Divinities are born of ritual, but theologies spring from myth."[4] Her distinctions among myth, legend, and fairy tale (*Märchen*) follow those underlying the study of the myths, sagas, and fairy tales which are so abundant in the early

* From *Language and Religious Language* by Jules Laurence Moreau. Copyright © 1961, W. L. Jenkins. The Westminster Press. Used by permission.
[1] Geddes MacGregor, *Introduction to Religious Philosophy* (Houghton Mifflin Company, 1959), pp. 269ff.
[2] R. G. Collingwood, *The Idea of History*, edited by T. M. Knox, Galaxy Books, 1 (Oxford University Press, 1956), p. 15 (italics his own).
[3] *Ibid.*, p. 17.
[4] Susanne K. Langer, *Philosophy in a New Key* (Harvard University Press, 1942), p. 169.

history of the Germanic peoples. The chief characteristics of myth, according to this view, are its confrontation of the actual world and its determination to understand and organize experience. That is to say, among those who have studied German saga literature, myth is a means of orientation to the world that actually is, and is not a vehicle for escape from it. This is an important refinement of the definition of myth, since it removes it from the realm of the merely untrue. Yet, even this refinement of what myth does will not satisfactorily account for the distinctive feature of the Hebrew myth—its concern with time and history.

If it be maintained that myth arises only when the relationships of mankind to cosmic forces, that is to nature, ". . . are conceived through the spontaneous metaphor of poetic fantasy,"[5] then myth does not designate the peculiar stance of the Biblical literature toward time. In fact, the Biblical myth, which provides the framework in which the entire story of salvation is recounted, is inextricably bound up with a keen awareness of time. No explanation of the cosmic outlook of the Old Testament—and this is equally true of the New Testament—which slights the Hebrew valuation of time and history as basic to that outlook can do any justice to the peculiarly Biblical view of reality. Alan Richardson sums up the Biblical preference for time as a fundamental category when, in the course of pointing out that the Bible is enclosed within two internally related myths, he says, ". . . whereas the one myth affirms: 'In the beginning God,' so the other declares: 'at the end Christ.' "[6]

At the one end of the Biblical narrative we encounter the creation myth, and at the other we are confronted with the myth of the *eschaton*, the end of time. Throughout the entire length of the Bible from Genesis to Revelation, however, these two myths not only recur but actually provide the locus of the story which orients man in the world. It is profoundly significant that neither the religion of the Old Testament nor that of the New is at all concerned with what happened *before* "the beginning" or what happens *after* "the end." The Christian proclamation somewhat alters the perspective by designating Jesus as the Christ or the bringer of "the end," but the end that God brings into history in Jesus the Christ is a foretaste of the real end toward which time and history move. Only the reintroduction of the dualistic world outlook, which the Hebrew-Christian myth excluded, has been able to turn the Christian proclamation into a promise of escape and extrication to some far-off paradise.

[5] *Ibid.*, p. 180.
[6] Alan Richardson, *A Preface to Bible Study* (The Westminster Press, 1944), p. 179.

The process by which the book of Genesis achieved its present form testifies to the primary concern for history of the community for whom this book was the first chapter of its sacred history. The earliest account, forming the basis upon which all later expansions were made, consisted largely of *legends;* the primary stratum of the book of Genesis is a series of *legends.* A legend contains a kernel of historical fact inside a story that is elaborated in the retelling and expanded until it reaches the proportions of a narrative of the size and complexity of the Abraham story or the Joseph story. The compiler of the earliest narrative in Genesis meant to relate a series of legends of diverse origins one to another in order that the legends belonging to various groups in the Israelite amphictyony might be brought into a coherent whole. His purpose was that of relating the pastoral tradition of the desert tribes to the indigenous Palestinian tradition so that the whole could serve as a continuous religious tradition for a people unified into one nation. At this stage of the Genesis tradition, the mythic element is practically nil. It was not until the first significant revision of this catena of legends that myth made its appearance in the tradition of Israel as a vehicle for expression.

Of the two Creation stories in Genesis (Gen. 1:1 to 2:4a; 2:4b–25), the J story (Gen. 2:4b–25) is clearly the older. This older narrative itself consists of two definitely discernible strata that have been fused into a single unit. As Dr. Simpson has adequately maintained,[7] the final form of this earlier narrative contained some distinctly modified version of the Babylonian creation myth as it was known to the Canaanites. In its original Babylonian or even its Canaanite context, this myth would qualify for Collingwood's characterization of myth; that is to say, it is not only theogonic, but it is cosmogonic as well—it relates the *origin* of the gods and of the world. In that context, however, the myth is not historical, nor does it relate necessarily to a concrete group of people or nation. The Israelite writer responsible for the developed version of the earlier stratum of the Genesis narrative used as much of the myth as he could profitably employ. His purpose was to show, by modification of the thrust of the myth, that the God of Israel, Yahweh, whom the Israelites had come to know in such concrete historical events as are related in the Song of Deborah (Judg., ch. 5) or in the Song of Miriam (Ex. 15:21) was not only more than a tribal deity—he was the foundation of the world that is. The manner in which he accomplished this purpose was to expand backward the catena of legend which preserved a series of encounters with

---

[7] C. A. Simpson, "The Book of Genesis," *The Interpreter's Bible* (Abingdon Press, 1952), 1, pp. 441–450, 491 f.; cf. pp. 195 f.

Yahweh—Abraham, Jacob, Joseph, etc. When the considerably modified form of the creation myth was prefaced to this expanded account, it served to identify the Yahweh of historical encounter as the creator and sustainer of the world. This order of identification is of vital importance to an understanding of the peculiarly Israelite use of myth, for it indicates most clearly that the earliest category of Israelite theological reflection was *history* and *not nature*. Corroboration of this viewpoint is supplied by the fact that the normal designation of Yahweh is ". . . the God of your fathers, the God of Abraham, the God of Isaac, and the God of Jacob" (Ex. 3:15 f.; 4:5; cf. chs. 2:24; 6:3, 8; 32:13; 33:1; Num. 32:11; Deut. 1:8; 6:10; 9:5, 27, etc.). Except for certain oblique references in the latter sections of the Second Isaiah, God is not designated as the creator until the apocryphal Book of Jubilees.

The final redaction of the Israelite sacred history as it is presented in the Pentateuch was accomplished by the Priestly writer. Although his hand is visible through the story from Genesis through Joshua, one of the most significant achievements of this writer is his revision of the Creation story. The Creation story which now opens the book of Genesis (Gen. 1:1 to 2:4a) is his restatement of the Babylonian myth purged of those cosmogonic remnants which the earlier writer had felt it necessary to retain in his own modification of that myth. The peculiarly Israelite orientation of the Priestly writer is evident from his concern for the primarily historical character of the act of creation. His interest in the historical depth of this act, cosmogonically conceived in his source, comes through in unmistakable outline, for this account contains the seeds of a doctrine of *creatio ex nihilo*, even if it does not articulately express such a doctrine.[8] It must not be construed, however, that the doctrine of *creatio ex nihilo* is a metaphysical generalization made by the Priestly writer.

In this mythic conception, as presented in Genesis, we encounter an instance par excellence of the distinction between mythic expression and philosophical speculation. If God's creative act was performed upon an already existent matter, then from the historical viewpoint, God is not ultimate; there is a basically dualistic foundation to the universe if this view is carried to its logical conclusion. Depending upon the way in which the first two Hebrew words are translated at the beginning of Genesis, one can arrive at either a monistic or dualistic conception of the ultimate character of the Israelite view of reality.

The mythic vehicle employed by the Priestly writer is not primarily

[8] *Ibid.*, pp. 466–468.

concerned with cosmogony, however, but it is a religious affirmation cast against what, to him, is an inadequate conception of ultimate reality—the Babylonian creation myth. Apparently, nothing was conceivable for him before the beginning of God's creative activity; hence, his view comes from the inside of the historical process which he projects backward. The metaphysical view would be an *exterior* view in which the narrator would be attempting to achieve an objective detachment, a platform from which he could view the process. He, like his fellow Israelites, construed God as active and historical rather than quiescent and atemporal. Consequently, the beginning of the creative process is the only point to which it is possible to attain, and anything behind this point would have to speak of a quiescent and atemporal God, a notion that is simply inconceivable to an Israelite. Because of the historical orientation of the community represented by the Priestly writer, he was under pressure to change the naturalistic orientation of the source myth so that it would reflect the primacy of history over nature as the fundamental category of Israelite conception of God and the world. The measure of his achievement is stamped over the entire structure of the Pentateuch, and it carries forward into the Former Prophets, reaching a type of conclusion in the Priestly version of history contained in the work of the Chronicler and Ezra-Nehemiah.

The nature myth was persistent in the milieu in which Israel hammered out its conception of Yahweh, the God who acts. The hardiness of this mythic conception is demonstrated by the prophetic literature. While the incipient theological viewpoint of the Pentateuch was taking shape as a challenge to the generalized Semitic myth of creation, the prophets were waging war in the name of Yahweh against the fertility ceremonials which are characterized by the name Baalism. The cultic observances of Baalism were a response to the Canaanite manifestation of that variety of myth which arises among a settled agricultural people. In some form or other, this myth of the regularity of the seasons of planting, growing, and harvesting appeared among all the ancient people of the Mediterranean and the Near East. The myths of Demeter, Ceres, Syra Dea, and even Isis and Osiris are all localized forms of mythic generalization based upon the cyclic occurrence of the seasons as well as the precarious plight of the man who depends for sustenance upon the whims of the seasonal rains. In another form, this mythic outlook rises among a people whose lives depend upon viticulture. The Dionysiac rites are related to this cycle of myth.

The consolidation of the Israelite community brought into close proximity tribes of people who had varied backgrounds. On the one hand, there were those whose lives had been bound up in the agricultural processes of Canaan. They were the settled peoples against whom the invasion by pastoral and nomadic tribes had been mounted. Their outlook was essentially a cyclic one, for they knew the endless round of seasons and the difficulties of extracting a living out of the land. Their entire mythic structure was based upon this experience. On the other hand, the pastoral and nomadic tribes who had come into the land and taken control by force were differently oriented. The precariousness of existence on the desert wastes where there was little grazing for the flocks emphasized the transitoriness of life. Being nomadic, they could not appreciate the meaning of settled existence, nor could they have had that kind of experience which speaks of regularity. Tomorow and another grazing land were their hope; hence, time and history were the ingredients of their mythic structure.

The fundamental insight of the prophets was the recognition of the primacy of history for the life of the world as well as for its beginning. Therefore, from the days of Elijah onward, the prophets continued to inveigh strongly against the tendency to turn the Yahweh of historical encounter into an image, however exalted, of the gods of nature and the natural processes. The stock in trade of the prophets as they made their declarations was the destructive power of Yahweh, whose sovereignty tolerated no manipulation by mimetic cult. The message of the prophets had two dimensions that were really but two aspects of the same dimension. Their twin targets were settled agricultural existence and settled political existence. These targets were represented by Baalism and the monarchy, both of which were manifestations of their having deserted the religion of the fathers.

The establishment of the monarchy in Israel meant that the nation had made certain concessions to settled political existence. The corollaries of this act of concession were to be found in the shifting alliances made by the Israelite nation in order both to preserve its identity and to engage in political activity in the seething Middle East. Despite the fact that there were gains in Israel's national status, its achievement signified that an idol had replaced Yahweh, for security became more important than service to God who had chosen this people for his own. The development of agriculture and viticulture was, on its own level, a manifestation of the same idolatry, for Baal replaced Yahweh. So bitter was the opposition to this agricultural religion that the festivals that belonged to its observance were radically transformed in the prophetic period. The two early festivals of Passover and Pentecost were agricultural in origin and represented the offering of the early harvests. The Old Testament witnesses to their transformation into feasts of a historical genre having to do with the *wandering* period of Israelite life.

Passover was related to the exodus and Pentecost to the giving of the law at Sinai; thus, even at the level of observance there was reflected a radical abhorrence of the generalized Semitic myth of the cyclic return of the seasons. Less successful was the transformation of the feast that related to viticulture, the Feast of Tabernacles. Nevertheless, there are clear indications that this feast was reoriented by likening the living in temporary dwellings, required once the grape harvest starts, to the wandering in the wilderness for forty years. The superficialities of this transformation were recognizable, since the more orgiastic features of the old grape festival were transferred to the temple court in the form of dances and other observances. The process continued even into the second century B.C. when the feast of the winter solstice, Chanukah, was invested with rites, ceremonies, and meaning, linking it to the victory of Judas Maccabaeus over Antiochus Epiphanes (167 B.C.).

Against these twin manifestations of trading precariousness for security, the monarchy and Baalism, the prophets declared the wrath of Yahweh. The orientation toward nature reflected both in Baalism and in dependence upon the monarchy dramatized the serenity and passivity of God, but the prophetic orientation toward the emergent nature of history made the judgment of God a prime category. Baalism looked toward predictability, but the prophets demanded response. In the face of the cult of action, the prophets seemed to say:

> If you would understand the character of Yahweh, the God of Israel, look not to the orderly pattern of day upon day, season upon season. The God of Israel has brought all that into being by his word, and he can put an end to it by his word. Hear the Word of Yahweh (the God of Abraham, of Isaac, and of Jacob): "You only have I known! See that I have chosen you in the nexus of historical event, and in those same events I can reject you." If you would learn what is your origin and destiny, what Yahweh requires of you, look what he has done for your fathers; then return to him in trust and faithfulness. He will forgive your rejection of him. But if you turn not, he can and will destroy—he will bring this whole round of regularity and endless cycle to an end tumbling about your ears.

Here, then, in the prophetic strain is also a sharp challenge to the primacy of nature as a category for understanding the ultimate meaning of the world and existence. The structure against which the theologians of the Pentateuch as well as the prophets struggled together was a mythic generalization of the natural processes as those generalizations had been made by Babylonian cosmogonists or Canaanite naturalists. Against the universalistic thinking of the Babylonian or the Canaanite, the Israelite Yahwists posed singularity—the category of a particular history as the key to an adequate understanding of the world as they experienced it.

The logical outcome of prophecy was apocalyptic. As the Pentateuchal writers reflected upon the historical meaning of creation, so the successors of the prophets worked out the historical meaning of finality. The infiltration of the eschatological myth, whose origin is to be sought in the same general region as that which produced the creation myth, follows a pattern similar to that which explains the Israelite use of the creation myth. As the Israelite community's successor Judaism developed the myth of the end, there was no longer a unified political entity with ecclesiastical jurisdiction. Hence, there are but hints in the Hebrew canon of a developed eschatology.

The only book in the Old Testament that contains anything approaching a systematic eschatology is The Book of Daniel; even here the rough outlines hardly suffice for a systematic discussion or presentation of the myth of the end in a way comparable to the creation myth. In its present form, The Book of Daniel reflects the last period during which Israel had independent hegemony. It is interesting to speculate upon what the eschatology might have looked like had it been permitted to take shape in a milieu similar to that in which the doctrine of creation reached fruition. The history of the last century or so of Roman domination of Israel's remnant successor prevents one from delving too deeply into this question, but one conclusion does seem inevitable. Just as the doctrine of creation was not arrived at by generalization from the observed regularity of natural processes, so the eschatology of Judaism was not derived from any observed devolution of natural processes. As a matter of fact, the origin of eschatology in the prophetic period took place in a milieu in which Israel enjoyed great prosperity. Both creation and the *eschaton* are historical categories and must be seen historically. The way in which this eschatology did develop can be seen by observing the mythic framework in which the person of Jesus was evaluated by the Jews in whose midst he appeared.

The Judeo-Christian faith affirms that the Creator God, as Source, Ground, Goal of everything that is, holds the worlds of nature and man within His grasp. But this appears to mean that He squeezes the life out of them. An all-powerful God must absorb the realm of nature into Himself. Such a God surely makes of human beings mere puppets under absolute and tyrannical control.

Atheists and "God is dead" theologians from Nietzsche to Altizer have interpreted belief in a Creator God in this way. This view, however, neglects an essential aspect of the doctrine of creation itself. The "wholly other" God, beyond all time and change, is yet dynamically related to *nature* and events of the *personal and social order*. He ". . . uses the forces of nature to serve his purposes without making them any less natural and actions of men without making them any less human . . .," and a patient God ". . . uses the conflicting desires and purposes of men to achieve his will, without destroying human freedom or converting man into a mere puppet in his hands.[1]

The Apostles' Creed affirms: "I believe in God the Father, Maker of heaven and earth." It quickly moves on in the second article to "and in Jesus Christ, His only Son. . . ." In his *Dogmatics in Outline*, Karl Barth states that these two articles belong together, for affirmation about God the Creator cannot be separated from God's relation to man. Faith in creation by God begins, as we have said, in man's experience in history. For the Christian the pivotal historical event is God's disclosure of Himself in Jesus, the Christ. God came into *this* world; ". . . the decisive point is the recognition that God does not exist for Himself, but that there is a reality distinct from Him—namely, the world."[2]

Man's basic doubt, then, is not about the being or character of God. The pressing question concerns the actuality of ourselves and the world around us. These seem at first glance to be unreal. Perhaps even my own self is just a dream.

[1] H. H. Rowley, *The Faith of Israel*, The Westminster Press, Philadelphia, 1956, p. 61.

[2] Karl Barth, *Dogmatics in Outline*, trans. by G. T. Thompson, Harper Torchbooks/The Cloister Library, Harper & Row, Publishers, Incorporated, New York, 1959, p. 52.

Faith in God the Creator expresses confidence in the positive status of the created world and man. These have been brought into being and are sustained by God's gracious love. The world is "something" in its own right, outside God. This realm of nature, of which we are a part, is not inherently evil but good. This life is not to be shunned but affirmed. As men, we exist in and of ourselves. We are free and autonomous beings. God ". . . does not grudge this world its existence, its own reality, nature and freedom." The Judeo-Christian view of man is basically this: *Man, as God's creature, is an independent person in his own right.*

Man enjoys freedom, therefore, but it is a freedom he has been given. Man's freedom involves responsibility and risk. Is man endowed by God with an absolute freedom to do what he pleases? The Judeo-Christian view of man answers "No." Man is not God. He is like God but as a creature of God. Since God gives man ability to accept or reject the claims, love and judgment of God Himself, possibility of destruction and loss threaten him at every turn. "Everything outside God is held constant by God over nothingness."[3] But God holds off this threat and maintains the reality of the actual universe and the autonomous existence of man. For what God in gracious concern has created He continues to re-create. "And God saw everything that he had made, and behold, it was very good" [Genesis 1:31].

The Creation of Man

The Old Testament records two different accounts of the act of God in which He made man, the early J version in Genesis 2:4b–3:24 and the later P version in Genesis 1:26–30. These passages are continuous with the "myths" of the beginnings of the world. The accounts are not factual descriptions of the actual origins of man, such as are developed by historian or scientist. Rather, these writers take their starting point in an interpretation of the meaning of history. Their language is imagic and pictorial. The faith they express is the conviction that human existence is rooted in the purpose and creative activity of God.

In the later P version (Genesis 1:26–30), by contrast, God reaches the climax of His creative activity in making man ". . . in the image of God, male and female he created them." Here the priestly author portrays God as resolving to make "man" and not simply a man. He does not, as in the J version, create the male and then the female to be his companion. But

<hr />

[3] *Ibid.,* p. 55.

He makes "man," in the plural, both men and women from the very beginning.[4]

We turn now to discussion of the J narrative. G. Ernest Wright indicates in the selected reading of Paradise and the fall that the Genesis 3 (J) account is not ". . . a history of man, but a traditional narrative which is employed to interpret the life of man in history—not so much the history of the origin of sin, as an interpretation of the fact of sin." Thus traditional materials from Babylonian sources are used to dramatize man's most poignant questions concerning himself: Why does God's creature find himself in such a state? Why does he refuse to acknowledge the sovereignty of his Creator? The biblical writer now affirms in a new form the covenant faith in God's gracious love and call to responsibility and what happens when Israel rebels against Yahweh's authority. In the Paradise story, the writer is saying that what is true for Israel in relation to God is true for the whole of mankind. Man's all-pervading problem, thus, is not ignorance or poverty or disease. Rather, the root of all these ills lies in man's decisions of will in relation to God's will; man's freedom and what he does with it; why man rebels and why this rebellion incurs divine judgment.

What Is Man?

The psalmist poses the ultimate question concerning human nature:

> When I look at thy heavens, the work of thy fingers, the moon and the stars which thou hast established; what is man, that thou art mindful of him? and the son of man that thou dost care for him? Yet thou hast made him little less than God, and dost crown him with glory and honor.[5]

This is not the question asked by psychologist or anthropologist. Nor does the biblical writer concern himself with the speculative questions of the traditional philosopher. These scientific and philosophical questions have been asked through the centuries, and today various options as to the nature of man have been proposed. Man is a complex being. There are many levels or dimensions on which we may move in our attempt to understand ourselves: from factual, scientific description of the actual conditions of human life to the religious dimension of depth, the question of man's ultimate destiny. These dimensions do not contradict one

---

[4] Ludwig Köhler, *Old Testament Theology*, trans. by A. S. Todd, The Westminster Press, Philadelphia, 1957, p. 132.
[5] Psalms 8:3–5.

another. Neither is any one of them reducible to any of the others. To give a scientific description of the conditions of human life does not negate theological affirmation, nor does the theological deny the scientific.

Optional Views Rooted in the Greek Tradition

In the final analysis, we live and act on one belief about the nature of man or another. Broadly speaking, two main positions stand over against the Judeo-Christian. Both of these are rooted in the Platonic, Aristotelian and Stoic traditions.

The first of these finds definitive expression in the Neoplatonism of Plotinus. But, besides reflections of Plato and the Pythagoreans, influences from the mystical tradition of the Orient may also be discerned. Here the soul is pictured as independent of the body. It is immortal or deathless in its essential nature and therefore belongs not to the flux of physical things but to the unchanging and the eternal.

The second perspective is also traceable to the Platonic tradition, but here the stress is on man's powers of reason. It comprises a central motif in Western thought: from the Renaissance, through the Enlightenment of the eighteenth century, to the idealism of the nineteenth century and the naturalistic humanism of our own times. Throughout these movements, man is regarded as essentially a rational being who is able to grasp general concepts and the order which pervades the cosmos. For the Greek view, the way to understanding reality is thus through man's ability to know universal structures—forms. To know universal good is to do good. This kind of knowledge brings freedom from slavery to the limitations of space and time, the senses, the impulses and thus enables man to achieve harmonious balance of body, mind and soul. Man's basic predicament stems from ignorance, and the solution lies in rational knowledge.

The Renaissance, on the very threshold of what we call the modern period, represents a melding of these strains of ancient thought into a new emphasis on humanity; freedom to choose good or evil and to determine one's own destiny; ability to use rational powers to cope with the problems of this world; capacity to create and appreciate works of art; increasing sense of the vastness of a universe awaiting scientific discovery; awareness of man's own place in the scheme of things as part of the natural order and yet ". . . lifted above other creatures by a soul that was rational and immortal like God Himself."[6]

During the nineteenth century, this confidence in man is reflected in

[6] George F. Thomas, *Christian Ethics and Moral Philosophy*, Charles Scribner's Sons, New York, 1955, p. 148.

philosophical idealism. Idealists hold that reality itself is of the nature of mind, psychical or spiritual in basic makeup but also rational, ordered and intelligible. Its meaning is grasped through the self, for there is an inner harmony between ultimate reality and man's own nature. Human existence is the expression or unfolding of the Universal Mind or Spirit. Man's self, then, is one phase in the cosmic process of development upon the plain of history.

Modern Naturalisms

Naturalism has had various forms of expression from the time of early Greek thought, but what has given this movement impetus in our day is the growth of the modern sciences. Naturalism is the philosophy which holds that nature is the whole of reality and that the experimental sciences give us the whole of truth. It therefore rejects the metaphysical speculations of idealism and the theological affirmations of traditional religion.

Among naturalistic positions is a vigorous contemporary movement called variously scientific or naturalistic humanism. Man is the child of nature. He is conditioned by his physical, organic and social environment. Yet he is able to deal with the obstacles which confront him. Through use of the tools provided by the physical, biological and social sciences, he may predict and control the forces of nature. Especially in recent days, man has become the social engineer in meeting the challenge of the problems of human relations.

Contemporary humanists agree with classical and Renaissance humanists that man is a rational being. He has the capacity to ask questions, appreciate the beautiful, control his environment, undertake self-development, pursue projected goals. For man is a free, creative and responsible self. He is also a social being who needs other persons and groups in order to develop his fullest capacities of intelligent and responsible freedom. Man's basic problems are of his own making: poverty, disease, crime, wasted lives, warfare. The trouble is that we have not developed our inherent resources of human ingenuity. Neither accidents of history nor a supernatural God, if any exists, will solve our difficulties for us. While humanists reject traditional faith, many commit themselves to causes of human well-being in a mood of religious fervor. Theirs is a confidence in the worth and dignity of man and the possibilities of full and complete personal and social life. The projection of such goals as these, beckoning on into the future, and man's constructive realization of these goals, *are* religion—all that is needed to achieve a perfected humanity.

What sort of statements are these affirmations on the part of humanists? Clearly they are not straightforward statements of fact, based on scientific evidence, describing the case of man. Nor are they scientific explanations of how man functions. Rather they are the expressions of personal commitment to certain causes and ideals. These are the affirmations of religious faith and therefore must be assessed as such. The choice is one faith or another.

The Judeo-Christian View of Man

What is man? For biblical faith, man is a creature of contrasts. He is an "in-between being" who is the child of the natural order. Yet he is that curious creature who transcends nature and in some measure is able to control the forces of nature. Blaise Pascal, pondering over the riddle of human life and the paradox of man's double existence, exclaimed: "What a novelty! What a monster, what a chaos, what a contradiction, what a prodigy! Judge of all things, imbecile worm of the earth; depository of truth, a sink of uncertainty and error; the pride and refuse of the universe."

But it is the conviction of the Judeo-Christian view of man that this paradoxical being of contrasts and contradictions is a whole self. Traditional Christianity (and contemporary popular conception) is often a reflection not of biblical thought but of the Greek, Neoplatonic tradition. Modern sciences and philosophy assert that man is a *whole* self and therefore has no use for the dichotomy or division between a *body* and a *soul*. As Arnold Come writes:

> Fortunately, recent Biblical studies and the existential analysis of faith have demonstrated that this dichotomous view of man is not "traditional" but is a perversion in the Christian tradition. Man does not consist of a tenuous synthesis of *a* body and *a* soul, and nothing more. When so regarded, man is a *negative* unity; i.e., the joining of the two is not considered to be essential to man's being and good. Rather, the essence of man is identified with the soul, and his good is realized in the freeing of the soul from the body.[7]

[7] From *Human Spirit and Holy Spirit,* by Arnold B. Come, p. 34. The Westminster Press. © W. L. Jenkins, 1966. Used by permission.

I am indebted to Professor Come for insight into recovery of the biblical view of man and its impact on contemporary thought. The "really old" has become "new" in our day.

By contrast, contemporary theological studies thus have recovered in new and exciting ways the biblical view of man as a positive and total personality. What we call soul and body are rather two dimensions or levels of this whole person, soulish and bodily.[8] The "bodily" points to man as creature, with his finite existence, bound to space and time, linked to the necessities of the natural order. The term "soulish" indicates man's existence as a person in relation to God, to the infinite, transcending the limits of space and time, moving freely and to some degree independent of the necessities of nature.

But there is a third dimension, designated as "spirit," "self," the complete unity of personality. Professor Come writes of the relation between this third dimension and the other two dimensions, the soulish and the bodily:

> And the two dimensions or factors are so united or related that if either were to be lost or become inoperative, man as man would lose his being and be incapable of that life and goodness designated as "human." Indeed, it is so impossible to identify man essentially with one or the other that man must be identified with the *unity* of the two as a third factor. This third dimension consists of man as self or spirit. Here another whole level of complexity in human nature comes to view.[9]

To use these terms "self," "spirit" or "person" is confusing to the modern-minded who rebel against what they understand as traditional Judeo-Christian faith. For to speak of man as spirit seems to involve a return to the concept of a separable "soul" or some kind of "nonmaterial substance," which inhabits this body like a "bird in a cage," waiting to be released at death for travel to some "heavenly realm." But this is a caricature of Christianity.

> It must be stated categorically that the Christian use of "spirit" in no way indicates an acceptance of the Greek trichotomous view of man as body (*soma*), soul (*psyche*), and mind (*nous*). Human spirit is not a third entity or power which, in itself, is the essence of man and which is capable of and actually seeks separation from the other factors by a union with the universal or divine truth.[10]

Contemporary Judeo-Christian perspectives have a great deal in common with the modern functional interpretation of human nature. They

---

[8] *Ibid.*, p. 35. See Søren Kierkegaard, *The Concept of Dread*, Princeton University Press, Princeton, N.J., 1944, p. 39.

[9] *Ibid.*, p. 35.

[10] *Ibid.*, p. 36.

are even close to naturalism, although not identical with that position. For Christian and naturalistic views are alike in one respect: when naturalism regards the "mind" or "spirit" of man as a function of the body. But ". . . idealism and naturalism are equally inadequate in their view of man . . .; it is misleading to designate one secular view of man as more Christian than another." To summarize, in Professor Come's words:

> Man qua man, then, is a realized indissoluble unity of body and soul, denoted by the term "spirit," or, in contemporary language, "self," or "person." To speak of body or soul in reference to man, then, is to speak of abstractions. They do not exist as such. "Human body" indicates body as always determined by soul. "Human soul" indicates soul as always determined by body. Man has found it difficult to speak directly of his spirit, or self, or person. So he has spoken of his body and soul. But in normative Biblical usage these terms are not meant as abstractions but as indicating the complex dimensions of the unitary man. Uniting the two is always the real but indefinite "I," the self, the person, the spirit.[11]

Further Perspectives on Man

The following paragraphs present in greater detail central points concerning the Judeo-Christian view of man. Here also, exciting new perspectives concerning the biblical view have been recovered. These serve to refute many popular misconceptions of the Judeo-Christian view.

First, the bodily dimension of man as indicated in the Bible by the Hebrew word *basar* ("flesh") is not evil in itself or the source of sin. "The Lord God formed man of dust from the ground" [Genesis 2:7]. Jesus brought healing to bodies as well as to souls. The Greek word *sozein* means "to heal," "to save," "to make whole." Man realizes his full humanity as a complete person when God gives life to the clay of the earth. Here again is the emphasis we made above: the bodily dimension of man points to man's difference from God, his independence, autonomy. Man, as a person, stands over against God. It is through the bodily that he expresses or extends his selfhood into all of life around him. As for death, the Hebrews viewed it not as escape of a soul from a decaying body but as loss of the total functioning of the whole person, in a state of impotence or weakness. But, most important, the bodily dimension is the medium of communion between man and God. For God moves and acts in and through this actual world in which man lives day by day.

[11] *Ibid.,* p. 37.

In short, the bodily is what separates man from God and yet makes possible communion with God. For it is as a creature of God, made in the image of God, that man achieves his essential manhood. In the New Testament, also, Paul especially stresses the bodily, "flesh" (*sarx*), as that dimension of the whole person which sets man off from God. This is man as part of the natural world, subject to weakness and death. But the Old Testament man as a whole person reaches sharper definition in the New Testament. That unified self is the "new creature," reconciled, restored to his rightful relationship with God in and through Jesus, the Christ. Man, while he becomes a transformed human being, never loses his identity over against God. However, for Christianity, man is never simply an animal or part of nature. He is always "creature-in-the-image-of God" or "creature-made-for-life-with God."[12]

Second, the soulish is indicated by the Hebrew word *nephesh*. Again, neither in Old or New Testaments is the soul regarded as a separate thing or entity which leaves the body behind at death. Rather to speak of body and soul (*nephesh*) is to be concerned about weakness and strength. *Nephesh* means "life." All forms of existence, including animals, have life, or soul. Thus "soul" means the "life" of anything, ". . . but it is that life in terms of its particular stamp, its special qualities, capacities, and powers which make this thing, this piece of life, a member of a particular genus of life and within that genus a unique sample."[13] As for man, then, he is a "living soul" of a unique kind. He is a creature who is potentially able to unify or integrate both flesh (*basar*) and soul (*nephesh*) into that wholeness of personality or selfhood called spirit. Again, this wholeness, spirit, is a unique quality of life which we call the image of God.

Closely related to the bodily (*basar*), soulish (*nephesh*), and spirit is the Hebrew term translated "heart" (*lebh*). Here also, the word *heart* (as in the case of *spirit*) ". . . does not refer to a piece or part of man but to a dimension or characteristic of his entire being and life. Basically, the term stands for man in his essentially and pervasively volitional nature. . . . the Israelite does not differentiate among need, desire, idea, will and act, but views them as a totality."[14] A man draws together in a total act all decisions and intentions to achieve what is desirable.

But, third, the persistent question is: How does man know what is desirable? How can he muster insight and power to realize the "image" of his real manhood? Again, in the words of Arnold Come: "The Hebraic-

12 *Ibid.*, p. 51.
13 *Ibid.*, p. 58.
14 *Ibid.*, p. 68.

Christian religion finds the answer in the nature of man as 'spirit' (*ruach*). The distinctive character of *human* soul, of the human form of life, has not been isolated until its whole sentient, emotional, desiring, self-projecting, idea-forming, and volitional nature has been qualified by the 'spiritual.' "[15]

Spirit (*ruach* in the Hebrew and *pneuma* in the Greek) originally meant "wind" or "breath," or also "life" that energizes. Yet it is not a thing different from soul or heart within a man but man living as a whole being, employing all his capacities. God's spirit (*ruach*) moved upon the face of the deep and created the world. This is the same God who also said, "Let us make man in our image, after our likeness" [Genesis 1:1–26]. This is the uniqueness of man, in the final analysis: the capacity to become fully spirit, as God is Spirit; not to be God but to be like God and always as the creature of God.

The ability to stand before God in a person-to-person or I-Thou relationship is thus rooted in man as spirit. The basic meaning of the covenant relationship, of which we have spoken so often, finally becomes clear. Man as spirit is the only kind of being who can enter with God into an agreement in which God chooses him for a sacred task and in which man may respond with all the powers of decision and action at his command. For man's spirit is not "something foreign to man" but is that God-given and distinctive form of life that is man's own and his alone. This is what it means to say that man is made in the image of God.

Yet, though man as spirit is made in God's image, he is, as we have stated, a free and responsible self capable of rejecting as well as accepting God's claim upon him. The consequences of this freedom spell out man's basic and ultimate predicament. Man, by asserting his independence, may distort the divine image that is within him, but he does not utterly destroy it. This is the predicament in which man stands before God. His very freedom leads him to seek to become more than man, to become his own center of meaning and significance, to become "god" instead of creature. But the result is separation in his total person from God and from his own essential nature! The myth of the fall is a parable of man's situation in every age. This is sin.

Sin does not result simply from man's bodily nature. It is the product of that very same capacity of soul, heart and will which relates man to God and himself to himself as a total person. This dual capability on the part of man makes the alienation called sin doubly tragic. Sin is not just doing things forbidden by convention. Sin is rather both a tendency and

---

[15] *Ibid.*, p. 70.

a state. Men seek all sorts of devices to find release from restlessness and insecurity. They are frequently content with partial answers in some cause, power or center of meaning less than God. The result is delusion, despair, meaninglessness and emptiness. Thus they miss the mark of that achievement of wholeness of personality or spirit which is man's God-given destiny. For another way to speak of sin is to recall what we have been saying about the dimensions of man's existence. To sin, for biblical religion, is to negate one dimension and seek to live completely in the other. Sometimes we try to deny the bodily and live as disembodied souls or as gods. At other times we vainly deny the soulish and try to live entirely in the realm of the bodily or the natural. Attempts like this lead to death, disintegration, separation instead of wholeness.

It is the Christian faith that ultimately only God Himself can break down the barriers of separation and reconcile alienated men to themselves, to each other and to Himself. But it is also the Christian conviction that He has done this and continues to do so in and through His Son. For the God of creation is also the Father of the Lord Jesus Christ. To the significance of this conviction we now turn. It is the core of Christian conviction.

5

G. ERNEST WRIGHT | *The Nature of Man:*
An Exposition of Genesis 3*

One of the crucial passages of Scripture in the history of Christian exegesis is the third chapter of Genesis. I venture to say that, because of what this chapter tells us about man, Christianity and Judaism possess a doctrine of man that differentiates them from other religions. Furthermore, this chapter constantly acts as a corrective to those in both faiths who would adopt more idealistic conceptions. An exegetical study of this chapter is perennially fruitful.

1. First, let us ask the question as to the authorship and date of the Adam and Eve stories in chapters 2–4 of the Book of Genesis. Fortunately, this is not a difficult question to answer. Nearly all critical scholars today are agreed about the authorship, and they do not diverge very widely in the matter of date. These chapters are considered to be a part of the J or Yahwist document. While many scholars of the previous generation dated this work to about the time of the prophet Elijah, that is, about 850 B.C., I suspect that a majority of the scholars of this generation would say without too much hesitation that it was the product of the court of David, or, more probably, of Solomon, in the tenth century B.C. But how should this document be conceived? Here again, we may say that modern scholarship is fairly well agreed on the supposition that the Yahwist was a collector of the early traditions of Israel, who edited and put them together in such a way that they would form a proper confessional epic for the nation of Israel, newly recreated in strength by King David. It is a remarkable piece of work, the earliest extensive collection of historiographical materials known from the ancient world. On the other hand, we understand that the unknown author of this epic was not writing simply for personal pleasure. He was collecting and interpreting the

* From *The Rule of God* by G. Ernest Wright. Copyright © 1960 by G. Ernest Wright. Reprinted by permission of Doubleday & Company, Inc.

traditional materials in such a way that they would adequately confess the nation's faith. Here was a people who could only explain what they were by telling the story of their past in terms of the mighty work of God. To tell the story was thus to confess the faith and to give praise to Israel's divine Lord.

The Yahwist document is the first written edition of this classic story of which we know, and it forms the basis of our present Hexateuch. It can be traced with considerable certainty in the books of Genesis, Exodus, and Numbers. After that, however, scholars are not at all sure as to its identity, and there is little agreement. The prehistoric traditions that were taught to Israel in Genesis 1–11 are basically those first presented in the court of Solomon by our historian. Subsequently, during the sixth or fifth century, the Jerusalem priesthood in exile in Babylon edited this old material by adding a new introduction in chapters 1–2:4a, by providing a genealogical framework in chapters 5–11 and by elaborating the older material by supplementation, particularly in the matter of the Flood story and the covenant with Noah. As far as can now be seen, however, the original purpose and intent of the Yahwist writer in chapters 2–4 was not changed by this later editing and supplementation.

2. Second, we must ask the question as to the form, or type, of literature contained within our chapter. It would appear to be a very individual type of material that is unlike anything else that is in the Bible. At first glance, it would appear to be one segment of a people's traditional history of the world and of human origins, such as was taught by one generation to another. Yet a closer look at the material suggests that it is not given as a series of obvious facts to be accepted or rejected as fact. It possesses a deeper dimension. To be sure, in the Bible as a whole, fact and event, history interpreted by faith, have a very close and inseparable relation. Yet here the didactic intent, or parabolic aim, is so obvious that for a parallel one might turn to the parables of Jesus. Yet the difference is also apparent, when we recall that this traditional story of human origins is not a fable or narrative made up to serve a particular teaching occasion. That is to say, the tenth-century writer was scarcely conscious of the problem of fact and faith in the way that we are today. *We* are very conscious of this problem, and we want to ask continually whether or not something really happened as a tradition says that it did. This very self-conscious type of inquiry is what separates us from our writer and those he taught. Even so, however, our center of interest must be at the point where his was. That is to say, we must primarily be interested in his question, not in ours, if we would exegete the passage. *Our* first question is: Did it happen? He is uninterested in such a question, perhaps because this is something which everyone amongst his people more or less took for granted. In telling the story, however, his question has to do with the problem of man as man; it is not primarily concerned with a factual history of creation. His problem has to do with the profound question as to why a creature of the wondrous God finds himself within history in such a miserable state.

In other words, an analysis of the literary form of the chapter suggests that we do not have in Genesis 3 a story, the central purpose of which is merely to present a history of man, but a traditional narrative which is employed to interpret the life of man in history—not so much the history of the origin of sin, as an interpretation of the fact of sin.

3. In the third place, what can be said about the traditional material behind this story? The author is surely not creating something out of nothing; he is using pre-existent material, though the exact form and history of his traditions are unknown. Central to the story, however, are the following: (a) the Garden of Eden, which is the primordial paradise; (b) the first man, who does not bear a proper name. The Hebrew word *Adam* was never used by the Israelites as a word suitable for a personal name. In this chapter *Adam* means "the man" in the most general sense. The fact that the term is used at all indicates that primordial man is considered in a generic aspect, that is, his name is mankind; (c) then there are the two trees in the Garden, the tree of life and the tree of the knowledge of good and evil, symbolic names obviously borne by no species of historical tree!

We know that ancient Babylonia also had a traditional picture of a paradise in primordial times. Furthermore, we know that western Asia had a great interest in the tree of life. This tree seems to appear very frequently in ancient art; it surely played a very much larger role in everyday life and thought than the mythological texts that have survived would indicate.

One of the central concerns of man in Biblical times was the problem of life, life in which there was no death. Death was the horror from which an escape was sought. The multitudinous forms of weakness, sickness, trouble, anything which circumscribed the freedom and joy of one's activity—these could be interpreted as a manifestation that death was in the midst of life. Life without death, therefore, was an important speculation to ancient man. In Egypt the meaningful reality of death was actually denied. The end of this mortal existence was but the transition point from life on earth to life in fellowship with the gods, from humanity to divinity.

The king was an incarnate god, and in the blessings enjoyed by him his people would likewise share.

In western Asia, however, life was much more difficult and fragile. Death was a grimmer and more problematical reality. One of the most interesting of the classic tales of western Asia was the Babylonian epic of Gilgamesh. This is the story of man's search for life, and of his failure to find it. He was a king of a city in southern Babylonia, a great hero and a mighty man of valor. So active and energetic was he that his people besought the gods that some outlet for his energies be provided and that they be delivered from his constant ministration! A great companion was provided him by the gods, and the two of them together performed mighty exploits until the friend killed the bull of heaven and for this himself was put to death by the gods. Gilgamesh now was inconsolable. Hitherto, his only thought of death was the glorious death of a hero, killed in some marvelous deed of valor. Now, however, his friend was gone, torn from him, leaving him without hope and with no way whereby this personal tie could be mended. Disregarding the advice of his people, he set out on a long search for life. He finally arrived at the River of Death, and the boatman ferried him across it. There in what was evidently the primordial paradise he found the Babylonian Noah, the one man in the history of the human race who had been granted immortality by the gods. To him Gilgamesh appealed for aid, but this appeal was without effect. The Babylonian immortal can only tell the story of the almost accidental circumstances in which he had received life. These circumstances involve the Babylonian story of the primordial flood. Enlil, the king of the gods and the personification of the storm, found man a most troublesome creature after his creation. The god's sleep was disturbed, and, in a fit of rage, he decreed a flood which would put an end to all mankind. The flood in the Babylonian account, therefore, is within the context of the search for life—a very different context than that given in the Bible. Furthermore, in Babylon in contrast to Israel the flood is a rash and irresponsible act of a god in anger. To counteract and to balance this rash act, the flood hero is told by another of the gods to build the ark and to save himself, his family, and two of every type of creature. As a reward for his deeds he is granted eternal life without death. Hence, he concludes his sorrowful tale to Gilgamesh by saying that what has happened to him can happen never again; his blessing cannot be transferred to all mankind. As Gilgamesh turns to leave, however, the flood hero's wife tells him of a certain plant at the bottom of the River of Death which, when eaten, has the power of rejuvenation. On his return, Gilgamesh found this plant and started across the desert with it, back to his own city. After a hot day, he encountered an oasis, stripped off his clothes for a bath. While he was thus refreshing himself, however, a serpent smelled the plant, darted from its hole, and took it away. Thus it comes about, the ancient Babylonian believed, that snakes never die— they merely shuffle off their skin—but man must die! On this bitter, and rebellious, note the great epic ends.

In the Bible, by contrast, we note, however, that the tree of life is no longer the central theme. At one stage in the history of the tradition it may well have played a larger role than it does in the final edition preserved for us in the canonical scriptures. But, for our unknown tenth-century theologian, it is a simple fact of existence which must be accepted without question that the tree of life is denied man. Man is mortal, death is his lot, to dust he shall return. Why is this the case? How did it come about that the wondrous goodness of God should have so decreed in the creation? It is this searching "why" which is our writer's central concern.

4. In the fourth place, we must look more closely at the second tree, the tree of the knowledge of good and evil. As far as we now know, there was no such tree amongst the mythologies of the neighboring peoples. Yet the story in the third chapter of Genesis shows certain indications of having had a background and history before it has reached its present form. The talking snake was certainly once a mythological element. In its present form, however, the snake is demythologized; it is not a god or goddess of wisdom; it is only a beast of the field which the Lord God has made. Its mythological background survives only in the function it performs and in the fact that it is allowed to speak. We note a similar ancient background for the snake in Jesus' reference when he says that his followers should be ". . . wise as serpents and harmless as doves." There is no reason why a snake should be particularly wise, unless one recalls the long mythological history behind the poor creature.

Furthermore, a pagan, or at least a very early, background of the story may be suggested in the sexual consciousness that still survives. At one stage, the Genesis 3 account may also have been a part of the ancient mythological search for life. To know good and evil, therefore, in its original context may have referred to the mysterious principle of fertility and reproduction in which the life of man shares the life of the gods which is the life of nature in polytheistic thought.

All this, however, is far in the background of the present narrative and can only be conjectured. The peculiar and distinctive part of the story as we have it now is that the whole focus of attention is upon the tree of the knowledge of good and evil; it is not upon the tree of life. We are not told precisely what is meant by the tree of knowledge; its meaning is only suggested, not defined. Whatever it precisely designated or was intended to designate, it immediately focuses attention upon the will of man rebelling against his Creator. This is a most unusual note, a most remarkable portrayal in either an ancient or a modern setting—a free man using his will power against his Creator and Lord. This is seen as the human problem; this is the center of the story. The knowledge man gets from his eating of the forbidden fruit is a knowledge which enables him to use the goodness of God's creation to evil ends. The central problem of human existence, then, does not lie in nature; it lies within the human will. Man's central concern, therefore, should not be eternal life—that is God's gift or prerogative—but with the relation of his will to the will of God.

5. From the story we note the fact of man's freedom, and the fact that free will is power which can be used against a divine command.

In one sense this is the source of the Biblical conception of the dignity of man. Human dignity does not lie in a divine nature, or even in an unlimited capacity for creativity. Man's dignity rests in the fact that he has been addressed by God; he is the recipient of the divine command. He alone amongst all the creatures of earth has an "ought" or a "must" addressed to him. But he has used his free will to rebel. Responsibility and freedom of decision in relation to that responsibility—this is surely what the Jerusalem priest who is responsible for giving to us the first chapter of Genesis must have meant by the phrase "the image of God." In these two terms, responsibility and freedom, what is meant by the similarity to the divine in man exists. But, we might say, for man freedom lies in the mystery of his creation by God, while responsibility lies in his election, his calling to labor as God's servant.

6. Furthermore, in the sixth place, the story implies a judgment on man. He rebels. His dignity, the office of kingship over the whole creation in which he has been installed by God, this is not the real point of the story for the Yahwist writer. The real question is: Why has he rebelled? Why has this noble creature refused his creaturehood? The Biblical understanding of man actually centers at this point; he is one who has betrayed his creaturehood. His power has become a lust for self-divinization. It is not that the power given him is an evil in itself; but it has surely been used to an evil end.

Man the rebel, man the sinner—this is scarcely a self-evident proposition. This is not the first thing that occurs to the normal human being when he seeks to describe himself and the lot of his kind. It is an insight, achieved only within the Biblical doctrines of election and covenant, only in the story of a people who have been addressed by God, and given their mission by God, but nevertheless whose history is a history of betrayal of covenant and disobedience to the goodness of God.

7. In the seventh place, man's sin has brought the divine judgment. Nature, of course, is far from the perfect creation it was meant to be. Why? Not because of an incomplete evolution, but because of judgment. The whole understanding of the world revolves around the judgment. Nature is under a curse for man's sake. Indeed, the story of civilization on earth also is to be seen as hanging from the fact of sin. By the very juxtaposition of traditional stories, our author presents his view of the progress of civilization. In chapter 4 the separation of nomadic and agricultural pursuits is accompanied by the first murder. The building of the first city is accompanied by the story of Lamech, whose life is a life of vengeance, a vengeance that elsewhere in scripture is something belonging to God alone and not to man. Lamech is the picture of man's ultimate degradation in a life apart from God. At the close of the Flood story (chapter 8), we are told about the introduction of vineyard culture, one of the basic industries of the Palestinian and Syrian areas. And this is accompanied by the picture of the good man. Noah, drunk! The distribution and blessing of the nations in chapter 10 is accompanied by the Tower of Babel story. In the latter mankind thrusts its creation into heaven itself, saying: "Let us get us a name!" Civilization at each stage is accompanied by its spiritual problems, and the meaning of the whole is that it knows nothing whatsoever of its responsibility to its sovereign Creator.

Evil in this early material is both an act of man's will and a state in which he lives. Man wills to sin and this also creates a state of sin, both as an aspect of man's willed act and as the judgment of God. Indeed, the Hebrew word for evil (ra) means both things. It can refer to an ethical decision, a willed act; but it can refer at the same time to the concomitant psychical, social, and material results or penalties. In this way the word can mean a sinful act of the will or it can mean the state of society in which we live, or even the suffering or harm that may come at any one moment in any situation. Hence, man sins, and he lives in a state of sin. He wills to sin and he is born into sin. Recall the well-known words in the Fifty-first Psalm: "Against thee and thee only have I sinned." This is the willed act. Yet these words are followed in the psalm by the following: "Behold I was brought forth in iniquity and in sin did my mother conceive me." This is not a direct reference to a willed act on the part of the mother, but to the sinful society in which we live. Recall the words of the prophet Isaiah who, after the vision of the holiness of God, confesses that he is an unclean man in the midst of an unclean people.

One of Israel's most ancient and marvelous confessions of faith is preserved in Exodus 34 (vv. 6–7). Here God, in revealing his name to Moses, expounds the meaning of the name through the quotation of the old liturgical confession. This confession speaks of the marvelous love and patience of God in his dealings with his people, but it adds that, while God keeps his loving-kindness for thousands, forgiving iniquity and transgression and sin, ". . . he will by no means acquit the guilty, visiting the iniquity of the fathers upon the children, and upon the children's children, unto the third, even the fourth generation." This is an empirical description of the fact of evil and suffering in the world, that the deeds of the father do cause consequences which are felt by the generations of the children. Such is the state in which we live in history.

The doctrine, so important in Christian theology, of human depravity, or of original sin, means just this. We are born into and live in a state of sinfulness. Cain, Lamech, the nations—they all possess an inner infection; there is no real soundness in them; there is a state of sinfulness, though specific acts of the responsible will continue.

How has this situation in human affairs come about? The tenth-century Yahwist writer can only tell a story, an old story about a tree of the knowledge of good and evil. Man (mankind) ate the forbidden fruit of all knowledge, a knowledge that gave him power for evil, an evil to which even the good can be used. Man has used his freedom and his power to attempt to acquire a divine knowledge, to become a god or a divine being in his own right; this is his denial of his creaturehood. This is the source of his woe.

A few years ago, Professor Richard Niebuhr of Yale University, in unpublished remarks at a meeting of the Theological Discussion Group in Washington, D.C., said that in his opinion there are two common ways of understanding man which are current amongst us. One is through the myth of the fall of Adam. The other is through the myth of *Pithecanthropus erectus*. The one is tenth century B.C. within the third chapter of Genesis. The other had to do with our ancestry, the long evolution of the human being, beginning within and perhaps before the Pleistocene age of geologic history. Which of the two is true?

Another way of putting the matter, Professor Niebuhr continued, is to think of man in terms of the vast ruin of the Colosseum in Rome. It is a spectacular, awe-inspiring building. Though it is in ruins, still it is awesome and one must respect it. Another way is to think of man in terms of a modern ranch house of the type being built by the thousands upon thousands around the edges of our cities. The ranch house can be an attractive, neat, and extremely comfortable small home. Furthermore, it has the capacity for great expansion. One wing can be added after another. Dreams and great possibilities go hand in hand in its construction. No one knows where it has to end!

Which of these two pictures presents a truer understanding of man? Which picture presents the greatest appreciation of the dignity of man? The Colosseum is a noble and tremendous structure even in its tattered state. The ranch house is attractive, small but perhaps adequate, convenient, and possessing great potential. In some sense, perhaps, both are true. Yet it perhaps must be remembered that modern totalitarianisms have grown, not out of the Colosseum, but out of the ranch house! Not out of the myth of Adam, but out of disillusion with *Pithecanthropus erectus!* Disillusionment cannot affect the ruined Colosseum; it perhaps may give one a more realistic appreciation of it. But the hopes and dreams behind the ranch house can quickly perish. And housing authorities are beginning to wonder whether or not our vast new suburbs may not be the slums of tomorrow.

Chapter 4 | The Problem of the Historical Jesus

We glance back briefly at the story of the Jewish people after their return from exile under the Babylonians (586–538 B.C.). Except for short-lived, precarious independence under priest-kings (143–63 B.C.), this peculiar people suffered under the political tyranny of a long succession of foreign powers: Persian, Macedonian, Egyptian, Syrian and Roman.

Jewish Religion in Jesus' Day

In response to difficult outward circumstances, the Jews sustained their distinctive inner resources of faith and worship. They had met their God in His demand and gracious concern through obedience and disobedience, plenty and want, on desert, on mountain and in cities. Yahweh knows no boundaries. Within His covenant and law His chosen people still found their sense of pride and confidence. But they did not dare count on their status before God as a matter of course. Whenever they took His promises for granted, Yahweh's judgment shattered their false security and recalled them to their origin in Himself.

But as outward conditions became more difficult, the Jewish people held more closely to the Torah (the Law) given by God as His will for their cultic practices and moral conduct. A discernible change now occurred. The ancient religion of Israel narrowed and hardened into sole concern as to how to relate the Torah to shifting practical situations. Now also the ritual observances of worship and sacrifice were regarded as binding with the same authority as moral obligation. The Temple, with its priesthood, became the center of these rituals of sacrifice.The synagogues also served as focal points of Jewish life and thought, and here the community assembled to hear the elders read and interpret the Law.

The Jews' hopes for deliverance by God for long centuries had centered in this world: recapturing of lost territory, purging and recovery of purely Jewish practices. But now in the era of later Judaism, they longed for the coming of God's kingdom or reign over all the world. Under the influence of ideas and myths from Babylonian and Persian sources, this hope was understood in dualistic terms. The world was pictured as a battleground of the opposing powers of God and Satan, with men choosing one side or the other. Yet the Jews were confident that God's righteousness would be vindicated.

The Book of Daniel, written soon after the outbreak of the Maccabean War, during the persecution of Antiochus Epiphanes, brought a new style of thought and expression in the form of vivid images. For example, two aeons were portrayed: this passing age under the curse of sin drifting toward catastrophe and the new age to come in which the righteous would see God's glory. The figure of the heavenly "Man" (Daniel 7:13) would surely appear on the clouds of heaven to bring the world under judgment and gather together God's people. Here also at this time the doctrine of the resurrection of the dead found its way into Jewish religious thought.

This kind of imagic portrayal of the *end* of things and God's ultimate triumph over the forces of evil is called "eschatology," indicating, in the Greek term, concern with the *eschaton,* or end. Another term used is "apocalyptic," again from the Greek, meaning revelation. For writers who deal with eschatology claim to bring to men disclosures about the last things.

In summation, we see two phases of Jewish life and practice, both centered in faith in *one* God, who is transcendent and righteous and yet is intimately related to the people as their God. One phase stressed the Law as the way to vindication before God both for individuals and for the whole nation. Closely linked to observance of the Law was the Temple with its rites of worship and sacrifice. But the second phase emerged when times were out of joint, when neither punctilious observance of the Law nor Temple rites completely satisfied. Then men dreamed of God's showing forth His judgment to deliver and save them. Although the Jews had always believed that God Himself would bring about the new age, there was a persistent tendency to hold that God's *Messiah, One sent by God,* would accomplish His divine purpose.

This is the hope which sustained the Jews in Jesus' time, as they yearned for God's decisive intervention in human history. For many, this aspiration took political forms. They identified evil with the actual powers that held them in bondage: the Seleucid kingdom and then Rome itself. When Jesus came as the Christ of the new community, drastic transformation of these forms of hope was demanded. For Jesus began His work by saying: "The Kingdom of God is at hand."

John Knox in his *Christ the Lord* says that the New Testament record shows how Jesus was "remembered," was known still and was interpreted. Through a new event God had disclosed Himself. Men made response and became members of the believing Christian community under the terms of the new covenant. They became participants in the revelatory event itself. For at the center of the event or series of events moved the person of Jesus, the Christ: His life, death, resurrection and continuing presence, together with the formation of the new community itself.

Our word *Gospel* (ευαγγελιον in the Greek) is of Old English origin and means "God story" or "good story." The Gospel is hence the good news itself: how God has acted in history through the person of Jesus Christ. In a derivative sense, the term is applied to the written records concerning this good news.

Bornkamm says, "No one is any longer in the position to write a life of Jesus."[1] Scholars generally agree that attempts, especially within the past two centuries, to recapture a biography of the historical Jesus have failed. Students may wonder about this, for writing a life of Jesus seems like a straightforward project. As Bornkamm observes, such undertakings have missed their intended goal because each writer inevitably brings into his portrayal of Jesus the spirit of his own age.

But more basic reasons for the fruitlessness of further attempts at lives of Jesus have to do with the character of the sources on which we must rely for knowledge of Jesus. These are the Gospels of the New Testament. There are Roman and Jewish documents, outside the biblical account, to which we might turn for evidence. The fact is, however, that except for a few instances[2] world history took little notice of Jesus.

The chief importance of these Roman and Jewish documents is their confirmation of the fact that even the fiercest enemies of Christianity did not doubt the historical existence of Jesus. (Such doubt is a trend of modern times.) But for knowledge of the person and work of Jesus Christ we must rely on the record of the New Testament itself.

The Gospel of Mark records the most direct account of Jesus' life and ministry. There we read how John the Baptist began his work along the shores of the Dead Sea. He demanded repentance and obedience to God. The people asked what they should do. He told them that they must about-

---

[1] From *Jesus of Nazareth* by Günther Bornkamm, p. 13, Copyright © 1960 by Hodder & Stoughton Ltd. and Harper & Brothers, Publishers, Inc. Copyright © 1956 Verlag W. Kohlhammer GmbH., Stuggart.

[2] Pliny, about A.D. 112; Tacitus, about A.D. 115, in his *Annals;* Suetonius, a contemporary of Tacitus; Joseph, a Jewish historian, about A.D. 90, in his *Jewish Antiquities;* the Talmud, a collection of rabbinic commentaries on the Law. See Archibald M. Hunter, *The Work and Words of Jesus,* The Westminster Press, Philadelphia, 1950, pp. 15–16.

face. He baptized them as a sign of repentance and warned them that
One greater than himself would soon come to institute judgment. Jesus
also received baptism in the River Jordan as a sign of His obedience to
the will of God. For a voice said, "You are my Son, my beloved. You
are my chosen." Jesus sojourned in the wilderness for forty days and
then announced the message of the kingdom of God.

He healed the sick, ate with tax collectors, associated with the outcasts,
forgave sins in God's name. Scribes and Pharisees soon mounted opposition against Jesus because of His disregard of the oral tradition. The
Sadducees saw in Him a threat to their vested interests in the Temple.
The Zealots distrusted Him for His refusal to join in armed revolt
against Rome. After strategic withdrawals and returns to His ministry
among the people, He made His fateful decision to journey to Jerusalem.

As He entered the city, the crowds hailed Him with shouts of "Hail!
Hosanna!" He challenged the priestly caste for turning the Temple into
a marketplace. He overturned the tables of the money changers and the
seats of those who sold pigeons. The Sadducees sought to destroy Him
in order to protect their authority. Jesus was betrayed by Judas and led
from the Garden of Gethsemane down across the brook Kidron into the
city for trial. He was crucified on a skull-shaped hill called Golgotha. By
this time His closest friends, save for a group of women, had all fled
in fear. Thus He was laid in a tomb. But on the first day of the week,
Mary Magdalene and Mary the mother of James came with spices to
anoint His body but found the stone rolled away. "Do not be amazed,"
said a young man dressed in a white robe, "You seek Jesus of Nazareth,
who was crucified. He has risen, he is not here; see the place where they
laid him. But go, tell his disciples and Peter that he is going before you
into Galilee; there you will find him, as he told you."[3]

How the Gospels Were Written

In the New Testament, as in the Old, living persons responding in community to God's self-disclosure precede the written literature. For some
thirty years (A.D. 30–60) the early Christian community had no written
Gospels; their only Scripture was the Old Testament. But within these
groups of believers, there was the proclamation of the "kerygma," or
preached message, which lies embedded in the written Gospels as we now
have them. A. M. Hunter summarizes this earliest form of the good news:

[3] Mark 16:6–7.

God's promises made to His People in the Old
Testament are now fulfilled.
The long-expected Messiah, born of David's
line, has come.
He is Jesus of Nazareth, who
went about doing good and wrought mighty
works by God's power;
was crucified according to the purposes of God;
was raised by God from the dead and
exalted to His right hand.
He will come again in glory for judgment.
Therefore let all who hear this message
repent and be baptized for the forgiveness of their sins.[4]

What these first members of the community of the new covenant took seriously as the Gospel was not a list of moral precepts or abstract ideas but rather a moving account of a series of climatic events: the coming of the Messiah, good deeds, a cross, resurrection, as "mighty acts of God." Then, with the passing years, believers remembered, told and retold stories about Jesus Himself: healing the sick, forgiving sinners, feeding the crowds, teaching the kingdom of God, standing against the religious authorities, breaking bread with His closest followers. In each of the centers where the early Christians gathered for worship and their common meals—Jerusalem, Antioch, Caesarea, Rome—there probably grew up cycles of stories about Jesus, which believers recounted to each other. As yet they felt no need of written records, but their memories were clear and retentive. Scholars refer to this word-of-mouth telling of Jesus' life and work as the "oral tradition."

The first writings of the New Testament (A.D. 50–60) are the letters of Paul, which were designed to meet practical situations within the various Christian groups. But forty years or so after Jesus' death, new generations of converts expressed a need for ordered instruction in the Christian faith. Thus about A.D. 70 John Mark wrote the Gospel which bears his name. He was associated with Paul and Barnabas and may have been the one who acted as Peter's interpreter among Christians in Rome. Mark took the bare outline of Jesus' work contained in the kerygma and added to it what he had heard Peter say in his sermons and other materials recounted among the Christian communities. Mark's Gospel is rugged and simple.

[4] From *Introducing the New Testament*, by Archibald M. Hunter, pp. 25–26. Published in U.S.A. by The Westminster Press, 1958, and SCM Press, Ltd., London. Used by permission. See C. H. Dodd, *The Apostolic Preaching*, Harper & Row, Publishers, Incorporated, New York, 1944.

He stated the story of God's saving acts in Jesus Christ and reiterated Jesus' challenge to take up one's own cross and follow Him.

The Gospel according to Matthew is the work of a Jewish Christian writer (ca. A.D. 85) who emphasized the continuity of events between the Christian movement and the history of Israel. This writer used Mark on which to base his work, but he used as well a hypothetical source called Q (from the German word *Quelle*, meaning "source"). He also added more than 300 verses of his own, such as those concerning Jesus' birth, narratives of His life and career, and parts of Jesus' teachings such as the Sermon on the Mount (Matthew 5–7).

The Gospel of Luke was written at about the same time. The author was a close associate of Paul. His Gospel was followed by a sequel, the Acts of the Apostles, dealing with the spread of the Christian movement throughout the Greco-Roman world. In addition to Mark and Q, Luke used special materials of his own. These consisted of more than 400 verses of narrative and teaching, including parables like those of the Good Samaritan and the Prodigal Son.

In addition to these three Synoptic Gospels of Mark, Matthew and Luke, a fourth Gospel, that of John, was written at a much later date (ca. A.D. 90–110). John's is a different perspective and style. This writer sees the whole life and meaning of Jesus in terms of the Ground and Source of the entire created world. "In the beginning was the Word, and the Word was with God, and the Word was God." The Word here signifies the "thought" of God Himself, spoken to His creatures. For many centuries God had been speaking His Word, but now, "when the fullness of time was come," God made His thought come alive in history in the life of an actual man. "The Word became flesh and dwelt among us."

Thus, in a single sentence, the author of the fourth Gospel expresses what all the Gospels are saying despite the many differences among them. These works were written not to relate the biography of just another great man. Rather, they were written to proclaim Jesus as the long-awaited Messiah. In the words of John's Gospel, "These are written that you may believe that Jesus is the Christ, the Son of God, and that believing you may have life in his name" [John 20:31]. Here speaking is a community remembering decisive events in history, interpreting what they have experienced and having their say because they believed.

Can We Recover the "Historical Jesus"?

In order to write a biography of Jesus "as He actually lived and worked," one would have to look through the eyes of these writers of the New Testament. But, as we have indicated, these authors were not objective, disinterested reporters of the passing scene at the turn of the centuries. They were themselves caught up in the dynamic movement of history within which Jesus, the Christ, is the living center.

Two phases, therefore, of this total situation are inseparable: the telling of the history, the record of what Jesus did and said; and the expression of faith in Him on the part of those same writers who witnessed as members of the community of the new covenant. The record of Jesus and the Christian community's faith in Him, as the Christ sent by God, are inseparable. A so-called bare history of Jesus cannot be obtained. But neither would such a history, if it were obtainable, assure our understanding of this central Event and Person of the Christian movement. "Fact" and "interpretation" belong together in this religion of the new covenant just as under the old covenant. However, this interpretation, expressive of the faith of the early church, is not an invention without reference to the events of Jesus' life. In Bornkamm's words, ". . . the Gospels justify neither resignation nor skepticism. Rather they bring before our eyes, in a very different fashion from what is customary in chronicles and presentation of history, the historical person of Jesus with the utmost vividness."[5]

A vigorous dialogue among biblical theologians centers in this very question: Can we penetrate behind the interpretive faith of the Christian community to recover "Jesus as He actually was"? Especially concerned are the so-called form critics. Form criticism holds, for instance, that Mark functioned as an editor who took from the oral tradition whole units of material that were already shaped into definite form through years of oral repetition. There were within the oral tradition itself certain kinds of stories: for example, pronouncement stories in which Jesus spoke a climactic word in a conflict situation, teachings, miracle stories, the account of death on the Cross. Thus the written Gospels are the literary deposit of the funded experience, memory and faith of the early church. If we take the form critics seriously, it seems impossible to reconstruct a "life of Jesus." That is, no writer can set down Jesus' travels in day-to-day diary form. For even the order of events in Mark's Gospel is an expression of his own interests and interpretation. What he did was to join together sections of the oral tradition by artificially contrived devices, such as "that evening at sundown," "in the morning," "when he returned to Capernaum after some days," "as he was setting out on his journey."

Recent discussion involves interpretation of the kerygma. This debate among experts is too technical and involved to report in detail here. But

---

[5] Bornkamm, *op. cit.*, p. 24.

important issues for understanding the problem of the historical Jesus are at stake. We have included the Bultmann reading because it dramatizes this problem. Bultmann states that we can know virtually nothing about the historical person of Jesus. Jesus' mission was to summon men to an *existential* or personal decision. The preached message, or kerygma, has practically no connection with the earthly life of Jesus. Jesus is, according to this view, not so much a person as a salvation event, known only by faith. But the historical person of Jesus has disappeared.

At one stage in modern discussion, so-called liberal theologians made an attempt to distinguish between the "Jesus of history" and the "Christ of faith." They separated Jesus, the ethical teacher, from Christ, the divine Savior of the world. Here emphasis was placed on the humanity of Jesus and His "religion" of the fatherhood of God and the brotherhood of man. Bultmann substituted for this religion of Jesus the kerygma, the proclamation that the saving eschatological event has happened. Liberal theology, in other words, extracted from the Gospels the moral and religious ideas; for the historical occurrences did not seem to matter. But Bultmann thinks that the religious ideas of Jesus are not part of the kerygma at all. In each case, liberal theologians and Bultmann would throw away the first-century mythological "envelope" in which the Gospels are cast to get at what, for them, is essential.[6]

What is essential for Bultmann lies beneath the mythological language in which the Gospel record is cast. For he holds that the world view of the New Testament is a mythical one. The universe is three-storied with God and angels dwelling in heaven, the earth in the middle and the underworld, which is the place of torment. God and His angels meet on earth with Satan and his demons. Man is caught between the contending forces. Supernatural powers perpetually intervene in this world. Now is the age of Satan's reign, but it moves toward that cosmic crisis when the heavenly Judge will come to raise the dead, save the good and destroy the evil.

Bultmann states that the saving event that will occur is also a mythical representation. This saving event encompasses Jesus Christ as preexisting, coming into this world, living, dying, rising again, continuing in presence to empower the church. This whole event is expressed in mythical language. For the kerygma itself is such a mythical expression. It is derived from the mythology of both Jewish apocalyptic and Gnostic sources.

In Chapter 2 we discussed contrasting meanings of "myth." Nature religions of biblical times understood the problems of human life over against the forces of nature. They interpreted history in terms of natural,

---

[6] See Alan Richardson, *The Bible in the Age of Science*, The Westminster Press, Philadelphia, 1961, p. 107.

recurring processes of fertility and productivity. But biblical writers saw the role of nature in terms of events in history. We have suggested that myth more properly belongs to the tradition of nature religions with its pictures of cosmic forces, origins of the gods themselves and the conflict of universal powers. For the biblical tradition, perhaps we need to abandon the use of "myth" with its references to the cycles of birth and death, morning and evening, etc. Karl Barth has suggested that we speak, for instance, of the "saga" of creation ". . . because creation as such is simply not accessible to myth." We have also suggested that, if we retain the term "myth" in the biblical context, we ought to speak of "historical myth."

This issue is relevant to discussion of Bultmann's understanding of myth. Clearly, he accepts the usage of the "History of Religions" school and employs the term "myth" in such a way as to refer to every possible religion—as depicting the divine in terms of the human and what is beyond this world in terms of the processes of this world. The critical question is: Does Bultmann consider whether or not his use of myth is appropriate to the New Testament? For here also, history is central in depicting man in relation to God.

Modern men, Bultmann claims, can no longer believe the myths of a three-storied universe, angels, Satan, demons and a preexistent Christ coming into this world. He says, "It is for the man of today unbelievable, because for him the mythical world picture is a thing of the past." If we cannot hold any longer to these ancient pictures of a three-storied universe, spirits, demons, the death of a preexistent Christ or a resurrection, what shall we do?

Bultmann's view is that it is possible to cut through and discard the outdated mythology and still retain the kerygma. There is religious truth independent of the mythological envelope in which the Gospel comes to us. For liberal theology, this truth is Jesus' teaching of religious and moral principles. For Bultmann, myth does not give us an objective picture of the world, but it does help us to understand our human, *existential* situation. We need therefore to "demythologize" or reinterpret these myths into terms of man's need in every age of reconciliation between his estranged self and God. According to this view, man's perennial problem, his personal predicament, his *existential* situation is lostness and aloneness. His existential situation has to do with his total life as a person, face to face with the ultimate.

Burton H. Throckmorton, Jr., interprets Bultmann's view in this way:

Myths have an existential purpose; they point to truth, not outside of man, but to truth about man. Myth expresses the belief that the origin and purpose of the world in which man lives are not to be found in the world, but that these lie outside the world; myth tells man that ". . . he is not lord of himself, that he is dependent not only upon the world he knows but above all upon outside powers that govern the world he knows;" and finally myth expresses the conviction that man can be delivered from the powers of the world. The process of demythologization has already begun, since its purpose is not to paint an objective picture, but to tell man something about himself.[7]

In contrast to the Existentialist stance represented by Bultmann, many British and American theologians seem to have held through the years to a steady, mediating viewpoint. C. H. Dodd believes, for instance, that we cannot know the historical life and teaching of Jesus by stripping away the kerygma, as Bultmann would bid us to do. For what we know of Jesus must be seen *through the kerygma* and not by cutting it away. Alan Richardson writes:

> At this point an acute difference of opinion arises between Dodd and the followers of Bultmann. Dodd has strongly argued that the apostolic *kerygma* itself contained an outline of the life and work of the historical Jesus; a skeleton outline of the history of the Lord's ministry was preserved in the primitive Christian tradition and was used by St. Mark in the writing of his Gospel.[8]

The entire volume from which the Bultmann selection is taken, *Kerygma and Myth*, contains a fuller account of his position. It also includes critical comment by other scholars and Bultmann's replies. More recently, a group of Bultmann's followers have attempted to move beyond their master to a "rediscovery of the historical Jesus." Especially helpful is Günther Bornkamm's *Jesus of Nazareth* (specifically pages 13–26), which we have cited above. The American James M. Robinson in his *A New Quest of the Historical Jesus* (Alec E. Allenson, Inc., Naperville, Ill., 1959) also represents an approach to the problem in a new way. A discussion of Existentialism is included in Chapter 11 and the reading selections related to that chapter. For a reflection of Bultmann's influence on contemporary religious thought on the popular level, students are reading, for instance, John A. T. Robinson's *Honest to God* and *The Honest to God Debate* (both The Westminster Press, Philadelphia, 1963).

We need not come to completely negative conclusions about knowledge

---

[7] From *The New Testament and Mythology*, by Burton H. Throckmorton, Jr., pp. 23–24. The Westminster Press. © W. L. Jenkins, 1959. Used by permission.

[8] Richardson, *op. cit.*, pp. 129–130.

of who and what Jesus Christ was. D. M. Baillie insists, as we have tried to do, that we must keep history and faith together. Yet, he asserts, it is absurd to say of the New Testament that it knows nothing of the human character and personality of Jesus Christ. He writes:

> It seems to me that a good deal of confusion would be averted if we reminded ourselves that the phrase, "the Jesus of history," means simply and precisely: "Jesus as He really was in His life on earth," which includes of course what He did and said, what He intended and whom He taught. . . . When we speak of "Jesus as He really was," we must not mean "Jesus as a figure which can be described and authenticated by a cold and detached criticism." For that would not be real history at all. I am sure that this is a fertile source of confusion in the whole matter: the habit of setting "history" and "faith" too sharply against each other. . . .[9]

Again, Bernhard Anderson makes a critical comment about form criticism's view that it is impossible to reach a historical Jesus:

> This does not mean that we are driven to skepticism about the historical Jesus, for we would face a similar problem in dealing with, say, Socrates, who left no writings and is known to us only by his impact on others. As a matter of fact, the fragments of the oral tradition are invaluable to us, for in many cases they give vivid glimpses of Jesus in action, small tableaux of various episodes in his ministry. Moreover with the limitations defined by the nature of the gospel tradition it is possible to reconstruct in outline the broad features of his career and the essential aspects of his message.[10]

[9] "The Paradox of the Incarnation" and other quotations by D. M. Baillie are reprinted with the permission of Charles Scribner's Sons from *God Was In Christ* by D. M. Baillie. Copyright 1948 Charles Scribner's Sons.

[10] By permission. From Bernhard W. Anderson, *Rediscovering the Bible*, Association Press, New York, 1951, pp. 184–185.

6

RUDOLPH BULTMANN | *The Task of Demythologizing*
*the New Testament Proclamation**

A. THE PROBLEM

1. The Mythical View of the World and the
Mythical Event of Redemption

The cosmology of the New Testament is essentially mythical in character.
The world is viewed as a three-storied structure, with the earth in the centre,
the heaven above, and the underworld beneath. Heaven is the abode of
God and of celestial beings—the angels. The underworld is hell, the place
of torment. Even the earth is more than the scene of natural, everyday
events, of the trivial round and common task. It is the scene of the supernatural activity of God and his angels on the one hand, and of Satan and
his daemons on the other. These supernatural forces intervene in the
course of nature and in all that men think and will and do. Miracles are
by no means rare. Man is not in control of his own life. Evil spirits may
take possession of him. Satan may inspire him with evil thoughts. Alternatively, God may inspire his thought and guide his purposes. He may grant
him heavenly visions. He may allow him to hear his word of succour or
demand. He may give him the supernatural power of his Spirit. History
does not follow a smooth unbroken course; it is set in motion and controlled by these supernatural powers. This aeon is held in bondage by
Satan, sin, and death (for "powers" is precisely what they are), and
hastens towards its end. That end will come very soon, and will take the
form of a cosmic catastrophe. It will be inaugurated by the "woes" of the
last time. Then the Judge will come from heaven, the dead will rise, the
last judgment will take place, and men will enter into eternal salvation
or damnation.

* By permission. From Rudolf Bultmann, *Kerygma and Myth*, vol. I, ed. and trans. by
Hans W. Bartsch, Society for the Promotion of Christian Knowledge, London, 1953;
Harper & Row, Publishers, Incorporated, New York, 1961, pp. 1–16. (Footnotes omitted.)

This then is the mythical view of the world which the New Testament presupposes when it presents the event of redemption which is the subject of its preaching. It proclaims in the language of mythology that the last time has now come. "In the fulness of time" God sent forth his Son, a pre-existent divine Being, who appears on earth as a man. He dies the death of a sinner on the cross and makes atonement for the sins of men. His resurrection marks the beginning of the cosmic catastrophe. Death, the consequence of Adam's sin, is abolished, and the daemonic forces are deprived of their power. The risen Christ is exalted to the right hand of God in heaven and made "Lord" and "King". He will come again on the clouds of heaven to complete the work of redemption, and the resurrection and judgement of men will follow. Sin, suffering and death will then be finally abolished. All this is to happen very soon; indeed, St. Paul thinks that he himself will live to see it.

All who belong to Christ's Church and are joined to the Lord by Baptism and the Eucharist are certain of resurrection to salvation, unless they forfeit it by unworthy behaviour. Christian believers already enjoy the first instalment of salvation, for the Spirit is at work within them, bearing witness to their adoption as sons of God, and guaranteeing their final resurrection.

2. The Mythological View of the World Obsolete

All this is the language of mythology, and the origin of the various themes can be easily traced in the contemporary mythology of Jewish Apocalyptic and in the redemption myths of Gnosticism. To this extent *the kerygma is incredible to modern man, for he is convinced that the mythical view of the world is obsolete.* We are therefore bound to ask whether, when we preach the Gospel to-day, we expect our converts to accept not only the Gospel message, but also the mythical view of the world in which it is set. If not, does the New Testament embody a truth which is quite independent of its mythical setting? If it does, theology must undertake the task of stripping the kerygma from its mythical framework, of "demythologizing" it.

Can Christian preaching expect modern man *to accept the mythical view of the world as true?* To do so would be both senseless and impossible. It would be senseless, because there is nothing specifically Christian in the mythical view of the world as such. It is simply the cosmology of a pre-scientific age. Again, it would be impossible, because no man can adopt a view of the world by his own volition—it is already determined for him by his place in history. Of course such a view is not absolutely unalterable, and the individual may even contribute to its change. But he can do so only when he is faced by a new set of facts so compelling as to make his previous view of the world untenable. He has then no alternatives but to modify his view of the world or produce a new one. The discoveries of Copernicus and the atomic theory are instances of this, and so was romanticism, with its discovery that the human subject is richer and more complex than enlightenment or idealism had allowed, and nationalism, with its new realization of the importance of history and the tradition of peoples.

It may equally well happen that truths which a shallow enlightenment had failed to perceive are later rediscovered in ancient myths. Theologians are perfectly justified in asking whether this is not exactly what has happened with the New Testament. At the same time it is impossible to revive an obsolete view of the world by a mere fiat, and certainly not a mythical view. For all our thinking to-day is shaped irrevocably by modern science. A blind acceptance of the New Testament mythology would be arbitrary, and to press for its acceptance as an article of faith would be to reduce faith to works. Wilhelm Herrmann pointed this out, and one would have thought that his demonstration was conclusive. It would involve a sacrifice of the intellect which could have only one result—a curious form of schizophrenia and insincerity. It would mean accepting a view of the world in our faith and religion which we should deny in our everyday life. Modern thought as we have inherited it brings with it criticism of *the New Testament view of the world*.

Man's knowledge and mastery of the world have advanced to such an extent through science and technology that it is no longer possible for anyone seriously to hold the New Testament view of the world—in fact, there is no one who does. What meaning, for instance, can we attach to such phrases in the creed as "descended into hell" or "ascended into heaven"? We no longer believe in the three-storied universe which the creeds take for granted. The only honest way of reciting the creeds is to strip the mythological framework from the truth they enshrine—that is, assuming that they contain any truth at all, which is just the question that theology has to ask. No one who is old enough to think for himself supposes that God lives in a local heaven. There is no longer any heaven in the traditional sense of the word. The same applies to hell in the sense of a mythical underworld beneath our feet. And if this is so, the story of Christ's descent into hell and of his Ascension into heaven is done with. We can no longer look for the return of the Son of Man on the clouds of heaven or hope that the faithful will meet him in the air (I Thess. 4. 15ff.).

Now that the forces and the laws of nature have been discovered, we can no longer believe in *spirits, whether good or evil*. We know that the stars are physical bodies whose motions are controlled by the laws of the universe, and not daemonic beings which enslave mankind to their service. Any influence they may have over human life must be explicable in terms of the ordinary laws of nature; it cannot in any way be attributed to their malevolence. Sickness and the cure of disease are likewise attributable to natural causation; they are not the result of daemonic activity or of evil spells. The *miracles of the New Testament* have ceased to be miraculous, and to defend their historicity by recourse to nervous disorders or hypnotic effects only serves to underline the fact. And if we are still left with certain physiological and psychological phenomena which we can only assign to mysterious and enigmatic causes, we are still assigning them to causes, and thus far are trying to make them scientifically intelligible. Even occultism pretends to be a science.

It is impossible to use electric light and the wireless and to avail ourselves of modern medical and surgical discoveries, and at the same time to believe in the New Testament world of spirits and miracles. We may think we can manage it in our own lives, but to expect others to do so is to make the Christian faith unintelligible and unacceptable to the modern world.

The mythical eschatology is untenable for the simple reason that the parousia of Christ never took place as the New Testament expected. History did not come to an end, and, as every schoolboy knows, it will continue to run its course. Even if we believe that the world as we know it will come to an end in time, we expect the end to take the form of a natural catastrophe, not of a mythical event such as the New Testament expects. And if we explain the parousia in terms of modern scientific theory, we are applying criticism to the New Testament, albeit unconsciously.

But natural science is not the only challenge which the mythology of the New Testament has to face. There is the still more serious challenge presented by *modern man's understanding of himself*.

Modern man is confronted by a curious dilemma. He may regard himself as pure nature, or as pure spirit. In the latter case he distinguishes the essential part of his being from nature. In either case, however, *man is essentially a unity*. He bears the sole responsibility for his own feeling, thinking, and willing. He is not, as the New Testament regards him, the victim of a strange dichotomy which exposes him to the interference of powers outside himself. If his exterior behaviour and his interior condition are in perfect harmony, it is something he has achieved himself, and if other people think their interior unity is torn asunder by daemonic or divine interference, he calls it schizophrenia.

Although biology and psychology recognize that man is a highly dependent being, that does not mean that he has been handed over to powers outside of and distinct from himself. This dependence is inseparable from human nature, and he needs only to understand it in order to recover his self-mastery and organize his life on a rational basis. If he regards himself as spirit, he knows that he is permanently conditioned by the physical, bodily part of his being, but he distinguishes his true self from it, and knows that he is independent and responsible for his mastery over nature.

In either case he finds *what the New Testament has to say about the "Spirit"* (πνευμα) *and the sacraments utterly strange and incomprehensible.* Biological man cannot see how a supernatural entity like the πνευμα can penetrate within the close texture of his natural powers and set to work within him. Nor can the idealist understand how a πνευμα working like a natural power can touch and influence his mind and spirit. Conscious as he is of his own moral responsibility, he cannot conceive how baptism in water can convey a mysterious something which is henceforth the agent of all his decisions and actions. He cannot see how physical food can convey spiritual strength, and how the unworthy receiving of the Eucharist can result in physical sickness and death (I Cor. 11. 30). The only possible explanation is that it is due to suggestion. He cannot understand how anyone can be baptized for the dead (I Cor. 15. 29).

We need not examine in detail the various forms of modern *Weltanschauung*, whether idealist or naturalist. For the only criticism of the New Testament which is theologically relevant is that which arises *necessarily* out of the situation of modern man. The biological *Weltanschauung* does not, for instance, arise necessarily out of the contemporary situation. We are still free to adopt it or not as we choose. The only relevant question for the theologian is the basic assumption on which the adoption of a biological as of every other *Weltanschauung* rests, and that assumption is the view of the world which has been moulded by modern science and the modern conception of human nature as a self-subsistent unity immune from the interference of supernatural powers.

Again, the biblical doctrine that *death is the punishment of sin* is equally abhorrent to naturalism and idealism, since they both regard death as a simple and necessary process of nature. To the naturalist death is no problem at all, and to the idealist it is a problem for that very reason, for so far from arising out of man's essential spiritual being it actually destroys it. The idealist is faced with a paradox. On the one hand man is a spiritual being, and therefore essentially different from plants and animals, and on the other hand he is the prisoner of nature, whose birth, life, and death are just the same as those of the animals. Death may present him with a problem, but he cannot see how it can be a punishment for sin. Human beings are subject to death even before they have committed any sin. And to attribute human mortality to the fall of Adam is sheer nonsense, for guilt implies personal responsibility, and the idea of original sin as an inherited infection is sub-ethical, irrational, and absurd.

The same objections apply to *the doctrine of the atonement*. How can the guilt of one man be expiated by the death of another who is sinless— if indeed one may speak of a sinless man at all? What primitive notions of guilt and righteousness does this imply? And what primitive idea of God? The rationale of sacrifice in general may of course throw some light on the theory of the atonement, but even so, what a primitive mythology it is, that a divine Being should become incarnate, and atone for the sins of men through his own blood! Or again, one might adopt an analogy from the law courts, and explain the death of Christ as a transaction between God and man through which God's claims on man were satisfied. But that would make sin a juridical matter; it would be no more than an external transgression of a commandment, and it would make nonsense of all our ethical standards. Moreover, if the Christ who died such a death was the pre-existent Son of God, what could death mean for him? Obviously very little, if he knew that he would rise again in three days!

The *resurrection of Jesus* is just as difficult for modern man, if it means an event whereby a living supernatural power is released which can henceforth be appropriated through the sacraments. To the biologist such language is meaningless, for he does not regard death as a problem at all. The idealist would not object to the idea of a life immune from death, but he could not believe that such a life is made available by the resuscitation of a dead person. If that is the way God makes life available for man, his action is inextricably involved in a nature miracle. Such a notion he finds incomprehensible, for he can see God at work only in the reality of his personal life and in his transformation. But, quite apart from the incredibility of such a miracle, he cannot see how an event like this could be the act of God, or how it could affect his own life.

Gnostic influence suggests that this Christ, who died and rose again, was not a mere human being but a God-man. His death and resurrection were not isolated facts which concerned him alone, but a cosmic event in which we are all involved. It is only with effort that modern man can think himself back into such an intellectual atmosphere, and even then he could never accept it himself, because it regards man's essential being as nature and redemption as a process of nature. And as for the pre-existence of Christ, with its corollary of man's translation into a celestial realm of light, and the clothing of the human personality in heavenly robes and a spiritual body—all this is not only irrational but utterly meaningless. Why should salvation take this particular form? Why should this be the fulfilment of human life and the realization of man's true being?

B. THE TASK BEFORE US

1. Not Selection or Subtraction

Does this drastic criticism of the New Testament mythology mean the complete elimination of the kerygma?

Whatever else may be true, we cannot save the kerygma by selecting some of its features and subtracting others, and thus reduce the amount of mythology in it. For instance, it is impossible to dismiss St Paul's teaching about the unworthy reception of Holy Communion or about baptism for the dead, and yet cling to the belief that physical eating and drinking can have a spiritual effect. If we accept *one i*dea, we must accept everything which the New Testament has to say about Baptism and Holy Communion, and it is just this one idea which we cannot accept.

It may of course be argued that some features of the New Testament mythology are given greater prominence than others: not all of them appear with the same regularity in the various books. There is for example only one occurrence of the legends of the Virgin birth and the Ascension; St Paul and St John appear to be totally unaware of them. But, even if we take them to be later accretions, it does not affect the mythical character of the event of redemption as a whole. And if we once start subtracting from the kerygma, where are we to draw the line? The mythical view of the world must be accepted or rejected in its entirety.

At this point absolute clarity and ruthless honesty are essential both for the academic theologian and for the parish priest. It is a duty they owe to themselves, to the Church they serve, and to those whom they seek to win for the Church. They must make it quite clear what their hearers are expected to accept and what they are not. At all costs the preacher must not leave his people in the dark about what he secretly eliminates, nor must he be in the dark about it himself. In Karl Barth's book *The Resurrection of the Dead* the cosmic eschatology in the sense of "chronologically final history" is eliminated in favour of what he intends to be a non-mythological "ultimate history". He is able to delude himself into thinking that this is exegesis of St Paul and of the New Testament generally only because he gets rid of everything mythological in I Corinthians by subjecting it to an interpretation which does violence to its meaning. But that is an impossible procedure.

If the truth of the New Testament proclamation is to be preserved, the only way is to demythologize it. But our motive in so doing must not be to make the New Testament relevant to the modern world at all costs. The question is simply whether the New Testament message consists exclusively of mythology, or whether it actually demands the elimination of myth if it is to be understood as it is meant to be. This question is forced upon us from two sides. First there is the nature of myth in general, and then there is the New Testament itself.

2. The Nature of Myth

The real purpose of myth is not to present an objective picture of the world as it is, but to express man's understanding of himself in the world in which he lives. Myth should be interpreted not cosmologically, but anthropologically, or better still, existentially. Myth speaks of the power or the powers which man supposes he experiences as the ground and limit of his world and of his own activity and suffering. He describes these powers in terms derived from the visible world, with its tangible objects and forces, and from human life, with its feelings, motives, and potentialities. He may, for instance, explain the origin of the world by speaking of a world egg or a world tree. Similarly he may account for the present state and order of the world by speaking of a primeval war between the gods. He speaks of the other world in terms of this world, and of the gods in terms derived from human life.

Myth is an expression of man's conviction that the origin and purpose of the world in which he lives are to be sought not within it but beyond it—that is, beyond the realm of known and tangible reality—and that this realm is perpetually dominated and menaced by those mysterious powers which are its source and limit. Myth is also an expression of man's awareness that he is not lord of his own being. It expresses his sense of dependence not only within the visible world, but more especially on those forces which hold sway beyond the confines of the known. Finally, myth expresses man's belief that in this state of dependence he can be delivered from the forces within the visible world.

Thus myth contains elements which demand its own criticism—namely, its imagery with its apparent claim to objective validity. The real purpose of myth is to speak of a transcendent power which controls the world and man, but that purpose is impeded and obscured by the terms in which it is expressed.

Hence the importance of the New Testament mythology lies not in its imagery but in the understanding of existence which it enshrines. The real question is whether this understanding of existence is true. Faith claims that it is, and faith ought not to be tied down to the imagery of New Testament mythology.

3. The New Testament Itself

The New Testament itself invites this kind of criticism. Not only are there rough edges in its mythology, but some of its features are actually contradictory. For example, the death of Christ is sometimes a sacrifice and sometimes a cosmic event. Sometimes his person is interpreted as the Messiah and sometimes as the Second Adam. The kenosis of the pre-existent Son (Phil. 2. 6ff.) is incompatible with the miracle narratives as proofs of his messianic claims. The Virgin birth is inconsistent with the assertion of his pre-existence. The doctrine of the Creation is incompatible with the conception of the "rulers of this world" (I Cor. 2. 6ff.), the "god of this world" (2 Cor. 4. 4) and the "elements of this world" $\sigma\tau o\iota\chi\epsilon\tilde{\iota}\alpha$ $\tau o\tilde{\upsilon}$ $\kappa o\beta\mu o\upsilon$ (Gal. 4. 3). It is impossible to square the belief that the law was given by God with the theory that it comes from the angels (Gal. 3. 19f.).

But the principal demand for the criticism of mythology comes from a curious contradiction which runs right through the New Testament. Sometimes we are told that human life is determined by cosmic forces, at others we are challenged to a decision. Side by side with the Pauline indicative stands the Pauline imperative. In short, man is sometimes regarded as a cosmic being, sometimes as an independent "I" for whom decision is a matter of life or death. Incidentally, this explains why so many sayings in the New Testament speak directly to modern man's condition while others remain enigmatic and obscure. Finally, attempts at demythologization are sometimes made even within the New Testament itself. But more will be said on this point later.

4. Previous Attempts at Demythologizing

How then is the mythology of the New Testament to be reinterpreted? This is not the first time that theologians have approached this task. Indeed, all we have said so far might have been said in much the same way thirty or forty years ago, and it is a sign of the bankruptcy of contemporary theology that it has been necessary to go all over the same ground again. The reason for this is not far to seek. The liberal theologians of the last century were working on the wrong lines. They threw away not only the mythology but also the kerygma itself. Were they right? Is that the treatment the New Testament itself required? That is the question we must face to-day. The last twenty years have witnessed a movement away from criticism and a return to a naïve acceptance of the kerygma. The danger both for theological scholarship and for the Church is that this uncritical resuscitation of the New Testament mythology may make the Gospel message unintelligible to the modern world. We cannot dismiss the critical labours of earlier generations without further ado. We must take them up and put them to constructive use. Failure to do so will mean that the old battles between orthodoxy and liberalism will have to be fought out all over again, that is assuming that there will be any Church or any theologians to fight them at all! Perhaps we may put it schematically like this: whereas the older liberals used criticism to *eliminate* the mythology of the New Testament, our task to-day is to use criticism to *interpret* it. Of course it may still be necessary to eliminate mythology here and there. But the criterion adopted must be taken not from modern thought, but from the understanding of human existence which the New Testament itself enshrines.

To begin with, let us review some of these earlier attempts at demythologizing. We need only mention briefly the allegorical interpretation of the New Testament which has dogged the Church throughout its history. This method spiritualizes the mythical events so that they become symbols of processes going on in the soul. This is certainly the most comfortable way of avoiding the critical question. The literal meaning is allowed to stand and is dispensed with only for the individual believer, who can escape into the realm of the soul.

It was characteristic of the older liberal theologians that they regarded mythology as relative and temporary. Hence they thought they could safely eliminate it altogether, and retain only the broad, basic principles of religion and ethics. They distinguished between what they took to be the essence of religion and the temporary garb which it assumed. Listen to what Harnack has to say about the essence of Jesus' preaching of the Kingdom of God and its coming: "The kingdom has a triple meaning. Firstly, it is something supernatural, a gift from above, not a product of ordinary life. Secondly, it is a purely religious blessing, the inner link with the living God; thirdly, it is the most important experience that a man can have, that on which everything else depends; it permeates and dominates his whole existence, because sin is forgiven and misery banished." Note how completely the mythology is eliminated: "The kingdom of God comes by coming to the individual, by entering into his *soul* and laying hold of it."

It will be noticed how Harnack reduces the kerygma to a few basic principles of religion and ethics. Unfortunately this means that *the kerygma has ceased to be kerygma:* it is no longer the proclamation of the decisive act of God in Christ. For the liberals the great truths of religion and ethics are timeless and eternal, though it is only within human history that they are realized, and only in concrete historical processes that they are given clear expression. But the apprehension and acceptance of these principles does not depend on the knowledge and acceptance of the age in which they first took shape, or of the historical persons who first discovered them. We are all capable of verifying them in our own experience at whatever period we happen to live. History may be of academic interest, but never of paramount importance for religion.

But the New Testament speaks of an *event* through which God has wrought man's redemption. For it, Jesus is not primarily the teacher, who certainly had extremely important things to say and will always be honoured for saying them, but whose person in the last analysis is immaterial for those who have assimilated his teaching. On the contrary, his person is just what the New Testament proclaims as the decisive event of redemption. It speaks of this person in mythological terms, but does this mean that we can reject the kerygma altogether on the ground that it is nothing more than mythology? That is the question.

Next came the History of Religions school. Its representatives were the first to discover the extent to which the New Testament is permeated by mythology. The importance of the New Testament, they saw, lay not in its teaching about religion and ethics but in its actual religion and piety; in comparison with that all the dogma it contains, and therefore all the mythological imagery with its apparent objectivity, was of secondary importance or completely negligible. The essence of the New Testament lay in the religious life it portrayed; its high-watermark was the experience of mystical union with Christ, in whom God took symbolic form.

These critics grasped one important truth. Christian faith is not the same as religious idealism; the Christian life does not consist in developing the individual personality, in the improvement of society, or in making the world a better place. The Christian life means a turning away from the world, a detachment from it. But the critics of the History of Religions school failed to see that in the New Testament this detachment is essentially eschatological and not mystical. Religion for them was an expression of the human yearning to rise above the world and transcend it: it was the discovery of a supramundane sphere where the soul could detach itself from all early care and find its rest. Hence the supreme manifestation of religion was to be found not in personal ethics or in social idealism but in the cultus regarded as an end in itself. This was just the kind of religious life portrayed in the New Testament, not only as a model and pattern, but as a challenge and inspiration. The New Testament was thus the abiding source of power which enable man to realize the true life of religion, and Christ was the eternal symbol for the cultus of the Christian Church. It will be noticed how the Church is here defined exclusively as a worshipping community, and this represents a great advance on the older liberalism. This school rediscovered the Church as a *religious* institution. For the idealist there was really no place for the Church at all. But did they succeed in recovering the meaning of the Ecclesia in the full, New Testament sense of the word? For in the New Testament the Ecclesia is invariably a phenomenon of salvation history and eschatology.

Moreover, if the History of Religion school is right, the kerygma has once more ceased to be kerygma. Like the liberals, they are silent about a decisive act of God in Christ proclaimed as the event of redemption. So we are still left with the question whether this event and the person of Jesus, both of which are described in the New Testament in mythological terms, are nothing more than mythology. Can the kerygma be interpreted apart from mythology? Can we recover the truth of the kerygma for men who do not think in mythological terms without forfeiting its character as kerygma?

5. *An Existentialist Interpretation the Only Solution*

The theological work which such an interpretation involves can be sketched only in the broadest outline and with only a few examples. We must avoid the impression that this is a light and easy task, as if all we have to do is to discover the right formula and finish the job on the spot. It is much more formidable than that. It cannot be done single-handed. It will tax the time and strength of a whole theological generation.

The mythology of the New Testament is in essence that of Jewish apocalyptic and the Gnostic redemption myths. A common feature of them both is their basic dualism, according to which the present world and its human inhabitants are under the control of daemonic, satanic powers, and stand in need of redemption. Man cannot achieve this redemption by his own efforts; it must come as a gift through a divine intervention. Both types of mythology speak of such an intervention: Jewish apocalyptic of an imminent world crisis in which this present aeon will be brought to an end and the new aeon ushered in by the coming of the Messiah, and Gnosticism of a Son of God sent down from the realm of light, entering into this world in the guise of a man, and by his fate and teaching delivering the elect and opening up the way for their return to their heavenly home.

The meaning of these two types of mythology lies once more not in their imagery with its apparent objectivity but in the understanding of human existence which both are trying to express. In other words, they need to be interpreted existentially. A good example of such treatment is to be found in Hans Jonas's book on Gnosticism.

Our task is to produce an existentialist interpretation of the dualistic mythology of the New Testament along similar lines. When, for instance, we read of daemonic powers ruling the world and holding mankind in bondage, does the understanding of human existence which underlies such language offer a solution to the riddle of human life which will be acceptable even to the non-mythological mind of to-day? Of course we must not take this to imply that the New Testament presents us with an anthropology like that which modern science can give us. It cannot be proved by logic or demonstrated by an appeal to factual evidence. Scientific anthropologies always take for granted a definite understanding of existence, which is invariably the consequence of a deliberate decision of the scientist, whether he makes it consciously or not. And that is why we have to discover whether the New Testament offers man an understanding of himself which will challenge him to a genuine existential decision.

Chapter 5 | Crucifixion and Resurrection

The whole message of Jesus' life, word and work is summed up in this way: "Now after John was arrested, Jesus came into Galilee, preaching the Gospel of God, and saying, 'The time is fulfilled, and the kingdom of God is at hand; repent, and believe in the Gospel'" [Mark 1:14–15]. Again: "From that time Jesus began to preach, saying 'Repent, for the kingdom of heaven is at hand.'" The first statement is that of the author of the earliest Gospel written. The other is the language of Matthew expressing the perspective of the first Jewish Christian community. For these latter folk avoided the direct use of the name of God and spoke of the "kingdom of heaven" instead of "the kingdom of God." The core of the message is the same: the kingdom is near!

The original Greek word is only roughly translatable into the English word *kingdom*.[1] The *reign* of God, or complete rule of God, expressed the Jewish conviction that this seemingly chaotic world is under the total and ultimate control of God. Thus, the people lived in the expectation of fulfillment to come at the end of time. Yet God was a living God, present and accessible in the immediate moment. Here lie the problem and paradox within both the older Jewish and the newer Christian faith.

Bernhard Anderson voices the sense of this tension between the now and the end time to come in the reading selection from *Rediscovering the Bible*. Jesus Himself announced the urgency of God's imminent reign. It is a time for repentance and decision under the demanding yet merciful judgment of God.[2] For in Jesus Himself the verge of the reign of right relationship under God becomes a present reality. In what He did and said, they recognized God's demand and gift. For, more important, they responded to what Jesus was in His own person. In truth He Himself is the living *sign* of the coming reign of God. He is the Messiah of their hopes, sent by God to reconcile to Himself all that is divided and separated.

[1] See Günther Bornkamm, *Jesus of Nazareth*, Harper & Row, Publishers, Incorporated, New York, 1960, p. 64, note 2 (Notes, p. 200).

[2] See Chap. 4, pp. 94–95, for the tone of the kerygma of the early Christian community, which echoes this urgent call to new direction and action.

Signs of God's Reign

Clearly, however, Jesus' word of hope is strikingly different from Jewish expectations. We have discussed the new age for which the Jews looked. But Jesus said nothing of national or political dreams in which the kingdom of David would be established in power and under which the destruction of their enemies would be accomplished. Yet Jesus' message linked itself to the apocalyptic expectations of His own day. The Synoptic Gospels record Jesus' shocking reminder of the violent day of reckoning (Luke 27:26ff; 21:34ff); the advent of the Son of Man, Judge of the whole earth (Matthew 8:38; 13:24ff); the harvest that is to be reaped throughout the world (Mark 4:26ff; Matthew 13:24ff); the feast to come (Matthew 8:11). But, despite these ways in which Jesus related His basic word to current expectations, He lashed out in sharp criticism of complacency, bizarre flights of fancy and fruitless attempts to find literal answers to age-old speculations. The ancient cry had been "How long, O Lord?"[3] Men looked for calculations concerning events in nature and history as signs and portents of the exact time of God's appearing. Jesus is significantly silent about these matters. No man can know the day or the hour. "Therefore you must also be ready; for the Son of Man is coming at an hour you do not expect" [Matthew 24:44].

"Then some of the scribes and Pharisees said to him, 'Teacher, we wish to see a sign from you.' But he answered them, 'An evil and adulterous generation seeks for a sign; but no sign shall be given to it except the sign of the prophet Jonah . . . and behold, something greater than Jonah is here' [Matthew 12:38–41]. The irony is that just before this question about a sign was asked, Jesus had given a sign of the love and promise of God in their midst. This He had done through an act of healing. As in the Old Testament record, signs are not intended by the Gospel writers to stand as ends in themselves. They are events which point beyond themselves to the God who reveals Himself. Again, by contrast, the Jewish leaders meant by "sign" a startling cosmic occurrence like light streaming from heaven at midnight or plucking a star from the sky. Nothing less than wonders and sleight-of-hand tricks could satisfy these men concerning Jesus. Or did they stand on the sidelines with caustic eye and tongue in cheek? At any rate, it is the conviction, attested to by the early Christian community, that only participation in revelatory events, not idle speculation, is the favorable stance for faith as response. Decision, a turning around of whole persons, will serve where indifference fails. Jonah

[3] See Psalms 80:4; 74:10; Daniel 9:4–19.

had been set by God to the people of Nineveh, but only repentance opened up their readiness to receive God's gift of reconciliation. This is the sign of Jonah. But Jesus' critics were not ready for His straight-forward demand.[4]

But what are the signs of the coming of God's kingdom? Jesus is no seer or magician. As Bornkamm puts it, "What distinguishes Jesus from these seers is that he himself enters the battlefield; God's victory over Satan takes place in His words and deeds, and it is in them that the signs of this victory are erected."[5] Jesus thus replies to the Pharisees' query as to when the kingdom would come: "The kingdom of God is not coming with signs to be observed; nor will they say, 'Lo here it is!' or 'there!' for behold the kingdom of God is in the midst of you" [Luke 17:20f]. God's reign is *already here*, and yet it is *still to come*.

The signs are these: first, Jesus amazed the people in the synagogue because He taught not as their scribes but as one whose words conveyed authority. Second, He brought merciful healing to the sick of body and tormented in mind. In His day, many disorders were thought to be caused by "evil spirits," or "demons." To exorcise these, to get rid of them, meant to bring healing and wholeness. Whose proper work is this? The Gospels affirm that this is definitely God's work. It is the business of the kingdom of God. For the kingdom of God is nothing less than God Himself, present and still to come. What Jesus did is the authentic sign of the coming reign of God. Yet God is even now effectively at work in the world.

Thus men came to Jesus to ask if He were the Messiah for whom they looked. He replied, in effect, that the signs were evident, although not the kind they had been taught to anticipate. Rather, He said, "The blind receive their sight." "The lame walk." "The lepers are cleansed." "The deaf hear." "The dead are raised." These are the signs of the reign of God, sign-events through which God disclosed Himself. Through Jesus' word, work and person, God was now bringing into being His own reign, a kingdom of right relations among men and between God and men.

The Gospel of Luke reports how Jesus went to the synagogue in Nazareth, His hometown, among His own people, read from the Scriptures and gave His comments (Luke 4:16–30). He chose words from Isaiah 61:1–2:

[4] See *The Interpreter's Bible*, Abingdon Press, Nashville, Tenn., 1951, vol. VII, pp. 402–403.

[5] From *Jesus of Nazareth* by Günther Bornkamm, p. 68, Copyright © 1960 by Hodder & Stoughton Ltd., and Harper & Brothers, Publishers, Inc. Copyright © 1956 Verlag W. Kohlhammer GmbH., Stuttgart.

The Spirit of the Lord is upon me,
Because he has
  anointed me to preach
  good news to the poor
He has sent me to proclaim release to the capitives,
And recovering of sight to the blind;
To set at liberty those who are oppressed,
To proclaim the acceptable year of the Lord.

He closed the book and said, "Today this scripture has been fulfilled in your hearing."[6]

Word, Work and Person

According to Christian conviction, there is an indissoluble connection between Jesus' *word*, His *work* and His own *person* as the effective agent of God's reign. This comes to climax in Jesus' death on the Cross and His resurrection.[7] He was done to death not because He talked abstractly about God's forgiving nature or taught an inspiring ethic. He was killed because He claimed to embody ". . . in his words and works the saving power of God. . . . He claimed to do what only God can do." To the Jews this was blasphemy. But to those who saw and heard in faith, what Jesus said and did were the signs of God's reign of right relationships breaking into history. They came to believe that through Jesus Christ, in His life and now in His sacrificial death and rising again, God took the initiative in reconciling men to Himself.

The Crucifixion and the Resurrection cannot be separated. In Christian conviction, these two phases of what was done for mankind through Christ belong together. The Crucifixion-Resurrection comprises the dynamic point of contact between God Himself and mankind. For this reason, the oldest forms of preaching and statement of faith, within the early Christian community, concentrated on the death and Resurrection. They declared thereby the end of this age that is past and the breaking in of a new world in judgment and deliverance wrought by God.[8]

The Crucifixion-Resurrection, thus linked together, is a total event. But it is an event as seen and interpreted from the post-Resurrection per-

[6] Luke 4:18–19, 21.

[7] See Bernhard Anderson, *Rediscovering the Bible*, Association Press, New York, 1951, p. 198.

[8] See Acts 3:13ff, 4:10ff, 5:30ff and compare I Corinthians 15:3ff.

spective. This is the response of the community, looking back, remembering and affirming. But, as Anderson reminds us, such interpretive faith as this, centered on the Passion, ". . . was no afterthought." Rather we have every warrant for holding that Jesus Himself conceived His role as that of the suffering servant sent by God to bring about, through His sacrificial death, a new covenanted relationship between God and man.[9]

The Cross for Man

As for man, all the evil which human beings can contrive is drawn into sharp focus on the Cross. The Christian holds that every man can discern himself, his motives, attitudes and acts among the cast of characters moving through this cosmic drama. Jesus was done to death by men's ambition, self-righteousness, greed, jealousy, pride, drive for power, fear and indifference. One way of stating Christian conviction about this event is: given man's sin, the Cross is necessary to the fulfillment of God's redemptive purpose in history. But this view of it does not say that men are mere puppets controlled and used by God. Rather the Crucifixion discloses everything that men actually are when they try to take things completely into their own hands and make "gods" of themselves. It is to this human situation of alienation called sin that the Cross speaks. For, as stated in Chapter 3, sin is not simply doing conventionally bad things. It is the deliberate denial of the soulish or bodily dimensions of human existence and ceasing to achieve full selfhood before God. Sin is a state and a condition of separation from God, from ourselves and from our fellowmen.

When a human being who has estranged himself from the Ultimate attempts by his own unaided power to restore that broken relationship, the result is only further alienation. From these denials of self and God, he is driven more deeply into tension, anxiety, conflict, futile idolization of his finite achievements. The solution to this human predicament, for the Christian, lies in reconciliation between God and man and, hence also, between man and man. God has created man in His own image with power to respond, to enter into covenant relationship with his Creator. This image may be lost for a while and defaced but never destroyed. It is the Christian faith, the heart of it, that restoration of man's God-given destiny takes place through this climactic event of the Crucifixion-Resurrection.

[9] See William Manson, *Jesus, the Messiah*, The Westminster Press, Philadelphia, 1946, chap. VII.

Jesus Christ and the Cross

Jesus Himself conceived His role as that of the suffering servant to bring about a new covenant between God and man.[10] Jesus deliberately chose His course. "Behold, we go to Jerusalem, and the son of man shall be delivered unto the chief priests and the scribes; and they shall condemn him to death, and shall deliver him unto the Gentiles, and they shall mock him, and shall spit upon him, and shall kill him, and after three days he shall rise again" [Matthew 20:18–19]. The Gospels of Mark and Luke also contain passages telling how Jesus Himself said: "The Son of Man must suffer many things." The Gospel writers record, in such passages, the forecast of events of the final week of Jesus' ministry which had not yet occurred. These tell how Jesus would be rejected by the elders, chief priests and scribes, condemned, mocked, scourged and crucified. Clearly these writers projected back into this earlier period of Jesus' life their knowledge as to how the story actually ended.

Two points are essential for our understanding of this situation. First, the New Testament writers believed that the Old Testament foretells, in veiled figures of speech and hidden symbols, the Gospel story.[11] The Jewish Scriptures comprised up to that time the only written record of God's disclosure to men. Therefore, they held, this record must contain, even if in symbolic form, an account of fulfillment to come through God's chosen Messiah. This deliverer *had* come and, beyond death, was *still alive* in their midst in a way more intense even than during His earthly career. Through His spirit they now grasped the significance of all that had been foretold in the Scriptures. Their purpose was to demonstrate that Christ died according to the Scriptures (I Corinthians 15:3). Thus many details of the Passion narratives were written to establish Christ's death as the fulfillment of Old Testament hopes.[12]

This leads us, second, to ask: In what precisely did this fulfillment consist? Christ was now for Christians rooted in Jewish expectation, in truth the new Moses. He became the new deliverer and mediator between God and man. "There is one God and one mediator between God and men, the Man Christ Jesus, who gave himself a ransom for all" [I Timothy 2:5f]. Moses, as giver of the Law and establisher of the old covenant, was called the mediator in Jewish literature. Now there is no need of a human mediator, the Christians said, since we have direct access to God through

---

[10] *Ibid.*

[11] From Alan Richardson, *An Introduction to The Theology of the New Testament*, Copyright © 1958 Alan Richardson, pp. 185–186. Reprinted with the permission of Harper & Row, Publishers, Inc., New York, and SCM Press Ltd., London.

[12] *Ibid.*, p. 187. See Luke 22:37.

Christ. Just as God through Moses established the covenant at Sinai, so now Christ has brought us into a new covenant. This has been accomplished through His giving of His very life's blood. For, indeed, the old covenant had been ratified at Sinai, as Moses sprinkled the blood of animal sacrificial victims over the people, saying, "Behold the blood of the covenant . . ." [Exodus 24:8].

This sounds repulsive to sensitive moderns. Yet it was in this fashion that covenants were ratified in sacrificial blood in those earlier days. Jesus clearly referred to Exodus 24:8 when He distributed the cup to His disciples at the Last Supper. "This is my blood of the covenant which is poured out for many [Mark 14:24]. Alan Richardson makes comment on these words:

> . . . the meaning of Jesus is perfectly clear, and it has nothing whatever to do with the question which so preoccupied the minds of later medieval and reformation theologians. He was not making any kind of mystical or metaphysical statement about the *esse* of the wine in the cup; he was saying, in the typically allusive biblical fashion, that his death, now imminent, was the sacrificial act by which God was making a covenant with a new people, replacing the old, broken covenant of Sinai. . . .
>
> It is not suprising that Jesus should have regarded the shedding of his blood as a necessary condition of the making of the new covenant between God and man, which he understood to be the purpose of his own mission and work. . . . Jesus steadfastly set his face to go to Jerusalem (Luke 9.51) with the deliberate intention of giving his body and pouring out his blood on behalf of the covenant of the people. For more than nineteen centuries the "people of God", which his death did in actual fact bring into being, has made solemn ἀνάνηϐις of his atoning sacrifice.[13]

God Was There

In the book about boyhood, *Bevis,* by Richard Jeffries, the young lad looked at a picture of the Crucifixion. Says the author: "The crucifixion hurt his feelings very much: the cruel nails, the unfeeling spear: he looked at the picture a long time, and then turned over the page saying, 'If God had been there, He would not have let them do it.' "[14] For the Christian, irony could go no deeper; for he believes that God *was* there.

The Cross draws into a single event all the evil which men can contrive.

---

[13] *Ibid.,* pp. 230–232.

[14] Quoted in J. S. Whale, *The Christian Answer to the Problem of Evil,* Abingdon Press, Nashville, Tenn., 1936, p. 66.

There Jesus Christ willingly laid down His very life. But it is the Christian faith that in that same event stand disclosed the power and love of God. To put it another way, man's evil was drawn to the Cross so that something decisive could be done about it once and for all. Christ was there as mediator between God and man willingly to endure the pain and ignominy of it. The all-powerful love of God was there to do the doing. In Christian conviction, the Crucifixion is no localized incident. The Cross is cosmic. J. S. Whale speaks of the Christian affirmation that the Cross is the ultimate fact in human history and adds: ". . . beyond it there is and can be nothing. God Himself can do no more; greater love is impossible; the uttermost even of the infinite grace of God is there. The cross is not only a scandalous fact of history; it is the triumphant act of God."[15]

From Crucifixion to Resurrection

Anatole France creates an imaginative scene in which a character named Lamia is speaking to Pilate, the Roman governor under whom Jesus met death. "I knew a Jewess. . . . Some months after I lost sight of her, I learned by chance that she had attached herself to a small company of men and women who were followers of a young Galilean. . . . His name was Jesus; he came from Nazareth, and he was crucified for some crime, I don't know quite what. Pontius," continued this speaker, "Pontius, do you remember anything about the man?" Pontius Pilate contracted his brows, and his hand rose to his forehead in the attitude of one who was trying desperately to remember. Then after a silence of some seconds, "Jesus?" he murmured, "Jesus—of Nazareth? I cannot call him to mind."[16]

Pontius Pilate, under whose sanction Jesus Christ was tried and condemned, had forgotten. But members of the early Christian community remembered. Yet Jesus, the Christ, in their midst, was more than a memory. They centered their faith in His very person, present with them even now. He was the heart of this whole event comprising a unique act of God in history. Embraced within this total event were not only His life, career, word and work but also His death, resurrection and continuing presence in the midst of the new community. Thus the Christ to whom

[15] *Ibid.*, p. 89. See John B. Harrington, *Essentials in Christian Faith*, Harper & Row, Publishers, Incorporated, New York, 1958, pp. 200–201.
[16] By permission. From Anatole France, *Mother of Pearl*, trans. by Frederic Chapman, Dodd, Mead & Company, Inc., New York, and the Bodley Head Ltd., London, 1924, pp. 26–27.

they were committed was the triumphant Messiah, conqueror of sin and death. And *through* Him they now worshiped the God of a *new* covenant, the Father of their Lord who had overcome death with newness of life. They also became heirs of a new creation, for they saw all that Jesus had said and done in the light of the Resurrection. It was from this climax of belief and worship that the Christian community proclaimed the good news of the reign of God.

Tension between Crucifixion and Resurrection

As A. Michael Ramsey suggests, there is within the thought of the early community a tension between the Crucifixion and the Resurrection. But, despite this tension, it is too simple a comparison to say that one is a symbol of stark tragedy and the other a symbol of life and hope. For the Cross itself is the very medium of God's empowering love. Ramsey states: "We discover as we read the New Testament that the two events, seen first as opposites, are found increasingly to be like two sides of a single coin." Even in the austere loneliness of the Cross itself the ". . . scene is not one of pathos, or tragedy or defeat." However, the triumph of the Cross finds its vindication in the Resurrection. The Gospels themselves, suggests Ramsey, draw the Cross and Resurrection together. Luke, for example, show how even through the Cross there is evidenced a ". . . serenity and mastery of love whereby the Son of Man reaches out in sympathy and tenderness to those around Him. It is they and not He whose need and plight are pitiable." "The Crucifixion is not a defeat needing the Resurrection to reverse it, but a victory which the Resurrection quickly follows and seals."[17]

The Hebraic View of Man and History

Members of the early Christian community believed not in *immortality* of the soul but in a *resurrection* from the dead. Also, they held to the reality of *history* and God as now disclosing Himself through the mightiest of all His mighty acts *in* history. On two counts, therefore, their orientation was Hebraic rather than Greek. For the Greek, body and soul belong to two different worlds, the body to this world of change and decay and the

---

[17] A. Michael Ramsey, *The Resurrection of Christ,* The Westminster Press, Philadelphia, 1946, pp. 18–20, *passim.*

soul to the immortal or the deathless. Also, for the Greek, history does not move toward a goal but revolves in endless cycles as a reflection of the eternal. Christian perspective out of the Hebrew tradition thus implies a certain view of man and a distinctive view of history. These come to climax in this New Testament account of the Resurrection.

First, the biblical interpretation of human nature pictures man not as an eternal soul imprisoned in a body but as a total personality responding in acceptance or rejection of God's demand upon him. At death, man's personal existence comes to a halt. A man's body returns to dust, and his "shade" goes down to Sheol. To have a future life, there must be a re-creation. God must raise up and restore man once more to relationship with God.

Second, the meaning of the Resurrection comes to focus in terms of God's ". . . transfiguration of history itself." Messianic expectations pointed toward fulfillment in God's rule over the whole of creation. In that climactic period God would raise the dead so that all generations might participate in His final victory.[18]

These distinctively Hebraic views of man and history find their completion in Christian affirmation. Resurrection of the dead is not escape into some eternal realm. Resurrection is to take place at the end of history when the fathful will be raised up to become members of the messianic community. This is the context of Jewish conviction within which the Resurrection of Jesus became meaningful for the early Christians. They held that the Crucifixion-Resurrection was a *sign* that the climax of all God's acts was even now taking place. This was the new Exodus, of greater consequence even than the old. Now God had wrought deliverance from sin and death. This is the enduring theme of biblical religion: God active in human history to bring about at-one-ment between man and Himself. As Anderson writes, "The Resurrection, then, is the dominant category of a religion which rests upon a conviction intolerable to Greek thought: God's action, his coming into history, his self-revelation in historical events."[19]

Easter Narratives and Message

The message of Easter, rooted in the faith of the first Christians, may be distinguished from the Easter narratives concerning the way in which the event took place. The Easter narratives, as presented in the Gospels

---

[18] See Isaiah 26:19; Daniel 12:2–3; I Thessalonians 4:14; Acts 24:15; John 5:19.
[19] Anderson, *op. cit.*, p. 216.

and in Paul's First Letter to the Corinthians (Chapter 15), differ in many details. The New Testament simply does not give us a consistent account of what happened at the Resurrection.

In addition to the Gospel records, the words of Paul comprise an earlier literary witness than those of the Gospel writers (see I Corinthians 15). Paul speaks for the entire Christian community: "Whether then it was I or they, so we preach and so you believed" [I Corinthians 15:11]. In this same chapter he also states that Christians' faith stands or falls with the Resurrection message. Theirs is the solid conviction that, through the risen Christ, God has now overcome sin and death. "If Christ has not been raised, then our preaching is in vain and your faith is in vain. We are even found to be misrepresenting God, because we testified of God that he raised Christ, whom he did not raise up. . . . If Christ has not been raised, your faith is futile and you are still in your sins" [I Corinthians 15:14–15, 17]. In this passage, Paul faces his readers with the awful consequences of rejecting the Resurrection faith. If we are deceived, he says, "Let us eat and drink, for tomorrow we die" [I Corinthians 15:32].

Despite all the variations among the Easter *narratives,* every one of the Gospel writers and Paul express the basic faith of members of the early Christian community. Christ had conquered death and still lived among them to give new creative power to that community. This is, historically speaking, the event which brought the Christian Church into existence. The New Testament is the living record of the Resurrection event. Also there is the establishment of the first day of the week (Sunday) as the Lord's day in observance of the risen Christ. In short, if the Resurrection had not occured, the company of His followers never would have become the Christian Church with its special day of observance.[20]

In summary, we cite the words of Bornkamm:

From what has been said, it follows that we are to understand the Easter stories too as evidence of the faith, not as records and chronicles, and that it is the *message* of Easter we must seek in the Easter *stories.* That is not to say by any means that the message of Jesus' resurrection is only a product of the believing community. Certainly the form in which it comes down to us is stamped with this faith. What became clear and grew to be a certainty for the Church was this, that God himself had intervened with his almighty hand in the wicked and rebellious life of the world, and had wrested this Jesus of Nazareth from the power of sin and death which had risen against him, and set him up as Lord of the world. Thus, according to the interpretation of the early Church, Easter is above all else God's ac-

[20] *Ibid.,* pp. 222–244.

knowledgment of this Jesus, whom the world refused to acknowledge, and to whom even his disciples were unfaithful. It is at the same time the intervention of God's new world in this old world branded with sin and death, the setting up and beginning of his kingdom. An event *in* this time and this world, and yet at the same time an event which puts an end and a limit to this time and this world. To be sure only faith experiences this (Acts x. 40ff), for it cannot be observed and demonstrated like any other event in time and space. And yet it concerns this world as an act of salvation and judgment, and must therefore be proclaimed to the ends of the earth. We note how Jesus' own message of the coming of the kingdom of God is heard here again in a new form, only that now he himself, together with his death and resurrection, has entered into this message and became the core of it.[21]

[21] Bornkamm, *op. cit.*, pp. 183–184.

7

BERNHARD ANDERSON | *God Was in Christ**

J esus' message was set in the context of the belief in the drawing near
of "the Kingdom of God." The phrase must not be construed to mean
primarily a *realm,* as we would speak of the British kingdom. The underlying Aramaic phrase means basically "Kingly Rule" or "Sovereignty."
The Jews of Jesus' day used the phrase in a twofold sense. The rabbis
taught that when a man obeyed the Law he took upon himself "the yoke
of the Kingdom." Thus God's rule was present wherever faith was found,
even though to all outward appearances the world was under the dominion
of evil. Also, in the spirit of the prophets and apocalyptic writers, the
phrase was used to refer to the time when God would finally manifest his
sovereignty by overthrowing the evil forces of history and graciously manifesting his day of favor ("the acceptable year of the Lord"). Thus paradoxically, the Kingdom was conceived as being both present (in faith)
and yet to come (in hope).

Jesus' message, belonging fundamentally in the prophetic-apocalyptic
tradition of Judaism, stressed the latter part of the paradox, and thus
brought the two poles of the magnet—present faith and future hope—
close together. According to Mark, he came preaching ". . . the gospel
of the Kingdom of God," saying, "The time is fulfilled, and the Kingdom
of God is at hand [or, "has come near"]: repent and believe in the
gospel" (Mark 1:14–15). Jesus preached with the urgency born of the
realization that men were living in the "zero hour" of history when God's
"time" was on the verge of being manifested. It was no situation for complacency or quibbling like children at their games (Matthew 11:16–17;
Luke 7:31–32). It was a time for action, decision, repentance. Just as
night watchers behold the first signs of day in the dawn hours before the
sun bursts in full radiance, likewise—even before the Kingdom of God
comes in glory—its powers were spreading through the world! In various

* By permission. From Bernhard W. Anderson, *Rediscovering the Bible,* Association
Press, New York, 1951, pp. 187–198.

parables Jesus described the Kingdom as being in the process of arriving. The Kingdom, he said, is like a lump of leaven diffusing its energy through meal, like a hidden treasure which a man stumbles upon in a field, like a tiny seed growing mysteriously and irresistibly, or like a field of wheat and tares ripening for the approaching harvest (see Matthew 13). Already its powers are at work—for those who have eyes to discern "the signs of the times." The near approach of God's Kingdom was the heart of the "good news" proclaimed by Jesus. We must be very careful to distinguish this conception of the Kingdom from modern evolutionary versions of "building the Kingdom on earth," that is, realizing the ideal society.

Closely connected with Jesus, preaching concerning the Kingdom is his teaching on the subject of God. Actually "God" and his "Kingdom" cannot be separated, except in discussion, for the Kingdom is the manifestation of God's sovereign power in history. However, when Jesus spoke about God he proclaimed the good news that God *takes the initiative* to seek and to save. He does not wait for men to approach him; he is like the Good Shepherd who went out into the wilderness to find his lost sheep. He does not wait for his children to ask forgiveness; he is like the father of the prodigal son who was always willing to forgive and who eagerly ran down the road to meet the returning youth and be reconciled with him. The Jewish scholar, Claude Montefiore, insisted that the unique element in Jesus' teaching which could not be paralleled in the Old Testament or rabbinical literature is this picture of God taking the initiative to reconcile his people unto himself. The remark is not quite fair to the prophets, since the belief in divine initiative is at the heart of the doctrine of Israel's election, but at least Montefiore has singled out a central element in Jesus' preaching. The God of Jesus is the God who acts even before men turn unto him. His is the love which goes the whole length in bridging the chasm of self-centeredness (sin) which separates the children of God from the Source of their life.

Jesus' message focused upon the good news of God's forgiveness. Of course, the receiving of forgiveness necessarily presupposes the sense of *a need to be forgiven*. Therefore, Jesus constantly attacked the "good" people of the day whose pride constituted a self-erected barrier separating them from God. With a fine touch of irony, he pointed out that those who are "well" (that is, who suppose that they are) need no physician; the physician can help only those who know they are sick. "I came," he said, "not to call the righteous, but sinners" (Mark 2:17). We miss the point of this remark if we suppose that Jesus accepted Judaism's neat distinction between the sheep and the goats: the righteous being those who fulfilled God's demands in the Law, and the sinners being the religiously outcast who failed to live up to the legal requirements. Jesus' ministry was directed toward those who made no claims for themselves, who knew their poverty-stricken spiritual condition, and who were therefore in a position to receive the forgiveness which God freely offers. Surely one of the main purposes of the sayings now classified under the "Sermon on the Mount" was to oppose the legalism of Judaism which made possible such self-righteousness. "It was said unto you of old [in the Law of Moses] . . . but I say unto you. . . ." The things Jesus says to us in the Sermon on the Mount make God's demand so absolute, so inward, so immeasurable, and, in the last analysis, so unattainable that no Christian who is honest can parade his righteousness before God and look down condescendingly upon the other man as a sinner. It is equally out of place for Americans self-righteously to boast, as has been done recently, that United States foreign policy is governed by the Sermon on the Mount, the implication being that our foes are the sinners.[1] The first word of Jesus' preaching is directed to all men alike: Repent!

This explains why Jesus attacked the Pharisees. The Pharisees were the good people of the day. They were religiously devout, morally respectable, and socially minded. Like Job's devout friends, they were representatives of the best of Judaism. But their very goodness and piety excluded them from God's forgiveness, for, as Jesus said in the parable of the Pharisee and Publican (Luke 18:9–14), they ". . . trusted in themselves that they were righteous." The man who went down to his house "justified"[2] was not the self-righteous Pharisee, but the man who in self-despair cried out for divine mercy: "God be merciful to me, a sinner!" The same point is made in the parable of the Prodigal Son and Elder Brother (Luke 15:11–32). Both boys were loved *equally* by the father. However, the elder brother, like the Pharisees, excluded himself from the father's love by his self-righteous attitude ("Lo, these many years do I serve thee, neither transgressed I at any time thy commandment"), while the younger boy, reduced to despair by his knowledge that he had wounded his father ("I am no more worthy to be called thy son"), was in a position to receive the forgiveness freely offered him. "Blessed are the poor in spirit" (those who realize their spiritual poverty), said Jesus in the Beatitudes, "for theirs is the kingdom of Heaven" (Matthew 5:3).

Not only did Jesus preach a message of repentance, but he shocked many people then (and now) by announcing that men could *do* nothing to gain salvation or make themselves worthy of God's forgiveness. If the

[1] See the forceful editorial in *The Christian Century*, "Mr. Truman's Spiritual Blindness," June 28, 1950, p. 782.

[2] "Justified" means accepted or approved by God. We shall encounter this word again in our later discussion of Paul's doctrine of "justification by faith."

barrier separating man from God is egocentricity, then, apart from God's grace, man is in a hopeless condition. For try as he will, man cannot extricate himself from *himself*. Effort merely aggravates the problem. As one student wrote in an examination: "When we read the parable of the Pharisee and the Publican, we inevitably thank God that we do not have the pride of the Pharisees, thus showing our pride in being humble!" In this connection one is reminded of a passage in the *Screwtape Letters* where Screwtape, the Devil's Advocate, advises his understudy, Wormwood, on the strategy to be used in undermining the faith of a young Christian:

> I see only one thing to do at the moment. Your patient has become humble; have you drawn his attention to the fact? All virtues are less formidable to us once the man is aware that he has them, but this is especially true of humility. Catch him at the moment when he is really poor in spirit and smuggle into his mind the gratifying reflection, "By jove! I'm being humble," and almost immediately pride—pride at his own humility—will appear. If he awakes to the danger and tries to smother this new form of pride, make him proud of his attempt—and so on, through as many stages as you please.[3]

The best commentary on the human predicament is found in the story of the so-called "Rich Young Ruler" (Mark 10:17–31 and parallels). The story opens with the question: "What shall *I do* to inherit eternal life [the life of the Kingdom]?" Jesus dealt with this young man, who had been nourished on Jewish legalism, by imposing a demand which in his case was impossible of fulfillment. When the astonished disciples asked, "Then who can be saved?" Jesus answered, "The things which are impossible with men are possible with God." Thus Christianity, unlike Judaism and all moralistic faiths, is not a religion of attainment, as though by doing something man could somehow lift himself by his own bootstraps and improve his spiritual condition. The sum and substance of the gospel of the Kingdom is that God's love does for man what man cannot do for himself. God graciously offers the forgiveness which no man can merit by effort, and thus brings men into relationship with him—reconciled, restored, and transformed.

Thus by means of preaching Jesus sought to awaken a sleeping generation to the momentous crisis in which they stood. We are told that his contemporaries remarked that ". . . he taught as one having authority and not as the scribes" (Matt. 7:29). The role of the scribes was to inter-

---

[3] C. S. Lewis, *Screwtape Letters* (Macmillan, 1943), p. 71.

pret the recorded revelation of the past. Jesus, however, spoke with the authority of the prophetic "thus saith the Lord" as he disclosed the nature of the contemporary crisis in which men were standing. By means of the spoken word he proclaimed that God's sovereign rule was being manifested in a new and dynamic way. He attempted to stir men out of their complacency, and to shatter the self-defensiveness and pride which made it impossible for them to receive the gift of God's grace. Always his message focused upon God's initiative, his action, his coming into human life not only to judge men but to reconcile them to himself. Here we encounter the theme of the Old Testament prophets: the judgment and mercy of God. It will be recalled that in the prophetic message of the Old Testament the present crisis invariably was viewed in terms of God's judgment; God's mercy lay "beyond the judgment." Jesus' message concerning the near approach of the Kingdom and the in-breaking of God's sovereignty, even before its imminent arrival, brought these two themes together. In this case divine judgment and divine mercy were blended together in a gospel that spoke urgently to the present in which men were living.[4]

JESUS' MIRACLES

Jesus' ministry involved more than proclaiming that already the redemptive rule of God was breaking in upon human life. Not only did he preach this good news; he was its "effective agent." He was the instrument through whom God was accomplishing his purpose to reclaim and to reshape human life. The reality of God's Redemptive Rule was made manifest in what Jesus was *doing*, in the effect of his deeds. This is the central meaning of the miracle stories preserved in the Gospels. To early witnesses, both Jesus' words and deeds were evidences that he had the *authority* of God's Messiah (see Mark 1:27).

For many of us, Jesus' miracles constitute one of the great stumbling blocks in the New Testament. At this point the New Testament does not speak our language. A few of the stories are sometimes explained on the assumption that Jesus was a kind of twentieth-century psychiatrist, but this approach does not carry us very far in dealing with the miracle story tradition as a whole. What can one say, for instance, about the claims that Jesus walked on the sea, raised Lazarus from the dead, or turned water

---

[4] These two themes are blended together with magnificent counterpoint in the Fourth Gospel. There it is pointed out that the coming of the Son is *both* God's judgment upon the world and the free offer of God's saving mercy (see, for example, John 3:16–21; 12:31–32).

into wine? Such stories seem to violate ordinary human experience and common sense. It is not surprising, then, that some biblical interpreters have treated the miracle stories as curious relics of a prescientific age and have attempted to reduce Christianity to the moral and spiritual teachings of the New Testament.

Many of the things said previously in our discussion of the Exodus would apply, *mutatis mutandis,* to the miracle question in the New Testament. A proper study of this subject would involve a careful consideration of the transmission of the miracle stories in the oral period, with the aid of the method of Form Criticism. Here we can only refer to more adequate treatments of the issue and confine ourselves to a summary of their conclusions.[5]

All the historical evidence we have at our disposal points to the conclusion that the earliest followers of Jesus, as well as his enemies, believed that he performed miracles. Mark, for instance, devotes almost one-third of his Gospel to the subject of miracle. Moreover, Form Criticism has shown that the miracle story was one of the "forms" by which the Church gave expression to the messianic faith from the earliest times. The early apostolic sermons of Acts appeal to Jesus' "mighty works and wonders and signs" (Acts 2:22; 10:38) as evidence that God had demonstrated him to be the Messiah. The historical evidence is impressive. As Alan Richardson observes:

> The evidence that Jesus worked miracles is just as strong, and is of precisely the same quality and texture, as that He taught that God is Father and that His disciples should forgive one another. We cannot *on historical grounds alone* accept the evidence for the one and reject that for the other. The evidence that Jesus healed a dropsical man on the Sabbath day is just as good as the evidence that He told the story of the Good Samaritan or the Prodigal Son.[6]

Now, this does not mean that the Christian is under obligation to accept each and every miracle as a literal happening which could have been "taken" with a movie camera. In the New Testament there is less emphasis upon the literal act than upon the meaning which the miracle act conveys. This is clearest in the Fourth Gospel where Jesus' actions, like the symbolic actions of the Old Testament prophets, are regarded as "signs" which have

---

[5] See especially Alan Richardson, *The Miracle Stories of the Gospels* (Harper, 1942). For a shorter treatment, see William Manson, *Jesus, the Messiah* (Westminster, 1946), chapter 3. I am deeply indebted to both of these scholars.

[6] *Christian Apologetics,* p. 170.

a deeper symbolic significance to those who see in faith. So, for instance, the feeding of the five thousand is less the satisfying of physical hunger than it is the sign of Jesus' power to satisfy men's spiritual hunger with the Bread of Life (John 6:1–59), and the raising of Lazarus is less the re-animation of a corpse than it is the sign of Jesus' power to raise men to new life (11:1–46). But this emphasis upon the *meaning* of Jesus' acts was native to the miracle tradition from the very first, whatever the original nucleus of miracle stories was. Form Criticism emphasizes that the miracle story by its very nature gave free rein to the imagination dur-ing the period of the oral transmission of the Christian faith. Nevertheless, the embellishing of the tradition was in itself an expression of the messi-anic faith of the Church, and this faith, in turn, rested upon the historical experience that Jesus, as God's Messiah, performed miracles. As Canon Richardson points out, the proper place to begin the discussion of this subject is not with the consideration as to whether such and such a miracle happened, but to inquire into the meaning of Jesus' miracles.

On this point the evidence seems clear and consistent. To the eye of faith, Jesus' miracles were *signs* that the power of the Kingdom of God already was active among men, even before its arrival. Perhaps the key sentence is Jesus' statement as recorded in "Q" (Matthew 12:28; Luke 11:20): "If I by the Spirit of God cast out demons, then is the Kingdom of God come upon you." Commenting on this passage, William Manson says:

> What is indicated . . . is that the Kingdom of God, the most tremendous of all mysteries, has made itself known. It is not only near, it is impinging upon present history: "the kingdom of God has come your length" or "has lighted upon you."[7]

Thus Jesus not only confronted men with the crisis of God's Kingdom through his preaching; the saving purpose and power of God were also revealed in his "mighty works," which were essentially victories over the demonic powers of evil.

According to the tradition, Jesus did not perform miracles to draw crowds or to give indisputable proofs of his divinity. It is a strange fact, often overlooked, that the majority of those who saw Jesus perform miracles did not *see* the real miracle at all, and were not moved to faith merely by the mighty works which took place before them. We cannot appeal to the fact that Jesus performed miracles as a proof which compels belief, any more than could early Christians. The gospel tradition seems

[7] *Op. cit.*, p. 70.

to indicate that faith was the prerequisite for perceiving Jesus' messianic identity, just as light is necessary for the vision of the eye. And such faith was no a product of any "flesh and blood" proofs (see Matthew 16:17); it was God's revelation, the miraculous cure of spiritual blindness. When Jesus found this faith, he performed miracles. To those who saw his acts through the glasses of faith, the mighty works were signs of his messiahship and of the Kingdom of God which was impinging upon their lives. To others, his actions were essentially no different than the accomplishments of wonder-workers to be found everywhere among the Jews and Gentiles.

An excellent example of the meaning of Jesus' miraculous acts is found in the story of the healing of the paralytic (Mark 2:1-12). On one occasion when Jesus was preaching in a crowded house, a paralytic was let down through the roof. When Jesus perceived the faith of those who had done this extraordinary thing, he said to the paralytic: "My son, your sins are forgiven." This utterance caused a great commotion among the skeptical Jews, who found therein the blasphemous claim that Jesus himself was wielding the power of God. In answer to their murmurings, Jesus said:

> Which is easier, to say to the paralytic, Your sins are forgiven; or to say, Rise, take up your pallet and walk? But that you may know that the Son of Man has authority on earth to forgive sins . . . I say to you, rise, take up your pallet and go home.

Perhaps it is justifiable to interpret this man's illness as a "functional" paralysis, and to cite the testimony of some modern psychiatrists that in many cases when an individual has received God's forgiveness, his inward conflicts have been removed and, as a consequence, disabling physical symptoms have vanished. So in this instance it was Jesus' announcement of God's forgiveness which released the man from his paralysis. The important point, however, is that the miracle was regarded as a sign of Jesus' messianic authority. Jesus manifested the redemptive power of God which was already at work in human experience, delivering men from the inner frustrations and anxieties resulting from their separation from God. Today a physician or a psychotherapist can heal a patient and say, "Rise, take up your bed and walk." It is only the power of God's forgiveness which can exorcise the demons which dwell in the unconscious, free men from the paralysis of guilt, and release them from the anxiety of pain and death. Of course, this makes sense only to those whose eyes have been opened to the nature of the human dilemma, as the New Testament discloses it. It assumes that the confusion of human life is the result of man's separation from God (and thus from his *true* self) and it proclaims that God himself has taken the initiative in reaching across the separating chasm with his forgiveness which transforms and makes whole.

It is impossible in this brief space to go into the question of the historicity of each one of the miracles. The miracle story tradition was so expanded in the period of the oral transmission of the Gospel, in terms of the practical interests of the Church, that probably we can never confidently recover the original nucleus. It is important to realize, however, that the real miracle perceived by early followers of Jesus was the power of God's redemptive rule, the renewing and re-creative power of his forgiveness manifested in the deeds of the Messiah. Each story was intended not as a proof compelling unwilling belief, but as a vehicle for communicating the discerned meaning of Jesus' actions. Jesus' exorcism of demons was a sign of God's triumph over the forces of evil. His healings were not so much bodily cures as evidences of God's saving power. The resurrection of Lazarus from the dead was a sign of God's victory over death— not just the death of the body, but the more terrible spiritual death which may beset the living. Jesus' walking on water or his calming of the tempest signified that the Lord of history was also Lord over nature, even as we sing in the words of the Crusaders' Hymm: "Fairest Lord Jesus, Ruler of all nature. . . ." Underlying all of these miracle stories—the original nucleus as well as the expanded material—was the faith that ". . . God was in Christ reconciling the world to himself." C. H. Dodd observes that

> . . . whatever we may make of particular "miracles," the miracle stories as a whole are saying precisely this: that where Jesus was, there was some incalculable and unaccountable energy at work for the dispersal of evil forces and the total renewal of human life; and that this was nothing less than the creative energy of the living God.[8]

In answer to John's question, "Are you he who is to come, or shall we look for another?" Jesus sent word to him saying, "Go and tell John what you *hear* and *see:* the blind receive their sight, and the lame walk, lepers are cleansed, and the deaf hear, and the dead are raised up, and the poor have good news preached to them" (a Q passage: Matthew 11:4–5; Luke 7:22).

[8] *The Bible Today*, p. 92.

We should ponder Canon Richardson's reminder that Jesus was not put out of the way merely because he discoursed on the forgiving nature of God or gave inspiring ethical teaching. He was destroyed because he claimed to manifest in his words and works the saving power of God, in particular God's power to forgive sin. He claimed to do what only God can do. To Jews this was blasphemy, but to those who saw and heard in faith Jesus' words and works were signs of the near approach of God's Kingdom. Indeed, they gave assurance that already the Kingdom was breaking into history.

8

OLIVER CHASE QUICK | *Theories of the Atonement**

The various theological theories, in which the Church's teaching on the atonement has expressed itself, are simply attempts to answer the great question: How has Christ wrought this great change in man's relation to God, of which Christian life and faith are themselves the evidence? Why and how has the coming of Christ made all this difference? We will begin by distinguishing in a quite general way four main types of answer which have been given.

(a) Some have said, "It is because Christ brought God's message of forgiveness, and his human life revealed God's fatherly love in a way which has stirred man's heart to fresh repentance." This answer leads to what we may call the "subjective" or "moral" theory of the atonement.

(b) Some have said, "It is because God in Christ has won the victory over all the forces of evil, sin, and death, and has broken the power of the devil over man." This answer leads to what we may call (using Bishop Aulén's terms) the "classic" or "dramatic" theory.

(c) Some have said, "It is because Christ as man has borne the penalty for sin in man's behalf, and thus made it possible for God to forgive man freely." This answer leads to what we may call the "juridical" theory.

(d) Some have said, "It is because Christ, the Son of God who is also the sinless man, has offered through death that life of perfect human obedience and self-surrender, which, having died, becomes the universal expiation and cleansing power for sin-stained souls." This answer leads to what we may call the "sacrificial" theory.

Of course, elements which belong to more than one of the types of

---

* "Theories of the Atonement" is reprinted with the permission of Charles Scribner's Sons from *Doctrines of the Creed*, pp. 221–237, by Oliver Chase Quick.

theory which I have distinguished have often been combined with one another; and the classification is to some extent arbitrary. On the other hand, theological controversy has intensified the opposition between different types, so that they are often represented as quite antagonistic to one another. Nevertheless, if we start from the fundamental and cardinal thought of God's act of love in Jesus Christ, and then follow the lines of the classification just suggested, I think we can reach a reconciling point of view, from which each type of theory is seen to make its essential contribution to the truth, although no one theory, nor any number of theories, can be sufficient to express its fullness.

THE SUBJECTIVE THEORY

A sharp dividing-line is often drawn between the first type of theory, the subjective, and all the others, which are called "objective" in opposition to it. The ground of the opposition may be stated thus. According to the subjective theory the life and death of Jesus Christ in themselves effect nothing except the clear declaration of something which has always been true, viz., the fatherly and forgiving love of God for man. Thus the effect of the atonement, and the change wrought by it, begin only when human souls perceive through the life and death of Jesus Christ the truth of God's love, and are moved thereby to repentance. In contrast with this doctrine the other theories maintain that the life and death of Jesus Christ in themselves brought into being some new relation, which did not previously exist, between man and God, and that of this newly established relation Christians by faith receive the benefit.

The line of division seems clear enough; but further reflexion will tend to blur it. We will begin by echoing Rashdall's praise of Abélard, the classic exponent of the subjective theory.

At last we have found a theory of the atonement which thoroughly appeals to reason and to conscience. There is of course nothing absolutely original in the idea. St. Paul is full of the thought. It is set forth in its simplest and purest form in the Johannine writings. It occurs over and over again in the fathers. Whatever else they teach about the death of Christ, they all with one consent teach this—that it was a revelation of the love of God, intended to call forth answering love in man. The theory of Abélard does but isolate and emphasize the element in the preaching of the atonement to which in all ages it has owed its moving and saving power. Whatever were men's theories about the grounds on which the death of Christ became necessary, it was the love exhibited by Christ in submitting to that death which has really moved the heart, touched the conscience, and regenerated the life of believers. . . . "Greater love hath no man than this, that a man lay down his life for his friends." And, if he who so lays down his life is taken as representing and revealing the character of God, then no other way of ending the earthly life of him in whom God made this supreme self-revelation could so fully embody and symbolize the fundamental thought of Christianity that God is love, nor is any event in the history of the world so calculated to awaken and stimulate that repentance for sin upon which the possibility of forgiveness depends.[1]

The eulogy is true, and finely expressed. But let us grant that the essence of the atoning value of Christ's life and death lies in the fact that they are a declaration or demonstration of God's love for man. Still we must press the question, *how* was God's love demonstrated by that life and death? And then we begin to see that the subjective theory is by itself insufficient, on its own premises, as an account of the atonement. Two lines of criticism suggest themselves.

(a) If Christ's life and death are in themselves *merely* a revelation or display of God's love, they cannot reveal or display that love which Christian thought has at its highest attributed to God. The love of the living and redeeming God can only be fully revealed and displayed in a divine *act*. If all we can say of Christ's human life and death is that they *symbolize* God's constant love, and *not* that they are God's own act, then the love which they symbolize is after all something different from what the highest Christian faith has held God's love to be. But if, on the other hand, the life and death of Christ symbolize God's love because they truly are God's act, we cannot think of that divine act as a mere gesture which effects nothing beyond the declaration of what was already true before it happened. A revealing gesture is something much less than an act of power.

(b) If the nature of sin and its effects in man are really such as we have taken them to be, a simple display of love, which is not an act effecting something of which man in his sinful condition can avail himself, could not have met man's need, and therefore would not have been a full demonstration of God's saving love. Doubtless, in so far as sinful man retains the ability to see and choose the good when it is shown to him, the revelation of love on the cross constitutes by itself the most powerful motive to impel him to do so. And it would be worse than folly to belittle the wonder of the conversions which the revelation of the cross has wrought in this way. Nevertheless, the trouble expressed in the seventh

[1] *The Idea of the Atonement*, pp. 360 *sq.*

chapter of Romans and in the familiar tag, *"video meliora proboque, deteriora sequor,"* bears witness to a more subtle influence of sin which no mere relevation can dispel. As long as a theologian finds the prophetic conception of sin to be adequate, he may also be satisfied with the subjective theory of the atonement. But to one who understands the power of sin as St. Paul understood it, that theory can never express the reality of God's saving act in Jesus Christ.

The truth is that to accept fully Abélard's affirmation that the cross is the supreme manifestation of God's love for man must, if we follow out its implications, carry us beyond Abélard's theory of the atonement.

THE CLASSIC OR DRAMATIC THEORY

In what then does the objective element in the atonement consist? How did the life and death of Christ in themselves establish a new relation between man and God, of which man by faith receives the benefits? According to the so-called "classic" theory, God's love by the cross and resurrection of Christ has won a great and final victory over all the powers of evil; these powers have been deprived of their dominion over man, and man by faith in Christ is henceforth established in a new and triumphant life of communion with God; even in this world ". . . he tastes the powers of the world to come."

Undoubtedly language and ideas of this sort have always been familiar to Christian orthodoxy, although, as Bishop Aulén[2] points out, from the Middle Ages onwards their full meaning and value have been obscured. That the language in question stands for some vital and central truth, hardly any Christian perhaps would seriously deny. But by itself it lacks precision. It has the great merits of declaring that the atonement is throughout God's work, and of safeguarding the truth that God was in Christ Jesus reconciling the world to himself. But it is not easy to see how and with what degree of exactness the notions of conflict and victory over an enemy are to be applied. On the one hand, we may take quite seriously the personification of the powers of evil which is at first sight suggested. But if we suppose that such powers have held mankind in bondage, and have now by Christ's death and resurrection been utterly and finally defeated, it is hard to explain the remarkable vigour which they still apparently display even with the life of the redeemed community of believers. On the other hand, we may take the victory of Christ to

---

[2] *Christus Victor.*

mean simply the victory of perfect holiness over all temptation and tendency to sin, a victory which takes away death's sting and makes death itself the gate of immortality. In that case the enduring power of evil over those who have not yet attained Christ's holiness is fully accounted for; but the way in which Christ's victory benefits them requires further explanation. If that victory is no more than a demonstration of the fact that the perfect holiness of love must always triumph over sin and death, it would seem that it provides for us only a supreme example and a moving appeal; and thus our theory of the atonement becomes in principle "subjective" after all.

Our criticism therefore of the "classic" theory is not at all to suggest that it is false, but rather to point out that, like the subjective theory, it is incomplete. We need to know more of what exactly Christ's victory was. The old forms of the classic theory, that the victory was won by means of a ransom paid to the devil to release mankind, or by deceiving the devil as with a baited hook, certainly supply the lacking precision; but they have never commended themselves for long either to the reason or to the conscience of Christians.

THE JURIDICAL THEORY

We turn to the third type of atonement theory, that which suggests that Jesus Christ as man bore the penalty for human sin, or offered satisfaction for it, in our stead.[3]

There seems to be no reason in principle why Christ's vicarious suffering of the penalty for sin should not be regarded both as a demonstration of God's love for man, and as a means of his victory over sin and death. For, to quote Harnack's criticism of Abélard, ". . . is not that love the highest which, by taking the penalty upon itself, reveals at the same time the greatness of the absolution and the greatness of the cancelled guilt?"[4] And again, if Christ's bearing of the penalty is the divinely purposed ground of the exaltation of his manhood to God's throne and of our own deliverance from the power of evil, may we not truly say that it is the method of God's victory in Christ? Indeed, it is only when they are thus interpreted that juridical theories of the atonement can have any legitimate place at all in Christian theology. Notoriously the weakest point in the doctrine of St. Anselm, who first stated the juridical theory in a precise form, is that its logic seems to attach too exclusive an importance to

---

[3] For the purposes of this quite general discussion Anselm's careful distinction between *poena* and *satisfactio* need not concern us.

[4] I take the quotation from J. K. Mozley, *The Atonement*, p. 133.

the part played by Christ's manhood in the atoning work. According to this doctrine it is as man that Christ bore the penalty and offered satisfaction for human sin. Thus the vital truth that the whole act of atonement proceeded from God's love is liable to be obscured, and the notion is suggested that Christ's sacrifice propitiated God in a way which is quite alien from the thought of the New Testament. Juridical theories must be interpreted in the light of the classic theory, if they are to be made acceptable.

St. Paul's language in several places[5] does undoubtedly indicate his belief that Christ on the cross bore the penalty for sin on our behalf. But, if he had been pressed on the point, he would not, I think, have hesitated to declare that it is God's love which in Christ has provided a way of deliverance from his own wrath. He would certainly have agreed that we must interpret all juridical language about the atonement in the light of the principle that both the cross and its effects are the work of God's own love.

Granted then that we are to understand the juridical theory as expanding the classic, and not at all as contradicting it, we have still to ask the question: how far and in what way may we believe that Jesus Christ on the cross endured penal suffering in man's stead?

We must not forget that the theory which we are now considering is in principle juridical rather than sacrificial. It was developed by the Latin theologians of the Middle Ages from the hints contained in St. Paul's Epistles. It is true of course that St. Paul does use sacrificial language about Christ's atoning death. But whenever he or any other New Testament writer suggests that Christ bore our sins or the penalty for them, the implied thought about the atonement is juridical, and is really irrelevant to religious ideas which underlay the sin-offerings of the Pentateuch. For there the victims *sacrificed* for sin were not regarded as *bearing* the sin, nor as receiving in death the penalty for sin in man's stead. On the contrary, they were held to be pure from sin, and therefore their blood availed in expiation. The only victim believed to *bear* the sins of the people was the scapegoat; and exactly for that reason the scapegoat was not sacrificed, because as a sin-bearer it was accursed and could not be offered to God. The body hanged on a tree was certainly not sacrificed.[6] And even in Isaiah liii. there is no close or obvious connexion between the words, "the Lord hath laid on him the iniquity of us all", and the later

---

[5] E.g., Gal. iii. 13; 2 Cor. v. 21.
[6] Gal. iii. 13; Deut. xxi. 23.

prophecy, "when thou shalt make his soul an offering for sin, he shall prolong his days".[7] In considering therefore the doctrine that Christ bore our sins on the cross, we do well to dismiss all sacrificial notions and analogies from our minds.

Can we, then, at all apply the notion of penal substitution to Christ's atoning death? Not if we understand the word "substitution" strictly; and that for two reasons.

(a) It is impossible to maintain that the sufferings which Christ voluntarily endured for man's sin were *the same* as those which sinners would have had to endure and must endure if they remain unforgiven, but which through faith in Christ they escape. In what could such suffering endured by Christ, and to be endured by the unrepentant sinner but not by the faithful Christian, consist? It cannot be physical death, or the pain connected with it; for these Christians still have to undergo. And as to any other and more terrible sufferings, to which we may believe that Christ submitted, it is impossible to equate these with any which we can suppose to fall on the guilty and the unrepentant. However we interpret the cry, "My God, why hast thou forsaken me?" it can hardly be denied that the suffering here expressed is that of a love which feels itself deserted by God—and that is precisely the kind of suffering which the hardened sinner could never know.

(b) Again, a substitute, strictly speaking, is one who acts or suffers in order that the person whose place he takes may be free to do what he would have done, had he not been under the obligation of which the substitute has relieved him. In other words, the person for whom the substitute acts or suffers is affected by the substitution only negatively, in so far as he is relieved of something which otherwise he would have had to do or undergo. Thus, in the old story of Genesis, the ram was sacrificed as a substitute for Isaac, simply so that Isaac need not be sacrificed. Now I venture to affirm that no Christian has ever really believed that Christ on the cross bore the penalty for sin strictly in substitution for the sinner. In so far as there was any real substitution, the purpose of the crucifixion must have been that the sinner might be unaffected by the cross, except in so far as he would be released from enduring the penalty for sin. But no Christian can seriously affirm that the cross had any such purpose. On the contrary, Christ died in order to raise the sinner from the death of sin to the new life of repentance and fellowship with God.

[7] Isa. liii. 6 and 12.

We conclude therefore that we must not seek to interpret with any logical exactness language which speaks of Christ as having suffered *instead of* the sinner. Indeed, such a saying as "One died for all, therefore all died",[8] excludes the idea of substitution strictly understood, and signifies rather representation. As we shall see, the notion of Christ's death as *representative* is best interpreted as belonging to the sacrificial theory of the atonement rather than to the juridical; but it is probable that St. Paul never made any clear distinction in his own mind between the two. The language of substitution then is but an imperfect attempt to express the truth that in the crucifixion the divine love showed itself willing to endure to the uttermost for man the terrible consequences of sin which in justice should have fallen on the sinner. Christ, we may truly say, endured for us and on our behalf, though not strictly *instead of us*, what we could never have endured for ourselves.

This vicarious suffering of the divine love moves us to penitence as nothing else could; and it also reconciles our conscience to the fact that the world is not ordered on the principle of the justice which demands that pain should fall on the sinner in proportion to his guilt, and happiness reward the righteous in proportion to his merit. It may even be true that, if we reckon in terms of quantity of pain endured, the innocent and the penitent always suffer more because of sin than the guilty and the hardened. Who shall measure the suffering which evil inflicts on one who loves much, against the suffering of an unrepentant sinner punished for his crime? Which suffered more, St. Peter when he went out and wept bitterly, or Judas when he went away and hanged himself? Pains, like pleasures, differ in quality, and a merely quantitative comparison is fallacious. That is why the justice of rewards and punishments is never really satisfactory. But he who through the atonement understands the law of vicarious suffering, will know why it is that justice, at least in this world, seems so incomplete. It is in order that love by self-sacrifice may win its greatest triumph of redemption.

Nevertheless, in the light of the atonement the law of justice still stands unshaken as a moral principle; and it is the main purpose and value of the juridical theory to emphasize this truth. It is only when the sinner acknowledges that the sufferings which another bears for him were justly his own due, that he can know the penitence which brings salvation. Christ's atonement therefore does not make the law of none effect. It establishes the law, even while it goes beyond it and exposes its imperfection. Because Christ on the cross suffers what the sinner cannot suffer and

[8] 2 Cor. v. 14.

yet what it is just that the sinner should suffer, therefore the cross becomes the ground and cause of the penitence which enables the sinner to be forgiven and restored. Justice is satisfied, because the penitent sinner at last recognizes the righteous authority of its law. Love triumphs over justice, because the sinner is delivered from doom. What he has to suffer henceforth is transformed from mere punishment into a discipline gladly accepted because by it he is made one with Christ.

The elaboration of the juridical theory, which brings out this aspect of the atonement, is appropriately the work of Latin-speaking theologians. The mind trained under Roman influences realizes that the impersonal and impartial law of justice must somehow be vindicated. Traces of this conception of the majesty of justice are to be found in St. Paul, especially in Romans; but it is certainly not characteristically Jewish. To the Jew justice was not an abstract and impartial law. Rather it meant the concrete vindication and deliverance of one person, and the concrete condemnation and overthrow of another. The Jew realized all values only in concrete and personal terms. It was his supreme and unique achievement to make religion the establishment of a personal relation to a personal God. But the terms in which he thought were apt to be too narrowly personal. In his triumphs he was constantly guilty of what the Greeks called $\dot{\epsilon}\pi\iota\chi\alpha\iota\rho\epsilon\chi\alpha\chi\iota\alpha$,[9] in adversity he was always apt to become "a man with a grievance". It was left to the Latin mind, in its theology of the atonement, both to vindicate the full majesty of God's justice and also to utter the cry in which justice is forgotten, "O felix culpa."

Yet it seems that the juridical theory of the atonement, as we have sought to expound it, remains by itself incomplete. For, according to the only interpretation of it which we have been able to accept, it is still in principle a "subjective" theory. For the atonement is represented as producing its redemptive effect only by stirring man to penitence through his recognition of what Christ has suffered for him. In itself therefore the cross remains only a manifestation or demonstration of God's love; in itself it leaves unchanged the relation between sinful man and God. The actual change in that relation begins only with man's penitence which the revelation of the cross produces. St. Paul gave objectivity to his doctrine of the atonement by combining elements of the sacrificial theory with those which belong properly to the juridical. Later theologians have found a strictly objective element within the juridical theory by suggesting that Christ, by bearing the penalty for human sin, actually turned away God's

---

[9] I.e., literally, "rejoicing over the evils of another." The "taunt-songs" of the prophets and psalmists would have shocked Plato.

righteous wrath and so changed God's attitude to man. But this doctrine is not only theologically intolerable, it is also quite alien from the thought of the New Testament. In the New Testament Christ's life and death are said to reconcile man to God, but never God to man. It remains for us therefore to consider what is the distinctive contribution of the fourth type of atonement theory, the sacrificial.

THE SACRIFICIAL THEORY

Unlike the others, the sacrificial theory finds a systematic and coherent exposition in the New Testament itself, viz., in Hebrews. But two circumstances have combined to prevent this Epistle from taking the place which is its due in the theology of the atonement.

(a) The first is the persistent mistake of supposing that sin-offerings must somehow have been intended to propitiate God by the killing of a victim in the offerer's stead, an idea which has been a source of endless confusion in the exegesis of the New Testament. The truth is that such an interpretation of sacrifice is characteristic of heathen, and not of Jewish, religion. The ram sacrificed instead of Isaac is of course a case of substitution. But in the form in which the story has come down to us, the object of the sacrifice is not propitiation; it is simply a proof of Abraham's obedience. In the New Testament, moreover, the story is never mentioned in connexion with Christ's sacrifice, although the author of Hebrews cites it as a type of resurrection.[10] Again, in the law of the first-born there seems to be another case of an animal victim substituted for a human life;[11] and in the story of David there is an unmistakable allusion to a sacrifice intended to propitiate God.[12] But these have nothing to do with the sin-offerings of the later law. Scholars now seem to be fairly agreed that the object of the sin-offerings was expiation rather than propitiation, and that the victim was regarded as the offerer's representative rather than as his substitute. The intention was that the blood, or offered life, of a sinless victim should cleanse the offerers, or things used in worship, from the defilement of sin. The sacrifice thus changed the relation of man to God by operating directly, not upon God, but upon man.[13] Dodd has argued powerfully that the word and its cognates, which in heathen

---

[10] Heb. xi. 17–19.

[11] Exod. xiii. 13.

[12] 1 Sam. xxvi. 19.

[13] I do not, of course, mean to exclude the idea that it was the blood of a life *offered to God* which effected expiation.

writers almost always signify propitiation and are sometimes so rendered in the English Bible, nevertheless usually in the Greek Bible signify expiation.[14] The object of the verb is usually, not God, but sin; and in the New Testament the verb is never used with God as its object. Be that as it may, the author of Hebrews clearly understood the object of sacrifice for sin to be the cleansing away of defilement by the blood of a sinless victim.

(b) The second reason for the failure to do justice to the theory of the atonement set forth in Hebrews is of a different kind. As we have already noticed,[15] the austerity of the author's religious temperament makes him reluctant to use the Pauline language of love and grace in connexion with God. Although he clearly teaches that Christ is the divine Son through whom the worlds were made, he presents the earthly life of the Son only as the life of perfect human obedience culminating in the death on the cross. The connexion of Christ's self-sacrifice with love, divine or human, is never explicitly made, and has to be supplied by an extension of the author's thought.

What, then, is the essence of his theory? We may render it somewhat freely as follows:

The real intention of the old sacrifices for sin was that the blood of an unblemished victim, representing a stainless life offered to God in death, might be applied so as to remove defilements caused by sin, in order that man might draw near to God in worship, and communion between man and God be established. In these sacrifices the victim was offered by a priest who was appointed by God to represent the people before him. But the ordinances of the old covenant were imperfect for two main reasons.

(a) The lives of the victims were unstained by sin only because, being animals, they were innocent. The only blood, or sacrificed life, which can really avail to take away sin is that of one who has conquered temptation. It was therefore in the nature of the case impossible that the blood of bulls and goats could ever cleanse man's conscience.

(b) The animal-victims were sacrificed against their will. But the only life which can really avail for cleansing, is a life which has undergone death in free and perfect obedience to God. It must therefore be self-offered. In the perfect sacrifice for sin, priest and victim must be the same person.

---

[14] See his Commentary on *Romans*, pp. 54 *sq.*, also J. T. S., Vol. XXXII, pp. 352–60.
[15] Pp. 113 *sqq.* [These page numbers refer to Quick's book, *Doctrines of the Creed.*]

A further requirement for a perfect sacrifice remains to be noted. The life offered, while it must not be below the level of human capacities, nevertheless must not be strictly superhuman. Only the life which has conquered temptation *in man's own nature* can thereafter apply to that nature in other men a fully sanctifying power. The one therefore who is to be the perfect priest and victim must himself be human.

At all these points the Epistle exhibits the perfection and finality of Christ's atoning sacrifice. He is the God-appointed priest and victim who offered himself to God for us. He was a man, tempted in all points as we are, yet without sin. He was completely obedient to the Father's will even unto death. And thus he made his death to be the one all-sufficient sacrifice of the perfect human life, which, having passed through death, becomes the one availing power for sanctification. The blood of Christ's offered life is sprinkled on our sin-stained consciences. It enters our souls and cleanses them with its own triumphant purity, so that we also can draw near to God and offer ourselves in a like obedience.

Christ, then, has indeed done something for us which we could never have done for ourselves. In that sense he has suffered vicariously. But there is no hint of substitution in the thought. Christ's sacrifice avails for us because the sanctifying blood, the symbol of his offered life, is sprinkled upon us his people, and restores to us that communion with God which enables us to follow him who is our forerunner and pioneer as well as our high-priest. Nor is there any suggestion that Christ's sacrifice has propitiated God. For the perfectly obedient life self-offered avails to change, not God's attitude to man but man's attitude to God, and to remove the barrier between man and God which man's sin has erected.

Thus interpreted the theory of Hebrews supplies a firm basis for the doctrine of an *objective* element in the atonement. We are enabled to see in Christ's death something in principle more than the most appealing display of God's love for man; we now see it as the means whereby Christ's offered life becomes the power of a perfect and glorified manhood, which from the unseen world can penetrate and transform human souls. Christ has actually opened for us a new way into heaven, and made available a new power to enable us to tread it. True, temptation, suffering and death lie before the Christian still. What the Schoolmen called the *poenalitates praesentis vitae*[16] are not removed; the Christian's obedience still has to be made complete by his submission to them. Yet the atoning sacrifice of Christ has in itself made a real and objective difference, be-

---

[16] These *poenalitates* are distinguished from the *poena*, or direct punishment, for sin, as those "penal conditions" of life in this world, to which even the redeemed and forgiven must submit.

yond the mere revealing of God's constant love. It has made available for Christians communion in and with that perfect humanity of their representative and high-priest, which has already through its sacrifice entered the heavenly world.

The one conspicuous point of incompleteness in the atonement theory of Hebrews is its failure to make evident how the whole work of atonement is from beginning to end the act of God's love. We miss in Hebrews just that vital element which St. Paul and St. John so clearly supply. The reason for this defect is probably to be found, as we have suggested, in the author's temperament. Perhaps, moreover, he regarded his theory of the atonement as a supplement to Pauline theology, and thought it the less necessary to reaffirm explicitly that aspect of the truth which St. Paul has already made unmistakably clear.

SUMMARY AND CONCLUSIONS

There is a real and important distinction between "subjective" and "objective" theories of the atonement. The former see in the atoning life and death of Christ only the demonstration of a divine love which had been real from the beginning; they find the saving effect of that life and death only in the penitence to which the sinner is freshly stirred by what they reveal. "Objective" theories, on the other hand, see in the atoning life and death an act which in itself effects a change in the relation of man to God; and according to them this change is antecedent to the faith and penitence whereby the sinner is made partaker of its benefits. Each of these two broad types of theory is specially relevant to a particular conception of the nature of sin. Those theologians who think "subjective" theories sufficient are on the whole those who, like the prophets, regard sin mainly as a matter of personal *reatus,* i.e., as something for which the sinner is personally responsible as a free agent. Those, on the other hand, who maintain "objective" theories are on the whole those who see in sin a corrupting *vitium,* a moral or spiritual disease in human nature which man's will is powerless to overcome. It was as a *vitium* or taint that the priestly religion of sacrifice treated sin, though very often it failed to distinguish between a taint that really affected man's moral and spiritual being, and one that was a matter merely of ceremonial uncleanness.

It is obviously consistent with this analysis that among types of "objective" theory we should have found the most satisfactory to be that which most clearly bases itself on sacrificial ideas, and finds in the sin-offerings of the Old Testament a true foreshadowing of the atonement. Juridical theories, we have suggested, can only defend themselves against theological criticism by abandoning the claim to be "objective". But this point is easily obscured by the failure to distinguish clearly between ideas and language which are properly juridical, and those which are properly sacrificial.

When, however, the juridical and sacrificial theories have been distinguished from one another, and each expressed in its most acceptable form, there seems to be no good reason for holding them to be mutually exclusive. The truth that the cross shows the willingness of divine love to suffer the consequences of sin in man's behalf, need not exclude the further truth that on the cross the sinless manhood was offered so that, having passed into the heavenly world, its sanctifying and life-giving power might be available to sinful man. This latter doctrine is robbed of all unethical and quasi-magical implications, if it be recognized that the new power thus made *available* only becomes actually *availing* when it is humbly and thankfully received as God's gift. When it is thus received, what it bestows is the grace of Christ-like life.

Taken then in conjunction with one another, the truths of the juridical and sacrificial theories do but give greater precision to the truth of the "classical" theory that by the cross God in manhood has won the victory which redeems mankind from the powers of evil. And thus, finally, the fullest truth is found in the great principle vindicated by Abélard that the cross is the supreme demonstration of God's love for man.

Chapter 6 | Jesus Christ, both Man and God

The student walked alone across the campus. He looked beyond the green valley to the mountain peak glowing pink against the setting sun. "What does this breathtaking sight mean? Can I say more than 'Oh! Ah!' in the face of all this majesty and power? Isn't this where I find the sheer immediacy of God? Certainly He is in this place! God makes Himself known to me in and through His world of order and beauty."

But we ask: What God? Probing more deeply: Do we ever simply find God out there in the beautiful mountain? The God we "find" is the God already mediated to us through the cultural heritage and community within which we live. Under the influence of the Judeo-Christian tradition, if God is seen in the realm of nature, He is the kind of God who has first disclosed Himself in and through significant events of history. As we have seen, the ancient Hebrews moved from God revealed in history to the God of creation. For Christians also, God comes to men in and through all the divers aspects of the world outside them. But this God of all loveliness, beauty, majesty makes Himself known in these experiences *because* He has first disclosed Himself in and through that central event of which the person of Jesus Christ is the center.[1]

This is the puzzling yet indispensable core of Christian faith and life. It is puzzling partly because so many generations of theologians have attempted to translate this living faith into intricate doctrinal systems. The technical name for this discipline is "Christology," and the basic doctrine of Christ's nature is called "the Incarnation" (literally en-fleshment). Just as the *atonement* is concerned, as we have seen, with the *work* of Jesus Christ through which God reconciles men to Himself, so the *Incarnation* refers to the *person* of Jesus Christ in whom God is believed to dwell. These are inseparable aspects of a total view of Jesus Christ.

But these matters are also baffling, to modern men and women especially, because the ultimate mystery of One who is both God and man

[1] Here we point not simply to the psychological fact that we are conditioned by the community and culture to "see" things in a certain way. For this is also a logical priority in which data experienced in the world presuppose an interpretive framework.

remains a mystery beyond all human understanding. It would be very simple if we could look directly at this Jesus of Nazareth who actually lived, taught, died and continued somehow in influence and then were led to conclude that He exhibited certain qualities which are the sure marks of "divinity." Some try this approach and soon see the difficulties involved. What qualities of divinity? By what criteria shall we judge? Thus, hoping to avoid such complexities, many turn back to what seems like a "simple" faith: God the Creator, Sustainer, Judge, Deliverer! Yes! And Jesus, the greatest seeker after God that ever lived! Our example! Our pioneer in the quest after God! Even the Way to God! But Jesus Himself divine, "very God"? Impossible! He can tell us about God and lead us to God without Himself being God. So many sincere students conclude.

Something Vital about God

D. M. Baillie leads up to the passages from *God Was in Christ* included in the reading selections by raising similar questions. What kind of God do we find in Jesus' teachings? "Is it a God who would wait to be discovered? No, indeed. It is a God who takes the initiative. . . ." To bring us authentic tidings of the character of God, need Jesus *be* God? Professor Baillie answers:

> Is that, then, all that Jesus did—to bring us authentic tidings, as from a distant realm, of a God who takes no initiative Himself to seek us out? If God is like that, then Jesus was wrong about Him, the tidings He brought were not authentic, and He was not even a true discoverer. But if He was right, then there is something more to be said, something Christological; and if we leave it out, we are leaving out not only something vital about Jesus, but something vital about God. That is to say, if we have not a sound Christology, we cannot have a sound theology either.[2]

Through the ages, Baillie suggests, most of the great heresies arose from ". . . an undue desire for simplification, an undue impatience with mystery and paradox, and an endeavour after common-sense theology."[3] It sounds uncomplicated and persuasive to believe in God the Father and Jesus the Teacher. But while it is easy to believe in some "divine Intel-

---

[2] "The Paradox of the Incarnation" and other quotations by D. M. Baillie are reprinted with the permission of Charles Scribner's Sons from *God Was In Christ* by D. M. Baillie. Copyright 1948 Charles Scribner's Sons.

[3] *Ibid.*, p. 65.

ligence," many today hold, it is difficult to believe in the Incarnation. As we shall discover in Part II, it is not a simple matter to believe in God. A great deal depends on the sort of God men accept or reject. The central question relates to what kind of God it is with whom men are confronted in Jesus. This is not some far-off principle of order (as in deism) or divine Intelligence (as in theism) awaiting our rational proofs. It is not a cozy American God who is the personification of all our accepted values and way of life. It is rather the God, traced clear through the biblical record, who disturbs and seeks men out, who acts as Creator, Judge, Redeemer.

Is it easy to believe in such a God? Is it easier than to believe in the Incarnation? Surely the Incarnation is not an added difficulty, but is rather the sole way in which the Christian conception of God becomes credible or even expressible. It is only an extreme theological naiveté that can be blind to the mystery and paradox of the word "God" in the Christian sense; and we shall never do justice to the height of that paradox—we shall never do justice to the love of God—if we leave out the supreme paradox of the Incarnation. Such an omission would fatally impoverish and compromise our faith in God. That is why it is necessary to retort: Are you sure that you know what you mean by "God"? "Whosoever denieth the Son, the same hath not the Father: he that confesseth the Son hath the Father also" [John 2:23]. That is as true against modern as it is against ancient Gnosticism. For the whole Christological question is a question about God.[4]

Some Christologies

To put the matter briefly, the Christian does not begin with some theories about God and simply add to these some theories about Christ. Rather, he holds that in Jesus Christ Himself God confronts him. Jesus Christ is a *man*, who in His life and death was an actual, historical person. Yet He brought to climax a whole series of events, of which the Old Testament is the record. Through Jesus as the center now of a new event or series of events, God acts decisively in insistent judgment and concerned love to establish a new covenant. The phenomena of nature and of human history reveal much of the nature of God. But it is in the Christian faith that He discloses Himself most decisively and clearly in and through the life personality, teaching, work, death, resurrection and continuing presence of Jesus Christ. *For Jesus Christ is both man and God.*

[4] *Ibid.*, pp. 65–66.

It is with these puzzling paradoxical claims that any Christology has to deal. The history and theory of these many centuries of Christological discussion are exceedingly complex and can only be alluded to in a book of this scope. D. M. Baillie's *God Was in Christ*, of all modern presentations, most effectively cuts through all the intricacies to the central issues.

Baillie points out how the church through the ages has worked out its creeds under the pressure of "heresies." A heresy is usually defined as a "false belief," but it is not utter falsehood that is involved in most cases. Rather a heresy is often a sincere attempt to grasp the core of faith. It may be well intentioned but often becomes extreme expression of half-truth. But only within the context of open dialogue, involving vigorous give-and-take, can the Christian community in any age arrive at consensus of faith.

"Creeds should be sung," said John Calvin. Creeds, in other words, can never be precise, all-embracing statements claiming the final "truth" about God. At best they are men's faltering attempts to express the inexpressible. Yet members of the community of faith keep trying to find words of joy and gratitude for what Paul called God's "inexpressible gift." Men cannot therefore remain silent—even in the face of that whereof they cannot speak.

The Nicene Creed (A.D. 325) and the Christological formula of the Council of Chalcedon (A.D. 451) are the classic statements of the so-called Eastern tradition. They are concerned primarily with the *person* of Christ, or Christology. Later Western and Protestant theology, especially, tended toward interest in the *work* of Christ, what his *death* accomplished in *atonement*. To this day there is and ought to be a healthy tension within Christianity between these two polar emphases. Contemporary discussion reflects renewed concern with the doctrine of the person of Christ to counterbalance conviction about the atoning work of Christ. This Jesus Christ, in and through whom God reconciles men to Himself, *is* both "very man" and "very God." So the Christian faith affirms.

Professor Baillie cites some of the heretical misconceptions about the person of Jesus Christ which persist to our day. It is in open dialogue with these extreme overstatements that the community of Christian faith has hammered out its creedal platform.

The Christian belief in Jesus Christ does not hold that He was not *really* man but "a manlike God," as represented by Gnosticism and Docetism. Nor is Jesus some sort of intermediate being, neither man nor God in the full sense, a created being and yet an agent in shaping the world. This is the view of Arianism (ca. A.D. 320). Then too, the eternal Son of God is not a "divine soul" which inhabited a "human body" for some thirty years as in Apollinarianism. Neither is adoptionism acceptable to normative Christian faith. This view affirms that Jesus began as a man and grew into divinity. Many today are attracted to adoptionism. Why, it is asked, did Jesus Christ join the human race and grow into divinity? In order, it is said, that we might become God. Note Baillie's critical comments in each of these cases.

Against these heresies, especially Arianism, the Council of Nicea declared that Christ is one in being with the Father. The Greek word used is *homoousios,* meaning "of one substance or essence." A group called Semi-Arians tried to express this relation between Christ and God through the word *homoiousios,* meaning "similar in being," "of like substance or essence." But this position involves the difficulty of saying Jesus is really a man, even though He is a godlike man.

The Council of Chalcedon carried the discussion further and defined Christ's relationship to *man* in the same terms which the Council of Nicea had used to define His relation to *God.* He is thus ". . . *homo-ousios* with the Father as to his Godhead, and the same *homo-ousios* with us as to his manhood."[5] By the use of this term the Council clearly meant more than that Christ was a man like other men; it meant that, just as it was true to say that 'God was in Christ,' so also there is a sense in which it could be said that 'man was in Christ.' "[6]

Contemporary Attempts at Understanding

We moderns have trouble with these categories of Greek metaphysics employed to express the paradox of Jesus Christ, the God-man. We stare at the words of the Chalcedonian formula: ". . . two natures . . . concurring in one Person and one Substance. . . ." Behind these words lie assumptions taken as self-evident. These men presupposed the universal solidarity of all mankind. Not just individual men were real, but the form, the concept of manhood in general. Thus it was essential for them to express Christ as mediator between God and man in terms of oneness of being with the whole human race. This is the salvation in which each individual may share. For Christ has come to reconcile mankind to God.

Contemporary writers such as Baillie attempt to cut through these metaphysical concepts to a mode of expression more congenial to both

[5] R. V. Sellers, *The Council of Chalcedon,* Society for the Promotion of Christian Knowledge, London, 1953, p. 210.

[6] George S. Hendry, *The Gospel of Incarnation,* The Westminster Press, Philadelphia, 1958, p. 44.

modern men and the biblical context. Referring to the Chalcedonian formula of the two natures, one divine, the other human, Baillie writes:

> This formula has been sharply criticized in the modern world, as making an unnatural dualism in the Christ whom we know from the Gospel story [Westminster Shorter Catechism, 21], and the criticism is not unjust. We should not naturally express the truth in those terms to-day. But the two-natures doctrine was obviously intended to safeguard the complete recognition of the humanity of Christ. If Chalcedon insisted on two distinct natures in Christ, it was because those who said "one nature", fusing the divine and the human into one, really meant that the human was lost in the divine. They did not really believe in the humanity of the life that Jesus lived on earth . . . except in the sense of inhabiting a human body. This is very different from the doctrine of the Incarnation.[7]

John Knox and Daniel Day Williams both attempt to interpret the Incarnation to contemporary men. Knox in his trilogy, *Jesus, Lord and Christ,* recaptures the historical perspective of the New Testament record on the meaning of Christ. Instead of the categories of *being* and *nature,* he suggests that ". . . in the New Testament the meaning of 'Jesus Christ' involves, in varying degrees of relevance, the three categories, event, person, community. The same thing is true, . . . of the actual empirical meaning of Christ for you and me."[8]

Knox expresses the relationship between these three aspects in this way:

> Granted that all of them are present and are essential, which has pre-eminence? A good case could be made for each of the three. The person is the center of the event and also of the community. . . . But the community is both the locus of the event and the place where alone the person is remembered and still known. But just as inclusive, at the very least, is the event in which the person played his decisive part and out of which the community emerged. The truth is that these three are one. . . . Nevertheless . . . the event has . . . a certain primacy. . . . Back of the Church, even though also present in and with it, stand the person and the event. . . . The person *was* the event; the event *was* the person . . . one reality. . . . But . . . *when we are seeking to define the meaning of the revelation of God in Christ,* event is the more appropriate and adequate category. . . . The revelation in Christ . . . is not most truly represented by the statement that Jesus Christ *was* God, as certain types of later Christian orthodoxy have

[7] Baillie, *op. cit.,* p. 152.

[8] From *Jesus, Lord and Christ* by John Knox, Copyright © 1958 John Knox. Reprinted with the permission of Harper & Row, Publishers, Inc., New York.

tried to say it, nor yet by the modern liberal view that Jesus was a *picture* of God, showing us "what God is like." The revelation is best represented by the statement that Jesus Christ was an *act* of God—or, if we prefer, that in him took place the revealing act of God. But if revelation is an act, the medium of revelation is an event.[9]

Daniel Day Williams underlines the shift to historical event as the most appropriate way to express God's self-disclosure to men. He writes:

> It is not two "natures" which have to be related, but two "histories." There is the history of our human existence with its fate, its freedom, and its course of events. In this history stands the real person, Jesus of Nazareth, who is just as truly "historical" as any other. There is also the history of God's creative and redemptive dealing with men which has come to its climax in the history of Jesus. It is these two histories which we have to relate to each other. When we look for God's redemptive action it is not supernatural existence but personal meaning which concerns us. The emphasis on miracle gives way to that of personal faith. To use Richard Niebuhr's terms in *The Meaning of Revelation,* in Jesus Christ outer and objective history has come together with inner and personal history which is known by faith. It may well be that this shift in the terms of the Christological problem is more important for theology today than any of the paricular solutions which have yet been put forth.[10]

Williams freely admits that this perspective which stresses the historical and personal response also has its difficulties. Can we relate "two histories" any more convincingly than "two natures"? By way of comment, we observe that the series of events centered in the person of Christ may be viewed as "objectively" as any others as proper phenomena of historical study. But, for the Christian community, so-called objective investigation can never yield conclusions concerning God's self-revelation in human history. That is a matter for the way in which these selfsame events are seen by the community of faith. Each is a dimension of the whole which is Jesus Christ. There is no contradiction between the historical-investigation stance and the faith stance. Jesus Christ is *seen as,* experienced as, the decisive self-disclosure of God in and through that actual, finite human being who grew to maturity within a given cultural environment.

[9] *Ibid.,* pp. 210–213.
[10] From *What Present-day Theologians Are Thinking* by Daniel Day Williams, pp. 102–103, Copyright © 1952, 1959 by Daniel Day Williams. Reprinted with the permission of Harper & Row, Publishers, Inc., New York.

Williams asks: Shall we regard His humanity as an embarrassment to the faith that claims His divinity? He writes:

Suppose now that rather than regard this finite element as an embarrassment to the Christian claim that God has spoken his decisive word in Christ we see it *as intrinsic to the revelation itself.* Could we say that the Christian faith claims final revelation in Christ just because it gives us the picture of a finite person who acknowledges his own limitation, and points beyond itself to God's truth which no finite structure can fully express? If this thesis can be cogently worked out, the reversal it brings to much traditional Christology is startling. We would now rest the case for the ultimately decisive character of the revelation in Christ, not upon miraculous signs that the limitations of existence have been set aside, but upon the discovery that there is a witness to God which comes through those limitations. We still have to say why it is that the revelation is given through Jesus. Not every finite person, but this One becomes an adequate vehicle for the revelation. But we are saying now that it is the very humility of Jesus and his trusting acceptance of the risks and uncertainties of our human lot that we find not a barrier to God's word, but the very means for the communication of that Word.[11]

It is Baillie's intention as well to keep history and faith in dynamic relationship with each other. For in an earlier chapter of his book he writes:

It seems to me that a good deal of confusion would be averted if we reminded ourselves that the phrase, "the Jesus of history", means simply and precisely: "Jesus as He really was in His life on earth", which includes of course what He did and said, what He intended and what He taught. The phrase does usually imply that in certain respects we must give a different account of this from what was given in the pre-critical period, but that will be pretty generally recognized. The phrase may doubtless be used with a false preconception of what "history" is, and that is not an altogether simple question, as we shall see in the next chapter [of *God Was in Christ*]. When we speak of "Jesus as He really was", we must not mean "Jesus as a figure which can be described and authenticated by a cold and detached criticism". For that would not be real history at all. I am sure that this is a fertile source of confusion in the whole matter: the habit of setting "history" and "faith" too sharply against each other, with the assumption, which Brunner actually seems to make, that a really historical study of Jesus could not give us the kind of figure that would be of any use to faith! By a historical picture Brunner means the "photographic" kind of portrait

[11] *Ibid.*, p. 108.

which would of necessity leave the deepest things out: he actually speaks of the historical "photograph", as if it were axiomatic that a camera could exhaust the possibilities of portraiture and do better work for the science of history than could the portraiture of a great artist. But that is a poor sense of the word "historical", and would give a quite arbitrary limitation of meaning to the phrase, "the Jesus of history". It is true in a sense that the science of history cannot directly introduce the supramundane and the divine into its nexus of causes and effects, cannot penetrate into a supra-historical "dimension". In that sense the "historical" is the "human"; the sphere of history is the life of man, the dimension of humanity. But even then, are we to forget that the *humanity* of our Lord is vital to Christian faith? And can even His humanity be worthily studied without the sympathy and insight of faith? Without this, surely the historical study of such a subject would be vain. It would not be soundly historical. The result would be bad history. It would not give us Jesus as He really was. It would not give us the Jesus of history. When we have understood this, we have disposed of the argument that the interest in the historical personality of Jesus is a kind of interest which is alien to the world of the New Testament and to the world of Christian faith.[12]

[12] Baillie, *op. cit.*, p. 47.

9

D. M. BAILLIE | *The Paradox of the Incarnation**

W̶e must now come to grips directly with the central problem of Christology, for which the foregoing chapters have been clearing the ground. What do we mean by saying that God was incarnate in Jesus? In what sense was Jesus both God and Man? How could that one life be both completely human and completely divine?

THE PARADOXES OF FAITH

There is a sense in which the *mysterium Christi* must always remain a mystery. The late Archbishop of Canterbury remarked that ". . . if any man says that he understands the relation of Deity to humanity in Christ, he only makes it clear that he does not understand at all what is meant by an Incarnation." Yet assuredly Dr. Temple did not mean that nothing at all can be said about the nature of the "hypostatic union," for that would itself be virtually a confession that we do not know what we mean when we speak of God being incarnate in Jesus. The Incarnation presents us indeed with the supreme paradox, and I do not believe that we can ever eliminate from it the element of paradox without losing the Incarnation itself. But this is not the only point at which we are beset with paradox in our Christian belief: this is rather the point at which the constant and ubiquitous paradox reaches its peak. And if we try to isolate absolutely the mystery of the Incarnation, failing to connect it with the all-round paradox of our Christian faith and experience, we shall end by having on our hands a mystery which is not a *religious* mystery at all and has no bearing on our actual religious life. The mistake is not to assert paradox in the doctrine of the Incarnation, but to miss the paradox everywhere else. I confess that certain schools of theology in the modern

* "The Paradox of the Incarnation" and other quotations by D. M. Baillie are reprinted with the permission of Charles Scribner's Sons from *God Was in Christ* by D. M. Baillie. Copyright 1948 Charles Scribner's Sons.

world seem to me to be sometimes in danger of that mistake, especially, perhaps, Anglican theology (of which I would always wish to speak with profound respect and with a sense of heavy debt). Modern Anglican theology has tended to be intolerant of paradox, smoothing out contradictions, sometimes almost turning itself into a common-sense Christian philosophy, semi-Pelagian rather than Augustinian or Calvinistic in its mood (is this the proverbial Semi-Pelagianism of British thought?)—until it comes to the doctrine of the Incarnation. Then it becomes quite different, treating the *mysterium Christi* as a solitary exception, a hard kernel which is never soluble in any howsoever powerful solvent of theological thought. The result is to make the theological system as a whole too "rational", and by contrast to make the Christological dogma too "irrational", too little connected with the rest of our theology, too much a sheer mystery, whose meaning we do not know. Paradox may then become a mere *asylum ignorantiae*, a theological mystification, instead of being a truly religious mystery, close to experience and to faith.

It may be worth while at this point to reflect for a moment upon the nature and place of paradox in Christian doctrine. There can be no doubt about the widespread recognition, in our time, of the presence of a paradoxical element in all religious thought and statement, whether it is called paradox, antinomy, dialectical contradiction and tension, or anything else. The thought of Sören Kierkegaard has been described as *par excellence* "the theology of paradox", and every student knows how deeply Kierkegaard has influenced the philosophical and religious thinking of our age. But there are many other historical sources of this tendency, and it betrays itself in one form or another in very diverse schools of theological thought. Without attempting to trace its sources or to distinguish its various expressions, I must try to indicate the sense in which it seems to me legitimate and sound.

The reason why the element of paradox comes into all religious thought and statement is because God cannot be comprehended in any human words or in any of the categories of our finite thought. God can be known only in a direct personal relationship, an "I-and-Thou" intercourse, in which He addresses us and we respond to Him. As it has sometimes been put, God cannot legitimately be "objectified". This does not mean that religion is thrown back upon the "subjective", against which we have so often been warned by the wise counsellors who tell us to turn away from our own feelings to the "objective realities" of our faith. In that sense, in contrast with religious subjectivism, it is wholesome to be reminded that God is an objective reality. Yet we cannot know God by studying Him as an object, of which we can speak in the third person, in an "I-It" relationship, from a spectator-attitude. He eludes all our words and categories.

We cannot objectify or conceptualize Him. When we try, we fall immediately into contradiction. Our thought gets diffracted, broken up into statements which it seems impossible to reconcile with each other. How then can we have any theology, since theology is bound to objectify God, to speak of Him in the third person, with human words and the categories of finite minds? The answer is that we must indeed do these things if we are to have any theology at all, and we must have theology; but we shall have to pay the price—it will always be a theology of paradox. The price is not too great to pay, for we must theologize; and indeed the very act of worship, particularly corporate worship, involves the use of words and thoughts about God, and to think or speak of God at all is to run into antinomy, dialectical contradiction, paradox. Father Bulgakov (who prefers the term "antinomy" to "dialectical contradiction", and maintains that they mean quite different things) writes as follows. "An antinomy simultaneously admits the truth of two contradictory, logically incompatible, but ontologically equally necessary assertions. An antinomy testifies to the existence of a mystery beyond which the human reason cannot penetrate. This mystery nevertheless is actualized and lived in religious experience. All fundamental dogmatic definitions are of this nature."

Father Bulgakov goes to the root of the matter when he says that while the mystery cannot be stated in words without contradiction, it is actualized and lived in religious experience, that is, in the direct faith-relationship towards God. The attempt to put our experience of God into theological statements is something like the attempt to draw a map of the world on a flat surface, the page of an atlas. It is impossible to do this without a certain degree of falsification, because the surface of the earth is a spherical surface whose pattern cannot be reproduced accurately upon a plane. And yet the map must be drawn for convenience' sake. Therefore an atlas meets the problem by giving us two different maps of the world which can be compared with each other. The one is contained in two circles representing two hemispheres. The other is contained in an oblong (Mercator's projection). Each is a map of the whole world, and they contradict each other to some extent at every point. Yet they are both needed, and taken together they correct each other. They would be either misleading or mystifying to anyone who did not know that they represent the surface of a sphere. But they can serve their useful purpose for anyone who understands that they are intended simply to represent in handy portable form the pattern covering the surface of this round earth which he knows in actual experience. So it is with the paradoxes of faith. They are inevitable, not because the divine reality is self-contradictory, but because when we "objectify" it all our judgments are in some measure falsified, and the higher truth which reconciles them cannot be fully expressed in words, though it is experienced and lived in the "I-and-Thou" relationship of faith towards God. It is only the paradoxes of which this can be said that are justifiable in theology. There is great danger in the habit of falling back too easily upon paradox in our religious thinking, and it would ultimately make all theological argument impossible. There should always be a sense of tension between the two opposite sides of our paradoxes, driving us back to their source in our actual religious experience or faith. That is where we must refine our theological statements, purging them of needless contradictions and testing them "whether they be of God". Thus no paradox in theology can be justified unless it can be shown to spring directly from what H. R. Mackintosh called "the immediate utterances of faith"; for since a paradox is a self-contradictory statement, we simply *do not know what it means or what we mean by it* unless it has that direct connection with the faith which it attempts to express.

Now it seems to me that Christian faith, when thought out, conceptualized, and put into human language, runs into paradox not only in the doctrine of the Incarnation, but at every vital point. We must not imagine that the other doctrines are easy and unparadoxical, and that mystery appears only when we come to the Incarnation. It is indeed the central paradox: how can the same life be explained as a completely human life in the continuum of history and as the life of God Himself? But there is similar paradox whenever in Christian thought we introduce God as the ultimate source of anything in our experience: He comes in, as it were, on the vertical line from the eternal world (*"senkrecht von oben"*) to touch the horizontal line on which we inevitably have another explanation in empirical terms. And the mystery of the Incarnation is the climax of all the Christian paradoxes. They all point to it, they all have an organic connection with it, and indeed they are all revealed by it. For these paradoxes are peculiar to Christian theology, and distinguish it from the various dualisms and pantheisms which beset it on opposite sides. These Christian paradoxes come of thinking out the religion of the Incarnation.

Let me indicate one or two main points where this paradoxical element is found.

(a) *The doctrine of Creation.* There is something quite distinctive about the Christian idea of *creatio ex nihilo*. It is not found anywhere else. It is peculiar to the religion of the Incarnation. It is highly paradoxical. It does not compete with anything that science may say about the temporal process by which things have come to be what they are.

If it is taken as an answer to the question of world-origins in a scientific sense, it sounds absurd. "God created all things out of nothing." Even when taken as answering a more ultimate question, it seems far less satisfactory, far more difficult to state, then the other answers which it is intended to exclude. On the one hand is the dualistic answer which conceives of God as a great artificer taking an already existing raw material and moulding His world out of it. That is quite easy to state. But it is quite a pagan view, and it gives us an unworthy conception of God, a false conception of matter as godless and inherently evil, and therefore ultimately even an inadequate ethic and an inadequate doctrine of immortality. On the other hand is the pantheistic answer, which conceives of God as creating all things out of Himself, out of His own substance. This is not really creation, but emanation. Again it is easily stated, and as it lent itself to the great pantheistic systems, so it has lent itself easily to absolute idealism in the modern world. But it also is quite a pagan view, destroying the true attitude of man both to God and to the world. No, says Christian faith, God did not fashion the world out of a raw material which He found, nor did He generate the world out of His own substance. He created all things out of nothing. This is highly paradoxical. It does not seem to be the kind of position that could ever be reached by a process of inference from the phenomena, or that can even be stated without paradox. In contrast to every theory of temporal origins, it probably involves the idea that time itself is part of creation, and this again is highly paradoxical. Yet these paradoxes are inescapable. Theology is driven to them. Moreover, it is *Christian* theology in particular that is driven to them. It is, we may say, in the endeavour to think out the religion of the Incarnation that the human mind has been led even to the paradoxes of Creation—to the peculiarly Christian and wholly paradoxical doctrine of *creatio ex nihilo.*

(b) *The doctrine of Providence.* It seems plain that this doctrine also is inseparable from paradox. Here again we have a paradoxical relation between the horizontal and the vertical plane. The whole texture of our life in this world is a network of causes and effects on the empirical level, and everything that comes to us comes through the continuum of history, with all its determinants, of natural law and human action around us; and on the horizontal plane that is all that is to be said about it by way of explanation. But every Christian believes also that whatever comes to him comes from God, by God's appointment, God's providence. And not simply in the sense that God works through the natural (including the psychological) laws of His own ordaining; as if, having "wound up" the universe to run by these laws, He had then left it to run its course. The

Christian believes that in some sense everything comes to him *directly* from God, whose working is always individual. And this becomes highly paradoxical when we reflect that in the historical or horizontal network of determinants there are many which are directly contrary to the will of God. The course of my life may be profoundly affected by some injury which has befallen me through the deliberately evil volition of a fellow-man, who seeks to do me harm and is thereby acting directly against God's will. Yet as a Christian I also believe that the thing has come to me from God, who is all-good and all-loving, and who makes all things work together for good to those who love Him. This is highly paradoxical. But it is impossible to escape from the paradox without running either into a dualistic doctrine of a finite or limited God, on the one hand, or into a pantheistic doctrine, which explains away the reality of evil, on the other. And if we take either of these courses, we lose the Christian doctrine of Providence altogether. Moreover, however paradoxical this doctrine may be when we try to think it out theologically, the mystery that lies behind it is grasped by countless unsophisticated Christian men and women in the actual life of faith. Here again the paradox arises out of actual religious experience, and indeed Christian experience. The doctrine of Providence in its fullest and most paradoxical form is peculiar to Christianity. Here again, as in the case of creation, we may say that it is in the endeavour to think out the religion of the Incarnation that the human mind has been driven to the paradox. We can see this happening in the New Testament with special reference to the scandal of the crucifixion of Jesus. Faithful souls in Israel had long been wrestling with the problem of how the belief in God's rule could be compatible with the dreadful things that were allowed to happen among men; and this came to a head when Jesus was condemned and crucified. This was the worst thing that had ever happened through the sin of men. Yet they came to believe that this was also the best thing that had ever happened in the providence of God. We can see it, with all its paradoxical contradictions, in the early chapters of the Acts of the Apostles. The crucifixion of Christ was the supreme instance, driving men to think out afresh the whole problem of divine rule in the world; and the result was the highly paradoxical Christian doctrine of Providence.

Now if it is thus true that the Christian faith, the religion of the Incarnation, runs into paradox at one point after another, may not these secondary paradoxes point us towards an understanding of the supreme paradox of the Incarnation itself? May they not give us some small hint of how it can be true that a phenomenon which emerges in the continuum of temporal and terrestrial history is also, and in a deeper sense, an incursion of the eternal, the Divine? That seems to be especially true of the paradox of Providence which we have just been considering. Indeed, if we could be content with the type of Christology [criticized in Chapter III (of *God Was in Christ*)] which makes Christ the "centre of history" but has nothing to say about His Person, then the doctrine of Providence would cover the whole, and Christology would be merely a special application of it to the supreme instance. But that is not enough; for though it would give us the incursion of the Word of God into human history, it would not give us the Word made flesh, God incarnate in a particular human life. Therefore it can only be said that the paradox of Providence points us from afar in the direction of the paradox of the Incarnation.

Is there any further paradox in our Christian experience of God which can give us a nearer approach?

Yes, I think there is.

THE CENTRAL PARADOX

A far greater and deeper paradox than those which we have been considering lies at the very heart of the Christian life and vitally affects every part of it. It is what we may call the paradox of Grace. Its essence lies in the conviction which a Christian man possesses, that every good thing in him, every good thing he does, is somehow not wrought but by God. This is a highly paradoxical conviction, for in ascribing all to God it does not abrogate human personality nor disclaim personal responsibility. Never is human action more truly and fully personal, never does the agent feel more perfectly free, than in those moments of which he can say as a Christian that whatever good was in them was not his but God's.

This astonishing paradox, so characteristic of Christianity, can be widely illustrated from Christian literature of all ages. We may begin with the familiar words of St. Paul: "By the grace of God I am what I am: and his grace which was bestowed upon me was not found vain; but I laboured more abundantly than they all: yet not I, but the grace of God which was with me." We may go on to St. Augustine, who after quoting the above words makes the following comment: "O mighty teacher, confessor and preacher of grace! What meaneth this: 'I laboured more, Yet not I'? Where the will exalted itself ever so little, there piety was instantly on the watch, and humility trembled, because infirmity confessed all the truth." Again: "Therefore, blessed Paul, thou great teacher of grace, I will say it without fear of any man. . . .: Thy merits are recompensed with their own crown of reward; but thy merits are the gifts of God." Again: "Even if men do good things which pertain to God's service, it is He Himself that brings it about that they do what He commanded." This extraordinary doctrine of a God who not only demands obedience of us but supplies it Himself is summed up in St. Augustine's famous prayer: "Give what Thou commandest, and command what Thou wilt." Or take this from St. Anselm of Canterbury in the eleventh century: "What a man has, not from himself but from God, he ought to regard as not so much his own as God's. For no one has from himself the truth which he teaches, or a righteous will, but from God." To which we may add this from a prayer attributed to St. Anselm: "Whatsoever our heart rightly willeth, it is of Thy gift." Or take what Thomas à Kempis in the fifteenth century hears Christ say about His saints: "They glory not of their own merits, for they ascribe no goodness to themselves, but all to me." Or take this from the Westminster Confession in the seventeenth century, concerning the good works of believers: "Their ability to do good works is not at all of themselves, but wholly from the Spirit of Christ. And that they may be enabled thereunto, besides the graces they have already received, there is required an actual influence of the same Holy Spirit to work in them to will and to do of his good pleasure." Or take the familiar words of a nineteenth-century hymn:

> And every virtue we possess,
> And every victory won,
> And every thought of holiness
> Are His alone.

We can never ponder enough upon the meaning of this paradoxical conviction which lies at the very heart of the Christian life and is the unique secret of the Christian character. It is this that makes so wide a gulf between the Christian way of life and any "mere morality", so that in a sense Christianity transcends morality altogether and there is no such thing as a Christian ethic. The question is often asked whether the impossible ethic of the Sermon on the Mount has any relevance to our life in this world, as a code to be practised or an ideal on which to mould our characters. But the truth is that in the last analysis a Christian does not live by practising any ethic or moulding himself on any ideal, but by a faith in God which finally ascribes all good to Him. To detach the ethic from the whole context of the Christian secret is to make it irrelevant because it is impossible. The main function of the impossible ethic is to drive us away from ourselves to God: and then there grows that peculiar kind of goodness which can never be achieved by mere moral endeavour, the Christian kind, which is all unconscious of itself and gives all the glory to God.

Thus the paradoxical Christian secret, while it transcends the moralistic attitude by ascribing all to God, does not make us morally irresponsible. That is part of the paradox. No one knows better than the Christian that he is free to choose and that in a sense everything depends upon his choice. Pelagius was quite right to insist upon that, if he thought it was being compromised by the extreme statements of the zealous Augustine. My actions are my every own, expressions of my own will, my own choice. No one else can choose for me or relieve me of the responsibility. When I make the wrong choice, I am entirely responsible, and my conscience condemns me. And yet (here is the paradox) when I make the right choice, my conscience does not applaud or congratulate me. I do not feel meritorious or glow with self-esteem—if and in so far as I am a Christian. Instead of that I say: "Not I, but the grace of God." Thus while there is a human side to every good action, so that it is genuinely the free choice of a person with a will, yet somehow the Christian feels that the other side of it, the divine side, is logically prior. The grace of God is prevenient. The good was His before it was ours. That comes first, and in a sense that even covers the whole. It is not as if we could divide the honours between God and ourselves, God doing His part, and we doing ours. It cannot even be adequately expressed in terms of divine initiative and human co-operation. It is false to this paradox to think of the area of God's action and the area of our action being delimited, each by the other, and distinguished from each other by a boundary, so that the more of God's grace there is in an action, the less is it my own personal action. That is precisely the mistake that misled the morally ardent Pelagius. From the historical and psychological standpoint the good actions of a Christian are purely his own actions. And even from the religious and Christian point of view that aspect is indispensable. Without it the other side would lose its true meaning, and the good man would be simply a perfect marionette, or an automaton, as Huxley wished he could be. We are not marionettes, but responsible persons, and never more truly and fully personal in our actions than in those moments when we are most dependent on God and He lives and acts in us. And yet the divine side is somehow prior to the human. Whatever good there is in our lives and actions (and it is but fragmentary) is "all of God", and it was His before it was ours, was divine grace before it was human achievement, is indeed a matter of God taking up our poor human nature into union with

His own divine life, making us more truly personal, yet also more disposed to ascribe it all to Him.

This is the deepest paradox of our whole Christian experience, and it runs right through it, woven into its very texture. It is, moreover, virtually peculiar to Christianity. More than all the other paradoxes, it is a distinctive product of the religion of the Incarnation.

What I wish to suggest is that this paradox of grace points the way more clearly and makes a better approach than anything else in our experience to the mystery of the Incarnation itself; that this paradox in its fragmentary form in our own Christian lives is a reflection of that perfect union of God and man in the Incarnation on which our whole Christian life depends, and may therefore be our best clue to the understanding of it. In the New Testament we see the man in whom God was incarnate surpassing all other men in refusing to claim anything for Himself independently and ascribing all the goodness to God. We see Him also desiring to take up other men into His own close union with God, that they might be as He was. And if these men, entering in some small measure through Him into that union, experience the paradox of grace for themselves in fragmentary ways, and are constrained to say, "It was not I but God", may not this be a clue to the understanding of that perfect life in which the paradox is complete and absolute, that life of Jesus which, being the perfection of humanity, is also, and even in a deeper and prior sense, the very life of God Himself? If the paradox is a reality in our poor imperfect lives at all, so far as there is any good in them, does not the same or a similar paradox, taken at the perfect and absolute pitch, appear as the mystery of the Incarnation?

St. Augustine is not afraid to connect the one mystery with the other. "The Saviour, the Man Christ Jesus, is Himself the brightest illustration of predestination and grace." "Every man, from the commencement of his faith, becomes a Christian by the same grace by which *that* Man from His formation became Christ." And Calvin, commenting on this, can say: "Therefore when we treat of the merit of Christ, we do not place the beginning in Him, but we ascend to the ordination of God as the primary cause." St. Anselm, after writing the sentences I have quoted earlier, goes on to make the same connection. "What a man has, not from himself but from God, he ought to regard as not so much his own as God's. For no one has from himself the truth which he teaches, or a righteous will, but from God. Christ therefore came not to do His own will, but the Father's, because the righteous will which He had was not from His human but from His divine nature." It might almost be said that in that passage at least St. Anselm treats the divine-human Christ as the supreme instance of the familiar Christian paradox.

THE GOD WHO WAS INCARNATE

Let us leave the above argument for a moment and make another beginning from a different point—it will come to the same thing in the end.

Let us ask: With what conception of God have we embarked on our Christological quest? What do we understand by the word "God"? When endeavouring to confront, in an earlier chapter [of *God Was in Christ*], those persons who are willing to believe in God but not in the Incarnation, I was constrained to ask: Are you sure that you know what you mean by "God"? And now I must pursue the question further. It is astonishing how lightly many people assume that they know what the word "God" means. But it is still more astonishing that even when we profess Christian belief and set out to try to understand the mystery of God becoming man, we are apt to start with some conception of God, picked up we know not where, an idol of the cave or of the market-place, which is different from the Christian conception; and then to attempt the impossible task of understanding how such a God could be incarnate in Jesus. If the Incarnation has supremely revealed God, shown Him to us in a new and illuminating light, put a fresh meaning into the very word that is His name, *that* is the meaning that we must use in facing the problem of the Incarnation, because that is what God really is. It is only as Christians that we can hope to understand the Incarnation. Why then should we as theologians work with any other conception of God than that which as Christians we believe to be true?

What then do we mean when we speak of "God"? We mean something unique, something that cannot be fully conceptualized. Thus if we rightly understand the word "God", if we give it the only meaning it ought to have, we cannot possibly speak of "Gods" of even strictly of "a God". The word "God", rightly understood, is (as I have said repeatedly) not a common noun but a proper name. That is why Brunner makes the idea of "the name of God" so important in his theology, and conceives of revelation as "God telling us His name", on the basis of the story of Moses and the burning bush, and many other biblical passages. And yet this is not like any other proper name. It does not indicate particularity, one instance of a class, for God is not in any class. Common names, say the logicians, possess connotation, but proper names possess only denotation. May it not be said, however, that "God" is the one proper name that does possess connotation? And yet it is a connotation that cannot be fully conceptualized. Its meaning cannot be expressed without paradox. What then does it mean? With what meaning shall we use the word, as we try to understand how God could be incarnate?

Does it mean, fundamentally, the Maker of all things? No, that is not enough, nor is it a true starting-point; for however truly that phrase may be used in its place, it does not, when taken by itself, give us the meaning of "God" at all. If we could say no more than that about God, we could not even say that, in its true sense. For if we could say no more than that, then it could only have been by such logical processes as the argument from design or the cosmological proof that we reached that conception. And by such routes we could only reach a pantheistic *deus sive natura*, or a *prima causa* in the natural sense at the beginning of a causal chain, or a supreme artificer, like Paley's invisible watchmaker inferred from the watch found lying on the ground. But none of these conceptions is what is meant by God. When Augustine questioned earth and sea and sky about God, they said with one accord, "He made us". But he knew that he could not have heard them say even this if he had not known of God in other and more inward ways. The science of religions is showing, I think, that even in the case of pagan and primitive religion, where the word "God" has its plural, it was not by such arguments from nature, in howsoever primitive form, that the idea of the divine was reached. Christian faith does in fact praise God as Creator of all things, but such arguments from nature do not in themselves even begin to tell us what Christianity means by "God".

Does the word then mean the Source and Guardian of the moral law? That represents roughly the new approach proposed by Kant, the road of moral faith proposed in place of the speculative proofs which he found fallacious. This route looks at first far more promising; and Kant's conception can be so interpreted as to contain a great deal of truth. And yet if it is taken as an inferential argument from our moral convictions, as premisses, to God the Moral Governor of the universe as conclusion, it does not give us what Christians mean by God. At best it would give us "the moral and providential order". If we took this as the essential meaning of the word, it would reduce the practice of religion to "mere morality", and it would give us a thoroughly Pelagian conception of the life of faith. From the Christian point of view this would be a falsification of morality itself. To accept it would be to forget that there is a sense in which the Christian secret transcends morality altogether. It is Christianity that has discovered and exposed what we may call "the paradox of moralism"—that the attempt to be moral defeats itself, leads to "Pharisaism" instead of real goodness. Christianity has a different method, because it has a different conception of God. Christianity means a much deeper mystery, a much greater marvel, when it uses the word "God".

What, then, does the word "God" mean, in its true and full Christian use?

It means something so paradoxical that it is difficult to express in a few words. It means the One who at the same time makes absolute demands upon us and offers freely to *give* us all that He demands. It means the One who requires of us unlimited obedience and then supplies the obedience Himself. It means the One who calls us to work out our own salvation on the ground that ". . . it is He Himself who works both the willing and the working" in our hearts and lives. It is not that He bestows His favour, His grace, upon those who render obedience to His commands. Such divine giving in response to human obedience is a sub-Christian idea, alien to the New Testament; and indeed if God's grace had to wait for man's obedience, it would be kept waiting for ever. But the Christian, when he has rendered his fullest and freest obedience, knows well that somehow it was "all of God", and he says: "It was not I, but the grace of God which was with me." This is the Creator-God who made us to be free personalities, and we know that we are most free and personal when He is most in possession of us. This is the God of the moral order who calls us every moment to exercise our full and responsible choice; but He also comes to dwell in us in such a way that we are raised altogether above the moral order into the liberty of the sons of God. That is what Christians mean by "God". It is highly paradoxical, but it is bound up with the whole message of Christianity and the whole structure of the Christian life; and it follows inevitably if we take seriously the fundamental paradox: "Not I, but the grace of God", as we are bound to do unless we are content to be Pelagians. It is God's very nature to give Himself in that way: to dwell in man in such a manner that man, by his own will choosing to do God's will (and in a sense it must depend on man's own choice) nevertheless is constrained to confess that it was "all of God".

Such is the Christian conception of God; and therefore it is with such a conception that we must work when we try to understand the Incarnation.

The question may well be asked at this point: Is this really the *distinctively* Christian conception of God? Do we not seem to have forgotten that the peculiarly Christian view of God is to be found in the doctrine of the Trinity? And if that is the case, ought not the Trinitarian conception to be our starting-point in Christology? To this I would reply: Are these two conceptions really different from each other? The conception of God that has worked itself out in the language of devotion in the foregoing pages—is it not identical with that which is expressed in doctrinal terms in the dogma of the Trinity? I shall return to this subject in the next chapter [of *God Was in Christ*], but it seems necessary to say a word about it at this point. The Christian doctrine of the Trinity is not a mysterious mathematical statement about three-in-one, nor a metaphysical statement about a logically necessary triad. It may be difficult to understand the idea which Barth derives for Aquinas, that the numerical terms in the doctrine of the Trinity are to be taken metaphorically, but the statement that God is three-in-one is virtually meaningless until we go on to indicate the relation of the three to the one concretely on a basis of the Gospel history and the Christian experience out of which the doctrine arose. What the doctrine of the Trinity really asserts is that it is God's very nature not only to create finite persons whom He could love, and to reveal and impart Himself to them, even to the point of incarnation (through His eternal Word) but also to extend this indwelling to those men who fail to obey Him, doing in them what they could not do themselves, supplying to them the obedience which He requires them to render (through His Holy Spirit). All of this, says the dogma of the Trinity, is of the eternal nature and essence of God. He is Father, Son and Holy Spirit, and the Son and the Spirit are consubstantial with the Father. And this outgoing love of God, His self-giving, is not new nor occasional nor transient, but ". . . as it was in the beginning, is now, and ever shall be, world without end". Surely this doctrine is the objective expression of the same great paradox which finds its subjective expression in the confession: "Not I, but the grace of God."

This is the God in whom Christians believe. And this apprehension of God seems to be distinctive of Christianity. I do not say that it was never in any measure foreshadowed, for if this is the very nature of God there would naturally be some foreshadowing of the paradox wherever there was any knowledge of God at all. But the full paradox is peculiar to the religion of the Incarnation. It may be asked: What of the paradox so deeply rooted in Indian religion where the divine Brahma so dwells in man that He is both the worshipped and the worshipper, not only the hearer of prayer but the prayer itself, not only the desired but also the desire, not only the goal but also the aspirant? Yet that is very different from the Christian conviction, and indeed completely misses the depth of the paradox, because it is pantheistic, giving us a religion of identity, in which human personality is a painful illusion and its true goal is absorption and annihilation. In such a system the true idea of incarnation is impossible, just as there is no room for the paradox which combines the fullest personal freedom with the fullest divine indwelling, "I, yet not I, but the grace of God". At the other extreme stands a system like Islam, and here also there is no room for the paradox, but for the opposite reason. Islam is too moralistic for such a paradox. Its God is too sheerly transcendent, the Lawgiver, but not the Gracegiver, not the indwelling source and author of the obedience which He demands. Thus Islam is repelled by the doctrine of the Trinity, and its conception of God leaves no room for an incarnation.

There is, then, something peculiar to Christianity in the paradoxical conception of God that we have been elaborating and that has its counterpart in what I have called the central paradox of our Christian experience. That is, distinctively, what Christians mean by "God". And therefore when we try to understand the Incarnation, when we ask how God could become man and what it means, *that* is the God about whom we must ask the question.

But if so, then we have *ipso facto* begun to find an *answer* to the question, the only kind of answer that we ought to expect. In that case the doctrine that Jesus Christ is both God and Man is not sheer mystification. We can begin to understand it. Not that the reality so described becomes less wonderful. But it is not more wonderful than the God in whom we believe. I am reminded of the teaching we find in some of the Logos-theologians of the Patristic age, especially Irenaeus, to the effect that, while God is in Himself incomprehensible, unknowable, yet it is also His very nature to reveal Himself to His creatures, even to the point of Incarnation, because that is the natural activity of the Logos, and the Logos is of the essence of God. I am reminded also of Karl Barth's remark, that ". . . while God's becoming *man* is not a matter of course, yet it can be justly considered as the most natural of all natural occurrences, because it was *God* who became man in Jesus Christ". It may be objected that thus to explain the Incarnation by showing how naturally it connects with the doctrine of the Trinity, or with the paradoxical Christian conception of God, is no explanation at all, since these conceptions have themselves arisen out of the Incarnation. In one sense this is perfectly true. But it is not disconcerting. For there is a sense in which we should not expect or attempt to "explain" the Incarnation. Our theological task is to try to make sure that we know what we mean by it, what it means and what it does not mean; to try to make sure that, while it remains the *mysterium Christi*, it is not sheer meaningless mystery, but becomes a truly Christian paradox to us. And I am suggesting that this can happen because in our own experience, however poor and fragmentary, we know something of the paradoxical grace of God, something of the God who was incarnate in Jesus.

Our two lines of argument have converged upon the one point, with a view to such an understanding of the paradox of the Incarnation.

TRUE GOD AND TRUE MAN

Let us try to trace more fully the connection and analogy between what I have called the paradox of grace and the paradox of the Incarnation.

Let us begin with the witness of the New Testament. It is plain that we find in the New Testament both the very highest claims for the divine revelation in Jesus and the very frankest recognition that He was a man. How far can we also find these two related to each other in a way that reminds us of the paradox by which a Christian says: "I, . . . yet not I, but God"? A very great deal has been written by biblical scholars during the last century on the question as to what Jesus held and taught about Himself and His place in God's purpose, and a common phrase which figured as the title of many discussions a generation ago was "the (messianic) self-consciousness of Jesus". The phrase was doubtless legitimate and useful. And yet it has a somewhat unnatural sound, because in the Jesus of the Gospels it is not "self-consciousness" that strikes us, but God-consciousness. Throughout the story we get the impression of one who, with all His high claims, kept thinking far less of Himself than of the Father. Even in Him—or should we say, supremely in Him?—self-consciousness was swallowed up in His deep and humble and continual consciousness of God. When He worked cures, it was to His heavenly Father that He looked up for aid, and it was to God rather than to Himself that He expected people to give the glory when they were cured. As regards goodness, He was not conscious of possessing it Himself independently, but looked away from Himself to God for it. When once a man addressed Him as "Good Master", he replied: "Why do you call me good? No one is good except God." If we take the reply seriously, we shall surely find in it the supreme instance of that peculiar kind of humility which Christianity brought into the world. It was not self-depreciation: it was rather a complete absence of the kind of self-consciousness which makes a man think of his own degree of merit, and a dominating sense of dependence on God. The Man in whom God was incarnate would claim nothing for Himself as a Man, but ascribed all glory to God.

It is, however, when we turn to the Fourth Gospel that we find on the lips of Jesus the most remarkable expressions of this central paradox of Christian experience. I cannot in this place discuss the question as to how far the great Johannine discourses give us the *ipsissima verba* of Jesus; but it is in any case sufficiently impressive that in the Gospel which gives us the most transcendently high Christology to be found in the New Testament, Christology is more than anywhere else interwoven with the paradoxical human confession: "I, . . . yet not I, but the Father." On the one hand there is Jesus making His human choice from moment to moment, a choice on which in a sense everything depends. "He that sent me is with me: he hath not left me alone; for I do always the things that are pleasing to him." "Therefore doth the Father love me, because I lay down my life, that I may take it again. No one taketh it away from me, but I lay it down of myself. I have power to lay it down, and I have power to take it again. This commandment received I from my Father." But on the other hand, all His words and all His choices depended on the Father. "I can of myself do nothing: as I hear, I judge: and my judgment is righteous, because I seek not mine own will, but the will of him that sent me." "Verily, verily, I say unto you, the Son can do nothing of himself, but what he seeth the Father doing: for what things soever he doeth, these the Son also doeth in like manner." "My teaching is not mine, but his that sent me. . . . He that speaketh from himself seeketh his own glory: but he that seeketh the glory of him that sent him, the same is true, and no unrighteousness is in him." "I am not come of myself, but he that sent me is true, whom ye know not. I know him; because I am from him, and he sent me." "I spake not from myself; but the Father which sent me, he hath given me a commandment, what I should say, and what I should speak." "The words that I say unto you I speak not from myself: but the Father abiding in me doeth his works."

In these remarkable passages we find Jesus making the very highest claims; but they are made in such a way that they sound rather like disclaimers. The higher they become, the more do they refer themselves to God, giving God all the glory. Though it is a real man that is speaking, they are not human claims at all: they do not claim anything for the human achievement, but ascribe it all to God. According to Barth, the holiness of Jesus means that He did not treat His own goodness as an independent thing, a heroic human attainment. His sinlessness consists in His renouncing all claim to ethical heroism. He did not set up at all as a man confronting God, but along with sinners—who do *not* take this attitude—He threw Himself solely on God's grace. The God-Man is the only man who claims nothing for Himself, but all for God.

It hardly needs to be said the New Testament is conscious of a great gulf between what Christ is and what we are even when we are His people; and to some it may seem that this should exclude all analogy between His experience of God and ours. Especially it may occur to some that experience of the *grace* of God belongs to sinful men and does not enter at all into the mystery of divine Incarnation. According to Newman's hymn, "God's presence and His very self, And essence all-divine", in the Incarnation is " a higher gift than grace". More than one critic has made the comment that there is no higher gift than grace, since the grace of God is simply His personal and loving action upon us or within us; but it is perhaps not necessary to quarrel with Newman's meaning. It does not follow, however, that we must not think of Jesus as the recipient or object of the grace of God, or that we must not take the "paradox of grace" as in any measure a pointer to the Incarnation. According to Thomas Aquinas, the grace given to Christ is twofold: *gratia habitualis*, given to Christ as man, like other men, and *gratia unionis*, given only to Christ; but this seems an artificial distinction. It is relevant, however, to remember that the New Testament, while it speaks of the grace of God as given to Christ, speaks much more of the grace of Christ as given to us. And that indicates exactly the relation between His experience of God and ours, as conceived in the New Testament. Ours depends upon His. If God in some measure lives and acts in us, it is because first, and without measure, He lived and acted in Christ. And thus, further, the New Testament tends sometimes to say that as God dwells in Christ, so Christ dwells in us. St. Paul can express the paradox of grace by saying: "I live; and yet no longer I, but *Christ* liveth in me"; as he can say to Christians: "You are of Christ, and Christ is of God." But that is only a part of the truth, and St. Paul can also speak of Christian men sharing, in a sense and in a measure, Christ's relation to God. It is God's purpose that these men should ". . . be conformed to the image of his Son, that he might be the first-born among many brethren". In the Epistle to the Hebrews we find strong emphasis laid on the analogy between Christ's human experience and the experience of those men whom He saves. "Both he that sanctifieth and they that are sanctified are all of one: for which cause he is not ashamed to call them brethren." In the Fourth Gospel the risen Christ speaks of the disciples as "my brethren" and of God as "my Father and your Father, and my God and your God". There also we find the purpose boldly expressed that all Christ's people should come to have the same kind of unity with Him, and through Him with the Father, as He has with the Father: "That they may all be one; even as thou, Father, art in me, and I in thee, that they also may be in us: that the world may believe that thou didst send me. And the glory which thou hast given me I have given unto them; that they may be one, even as we are one; I in them, and thou in me, that may be perfected into one; that the world may know that thou didst send me, and lovedst them, even as thou lovedst me."

"He was made what we are", wrote Irenaeus, "that He might make us what He is Himself."

If then Christ can be thus regarded as in some sense the prototype of the Christian life, may we not find a feeble analogue of the incarnate life in the experience of those who are His "many brethren", and particularly in the central paradox of their experience: "Not I, but the grace of God"? If this confession is true of the little broken fragments of good that are in our lives—if these must be described on the one hand as human achievements, and yet on the other hand, and in a deeper and prior sense, as *not* human achievements but things actually wrought by God—is it not the same *type* of paradox, taken at the absolute degree, that covers the whole ground of the life of Christ, of which we say that it was the life of a man and yet also, in a deeper and prior sense, the very life of God incarnate?

It seems plain that it is the presence of this paradox that has always made it so difficult to express the doctrine of the Incarnation without running into error on the one side or on the other, so as to lose either the divinity or the humanity. And it appears to me that the method of approach which I have indicated is a certain safeguard against these errors, because it can be a continual reminder of the need of holding fast the two sides of the paradox and letting them correct each other. On the one hand, there was from the beginning the "Adoptionist" or "Ebionite" type of error, by which Jesus was regarded as a man who achieved such goodness that God exalted him to divinity or quasi-divinity. The reason why the Church could not rest content with such a view was not because they objected to the idea of deification (for the Greek Fathers tended too much to conceive even of salvation as deification) but because the Adoptionist Christology began with the human achievement of Jesus and brought God in at the end, so that it was a case of "first man, then God" or a man becoming God, instead of "first God, then man" or God becoming man. It was, of course, perfectly right to regard the life lived by Jesus as a human achievement. To deny that or to obscure or minimize it would be to fall into the opposite type of error, with Docetists, Apollinarians, and Monophysites. Jesus was a real man, subject to the conditions and limitations of humanity, with a human will that had to make its continual choices in face of life's temptations, and thus His goodness must be quite realistically regarded as a human achievement. But goodness in a human life, even in small proportions, is *never* simply a human achievement. To regard it as such would be pure Pelagianism. And ". . . no New Testament thinker could think of Jesus in Pelagian terms". All goodness in a human life is wrought by God. That is the other side, and somehow that side comes first, without destroying the human. And therefore the goodness of Jesus can ultimately be described only as the human side of a divine reality, which, so to say, was divine before it was human. The divine is always prevenient, so that however far back one may go in the life of Jesus, one can never reach a point that would meet the requirements of "Adoptionism", just as one can never reach a point of which a "Pelagian" account would be satisfactory. It is not adoption that we have to deal with, but Incarnation.

The whole problem of the Incarnation is contained in the old question, which can be asked in so many ways: Was Jesus divine because He lived a perfect life, or was He able to live a perfect life because He was divine? To put it otherwise: Did the Incarnation depend upon the daily human choices made by Jesus, or did He always choose aright because He was God incarnate? If our whole line of thought has been correct, this question does not present us with a genuine dilemma. It must, of course, be true that His choices were genuine human choices, and that in a sense everything depended upon them. "He that sent me is with me; he hath not left me alone; for (or because) I do always the things that are pleasing to him." All depended on those human choices from moment to moment. And yet as soon as we have said that, we must inevitably turn round and say something apparently opposite, remembering that in the last analysis such human choice is never prevenient or even co-operative, but wholly dependent on the divine prevenience. We must say that in the perfect life of Him who was ". . . *always* doing the things that are pleasing to God", this divine prevenience was nothing short of Incarnation, and He lived as He did because He was God incarnate. Thus the dilemma disappears when we frankly recognize that in the doctrine of the Incarnation there is a paradox which cannot be rationalized but which can in some small measure be understood in the light of the "paradox of grace". Somebody may wish to press the question in another form: Would *any* man who lived a perfect life be therefore and thereby God incarnate? But such a questioner would indeed be a Pelagian, showing by his very question that he regarded the human side of the achievement as the prevenient, the conditioning, the determinative. When we really accept the paradox of grace, when we really believe that every good thing in a man is wrought by God, when we have really understood the confession: "I . . . yet not I, but God", and have taken that divine priority in earnest, the question loses its meaning, and, like the proposed dilemma, fades away into the paradox of the Incarnation. And if we take these things in earnest, we have, as it appears to me, at least an approach to the *mysterium Christi* which will enable us to combine the most transcendent claims of a full and high Christology with the frankest recognition of the humanity of the historical Jesus.

It seems certain that whatever restatement of Christology may be necessary in the modern world, it will be in the direction of fuller and ever fuller recognition of both these sides of the truth. On the one hand there will be no abatement, but rather, if it were possible, an enhancement, of the highest predicates that Christian faith has ever given to Jesus Christ as God incarnate.

> The highest place that heaven affords
> Is His, is His by right:
> The King of kings and Lord of lords
> And heaven's eternal Light.

The Church must indeed break out continually into such lyrical notes to make up for the shortcomings of theological prose, and no expression can be too high. Nothing can be too high; and nothing can be too lowly or too human. Nothing can be too high, if only we save it from Docetic and Monophysite unreality by treating His life as in every sense a human life. A toned down Christology is absurd. It must be all or nothing—all or nothing on both the divine and the human side. That is the very extreme of paradox; but I have tried in this chapter to show how, as it seems to me, the derivative paradox which is the distinctive secret of the Christian life may help us to interpret in a truly Christian way the paradox of the Incarnation.

Part II | Can the Christian Theist Justify
His Central Claim?

A group of students asked me to speak in chapel on the question "Can a student of philosophy be a Christian?" I began by suggesting we could set a record for the shortest chapel talk yet. "Answer to the question? Yes! Let us pray!"

On one other occasion and on another campus after a chapel service, an eager student expressed surprise that a "professor of philosophy" would speak directly, without philosophical jargon, of the main motifs of the Christian message. For I tried to give voice in that place of worship to God's gift of love and man's response through Jesus Christ. One could only reply, "I do not stand in the pulpit as a philosopher but as a member of a believing community."

There is always the danger of confusing the sanctuary with the lecture hall, but more serious is failure to distinguish the role of worship, through expression of word, act and living symbol, from that of philosophical analysis. Surrounded by the symbols and sacred memories of a continuing tradition, worshipers celebrate "the faith of our fathers living still." They do so not in *second-order* language of theory and analysis but in *first-order* language, expressive of personal affirmation and commitment. For these are different but related *uses* of language. In the midst of the worshiping community, the modes of expression are those of living religious faith and theological belief. But to talk about these—to exhibit what sort of language is being used, to relate these utterances to other areas of human concern (such as science, morality, the arts)—to do this job is to become the student of philosophy. It is an important task, although not a task we normally carry out in the sanctuary of worship.

Differing Views of the Philosophy of Religion

Traditional philosophy of religion is primarily a nineteenth-century product and is associated with philosophical and theological movements which came under Hegelian influence. As a result there developed the conviction that philosophy and theology can be fused into a single rational enterprise. Men of religious conviction need not fear the onslaughts of the intellect that would destroy faith. For there is no conflict between reason and revelation. They are two sides of the same coin. Reason can reach out for the same "truths" which are disclosed through revelation. These truths may be established by rational criteria, and they are consonant with "spiritual truths."

After all, according to this point of view, any man of clear and ordered thought may arrive at the same conclusions as those of religion. The best and most disciplined philosophy is the best theology. For it is assumed that reason is competent to undertake the systematic exposition and defense of religion. Thus philosophy of religion becomes identical with rational or natural theology. *Natural* theology is made up of all those truths which can be reached by the unaided intellect of rational men. By contrast, *revealed* theology is said to consist of all those truths which are not open to unaided human reason. The latter can be apprehended only as they are revealed specifically by God. In both instances, theological truths are held to be "propositional"; for these were known by men just as statements (as in the sciences or commonsense experiences) are made and held about the empirical world. We shall refer in Chapter 10, by contrast, to a nonpropositional view of revelation and faith. This perspective, as a live option, we shall discuss in greater detail at that point.

Concerning the relations between philosophy of religion and theology, the writings of George Galloway, William Temple and Paul Tillich stand in clear contrast. Galloway represents British advocates of a Hegelian approach to the philosophy of religion. This view stresses the harmony and fusion between philosophy and theology, for ". . . the Philosophy of Religion is just the application of philosophical principles and methods to religion regarded as a matter given." Temple, on the other hand, asserts that although there is tension between these two different enterprises, still each can help the other. This tension can be positive and creative as mutual search leads to common ground for agreement, at least on some basic issues. Tillich takes the position that philosophy, through examination of the structure of being, raises questions about man's purpose and significance. But the task of theology is to make clear explication of the answers which religion offers to those questions. Thus, the relation between philosophy and theology is that of correlation and mutual assistance.

I would cite with approval still another view of the role of the philosophy of religion. It is frankly an approach stressing the *analytical* and *functional* task of philosophy in its relation to whatever specific subject matter it studies, in this case, religion.

Contemporary Philosophy of Religion

Philosophy (philosophy of religion or philosophy of science, for example) is thus in this newer viewpoint a second-order activity, standing at one step removed from, and yet significantly related to, its appropriate subject matter. Philosophy of religion is not itself a part of the religious realm. But it is related to it as philosophy of science, philosophy of law, philosophy of morality and philosophy of art are related to their proper realms.[1]

Philosophy of religion studies the concepts and statements of theologians and the basic religious utterances, concepts, experiences and activities out of which theology arises. Philosophy of religion listens to worshipers praying, confessing sin, giving thanks, making intercessions, reading Scripture, retelling sacred myths, affirming faith, interpreting convictions, receiving sacraments, responding to visible symbols, singing hymns and anthems, making resolves in the light of specific life-orientation images, giving voice to new aspirations and concerns for the world of societies and nations. The philosopher of religion does not tell lay worshiper or professional theologian what he shall or should mean by these expressions. Rather, he tries to grasp what these folk, within the religious and theological circle, do mean. The philosopher may be also worshiper and/or theologian and vice versa, but it is essential to distinguish the functions, concepts and language peculiar to each context. If we do not do so, we cannot relate them significantly.

Thus philosophy as an ordered discipline, from this perspective, is not what is vaguely and popularly called "philosophy of life" or a "world view." It is precise, rigorous and challenging. But philosophy can help honest searchers discover the grounds on which a world view or philosophy of life may be developed. However, those grounds, as applied in practical life situations, are religious and moral and arise out of personal existence itself. Can a student of philosophy espouse any given religious faith? Can he be a Christian? Of course, but not necessarily because he is a student of philosophy, although being one will aid in clarity and critical awareness of who he is. Can a Christian be a student of philosophy? He can if he is willing to undergo the rigorous discipline required.

[1] John Hick, *Philosophy of Religion*, © 1963, pp. 1–2. Reprinted by permission of Prentice-Hall, Inc., Englewood Cliffs, New Jersey.

We suggest, then, that it will not do to be a halfhearted religious believer dabbling in what is commonly called philosophy. There are no glib or easy answers. There are no creeds to mouth nor any sure outward signs of piety nor any fixed, "eternal" systems of abstract "truths." Someone may reply: "But I thought *both* Christianity and philosophy played around with nothing but certainties, the fixed, the final, the eternal." There are forms of religion and traditional philosophy which make this pitch. But these are not the kinds that are in the air today, both as to Christian belief and practice and as to the contemporary way of doing philosophy.

In this chapter and in those that follow, we need to attempt to clarify further some of the issues revolving around this relationship of philosophical to religious and theological concerns. Problems as to the relation of *reason* to *faith* and *revelation* still remain. How do we "verify" men's claims to the reality of a transcendent God? What *rivals* to the Judeo-Christian tradition are current today? How do we decide between them? Obviously, these are questions to be decided in a lifetime of continuing, serious search. But we can perhaps suggest some of the terms on which answers may be found.

Religion and Theology

The man of religious conviction and practice who at the same time attempts to understand what he is doing is caught in a dilemma. As Professor Wilbur M. Urban suggests, religion is always suspended between two worlds.[2] Man finds it difficult to live without religion or with it. He is born to a given tradition (or adopts it by becoming a member of a specific community). But this very concrete expression he finds hard to accept. Man attempts to express the ultimate and finds he cannot do so in literal terms. He employs imagic language and yet seeks to understand the non-conceptual in conceptual language. Urban suggests a basic postulate for the task of understanding religion. It is that religious expressions refer not simply to what is felt but to what is somehow known: a common reference, pronouncements and meanings clearly communicable. But are religious utterances expressible in conceptual language? Urban answers that they are not, in a direct, literal fashion. And yet we must presuppose what he calls "conceptual equivalents." This is our dilemma: the language of religion communicates what is not expressible in any other language

---

[2] W. M. Urban, *Humanity and Deity*, George Allen & Unwin, Ltd., London, 1951, p. 20.

and so not sayable in conceptual language. Yet, if we are to grasp and give voice to the essence of religion, we must do so in conceptual terms. This is the language of theology.[3]

Three Factors in the "Logic" of Religion

Thus one solution is to presuppose, with Urban, conceptual equivalents to the first-order, nonconceptual utterances of religious faith and practice. Frederick Ferré suggests another approach.[4]

There are, he reminds us, three factors in every situation in which men use language to convey to each other what they mean. These must be clearly distinguished, and yet they are all three present in every language situation: (1) the logical structure of the language itself, called "syntax" or the "syntactic dimension"; (2) the relation of what is said by the interpreter, the language-using agent, called "interpretics" or, generally, "pragmatics"; (3) an object to which reference is made by the interpreter, that is, content signified, a dimension of language called "semantics." Each of these three apart from the others is an abstraction.

First, as for the syntactic dimension as applied to our areas of concern, the syntactic rules for religious language differ from those of theological language. Yet they interact. This aspect of language study inquires as to how to test the adequacy of religious expressions. Here we ask about norms by which to judge the firsthand utterances of the worshiper engaged, for instance, in prayer of thanksgiving, confession or praise. We are concerned with criteria by which, for example, to gauge the authenticity of the acts and signs used in the sacrament of Communion or the Mass. ("This do in remembrance of me.")

The standards for adequacy of first-order faith utterances, Ferré states, are internal language norms.[5] For Christians, these language norms are those of Scripture, church tradition, creeds, the usages of rite and ceremony of worship. These are given. Today's utterances are syntactically correct insofar as they give new voice here and now to the "faith of our fathers living still." Thus the logic of religious expression is that of equivalence between the utterances of today's believer and the given forms of discourse used by the faithful through the ages. Ferré suggests that this stress on equivalence contrasts with the norms for theological

---

[3] *Ibid.*, pp. 52–66.

[4] From *Language, Logic and God* by Frederick Pond Ferré, Copyright © 1961 Frederick Pond Ferré. Reprinted with the permission of Harper & Row, Publishers, Inc., New York.

[5] *Ibid.*, p. 151.

uses of language. For equivalence does not mean entailment, that is, systematic relations of implication between what the believer says at one moment and what he says in the next.

Insofar as he, the believer, is engaged in first-order religious expression, then, we do not ask him about formal consistency but about equivalence. But this is not to say that he is utterly irrational or arbitrary. We acknowledge rather that his religion is gauged by standards from within itself. For we do not, for instance, bring some criteria from another discipline (scientific or mathematical) to judge the "truth" of Christians' claims about Jesus Christ.

Consider somebody whom you love. Suppose that person asks, "Why do you love me?" If a man were to say to his wife, "Because you perform such miracles with your cooking," she would probably hit him on the head with a frying pan. But would it be any better to say, "Because you have such a brilliant mind or a profound system of values"? So, if she were to do something stupid, he would disown her? There is only one adequate answer. It sounds childish. But it is the "logic" of love and of first-order religion. "I love you because *you are you!*" And this *includes* cookery, wisdom, values and all the rest, but ". . . does not leave the love at the mercy of any of these. It means that the loved one makes a total impact upon the lover, so that his only possible answer is that of love."[6]

By the same token, why does the Christian believer affirm, with response of his whole being, Christ as God incarnate? Because Jesus Christ is Jesus Christ! Neither formal deductive arguments nor empirical arguments can win or lose love between man and woman. No argument can create faith. But where faith is utter response of the entire self, no argument can destroy it. For the believer is not defending a set of abstract propositions, at this level of religious affirmation, but confessing to a focused orientation for his life that calls for momentous consequences for thought and action no matter what his particular vocation may be.

We must keep in mind that even the simplest worshiper at some point or other becomes theologian. Certainly, the theologian is also a member of the worshiping community. The symbols of his religious faith point to the principles that comprise the starting points for his theology. But the syntactic structure of theological statement is different from that of religious utterance. The syntactic structure of theological discourse follows the rules for both equivalence and entailment. Entailment means that the relation of implication holds between the statements comprising the theological system. But the rules of entailment are not simply those of

[6] I am indebted here to William Hordern, *The Case for a New Reformation Theology*, The Westminster Press, Philadelphia, 1959, pp. 84–85.

traditional formal logic, abstract and devoid of specific content. A newer philosophy reminds us that there is a wide variety of syntactic "rules" which are framed in the light of our practical experience in many different areas of concern.

Traditional formal logic insists that the rules of implication, contradiction and the like are purely abstract and have no reference to any particular subject matter. By contrast, contemporary functional logic recognizes, in addition to formal rules, that the specific content of given utterance is important.

Again Ferré states:

> But logical theorists in recent years have come to recognize that other kinds of rules for implication, contradiction and the like, play an important part in rational discourse. These are syntactical rules which are not irrelevant to the specific content being discussed, as are the rules of formal logic, but are openly dependent upon the definitions that establish inferences *within the language of a given subject matter.* In the language of the game of checkers, for example, the statement, "It is permissible to jump your opponent's piece" *entails* "You are required to jump your opponent's piece." But such an entailment-rule does not have the complete generality associated with formal logic; in "the language of chess," for example, no such entailment holds. In ordinary language our speech is heavily dependent upon this non-formal (or, as we shall call them "informal") kind of entailment and equivalence. . . . The study of both major kinds of syntactics, formal and informal, is proving to be of considerable importance for the understanding of language.[7]

This is true of the study of theological language, which exhibits both kinds of logic, formal and informal. Formal logical structures are essential to the utterances of theology: "and," "or," "not," "some," "all." But, in addition, what theologians say must be understood in terms of certain "informal" rules of inference which belong to specific contexts. Ferré cites an instance of informal rules in theology. One might say, "If salvation is possible, then God cannot be merely a conditioned *part* of the world and *subject to* change." Another rule states, "If salvation is possible, then God cannot be completely *apart from* the world and *unrelated to* change." The formal logician immediately sees that one of these rules contradicts the other; for if one is true, the other is false. But in the informal logic of theological discourse, what appears to be contradiction may be occasion for growth in insight. For the Christian, God both tran-

[7] Ferré, *op. cit.*, pp. 151–152.

scends the world and discloses Himself in and through events in the world.[8]

In everyday situations, we deal in informal logic. On an unpleasant day, we say of the weather, "It's raining, and it's not." Or we say, "She's pretty, and she's not" or "He's admirable, and he's not." In each instance, greater precision in expression and concept is needed in order to disclose exact meaning. Yet in a context like that of theology, the very meanings it would convey depend on exploiting just such fine nuances of significance. The formal logician's instrument cuts too sharply sometimes, even though in certain areas this is essential to clarity. Theology involves the understanding of certain key concepts. For this, the informal logician's approach points the way to imaginative grasp of intended meanings and to the search for more and more adequate means of expression.[9]

What now is the precise relation between theology and religion? The academic theologian must, we have seen, seek for systematic coherence, by the rules of both formal and informal logic. For these are the rules of entailment between some of his statements and others which he makes. But we recall that, like religious expression, theological utterance exhibits not only the relation of entailment but also equivalence. The theologian stands with worshiper within the context of the community of living faith. For the starting points of his theology are rooted in the expressions of that living faith.

Theology is the reasoned explication of faith's affirmations. These latter become the axioms of the theologian's system. In turn his reasoned pronouncements are reflected back on the creeds which become authoritative for a given community of faith. Thus religion and theology interact with each other within that believing community. This leads to the second dimension of language.

Interpreters within Community

We have already implied a great deal about the second dimension of language: interpretics, or pragmatics. For language affects its interpreters not simply in reaction but also in response. Religious language is expressive. Its function is not to inform us of some facts or some abstract concepts. Thus those who hear or read the words of Scripture or sermon respond to certain illuminative images and symbols. Theological discourse also deals with symbols which demand response of the whole person. Christian language speaks of birth, baptism, Lord's Supper, Cross, Resur-

[8] *Ibid.*, p. 153.
[9] *Ibid.*, pp. 153–154.

rection, covenant. Ferré writes of these: "Not the words or phrases themselves but the content of the words and phrases of theological speech possess the greatest power to affect the interpreter of this language."[10] Thus Christians who hear and/or use the expressions of religious and theological discourse respond to the symbols of their heritage within the church, the distinctive society, the community within which worshiper and theologian alike speak and listen. For theology is dynamically and reciprocally related to the living faith.

Reference to the Religious Object

But, third, language refers beyond itself and its interpreters to an object. The study of this dimension of the language situation is semantics proper, and the object is called the semantic reference. Theological discourse points beyond itself to "reality," what is "outside" and "over against" ourselves, our thoughts and our utterances. Here is involved belief in the reality of that object intended. Thus, belief is an indispensable ingredient, along with the syntactic structure of the language as used by the interpreter living within a specific community.

In some sense, "facts" are the object of such belief and affirmation. But are such facts of the same order as those involved in the sciences? More than natural facts are involved, we say. But will it do to speak of "supernatural facts," as if this phrase added some special quality of a specific entity, call this God or Reality? As suggested later, the claim "God exists" may not refer to such an entity said to be "out there." Rather "God exists" speaks out eloquently as an affirmation of an actual human person. He is possessed of certain attitudes, values, a specific life orientation. He sees, experiences, the world and Himself in distinctive ways. Certain life-orientation symbols, images, signs, acts, words form the core in which His whole existence centers. Around these images, He builds clusters of ideas, beliefs, systematic statements of theological affirmation.

He intends these clusters now to refer to an object, reality. This is then what we call metaphysics. Metaphysics is that enterprise which constructs theories of the nature of reality. A part of this enterprise is ontology, which is concerned with theories about *what is*. These theories, revolving around specific images, metaphors, analogies, comprise systematic conceptual schemes. A conceptual scheme of this metaphysical kind is designed to provide coherence for all the "facts" of the world. But this

[10] *Ibid.*, p. 157.

scheme is centered in models drawn from among the facts themselves. Theology, at this point of semantic reference to reality, *is* part of this enterprise called metaphysics, or, specifically, ontology.

The Search for World Hypotheses

I have recorded elsewhere[11] a suggested view of the nature of this metaphysical quest. This view still holds, I believe. But I now would connect the metaphysical concern more closely with the semantic reference of theological language, as advocated by Ferré and discussed in the foregoing paragraphs. Also I now would suggest a shift in the relation of metaphysics to science. For, with respect to the use of models to provide coherence for the facts under investigation, metaphysics is not unlike science.

There is thus a fruitful method of procedure in metaphysics without the dogmatic claims of the older schools of thought. We can overcome the strictures against metaphysics as carried on for a time by logical empiricists. For the latter took seriously the verification theory of meaning. Under this theory of meaning, the cognitive claims (that is, claims as *knowledge*) of moralists, theologians and metaphysicians were rejected. What these latter folk say cannot be regarded as knowledge because their claims cannot be verified by stating the conditions under which they might be shown to be true or false. These conditions are determined by methods effectively employed in mathematics and the empirical sciences. Mathematical and all matters-of-logic statements may be shown to be true or false, and therefore meaningful, by virtue of their form only and make no reference to the empirical world. Empirical statements may be shown to be factually true or false, and therefore meaningful, if conditions can be exhibited by which they could be verified by experiment and observation of the given phenomena of nature. Obviously, the claims of metaphysics and theology can measure up to neither of these criteria of meaning and were regarded therefore as meaningless. But more recent philosophical analysis has moved beyond this exclusive theory of meaning. There are wider uses of language than those of science. The methods we are urging in this chapter regard religious, theological and metaphysical statements as performing quite a different function and therefore *meaningful* in their own terms. The criteria by which they are to be judged are internal criteria.

[11] John B. Harrington, *Essentials in Christian Faith*, Harper & Row, Publishers, Incorporated, New York, 1958, pp. 39–44.

Of course, even the scientist uses creative imagination to construct definitive models which enable him to deal with a given set of phenomena. He does not suppose that his model (say, in the cryptic language of a formula) pictorially describes some corresponding state of affairs in the phenomenal order. Rather his model is a handle which he can use to explain and to cope with the particular processes in nature with which he is experimenting. Thus, even the scientist's understanding of the nature of truth is not that of point-for-point correspondence between his theory and the facts out there. Rather it is that of coherence within the conceptual schemes built up around his key explanatory models. The test is not that of "truth that pictures exactly." There is no entity out there with which to compare it. The test is rather that of the "adequacy" of the scientist's explanatory concepts in enabling him to deal experimentally with a given area of the natural order and explain what happens there in functional terms.

If this is so of science, the method of metaphysics bears a closer resemblance still to this process of imaginative construction of coherent conceptual schemes around certain models. But the difference between science and metaphysics lies in the use to which such an enterprise is put. Obviously, mathematical accuracy and experimental operations are also essential to scientific procedure. But the metaphysician proposes to use his conceptual scheme to deal with and relate various areas of human concern, including that of the sciences. No one science pretends to do this. The metaphysician selects, from among all the "facts" of these various orders, certain key models, images around which to build his conceptual scheme. But his motive may be religious and theological as well as metaphysical. For he may aspire to discovering certain images and clusters of concepts by which he can orient his whole existence to a whole world. Once again, the test cannot be exact picturing correspondence between his ordered images and the facts out there. For the criteria by which the images are gauged are those of adequacy in enabling the whole person to act coherently, to see things synoptically, to decide with precision and effectiveness the direction of his life. Thus theology, at the point of semantic reference to reality, is metaphysical in its aim and method.

My *Essentials in Christian Faith* records the suggestions of Stephen C. Pepper concerning "world hypotheses." For it is with these that the seeker after a world view may be said to deal:

> The peculiarity of world hypotheses is that they cannot reject anything as irrelevant. When certain inconvenient matters are brought to a mathema-

tician, he can always say, "These are psychological (or physical or historical) matters. I do not have to deal with them." Similarly with other students of restricted fields. But students of world hypotheses can never have that way out. Every consideration is relevant to a world hypothesis and no facts lie outside it.[12]

A world hypothesis thus becomes a point of view which seeks to see broad reaches of experience. Yet it begins with taking seriously a small segment of that experience. A man in search of a metaphysical view becomes sensitively aware of certain kinds of objects in his world and of the ways he responds to them. These are his own. They are all he has to deal with. But beginning with his own experiences does not condemn him to subjectivity. For since he cannot know everything, he must select, from among those things he does know, those keys or clues which suggest to him the nature of reality. Then, I have suggested, in *Essentials in Christian Faith*, it is like projecting a miniature color slide onto a huge screen. In the search for a world view, that selected segment becomes an *analogy* or "root metaphor" suggestive of the nature of the whole of reality.[13]

Pepper describes what he calls the root-metaphor method in this way:

The method in principle seems to be this: a man desiring to understand the world looks about for a clue to its comprehension. He pitches upon some area of common-sense fact and tries if he cannot understand other areas in terms of this one. This original area becomes then his basic analogy or root metaphor. He describes as best he can the characteristics of this area, or, if you will, discriminates its structure. A list of its structural characteristics becomes his basic concepts of explanation and description. We call them a set of categories. . . . Since the basic analogy or root metaphor normally (and probably at least in part necessarily) arises out of common sense, a great deal of development and refinement of a set of categories is required if they are to prove adequate for a hypothesis of unlimited scope. Some root metaphors prove more fertile than others, have greater powers of expansion and adjustment. These survive in comparison with others and generate the relatively adequate theories.[14]

When we choose one metaphysical model or root metaphor over another, it is a matter of deciding between different conceptual schemes. We have been saying that we are involved here in the semantical dimension of

---

[12] By permission. From Stephen C. Pepper, *World Hypotheses*, University of California Press, Berkeley, 1948, p. 1.

[13] *Ibid.*, p. 41.

[14] *Ibid.*, pp. 91–92.

language's reference to "an object." But we must not conclude that this is merely a semantic or linguistic problem. We are involved as well in what there is, in *ontology*. Willard Van Orman Quine writes:

> But we must not jump to the conclusion that what there is depends on words. Translatability of a question into semantical terms is no indication that the question is linguistic. To see Naples is to bear a name which, when prefixed to the words "see Naples," yields a true sentence; still there is nothing linguistic about seeing Naples.
>
> Our acceptance of an ontology is, I think, similar in principle to our acceptance of a scientific theory, say a system of physics: we adopt, at least insofar as we are reasonable, the *simplest conceptual scheme into which the disordered fragments of raw experience can be fitted and arranged.* Our ontology is determined once we have fixed upon the over-all conceptual scheme which is to accommodate science in the broadest sense; and the considerations which determine a reasonable construction of any part of that conceptual scheme, for example, the biological or physical part, are not different in kind from the considerations which determine a reasonable construction of the whole.[15]

In this metaphysical-theological enterprise, it is the *whole* conceptual scheme which is at stake. How shall we judge its adequacy? Simplicity, as just stated, is important. But simplicity is not sufficient. In addition, two further kinds of criteria and perhaps a third are essential. One of these kinds may consist of internal criteria and includes both consistency and coherence.[16] Consistency means, within a conceptual scheme, the absence of explicit logical contradictions and is a negative criterion. "Consistency is a necessary but not a sufficient condition for the acceptance of a metaphysical system." Therefore in addition to consistency, we must look for coherence in a conceptual scheme. "Since the role of the system is to provide unity in place of conceptual fragmentation, there can be no disconnection between the fundamental principles of the system. The model chosen for the metaphysical unification of thought must not itself be fragmented or permit of exceptions."[17]

External criteria for gauging the adequacy of metaphysical schemes are applicability to experience and illuminative value. The first of these simply stresses the relevance of our theories to the world and the human situation as it is. This means the adopted scheme must in some sense be

---

[15] By permission. From Willard Van Orman Quine, *From a Logical Point of View,* Harper Torchbooks, Harper & Row, Publishers, New York, 1953, 1961, pp. 16–17.

[16] Ferré, *op. cit.,* p. 162.

[17] *Ibid.,* pp. 162–163.

open to falsification as well as to verification. This aspect of our search for tests of adequacy is precisely the problem of verification in theology. We propose to discuss it in greater detail in Chapter 10. The question persists: How do we test, verify, have some sort of objective reason to accept one conceptual scheme and reject another? As to the second of these external criteria, illuminative value, our chosen theory must somehow "light up," illuminate the human situation, show it for what it is, without distortion. It is not a narrow segment of experience which a metaphysical scheme opens up to understanding but broader areas. We seek to discover a system which interpretively illuminates the widest ranges of the human scene, possibly *all* of experience.

This is the point at which it is helpful to recall our earlier discussion of H. Richard Niebuhr's and Will Herberg's suggestions concerning sacred history. Each person has the kind of history at the core of his existence which is definitive and gives significance to all his other histories. For the Christian, this illuminative center is the revelation which brings all existence into coherence. The key models here are those of personality itself and history itself. With these, made specific in terms of those climactic events, culminating in Jesus, the Christ, and the founding of the community of the new covenant, the Christian "sees" all of existence in a new way. Thus to see, to experience, to act means not simply to entertain a theory. It means to commit oneself to a way of life. For the final criteria for adoption of a theologicometaphysical scheme may be existential, that is, involve *decision* of the whole person. Such a leap may involve practical risk and theoretical uncertainty. But in the end there may be no other way to put religious thought into action.

10

GEORGE GALLOWAY | *The Philosophy of Religion in Relation to (1) Philosophy, and (2) Theology**

It will help to give greater definiteness to our conception of a Philosophy of Religion, if we consider briefly the relation in which it stands to Philosophy and to Theology. The answer to the first question would seem at first sight to be quite simple: the Philosophy of Religion is just the application of philosophical principles and methods to religion regarded as a matter given. The speculative mind is directed to a certain aspect of experience, and reports the results of its examination. Formally this is clear enough, but in the practical working out of the problem a great deal will depend on our conception of the actual scope and powers of philosophical thought. If we maintain the possibility of a completed System of Philosophy, then we cannot concede to the Philosophy of Religion any independence of the System. Like a member of an organism, it has a well-marked place and function assigned to it, and its meaning essentially depends on its relation to the whole of which it is a part. Now it will probably be granted by most people that the aim of Philosophy is system: it seeks to rationalize, it strives to make manifest the systematic unity of the universe upon which the connexion and coherency of its elements rest. Accomplishment, however, may come short of intention; and it matters much in settling the question we have in mind whether a speculative system is an ideal, a regulative conception which we use to guide our thought, or is a realised fact. The latter, it is well known, was the belief of Hegel, though it is not likely that many thinkers in our own day would admit that Philosophy has achieved so much. Still his idea of the organic whole of the speculative sciences is of interest to us in the present connexion, for it is a profound and suggestive attempt to show the precise

* By permission. From George Galloway, *The Philosophy of Religion*, T. & T. Clark, Publishers, Edinburgh, 1922, pp. 41–53.

place which a Philosophy of Religion occupies in a fully articulated speculative System.

According to Hegel, Philosophy, in its dialectic movement or process of explicating itself, is also the explication of religion. The speculative System as well as the Philosophy of Religion has God for its object, God conceived as the Absolute. But the Philosophy of Religion differs from the other philosophical sciences in beginning with the idea of God instead of reaching it at the last: in the one case it is the *terminus a quo*, in the other the *terminus ad quem*. Again, while Philosophy treats the Absolute as primarily Logical Idea, the Philosophy of Religion regards it as object, the mind or spirit which appears or reveals itself. Religious doctrine presents the idea of the self-revealing God in the form of figurative thought: the Philosophy of Religion criticises and purifies these representations in order to raise them to the speculative form. To put the theory succinctly: the Philosophy of Religion shows that the truth of religion is the speculative Idea of God; while Philosophy shows us how the Idea or Absolute has differentiated itself in nature, in spirit, and in religion as a phase of the movement of spirit.

Without entering into detail criticism, certain general remarks suggest themselves. There is, it appears to me, an element of truth in the Hegelian conception of the relationship now under review. A Philosophy of Religion depends on Philosophy: it is the application of philosophical thought to a specific phase or stage of experience in order to determine its general meaning and value. The explanation of any aspect of experience must be governed in its methods and principles by the methods and principles by which we explain experience as a whole. The idealistic interpretation of experience, for example, carries with it as a consequence a Philosophy of Religion constructed on idealistic lines. But the assertion that Philosophy can develop a complete System which gives a full and final meaning to each of its parts, must be subjected to serious qualifications. Reality can never be entirely absorbed in the process of rationalising it, and explanation itself rests in the end on postulates that cannot be transformed into logical elements in a system. We do not comprehend a thing by bestowing a name upon it; and the constant presence of unrationalised elements makes a final System an unattained ideal. We therefore deny that Philosophy has such a mastery over its materials, that it can exhibit in the light of a system the precise meaning and value of every aspect of experience. Owing to the presence in the universe of much which is unexplained, ultimate unification cannot be other than provisional. And if this be so, we must claim for the special philosophical disciplines a greater measure of independence than was conceded to them by Hegel. For each in its way is contributing to the development of a system rather than exactly determined by it. This is apparent enough in the case of religion. There is more in the religious consciousness than can be derived from any dialectic development of consciousness in general, and religious philosophy has the facts directly before it and handles them on its own responsibility. It should deal faithfully with the many and varied phenomena of religion, whether it succeed in giving them an adequate philosophical interpretation or no. The relation of the Philosophy of Religion to Philosophy is rather one of interaction and co-operation than of complete logical dependence. In practice at all events this is so; and it cannot be otherwise, since the idea of a completed philosophical System remains an ideal.

But the claim for a certain independence on the part of a Philosophy of Religion ought not to be pressed too far. The general standpoint from which it treats experience, and the forms and conceptions it uses in dealing with religious experience, are derived from Philosophy. It cannot arbitrarily create special forms and methods for its own service; it must draw them from the common speculative inheritance that has come down from the past. The dominant Philosophy of the age supplies the principles which men apply to religion in order to develop a theory of religious experience, and it determines in a general way the character of a religious philosophy. If the prevailing type of philosophical thought at a particular period be idealistic, dualistic, or realistic, it will be reflected in the way men interpret the meaning of religion. The Deistic notion of religion, for instance, is the reflexion of a general philosophical tendency or temper of mind: so likewise, the speculative theologies and religious philosophies of the post-Kantian epoch are deeply influenced by the far-reaching idealism which prevailed. It may be added that Idealism is the form of philosophical thinking which leads most readily to a philosophy of religion, inasmuch as mind or spirit is of primary value both for idealism and religion. Materialism, on the contrary, is a form of thought which is antagonistic to religion, and when it is accepted, it leaves no room for a philosophical theory of spiritual experience. The only task left for the materialist in respect of religion would be to demonstrate that it is and and must be an illusion.

The difficulties of any attempt to isolate the Philosophy of Religion from Philosophy become plainer when we remember that the philosophical treatment of religion is not a simple process. It involves Psychology and Epistemology, Ethics and Metaphysics; and to suppose that a religious thinker can evolve principles for himself in each of these departments is absurd. In every case he is dependent on the work already done in these provinces, and this even when he tries, as he ought to do, to think things out for himself. Were he foolish enough to attempt to cut himself loose from the philosophical inheritance of his age, he could not entirely succeed in doing so. A purely religious philosophy, standing on its own ground, though it appeals to a certain type of mind, is not a workable conception; for it is not possible to dissever religious experience from other forms of experience, and in striving to understand religion it is also necessary to look beyond it.

The objection to a Philosophy of Religion which recognises a general dependence on Philosophy, has been urged from the side of Theology, and especially by theologians who are hostile to Metaphysics. The supreme truth of religion, it is held, is contained in Christianity, which is the revealed religion, and the most and best we can do is to explicate and state systematically the truths it contains. In recent times, Ritschl has given outspoken expression to this view, and has argued strongly against the intrusion of metaphysics into the sphere of religion. In his short work, *Theologie und Metaphysik* (1881), he takes his stand on Christianity as a historical revelation, and protests, not without force, against the fashion of importing into it metaphysical ideas which are alien to its substance. If men are resolved to philosophise about religion, he tells us, there is but one way to do so to any profit, and that is to set out from the Christian idea of God as scientifically valid, and to develop a world-view in dependence upon it. In other words, we cut the Philosophy of Religion clear from Philosophy by identifying it with a Philosophy of Christianity, and by developing our own religious categories and principles. This conception of a Christian Philosophy of Religion finds favour with some in our own day, and one can understand the desire for a kind of spiritual philosophy, preserving the religious interest throughout, and removed from the fluctuations of speculative opinion. Yet the conception does not appear to be tenable, and it would be hard to defend it successfully against various objections. We have already argued that it is impossible to develop a religious metaphysics which neither draws from nor depends on metaphysics in general. There is a fallacy in the notion that you can find the whole truth in any particular phase of experience, however important; and for a like reason no religion can be isolated from the rest without losing significance in consequence. It has been said that the man who knows no book but the Bible, does not even know it rightly; and it is the same with a religion. No single aspect of reality is "cut off with a hatchet" from the remainder, and to know any one thing you must see its relations to other things. Only to this large outlook do the characteristic elements in a given religion stand forth; and to understand the ethical and spiritual value of Christianity, one must recognize not merely its distinction from, but its relations to other religions. Christianity is supreme not because it is severely separate from all other types of religion, but because it is their goal and completion. Hence a Philosophy of Christianity, if it were to rise to the fulness of its task, would perforce widen out into a Philosophy of Religion. And the latter, in its turn, cannot successfully deal with religious experience in abstraction from the rest of experience. In other words, it must perform its work, recognising its relations to and receiving help from Philosophy as the universal Science. We cannot philosophise in compartments, and in the search for truth, breadth is necessary as well as concentration. The idea, then, of a Christian Philosophy of Religion which has its own form and content, while it is inspired by a sincere purpose, is not right in theory nor feasible in practice. We can either have a Christian Theology or a Philosophy of Religion, but we cannot properly combine the two. It is not possible at one and the same time to preserve the religious authority which is claimed for the one, and to maintain the freedom and largeness of vision which are demanded by the other.

We pass now to the second question, the relation in which the Philosophy of Religion stands to Theology. The two differ distinctly in their scope, and this is evident after the slightest examination. When we use the term *Philosophy of Religion,* there is no doubt about the field of study to which we refer. It is religion, as a universal phenomenon in human experience, which we are proceeding to examine. But the word *Theology,* used to denote a system of Dogmatics, is ambiguous. The further query will follow: What theology? Is it Jewish, Christian, or Mohammedan? If it be Christian, we have still to find out whether it is Roman Catholic or Protestant. The term therefore requires qualification ere we understand definitely what is meant. In its nature a theology is an articulated system of religious beliefs or doctrines which has been developed from some historic religion. In intention it is a statement of the truths which have proved themselves the working-values of a given religion: and it strives to present them in an intelligible form, so that they can be taught, and serve as a bond of union for a religious community or Church. The proper office of theology is not to criticise the religious experience out of which it grew, but rather to deal faithfully with that experience, and report what is implied in it. What is called "Speculative Theology," which seeks to raise religious doctrines to a philosophical form by exercising a free criticism upon them, is better ranked with religious philosophy.

The significance of theology in relation to religion will be better appreciated if we indicate briefly the process by which it comes to birth and develops. Theology always presupposes the existence of a living religion, and religions which have advanced to a certain stage naturally produce theological doctrines. Theology is anticipated and prepared for by tendencies, which exist in the early forms of religion. The centre of a religion is the cultus, and the primitive way of explaining the traditional acts done in the cultus is to recite myths or legends about them. This was a crude though obvious plan of imparting a kind of meaning to religious usages handed down from the immemorial past, from the days when men moved in a world of instinctive beliefs, and reflective thought had not asserted its claims. With the great development of the personal consciousness which took place after the formation of national religion the rude form of reflexion passed into a higher form, and man began to make a conscious endeavour to explain and generalise the meaning of his religious rites and customs. The cultus is still the centre which offers a relatively stable material upon which reflexion is exercised and out of which religious doctrines are fashioned: these express the meaning and value which the community attaches to its religious activity. There are various causes which stimulate theological construction in a religious society: for instance, the expediency of presenting religious truth in a shape which can be taught; the need of defining what is true in opposition to rival religions and to heretical doctrines; and, finally, the felt obligation of meeting the demands which science and philosophy have made articulate. A decadent religion will not respond to these stimuli, but a vigorous faith will meet these needs and answer these demands by developing its doctrines and connecting them in a systematic way. Primarily, religious doctrines are designed to set forth the values of religious experience; but in the higher stages of culture, theology seeks to invest religious beliefs with a degree of reasonableness. It strives to become a system whose parts cohere with and mutually support each other. From the nature of the case, theology cannot be philosophy; yet in its maturer age, when science and philosophy are exercising an influence in the world around it, theology is prompted to enlarge its scope and to broaden out in the direction of a religious philosophy. The theologian passes beyond the original view of his office, which was to report faithfully the working conceptions and values implied in a given religion. He seeks now to unfold a world-view, based on religious postulates, but for which he also claims rationality. The motives that inspired this movement are not difficult to discern: the methods of explanation used in science and philosophy could not be altogether ignored by the theologian. Hence we find theology offering explanations of the nature of God, the creation and development of the world, and the origin of man. Doctrines bearing on these themes have entered into the structure of Christian Dogmatics, and have been embodied in the creeds of all the Christian Churches. When we consider the way in which theology was developed on these lines, we recognise that, in intention at least, it occupies a mediating position between faith on the one hand and reason on the other. Beginning with an explication of faith-experiences, it ends by offering what purports to be a rational view of the world. In this latter aspect of its development, however, Christian theology has become entangled in controversy, and has had to bear the brunt of criticism. Theology has failed to advance with scientific and philosophical culture, and in consequence its doctrines on the nature and origin of the world and man have fallen out of harmony with the knowledge of the age. Hence the so-called conflict between Science and Religion, about which so much was heard in the middle of the last century. The dispute, when closely examined, was seen to gather round doctrines which theology had pushed forward under the shield of religious authority, but which really fell within the province of science. A dispute of the kind could only end in one way; theologians have been forced to resile from untenable positions, though time has shown the issues at stake were greatly magnified.

The controversy to which I have referred draws attention to a difficulty which attends an endeavour on the part of theology to mediate between faith and reason. The difficulty arises from presuppositions from which Christian theology set out in forming its doctrinal system. The Sacred Writings, it assumed, were an authoritative basis, and the truths which could be gathered from them were divinely sanctioned, and provided an assured ground for inference. The appeal in this instance was not to a continuous spiritual experience which could be examined, but to statements in documents of very different dates and character. When theology, therefore, building on statements taken as authoritative, proceeded to develop doctrines for which the claim of rationality was made, the position became insecure. The scientist refused to admit some of the premises from which the theologian set out: the latter retorted by declaring he took his stand on truths divinely revealed. The awkwardness of the theologian's position resulted from the double method he had employed: on the one hand claiming *rationality* for his doctrines, and on the other repelling criticism by an appeal to *authority*. He laid himself open to the objection that he ought to employ one method or the other, for it was impossible to use both consistently. And it must be granted that many of the difficulties which have beset theology in modern times are the result of an attempt to fuse together methods and principles which will not naturally blend. This remark applies to Protestant as well as to Roman Catholic theology.

If theology is to enter into some kind of organic relation with a Philosophy of Religion, and to prove a connecting link between faith and reason, the principle of authority which it invokes should be wider and more convincing than documentary evidences. In the end, the ground of authority must be the character of the spiritual experience itself, with the historic values which have grown out of it, and the faith which is its living expression. The degree of authority which attaches to Sacred Books is secondary and derivative: it depends upon the purity and fulness of the spiritual experience they embody and the worth they possess for the religious life. The authority of Christian theology centres in the intrinsic superiority of the spiritual values which it sets forth—values not for one age merely, but for every age.

It is not consistent to maintain that the sole sources for authoritative theological doctrines are spiritual, and yet to say they are limited to certain inspired periods and spiritual movements which lie in the distant past. And this not because such periods do not possess a supreme value for the religious development of man, but because every attempt by a later age to generalise the religious meaning of these great movements must be influenced by its own life and culture. Thus successive epochs of Christian history show us the Christian Church of the time reading, unconsciously often yet none the less really, its own temper and ideals into the primitive record of the origins of our faith. So it is that the Present steadily contributes, albeit without observation, to the meaning and value of the Past. Ignoring this truth, theologians imagined they could express the meaning of religion in doctrinal forms which would be valid for all time, and would serve from generation to generation as the authoritative embodiment of the Church's faith. Still fettered by these prejudices, theology in modern times has progressed with difficulty, and the modern religious consciousness is finding it increasingly hard to take the ecclesiastical creeds for the expression of its own meaning and aspirations. The Philosophy of Religion has thus to some extent displaced the older Dogmatics in the regard of thoughtful people, and in the circumstances the relations between it and ecclesiastical Theology are somewhat strained. Nor is it likely they will be different until theology renounces the claim to finality and frankly accepts the principle of doctrinal development.

It may be well to say at this point, that philosophy need have no quarrel with theology because the latter accepts postulates of faith made on grounds of value. The Christian experience, of which theology is the explication, ultimately rests on truths which are held on the assurance of faith, not on logical demonstration. No rational deduction, for instance, can give for its conclusion the Christian idea of God: faith makes it real, not logical proof. In view of the stress philosophy lays on the principle of rationality, it might seem that the presuppositions of theology were unfavourable to any close relation on its part with a Philosophy of Religion. This is true, no doubt, if the theologian takes faith in the narrow sense of beliefs held upon authority: it is not the case if he sets out from postulates of the religious life. Faith, conceived as postulates or demand which our inner life makes on the world, is by no means limited in its operation to religion. It pervades practical life, and neither science nor philosophy can dispense with it. The process of rationalising is never complete, and the exercise of reason rests in the last resort on postulates which cannot be rationally deduced. In this respect the difference between theology and religious philosophy is one of degree only: the one lays greater stress on faith, the other on reason; but reason cannot work without faith, and faith has its proper ally in reason.

The conclusions we draw may now be brieflly stated. Theology is and must remain the exposition of the doctrines of a definite and historic religion. The principle of authority to which it appeals must not be external, but the enduring spiritual experience of which the religion is the practical and institutional expression. That experience, however, ought not to be arbitrarily limited to a particular epoch: it should not be conceived to begin at one point in history and to end at another. In other words, the theologian must take his stand on the development of religious experience, and he must abandon the idea that theological doctrines can assume a stereotyped and final form. This is only to give its due scope to the principle of the spirit leading the spiritually minded into fuller truth. But while thus enlarging its idea of experience, theology ought to abstain from excursions into the domain of metaphysics. It will not be denied that a good deal of metaphysics has found its way into Christian theology, and some of it, to say the least, is of questionable value. The objection to this intrusion is that theology is going beyond its legitimate sphere in developing metaphysical theories, for they stand in no direct and vital relation to the religious experience and the spiritual values of the religious life. Authority is not to be claimed for them, inasmuch as they cannot invoke the principle which alone would invest them with authority, the witness of spiritual experience. This is far from saying that religion ought not to be brought into contact with metaphysics at all; but it does mean that theology is not the proper science to deal with the meta-

physical issues involved. Theology may be well content to leave the speculative problems of religion unanswered, and to hand them over for solution, if a solution be possible, to the Philosophy of Religion. The latter
in virtue of its larger outlook is in a better position to deal with them;
and so the religious philosopher comes in to complete the work of the
theologian. The latter in consequence of the definitely limited task before
him should be satisfied to allow others to handle the ultimate metaphysical
problems connected with religion. Yet it is impossible for man, rationally
constituted as he is, to set these problems aside, or to acquiesce in treating
them as insoluble. And the growing importance of the Philosophy of
Religion in the present day is partly due to the knowledge that it occupies
ground on which the full and free discussion of these topics of perennial
interest may properly take place.

In practice, it may be granted, it will sometimes be difficult to keep
theology strictly apart from a Philosophy of Religion. For they deal with
the same materials, and the exposition of the meaning of a theological
dogma passes easily into a philosophical interpretation of it. And for the
theologian who has no antipathy to metaphysics, the temptation to develop a speculative theory is not readily to be resisted. Nor will any harm
ensue, provided his speculations are put forward as speculations, not as
theological doctrines. What must be deprecated is an unwitting confusion
of the two points of view. Hence it is right to insist that any speculative
treatment of theological doctrines really belongs to the province of religious philosophy, and must be judged as such.

WILLIAM TEMPLE | *The Tension between Philosophy and Religion**

The main type of that tension, then, which we have now to consider, is not caused by particular doctrines either of Religion or of Philosophy, but consists in a sharp difference in mental habit and outlook with reference to the same objects of attention. This may be briefly expressed by saying that *the primary assurances of Religion are the ultimate questions of Philosophy*. Religion finds its fullest expression in absolute surrender to the Object of its worship. But the very existence of that Object is a main theme of philosophical disputation. It is not possible to surrender one's self to what is felt to be an unverified hypothesis; it is not possible to discuss impartially the existence of a Being to whom one is utterly self-surrendered. How then can a religious person be a true philosopher? Or how can a philosopher who has not yet solved the problems of existence permit himself the exercise of religion? And if he do not permit himself this exercise, how can he know Religion from within in such a fashion as to qualify himself to pronounce upon its validity and to place it rightly within, or exclude it justly from, his ultimate construction?

That these are grave questions no one who has seriously attempted to combine the two activities is likely to deny. Yet the difficulties are not insuperable in principle, and it seems to be the special duty of some persons at least to engage in the enterprise of overcoming them.

The divergence of view is specially evident in relation to three central convictions of Religion in its higher forms. These are perhaps different expressions of one truth, but as expressions of it they differ, and it is well to state them separately:

First is the conviction that Spirit is a true source of initiation of processes—a real $\overset{\backprime}{\alpha}\rho\chi\acute{\eta}$, a *vera causa;*

* By permission of Mrs. William Temple. From William Temple, *Nature, Man and God*, Macmillan & Co., Ltd., and St. Martin's Press, London; The Macmillan Co., New York, 1934, pp. 34–39, 44–45, 51–56.

Second is the conviction that all existence finds its source ($\overset{\text{'}}{\alpha}\rho\chi\acute{\eta}$, *vera causa*) in a Supreme Reality of which the nature is Spirit;

Third is the conviction that between that Spirit and ourselves there can be, and to some extent already is, true fellowship, at least such as is involved in our conscious dependence on that Spirit.

The first of these convictions is, as stated, little more than the denial of materialism; but this denial carries positive implications of momentous import. The true nature of spiritual freedom must occupy our attention later, but some aspects of it concern us now. If it were true that by inspection of the Nebula, from which our solar system formed itself, an intelligence of sufficient scope could have predicted all the acts of moral choice that would ever be made by human beings living on this planet, then the whole aspiration and endeavour of Religion would be dismissible as part of the phantasmagoria of a consciousness which emerged only to take note of, never to direct, the process in which it was a transient and ineffectual episode.

Now the sense of the inherent determinism of the physical system, including our bodily organisms, is so strong that some great religions have to a certain extent made terms with it. The Hindu doctrine of Maya is such a compromise. It expresses despair of the spiritual domination of matter; but in order to safeguard both the reality and the supremacy of spirit, it dismisses the material as illusory; the great aim of life which it proposes, is to be delivered from the Wheel of Change (the figure of materialistic Determinism) so that the spiritual reality may exist in its own freedom. This attempt altogether to exclude matter from reality issues in a curiously uncontrolled empire of matter, so that Hinduism, which finds expression in some of the loftiest spiritual philosophy of the world, also makes room for obscenity in connexion with worship itself. You cannot regulate what you do not recognise. If matter is so unreal that spirit, which is real, has neither need for it nor control of it, then in its own sphere it will make havoc. The way to be spiritually effective is not to ignore matter but to use it.

Yet to deny the reality of matter in order to assert that of spirit is less disastrous to Religion than to let the spiritual be swallowed up in the material, as the West is always liable to do. The assertion of the reality and independence of Spirit in the Universe and in Man is a primary necessity for Religion. In the case of Man we may, for the moment, put this at the very lowest and be content to say that the causal process, as it affects human conduct, passes through consciousness and is modified by this passage. If preferred, the same thought may be expressed by saying that, attention having been attracted to the causal process, volition intervenes as an additional determinant of the result. The main point is that consciousness does affect the result, but this does not make the process leading to it other than causal, so that human beings act differently because they are conscious and self-conscious from the way in which they (or rather their bodies) would act if they had no consciousness and self-consciousness.

But while this alone is enough to break the chain of sheer materialistic Determinism, much more is required for the assertion that the Ultimate Ground of the Universe and all things in it is spiritual. This is a claim, not only for the independence of Spirit, but for the universal supremacy of Spirit. It is the claim that Spirit is not only *a* source of initiation, one among others, but is the only ultimate source of the whole World process. All the more developed religions, which do not deny the reality of matter, have advanced this claim. It is the doctrine of Creation. It is not of direct importance to Religion to assert a date for the act of Creation, or even to assert that it is an act having any date at all; it may be a never-beginning and never-ending activity. But it is of vital importance to Religion to assert that the existence of the world is due to the Will of God. This is the essential notion of Creation, and Religion dare not let it go, unless it is prepared to deny the real existence of the material world. For the only remaining alternative is the acceptance of limitation in the conception of the Supreme Spirit, not only in the sense of an actual finitude which none the less includes or controls all existence, but in the sense of leaving some part of eixstence outside its control. Such a dualism would be repudiated by Philosophy, which cannot rest in a multiplicity or duality of ultimate principles; and it is entirely fatal to Religion, because to a limited authority only a limited allegiance is due, and absoluteness of allegiance is the very life-breath of Religion.[1]

But this claim to absolute allegiance is one which Philosophy must investigate. Enquiry must be made into its precise meaning, and then into the relation of the claim so interpreted to the facts of common experience. If, for example, it is meant that all things exist only in dependence upon the Will of a Spiritual Being who is good and wise in the ordinary sense of those words, then there is a great deal of experience which cannot be treated as unreal and yet is very hard to appreciate as illustrating the goodness and wisdom of its Author. This is, of course, the familiar prob-

---

[1] Of course this does not mean that no one may properly be called religious who has not in practice attained to this absoluteness of allegiance; but it is essential to Religion in all its higher phases that the worshipper should regard his Deity as entitled to such allegiance and himself as under obligation to render it.

lem of Evil, which becomes acute in exact correspondence with the moral sensitiveness of the mind reflecting on it. A mind of low moral sensitiveness may be little troubled by this problem, for it will have a less exalted conception of the divine goodness, and will also be less afflicted by the evil elements in experience. As sensitiveness to moral issues develops, bewilderment before the problem of Evil deepens. It has found no more passionate expression than that given to it in many of the Hebrew Psalms.

That fact alone is sufficient evidence that this problem is not the creation of an alien criticism, but arises out of the heart of religious faith itself. Yet it is inevitable that when rationalising criticism sets to work, it should intensify the perplexity of religous people by seeming to exploit it in a hostile manner. For the aim of the religious person is to stabilise and deepen his faith; the aim of the philosopher is to understand, to "follow the argument wherever it leads," and to regard nothing as assured which is not supported by sufficient evidence. Between these two there is manifest tension; but no one is so intimately aware of that tension as a person who tries wholeheartedly to play both rôles at once. . . .

This reflection leads to a new consideration. The difference between Religion and scientific Philosophy[2] in relation to the Object of attention is not only one of temper but also one of method. The latter results from the former. In temper the attitude of Religion is that of assurance; the attitude of Philosophy is that of enquiry. It is hard enough to combine these, and probably it can only be done by deliberate alternation. But to combine the resultant methods is harder still. Religion, of which the essence is assurance of fellowship with, or at least of dependence on, the Supreme Spirit, and therefore also of the existence of that Supreme Spirit, necessarily makes its start from that point, and, so far as it enters on the field of Philosophy, seeks to offer explanations of the facts of experience by reference to the character of the Supreme Spirit. This is Theological Philosophy, and I had better here confess my belief that it is in the end the only Philosophy which has any hope of being altogether satisfactory. But it is also most hazardous, and is certain to lead the mind that follows it into all manner of fantasies unless it is constantly checked by a purely critical Philosophy which makes its approach from the other end. In the Middle Ages the course was clear for Theological Philosophy, and the

---

[2] By the phrase "scientific Philosophy" I mean any philosophy which takes its start from the departmental sciences, ranging from Physics to Epistemology or Ethics, as distinct from a philosophy which takes its start from the deliverances of religious experience as formulated by Theology. Wherever I speak of "Philosophy" without any epithet it is to be understood as "scientific Philosophy" in this sense. Of course Theological Philosophy is no less scientific than this in its own procedure.

wonder is that it avoided the fantastic as much as it did; yet that element is present in it in sufficient quantity to show the danger.

Theology, which is the science of Religion, starts from the Supreme Spirit and explains the world by reference to Him. Philosophy starts from the detailed experience of men, and seeks to build up its understanding of that experience by reference to that experience alone. Its inevitable and wholesome kinship to Science inclines it to account for everything by the "lowest" category that will in fact account for it; Theology begins with the "highest" category of all and fits in the "lower" categories in the most orderly hierarchy that it can devise in subordination to that "highest" principle. And this difference is inevitable, though it has been exaggerated by the dominant tendencies of European thought from the time of Descartes onwards. With that exaggeration, its causes, and the way to correct it, we shall be concerned in later lectures. Our present concern is with the difference itself, which would still exist if there were no exaggeration at all. The source of the method of Theological Philosophy in the nature of Religion itself has already been made clear. But the method of critical Philosophy is equally inevitable. . . .

The inevitability of tension between Religion and Science of the Philosophy which is in line with the scientific impulse is now clear. The method of Natural Theology no doubt requires ideally that the validity of Religion itself should be established before we consider, even cursorily, how this tension may be relieved. For if one of the two parties to it has no real right to exist, the tension is only to be properly relieved by the abolition of that party. Yet for purposes of exposition it is convenient to deal with this whole question of tension together, and the principles to be observed with a view to reconciliation are easily stated, though their detailed application is difficult enough.

First, then, the adherents of Religion must be ready to distinguish between the elements of expression of their faith which are of real spiritual importance, and those which have come to have sentimental value through association with the former. They will not be agreed among themselves about this distinction with regard to any point which is newly called in question. Some will be specially eager to say the point does not matter, so as to avoid the spiritual loss always involved in the tension between Religion and Science; these will be called Latitudinarians or Modernists, according to the fashion of the day; they will usually have intellectual clarity but little spiritual *élan*. Others will hold on till the last possible minute to every questioned phrase, lest what is lost be not only of sentimental but also of spiritual value. These will be called Traditionalists or Obscurantists; they will often have great spiritual force, and often, too, great learning, but as a rule, little intellectual enterprise. Between these two there will be others representing every possible gradation. But all may be loyal to the principle just stated, and may fulfill various necessary parts in winning for it a justly discriminating application. What must be excluded, and is very hard to exclude, is the element of purely personal sentiment. To cling to some belief, when it appears to have no inherent spiritual value and to be discredited by scientific advance, on the ground that it is bound up with what has spiritual value by ties of mere association, is a form of self-assertion which must be condemned by Science and Religion alike. But the nature of spiritual value is such that it is very hard to distinguish between it and personal attachment so that great sympathy is due to those who are perplexed by the need of making such a distinction at all.

The requirements to be made of scientific enquirers are different, though these too are largely various forms of the demand to avoid all self-assertion. Two are perhaps the most important. First it is to be remembered that Science, in following its method of using the "lowest" category applicable, is not entitled to deny the applicability of "higher" categories but is only seeing how far it can go without them. Even if it can cover all the facts and hold them togther by means of "lower," as for instance mechanical, categories, it does not necessarily follow that the "higher" categories, such as purpose, have no rightful application at all. Indeed, while an actual machine is an entity of which the unifying principle is mechanical, the natural inference from its existence is that a living intelligence designed and constructed it.[3] And if that is true of a steam-engine, it is hard to see why it should not be true of the stellar system or of the cosmos generally. It would be hard to refute the argument which urges that the more perfect the universe is in itself as mechanism, the more forcibly does it suggest an intelligent Creator as its cause. But this carries us past the main point, which is that the positive work of Science, in giving an account of observable facts by its own method, never justifies Science in proceeding to negative inferences concerning other methods of interpretation, provided that these in their turn do not exclude the method of Science.

Secondly, it is to be remembered that there are spheres in which the most characteristic methods of Science are inapplicable. This is true in

---

[3] I.e. "living" when it so designed and constructed. All arguments of this type are open to Hume's devastating suggestions in the *Dialogue* of which the following may be quoted: "This world, for aught (any man) knows, is very faulty and imperfect compared to a superior standard; and was only the first rude essay of some infant deity, who afterwards abandoned it, ashamed of his lame performance."

varying degrees of Ethics and of Art. Our appreciation of Right and Good is independent of argument and experiment. These may certainly affect our estimate of various actions or relationships; we may be persuaded that an action or a social order which we had thought good was in truth bad. But this never touches the ultimate objects of moral judgement. If a man tells me that he finds indulgence in cruelty one of the best things in life, I may try to make him contradict himself, as Socrates did with Callicles in a similar connexion,[4] and so show that he did not really mean what he was saying; or I may try to have him shut up in a prison or an asylum; but I cannot directly attack his proposition by argument. "Our sense of value, and in the end for every man his own sense of value, is ultimate and final."[5]

The realm of Art offers an illustration as clear as that of Ethics. In these days when our minds are chiefly influenced by scientific activity people are often inclined to say that they cannot believe where they have no proof; or at least they demand a balance of probability calculated by formulable laws of evidence. Yet they will without hesitation affirm and even passionately insist on (say) the superiority of Schubert to Mendelssohn, though it would puzzle them to prove it or show it to be manifestly probable.

But it is in personal relationships that the inadequacy of Science is most manifest. We should not recommend a pair of lovers to test the advisability of marriage by making each a psychological analysis of the other. We even use the word "understand" with a different sense in relation to other persons from that which it bears in relation to impersonal objects. To "understand" a person is to have that insight into his character and motives which is another aspect of what is also called sympathy. A wise scientist does not follow only scientific methods, as these are commonly understood, in choosing his wife or expressing his affection for his children.

The heart of Religion is not an opinion about God, such as Philosophy might reach as the conclusion of its argument; it is a personal relationship with God. Its closest analogy is not found in our study of astronomy or any other science, but in our relation to a person whom we trust and love. If Science is not the best of aids in helping the child to determine his relation to his father, no more is it—still less is it—the best of aids in determining the relation of a man to his God.

We have seen that tension between Philosophy and Religion is inevitable; and as both are here assumed to have a rightful place in life,

[4] Plato, *Gorgias*, 494–495.
[5] F. H. Bradley, *Essays on Truth and Reality*, p. 132.

this tension must even be regarded as good. We have seen ways in which it may be alleviated, through the recollection by the adherents of each, what is the real nature and concern of that activity to which they are committed. We may reasonably hope to find here the grounds for an ultimate reconciliation in principle; but that can only be when each is perfect in its own kind. Till then the tension will remain, to the special bewilderment of those who are conscious of an obligation to be loyal to both at once. Yet these may hope that through their travail the progress towards ultimate reconciliation is being made.

Prof. A. Wolf ends his admirable chapter on "Recent and Contemporary Philosophy" in *An Outline of Modern Knowledge* with a warning against the dangers involved in ". . . the unusually friendly relationship which is loudly proclaimed to exist now between science and the Churches"; and he adds this paragraph:

> Contemporary philosophy likewise seems to stand in need of an analogous warning. Considering the fact that so many philosophers were formerly students of theology, the relations between philosophy and theology are naturally expected to be friendly. Among British philosophers, indeed, the number of defenders of the faith seems to be abnormally large. It may be that academic conditions, and institutions like the Gifford Trust, either encourage this tendency or give undue prominence to those who follow it. But philosophy will be in a healthier condition when it has entirely ceased to be a handmaid to theology, and pursues its cosmic problems as independently as possible of vested interests.[6]

Prof. Wolf is more concerned with the welfare of Philosophy; I am, no doubt, more concerned with the welfare of Religion. Consequently my phraseology would differ from his. Yet I agree with him in substance. There not only is, but there ought to be, a tension between Philosophy and Religion. That tension is only relaxed when one of the two assimilates itself excessively to the other. The present atmosphere of friendliness may blunt the edge of philosophic criticism because there is an unwillingness to wound the feelings of religious people; it may also lead Religion to tone down its note of Authority because it does not wish to antagonise its philosophic friends. But the tension is not to be regretted; it is right in principle and stimulating in effect. And it can be delivered from the danger of doing harm if both parties respect the principle of Justice— τὸ τὰ αὑτοῦ πράττειν. But let no one suppose that this principle is as easy to practice as it is to enunciate.

---

[6] *Op. cit.,* p. 592.

PAUL TILLICH | *Theology and Philosophy:*
*A Question**

Theology claims that it constitutes a special realm of knowledge, that it deals with a special object and employs a special method. This claim places the theologian under the obligation of giving an account of the way in which he relates theology to other forms of knowledge. He must answer two questions: What is the relationship of theology to the special sciences (*Wissenschaften*) and what is its relationship to philosophy? The first question has been answered implicitly by the preceding statement of the formal criteria of theology. If nothing is an object of theology which does not concern us ultimately, theology is unconcerned about scientific procedures and results and vice versa. Theology has no right and no obligation to prejudice a physical or historical, sociological or psychological, inquiry. And no result of such an inquiry can be directly productive or disastrous for theology. The point of contact between scientific research and theology lies in the philosophical element of both, the sciences and theology. Therefore, the question of the relation of theology to the special sciences merges into the question of the relation between theology and philosophy.

The difficulty of this question lies partly in the fact that there is no generally accepted definition of philosophy. Every philosophy proposes a definition which agrees with the interest, purpose, and method of the philosopher. Under these circumstances the theologian can only suggest a definition of philosophy which is broad enough to cover most of the important philosophies which have appeared in what usually is called the history of philosophy. The suggestion made here is to call philosophy *that cognitive approach to reality in which reality as such is the object.* Reality as such, or reality as a whole, is not the whole of reality; it is the structure which makes reality a whole and therefore a potential object of knowl-

* By permission. From Paul Tillich, *Systematic Theology,* The University of Chicago Press, Chicago, 1951, vol. I, pp. 18–28.

edge. Inquiring into the nature of reality as such means inquiring into those structures, categories, and concepts which are presupposed in the cognitive encounter with every realm of reality. From this point of view philosophy is by definition critical. It separates the multifarious materials of experience from those structures which make experience possible. There is no difference in this respect between constructive idealism and empirical realism. The question regarding the character of the general structures that make experience possible is always the same. It is *the* philosophical question.

The critical definition of philosophy is more modest than those philosophical enterprises which try to present a complete system of reality, including the results of all the special sciences as well as the general structures of pre-scientific experience. Such an attempt can be made from "above" or from "below." Hegel worked from "above" when he filled the categorical forms, developed in his *Logic,* with the available material of the scientific knowledge of his time and adjusted the material to the categories. Wundt worked from "below" when he abstracted general and metaphysical principles from the available scientific material of his time, with the help of which the entire sum of empirical knowledge could be organized. Aristotle worked from both "above" and "below" when he carried through metaphysical and scientific studies in interdependence. This also was the ideal of Leibniz when he sketched a universal calculus capable of subjecting all of reality to mathematical analysis and synthesis. But in all these cases the limits of the human mind, the finitude which prevents it from grasping the whole, became visible. No sooner was the system finished than scientific research trespassed its boundaries and disrupted it in all directions. Only the general principles were left, always discussed, questioned, changed, but never destroyed, shining through the centuries, reinterpreted by every generation, inexhaustible, never antiquated or obsolete. These principles are the material of philosophy.

This understanding of philosophy is, on the other hand, less modest than the attempt to reduce philosophy to epistemology and ethics, which was the goal of the Neo-Kantian and related schools in the nineteenth century, and less modest also than the attempt to reduce it to logical calculus, which has been the goal of logical positivism and related schools in the twentieth century. Both attempts to avoid the ontological question have been unsuccessful. The later adherents of the Neo-Kantian philosophy recognised that every epistemology contains an implicit ontology. It cannot be otherwise. Since knowing is an act which participates in being or, more precisely, in an "ontic relation," every analysis of the act of knowing must refer to an interpretation of being (cf. Nicolai Hartmann).

At the same time the problem of values pointed toward an ontological foundation of the validity of value-judgments. If values have no *fundamentum in re* (cf. Plato's identification of the good with the essential structures, the ideas of being), they float in the air of a transcendent validity, or else they are subjected to pragmatic tests which are arbitrary and accidental unless they introduce an ontology of essences surreptitiously. It is not necessary to discuss the pragmatic-naturalistic line of philosophical thought, for, in spite of the antimetaphysical statements of some of its adherents, it has expressed itself in definite ontological terms such as life, growth, process, experience, being (understood in an all-embracing sense), etc. But it is necessary to compare the ontological definition of philosophy, suggested above, with the radical attempts to reduce philosophy to scientific logic. The question is whether the elimination of almost all traditional philosophical problems by logical positivism is a successful escape from ontology. One's first reaction is the feeling that such an attitude pays too high a price, namely, the price of making philosophy irrelevant. But, beyond this impression, the following argument can be put forward. If the restriction of philosophy to the logic of the sciences is a matter of taste, it need not be taken seriously. If it is based on an analysis of the limits of human knowledge, it is based, like every epistemology, on ontological assumptions. There is always at least one problem about which logical positivism, like all semantic philosophies, must make a decision. What is the relation of signs, symbols, or logical operations to reality? Every answer to this question says something about the structure of being. It is ontological. And a philosophy which is so radically critical of all other philosophies should be sufficiently self-critical to see and to reveal its own ontological assumptions.

Philosophy asks the question of reality as a whole; it asks the question of the structure of being. And it answers in terms of categories, structural laws, and universal concepts. It must answer in ontological terms. Ontology is not a speculative-fantastic attempt to establish a world behind the world; it is an analysis of those structures of being which we encounter in every meeting with reality. This was also the original meaning of metaphysics; but the preposition *meta* now has the irremediable connotation of pointing to a duplication of this world by a transcendent realm of beings. Therefore, it is perhaps less misleading to speak of ontology instead of metaphysics.

Philosophy necessarily asks the question of reality as a whole, the question of the structure of being. Theology necessarily asks the same question, for that which concerns us ultimately must belong to reality as a whole; it must belong to being. Otherwise we could not encounter it, and it could not concern us. Of course, it cannot be one being among others; then it would not concern us infinitely. It must be the ground of our being, that which determines our being or not-being, the ultimate and unconditional power of being. But the power of being, its infinite ground or "being-itself," expresses itself in and through the structure of being. Therefore, we can encounter it, be grasped by it, know it, and act toward it. Theology, when dealing with our ultimate concern, presupposes in every sentence the structure of being, its categories, laws, and concepts. Theology, therefore, cannot escape the question of being any more easily than can philosophy. The attempt of biblicism to avoid nonbiblical, ontological terms is doomed to failure as surely as are the corresponding philosophical attempts. The Bible itself always uses the categories and concepts which describe the structure of experience. On every page of every religious or theological text these concepts appear: time, space, cause, thing, subject, nature, movement, freedom, necessity, life, value, knowledge, experience, being, and not-being. Biblicism may try to preserve their popular meaning, but then it ceases to be theology. It must neglect the fact that a philosophical understanding of these categories has influenced ordinary language for many centuries. It is surprising how casually theological biblicists use a term like "history" when speaking of Christianity as a historical religion or of God as the "Lord of history." They forget that the meaning they connect with the word "history" has been formed by thousands of years of historiography and philosophy of history. They forget that historical being is one kind of being in addition to others and that, in order to distinguish it from the word "nature," for instance, a general vision of the structure of being is presupposed. They forget that the problem of history is tied up with the problems of time, freedom, accident, purpose, etc., and that each of these concepts has had a development similar to the concept of history. The theologian must take seriously the meaning of the terms he uses. They must be known to him in the whole depth and breadth of their meaning. Therefore, the systematic theologian must be a philosopher in critical understanding even if not in creative power.

The structure of being and the categories and concepts describing this structure are an implicit concern of every philosopher and of every theologian. Neither of them can avoid the ontological question. Attempts from both sides to avoid it have proved abortive. If this is the situation, the question becomes the more urgent: What is the relation between the ontological question asked by the philosopher and the ontological question asked by the theologian?

THEOLOGY AND PHILOSOPHY: AN ANSWER

Philosophy and theology ask the question of being. But they ask it from different perspectives. Philosophy deals with the structure of being in itself; theology deals with the meaning of being for us. From this difference convergent and divergent trends emerge in the relation of theology and philosophy.

The first point of divergence is a difference in the cognitive attitude of the philosopher and the theologian. Although driven by the philosophical *erōs,* the philosopher tries to maintain a detached objectivity toward being and its structures. He tries to exclude the personal, social, and historical conditions which might distort an objective vision of reality. His passion is the passion for a truth which is open to general approach, subject to general criticism, changeable in accordance with every new insight, open and communicable. In all these respects he feels no different from the scientist, historian, psychologist, etc. He collaborates with them. The material for his critical analysis is largely supplied by empirical research. Just as all sciences have their origin in philosophy, so they contribute in turn to philosophy by giving to the philosopher new and exactly defined material far beyond anything he could get from a pre-scientific approach to reality. Of course, the philosopher, as a philosopher, neither criticises nor augments the knowledge provided by the sciences. This knowledge forms the basis of his description of the categories, structural laws, and concepts which constitute the structure of being. In this respect the philosopher is as dependent on the scientist as he is dependent on his own pre-scientific observation of reality—often more dependent. This relation to the sciences (in the broad sense of *Wissenschaften*) strengthens the detached, objective attitude of the philosopher. Even in the intuitive-synthetic side of his procedure he tries to exclude influences which are not purely determined by his object.

The theologian, quite differently, is not detached from his object but is involved in it. He looks at his object (which transcends the character of being an object) with passion, fear, and love. This is not the *erōs* of the philosopher or his passion for objective truth; it is the love which accepts saving, and therefore personal, truth. The basic attitude of the theologian is commitment to the content he expounds. Detachment would be a denial of the very nature of this content. The attitude of the theologian is "existential." He is involved—with the whole of his existence, with his finitude and his anxiety, with his self-contradictions and his despair, with the healing forces in him and in his social situation. Every theological statement derives its seriousness from these elements of existence. The theologian, in short, is determined by his faith. Every theology presupposes that the theologian is in the theological circle. This contradicts the open, infinite, and changeable character of philosophical truth. It also differs from the way in which the philosopher is dependent on scientific research. The theologian has no direct relation to the scientist (including the historian, sociologist, psychologist). He deals with him only in so far as philosophical implications are at stake. If he abandons the existential attitude, as some of the "empirical" theologians have done, he is driven to statements the reality of which will not be acknowledged by anybody who does not share the existential presuppositions of the assumedly empirical theologian. Theology is necessarily existential, and no theology can escape the theological circle.

The second point of divergence between the theologian and the philosopher is the difference in their sources. The philosopher looks at the whole of reality to discover within it the structure of reality as a whole. He tries to penetrate into structures of being by means of the power of his cognitive function and its structures. He assumes—and science continuously confirms this assumption—that there is an identity, or at least an analogy, between objective and subjective reason, between the *logos* of reality as a whole and the *logos* working in him. Therefore, this *logos is* common; every reasonable being participates in it, uses it in asking questions and criticising the answers received. There is no particular place to discover the structure of being; there is no particular place to stand to discover the categories of experience. The place to look is all places; the place to stand is no place at all; it is pure reason.

The theologian, on the other hand, must look where that which concerns him ultimately is manifest, and he must stand where its manifestation reaches and grasps him. The source of his knowledge is not the universal *logos* but the Logos "who became flesh," that is, the *logos* manifesting itself in a particular historical event. And the medium through which he receives the manifestation of the *logos* is not common rationality but the church, its traditions, and its present reality. He speaks in the church about the foundation of the church. And he speaks because he is grasped by the power of his foundation and by the community built upon it. The concrete *logos* which he sees is received through believing commitment and not, like the universal *logos* at which the philosopher looks, through rational detachment.

The third point of divergence between philosophy and theology is the difference in their content. Even when they speak about the same object they speak about something different. The philosopher deals with the categories of being in relation to the material which is structured by them. He deals with causality as it appears in physics or psychology; he analyses biological or historical time; he discusses astronomical as well as microcosmic space. He describes the epistemological subject and the relation of person and community. He presents the characteristics of life and spirit in their dependence on, and independence of, each other. He defines nature and history in their mutual limits and tries to penetrate into ontology and logic of being and nonbeing. Innumerable other examples could be given. They all reflect the cosmological structure of the philosophical assertions. The theologian, on the other hand, relates the same categories and concepts to the quest for a "new being." His assertions have a soteriological character. He discusses causality in relation to a *prima causa*, the ground of the whole series of causes and effects; he deals with time in relation to eternity, with space in relation to man's existential homelessness. He speaks of the self-estrangement of the subject, about the spiritual center of personal life, and about community as a possible embodiment of the "New Being." He relates the structures of life to the creative ground of life and the structures of spirit to the divine Spirit. He speaks of the participation of nature in the "history of salvation," about the victory of being over nonbeing. Here also the examples could be increased indefinitely; they show the sharp divergence of theology from philosophy with respect to their content.

The divergence between philosophy and theology is counterbalanced by an equally obvious convergence. From both sides converging trends are at work. The philosopher, like the theologian, "exists," and he cannot jump over the concreteness of his existence and his implicit theology. He is conditioned by his psychological, sociological, and historical situation. And, like every human being, he exists in the power of an ultimate concern, whether or not he is fully conscious of it, whether or not he admits it to himself and to others. There is no reason why even the most scientific philosopher should not admit it, for without an ultimate concern his philosophy would be lacking in passion, seriousness, and creativity. Wherever we look in the history of philosophy, we find ideas and systems which claim to be ultimately relevant for human existence. Occasionally the philosophy of religion openly expresses the ultimate concern behind a system. More often it is the character of the ontological principles, or a special section of a system, such as epistemology, philosophy of nature, politics and ethics, philosophy of history, etc., which is most revealing for the discovery of the ultimate concern and the hidden theology within it. Every creative philosopher is a hidden theologian (sometimes even a declared theologian). He is a theologian in the degree to which his existential situation and his ultimate concern shape his philosophical vision.

He is a theologian in the degree to which his intuition of the universal *logos* of the structure of reality as a whole is formed by a particular *logos* which appears to him as his particular place and reveals to him the meaning of the whole. And he is a theologian in the degree to which the particular *logos* is a matter of active commitment within a special community. There is hardly a historically significant philosopher who does not show these marks of a theologian. But the philosopher does not intend to be a theologian. He wants to serve the universal *logos*. He tries to turn away from his existential situation, including his ultimate concern, toward a place above all particular places, toward pure reality. The conflict between the intention of becoming universal and the destiny of remaining particular characterizes every philosophical existence. It is its burden and its greatness.

The theologian carries an analogous burden. Instead of turning away from his existential situation, including his ultimate concern, he turns toward it. He turns toward it, not in order to make a confession of it, but in order to make clear the universal validity, the *logos* structure of what concerns him ultimately. And he can do this only in an attitude of detachment from his existential situation and in obedience to the universal *logos*. This obliges him to be critical of every special expression of his ultimate concern. He cannot affirm any tradition and any authority except through a "No" and a "Yes." And it is always possible that he may not be able to go all of the way from the "No" to the "Yes." He cannot join the chorus of those who live in unbroken assertions. He must take the risk of being driven beyond the boundary line of the theological circle. Therefore, the pious and powerful in the church are suspicious of him, although they live in dependence upon the work of the former theologians who were in the same situation. Theology, since it serves not only the concrete but also the universal *logos*, can become a stumbling block for the church and a demonic temptation for the theologian. The detachment required in honest theological work can destroy the necessary involvement of faith. This tension is the burden and the greatness of every theological work.

The duality of divergence and convergence in the relation between theology and philosophy leads to the double question: Is there a necessary conflict between the two and is there a possible synthesis between them? Both questions must be answered negatively. Neither is a conflict between theology and philosophy necessary, nor is a synthesis between them possible.

A conflict presupposes a common basis on which to fight. But there is no common basis between theology and philosophy. If the theologian and the philosopher fight, they do so either on a philosophical or on a theological basis. The philosophical basis is the ontological analysis of the structure of being. If the theologian needs this analysis, either he must take it from a philosopher or he must himself become a philosopher. Usually he does both. If he enters the philosophical arena, conflicts as well as alliances with other philosophers are unavoidable. But all this happens on the philosophical level. The theologian has no right whatsoever to argue for a philosophical opinion in the name of his ultimate concern or on the basis of the theological circle. He is obliged to argue for a philosophical decision in the name of the universal *logos* and from the place which is no place: pure reason. It is a disgrace for the theologian and intolerable for the philosopher if in a philosophical discussion the theologian suddenly claims an authority other than pure reason. Conflicts on the philosophical level are conflicts between two philosophers, one of whom happens to be a theologian, but they are not conflicts between theology and philosophy.

Often, however, the conflict is fought on the theological level. The hidden theologian in the philosopher fights with the professed theologian. This situation is more frequent than most philosophers realise. Since they have developed their concepts with the honest intention of obeying the universal *logos*, they are reluctant to recognize the existentially conditioned elements in their systems. They feel that such elements, while they give colour and direction to their creative work, diminish its truth value. In such a situation the theologian must break the resistance of the philosopher against a theological analysis of his ideas. He can do this by pointing to the history of philosophy, which discloses that in every significant philosopher existential passion (ultimate concern) and rational power (obedience to the universal *logos*) are united and that the truth value of a philosophy is dependent on the amalgamation of these two elements in every concept. The insight into this situation is, at the same time, an insight into the fact that two philosophers, one of whom happens to be a theologian, can fight with each other, and that two theologians, one of whom hapepns to be a philosopher, can fight with each other; but there is no possible conflict between theology and philosophy because there is no common basis for such a conflict. The philosopher may or may not convince the philosopher-theologian. And the theologian may or may not convert the theologian-philosopher. In no case does the theologian as such stand against the philosopher as such and vice versa.

Thus there is no conflict between theology and philosophy, and there is no synthesis either—for exactly the same reason which ensures that there will be no conflict. A common basis is lacking. The idea of a synthesis between theology and philosophy has led to the dream of a "Christian philosophy." The term is ambiguous. It can mean a philosophy whose existential basis is historical Christianity. In this sense all modern philosophy is Christian, even if it is humanistic, atheistic, and the intentionally anti-Christian. No philosopher living within Western Christian culture can deny his dependence on it, as no Greek philosopher could have hidden his dependence on an Appolonian-Dionysian culture, even if he was a radical critic of the gods of Homer. The Modern vision of reality and its philosophical analysis is different from that of pre-Christian times, whether one is or is not existentially determined by the God of Mount Zion and the Christ of Mount Golgotha. Reality is encountered differently; experience has other dimensions and directions than in the cultural climate of Greece. No one is able to jump out of this "magic" circle. Nietzsche, who tried to do so, announced the coming of the Anti-Christ. But the Anti-Christ is dependent on the Christ against whom he arises. The early Greeks, for whose Culture Nietzsche was longing, did not have to fight the Christ; indeed, they unconsciously prepared for his coming by elaborating the questions to which he gave the answer and the categories in which the answer could be expressed. Modern philosophy is not pagan. Atheism and anti-Christianity are not pagan. They are anti-Christian in Christian terms. The scars of the Christian tradition cannot be erased; they are a *character indelebilis*. Even the paganism of Nazism was not really a relapse to paganism (just as bestiality is not a relapse to the beast).

But the term "Christian philosophy" is often meant in a different sense. It is used to denote a philosophy which does not look at the universal *logos* but at the assumed or actual demands of a Christian theology. This can be done in two ways: either the church authorities or its theological interpreters nominate one of the past philosophers to be their "philosophical saint" or they demand that contemporary philosophers should develop a philosophy under special conditions and with a special aim. In both cases the philosophical *erōs* is killed. If Thomas Aquinas is officially named *the* philosopher of the Roman Catholic church, he has ceased to be for Catholic philosophers a genuine partner in the philosophical dialogue which goes on through the centuries. And if present-day Protestant philosophers are asked to accept the idea of personality as their highest ontological principle because it is the principle most congenial to the spirit of the Reformation, the work of these philosophers is mutilated. There is nothing in heaven and earth, or beyond them, to which the philosopher must subject himself except the universal *logos* of being as it gives itself to him in experience. Therefore, the idea of a "Christian philosophy" in the narrower sense of a philosophy which is intentionally

Christian must be rejected. The fact that every modern philosophy has grown on Christian soil and shows traces of the Christian culture in which it lives has nothing to do with the self-contradicting ideal of a "Christian philosophy."

Christianity does not need a "Christian philosophy" in the narrower sense of the word. The Christian claim that the *logos* who has become concrete in Jesus as the Christ is at the same time the universal *logos* includes the claim that wherever the *logos* is at work it agrees with the Christian message. No philosophy which is obedient to the universal *logos* can contradict the concrete *logos*, the Logos "who became flesh."

Chapter 8 | Language and God

For many moderns, *God* has become a conventional word to be spoken on stated occasions. Marriages, burials, openings of legislative sessions, times of national crisis demand proper and pious use of this name for "something beyond ourselves we know not what."

But also among our contemporaries, many thoughtful folk are engaged in a quest for grounds, if any can be found, for God's existence. It is strange but true that those standing in the biblical tradition did not raise this question. The problem of God's existence is the preoccupation of Western man, who has been grasped by the thought forms of Greek philosophy and the methods of rational inquiry. Indeed the very terms to speak about God in our Western tradition are derived from the Greek *theos* and the Latin *deus*. For example, various points of view are designated by these root terms: a-theism (no God); a-gnosticism (I do not know whether there is a God or not); deism (an absentee God who has set the world going and left it to its own ordered operation); theism (belief in a personal God); mono-theism (one God); poly-theism (many gods); heno-theism (many gods but loyalty to only one); pan-theism (God is identical with the whole universe). Monotheism involves the central tenet of the Judeo-Christian faith in one transcendent Source, Ground and Goal of all that exists and yet the God who discloses Himself in and through both human history and the orders of nature.

Language: A Recurring Theme

This chapter and much of the discussion which follows will be concerned with modern man's problem of grounds for God's existence. More specifically, in this chapter we shall raise and attempt to answer the *prior* question: How do we speak of God anyway? In our discussion thus far we have talked frequently about the religious use of language. In doing so we have tried to relate this issue of religious language to the specific contexts in which it normally arises within the old and new covenants.

226

Now we need to see how these insights focus on our use of language about God.

"The Word" is central to Judeo-Christian faith. It is God who "speaks" to men in specific historical situations. But, as we have seen, to speak is to act. God acts through particular events in human history. Indeed, these are sign events which point beyond themselves to the God who is their Source and Ground. These climactic events, the Exodus and the life, death and resurrection of Jesus Christ, especially, become media of God's self-disclosure. For revelation is, we recall, not the utterance of propositions, nor is faith simply assent to propositions or abstract knowledge of "eternal truths." In this perspective, both revelation and faith are non-propositional. Faith is responsive and personal acceptance of what God has done, is doing and will do. Thus the words of the Bible are the record of God's acts (Word) and men's responses, sometimes of obedient commitment and sometimes of rejection.

In this perspective, then, religious faith uses language in a distinctive way. The biblical writers were concerned to relate the whole story of their past in terms of the mighty works of God. The Exodus and establishment of the covenant, the coming of Jesus Christ in their midst, are focal events which illuminate all the rest of history including personal existence. They are revelatory events. What language then can tell this cosmic story? The problem is concerned with how mere men can put into words the wonder of ordinary occurrences in human experience *seen as* the acts of God.

There are many styles and levels of writing in the biblical record: narrative, history, poetry, legend, story, parable, myth, saga. But the biblical writers always centered what they had to say in the sacred history (*Heilsgeschichte*) of the community of faith. However, they did not pretend to make factual, total recall of what had "actually" happened. Theirs was an interpretive perspective. They were concerned to elicit response on the part of present and future generations as these relived the revelatory events of the past. In particular, myth is rooted in this historical concern. For biblical writers used myth not to abstract from history but to affirm even the creation of all nature as the first of God's acts in history.[1]

But how indeed shall men use language to refer to the Creator and Sustainer who is beyond human comprehension and expression? The reading selection by Robert L. Calhoun, "The Language of Religion," bears on this issue.

---

[1] See Chap. 2, Reading 4, Chap. 4 and Reading 6.

Dilemma and Paradox

As we use the language of *human* speech and act to refer to a *God* who transcends human existence, we are caught in a dilemma. Are we so bound by the limitations of the finite that we are forced to speak not so much of an infinite God as of a very great man? On the other hand, do the being and character of such an infinite God so far outreach human grasp that men cannot know or speak of Him at all? In the first case, all statements referring to God are bound to be anthropomorphic (in the form of a man) and cannot be about *God* but only about man. In the second case, our utterances lead into agnosticism and thus cannot be *about* God. This dilemma is not new in the history of human thought. Men of every age, whenever they venture to speak seriously about their relation to the Ultimate, run this double danger of anthropomorphism and agnosticism.

Frequently a student exclaims, "I no longer believe in God!" But what sort of God is he rejecting? What is his picture of God? He often insists on carrying about with him images of God from childhood days. Either he goes on believing in that kind of God, perhaps turning later to skepticism, or he may reject all belief on the ground that if God is like these childish pictures, He is scarcely believable.

The student needs to put to himself certain basic questions: In either acceptance or rejection, what conception of God's nature do I have in mind? In what sorts of deities do I believe, and how many have I outgrown? In the words of J. B. Phillips, "Is your God too small?" These are the same recurring questions that we raised in Chapter 6 and which Reading 9 from D. M. Baillie discusses. For the Christian especially, the issue is sharp. We do not simply *find* God out there but rather take with us some idea or other of His character. We may picture God as a cosmic "errand boy," or a "policeman," or a "big papa and mama in the sky" or a "tribal god," in short, a god who is just a projection of man's small wishes, serving human purposes. These "do-it-yourself" religions are inadequate. For the Christian, God is that Ground, Source and Goal of all being that transcends and yet is dynamically related to, and revealed in, this order of things within which men actually live.

How shall a man express what he can understand of the nature of such a God? What symbols can he use? We must somehow find metaphors or analogies derived from finite existence and yet somehow use these to grasp the nature of the infinite. This is precisely what man, the symbol-making creature, attempts to do. He selects key images from among the actual objects which surround him in his attempt to discover adequate symbols through which to speak of God: shepherd, judge, mighty rock, guide, light, father. Around such images as these he builds his convictions concerning his relationship to the Ultimate.

In Chapter 3, "The Nature of Man," we noted that, throughout Western culture, the Greek Platonic and Neoplatonic views of history, man and the cosmos stand as challenge to Judeo-Christian perspectives. In the Greek perspective, history is a cyclical reflection of the timeless forms and the soul of man is a separable entity belonging to the realm of the Eternal. But the biblical writers viewed history as moving purposively toward a Goal and this world of events as actual in its own right. Men live in terms of climactic events through which God discloses Himself. Man is not a soul linked temporarily to a body but a whole person responding to God in terms of faithfulness and obedience.

Involved here also are contrasts between two different approaches to the knowledge of God and the very character of God. The Hebraic is often called the "way of affirmation," while the Greek is called the "way of negation." Culminating in the mysticism of Plotinus, the Greek search for ultimate Reality begins with the soul's journey from this actual world of sense experience and progresses through the realm of rational understanding to final union with the One. That Reality which is absolute cannot even be known or spoken of as an object over against us. What then can anyone say in words and sentences about such an unknowable and transcendent One? For the Neoplatonist only one way of speaking is possible: the way of negation.

This negative approach to the Ultimate out of the Greek tradition stands as challenge to the way of affirmation expressed through the biblical documents. The Bible represents God not as a remote, lofty Absolute abstracted from this world of actual human strivings, successes and failures. Men portrayed in the biblical account do not seek to know Him through a philosophical method which finally fails them. God moves, acts, discloses Himself in events of history as Person, Purpose and Will. Those who respond to Him need not do so by straining after the bliss of mystical absorption and ecstasy. For the God who reaches beyond the finite is yet the same God who is Creator of the world and, as Father, has shown Himself to men in Jesus Christ. He calls folk to fulfill a specific destiny. He is a loving God and yet a God who judges and condemns. He uses the resources of nature and human society for His own purposes and yet does not absorb these into Himself or rob them of their own significance.

The language of the Bible thus speaks affirmatively of what God is and does, and that language is clearly anthropomorphic. Can the Greek way of negation and the biblical way of affirmation make any sense of each other?

This is precisely the problem which Christian thinkers, under influence of both Greek and Hebraic points of view, attempted to solve. They found themselves committed to these two ways at once: one claiming that the nature of God ever exceeds human grasp and expression and the other affirming the positive character of a God who makes Himself known to men. In view of this dilemma, some theologians were led to develop a third way, the "way of paradox or analogy." For God is known and yet never completely known.

For this way of analogy or paradox, we are justified in speaking affirmatively and negatively of God at the same time. We may legitimately employ analogies found in human existence to refer to God. These analogies become images which are genuinely revelatory despite the limitations of finite experience. We use them, however, not to prove but to illustrate the understanding of God held within the Christian tradition.

The Doctrine of Analogy

The same approach finds expression in the principal works of Thomas Aquinas and those of more recent writers.[2] The doctrine of analogy is complex. Yet the basic idea involved is not difficult to understand. We ask the question: What are we trying to say when we state, "God is good"? Is God good in precisely and literally the same sense in which we say our neighbor is good? When we apply a term to two cases with exactly the same meaning, we are using that term *univocally*. But it is clear that an infinite God is not good in the identical sense in which a finite man is good. Thus when a word is applied both to created being and to God, it is not employed univocally. But, on the other hand, is the word *good* then applicable to both man and God *equivocally*, that is, with utterly different and unrelated meanings? For example, the word *club* is equivocal when it is not clear whether it denotes an instrument used for hitting a golf ball or an organization which people join. But the doctrine of analogy holds that *good* as applied to both man and God is not being used equivocally. The reason is, according to this view, that there is a specific connection between God's goodness and man's goodness. This connection is based on

[2] See E. L. Mascall, *Existence and Analogy*, Longmans, Green & Co., Inc., New York, 1949, pp. 94–115.

the fact that God has created man. Man's goodness is therefore an effect which has its cause in God, who is good. Thus *good* may be applied to both Creator and creature neither univocally nor equivocally. It is used *analogically*.

John Hick suggests an illustration of the way analogical predication works.[3] Suppose we think of an analogy "downwards" from man to a lower form of life. A pet dog is said to be "faithful." We also evaluatively commend a man as "faithful." In each case, we use the same word because we discern a similarity between a specific quality in the behavior of a dog and the steady loyalty called faithfulness in a human being. We do not use the word *faithful* equivocally (with an entirely different meaning) because there is this similarity. Yet there is also a decided difference between the way a dog behaves and the conduct a man exhibits. Hick writes of this difference:

> The one is indefinitely superior to the other in respect of responsible, self-conscious deliberation and the relating of attitudes to moral purposes and ends. Because of this difference we are not using "faithful" univocally (in exactly the same sense). We are using it analogically, to indicate that at the level of the dog's consciousness there is a quality which *corresponds* to what at the human level we call faithfulness. There is a recognizable likeness in structure of attitudes or patterns of behavior which causes us to use the same word for both animal and man. Nevertheless, human faithfulness differs from canine faithfulness to all the wide extent that a man differs from a dog. There is thus both similarity within difference and difference within similarity of the kind that led Aquinas to speak of the *analogical* use of the same term in two very different contexts.[4]

As we draw comparisons between man's faithfulness and that of a dog, "true or normative" faithfulness is that which we find in man. For a dog's faithfulness is imperfect by contrast and therefore derived. But when we drawn an analogy "upward" between man and God, the situation is the other way around. Our own goodness, wisdom and love are imperfect approximations to the perfect qualities of God. But we know these only in ourselves and only by analogy in God. It is presupposed by the logic of analogy that these qualities are possessed by God in their true or normative nature and only in a distorted and fragmentary way in man.

But the question persists: If God and what He is like are forever hidden from us, how can we limited men know what these perfect qualities of

[3] By permission. From John Hick, *Philosophy of Religion*, Prentice-Hall, Inc., Englewood Cliffs, N.J., 1963, pp. 79–81.

[4] *Ibid.*, p. 80.

goodness, love and wisdom are? The doctrine of analogy replies that indeed we do *not* know. Aquinas held that we humans do not pretend fully to delineate all the qualities of perfection that belong to God. All we can possibly do is to point to the contrast between the different ways a word is applied both to man and to God. Professor Hick states:

> Analogy is not an instrument for exploring and mapping the infinite divine nature; it is an account of the way in which terms are used of the Deity whose existence is, at this point, being presupposed. The Doctrine of Analogy provides a framework for certain limited statements about God, without infringing upon the agnosticism, and the sense of the mystery of the divine being, which have always characterized Christian and Jewish thought at their best.[5]

Frederick Ferré suggests that the use of analogy does not ". . . provide us with information about real properties of supernatural entities." Rather the logic of analogy is ". . . one means of providing criteria for the disciplined use" of language derived from ordinary human experience and applying such language to theological contexts. Thus a word like *good* from a secular context may be employed theologically where a ground has already been established in theistic faith and the systems of doctrine and belief built upon that faith.[6] For the Judeo-Christian faith, the key analogies are those taken from the contexts of the personal and the historical: redeemer, creator, judge, father, love, everlasting presence.

This background is essential to our understanding of the classical arguments for belief in God to be discussed in the next chapter. Do I "prove" God by demonstrative or empirical argument? Or does God discover me in and through my responsive act of faith, involving commitment, belief and deeper intensity of awareness as to who I am and to whom I belong? Again, it is important to ask what kind of God I am affirming or denying. It makes a difference whether He is a small magic-working God who is dispensable or that Being who gives significance to everything else, including my own existence.

The scholastic thinkers of the Middle Ages employed a specific, basic term to characterize this infinite, creative, just, loving and holy God of the Judeo-Christian tradition. That term is "aseity." The Latin is *a se esse*, literally "being from oneself." This means that God is self-existent. He

---

[5] *Ibid.,* pp. 80–81.

[6] From *Language, Logic and God* by Frederick Pond Ferré, Copyright © 1961 Frederick Pond Ferré. Reprinted with the permission of Harper & Row, Publishers, Inc., New York. In addition to pp. 76–77, see also pp. 70–71 for distinctions between the "analogy of attribution" and the "analogy of proportionality."

does not depend for His existence or nature upon any being or reality other than Himself. No "higher" being has created Him, nor can any destroy Him. To say God is infinite and unconditioned means that He is that reality upon which all else depends. Likewise, He is before anything was. He will be when everything finite ceases to exist. For He is, by definition, the Eternal, without beginning or end.

We are here introducing the kind of terms which we must use in the next chapter. Does God exist? Can unlimited divine Being, upon which all that exists depends, Itself exist? Paul Tillich holds the challenging view that we cannot even say that God exists, for this would limit God:

> Thus the question of the existence of God can be neither asked nor answered. If asked, it is a question about that which by its very nature is above existence, and therefore the answer—whether negative or affirmative—implicitly denies the nature of God. It is as atheistic to affirm the existence of God as it is to deny it. God is being-itself, not *a* being.[7]

This seems a strange way to prepare ourselves for understanding the basic tenet of all theology. How can an avowed "believer" say, "God does not exist"? But what Tillich is affirming is that God is not just one being or existence among all the others. Chairs exist, mountains exist, atoms exist, persons exist—in the empirical, finite world of space and time. Tillich is thus restricting the term "exists" to the latter kind of usage. But God is not an existent in the same sense as, or alongside, all these others. God, then, does not exist. Rather He is the Source and Ground of all that exists. He is Being Itself. In this way, the scholastics and others who have followed their lead seek to establish the *being* of God. Thus the theological term "God" and the philosophical (ontological) term "Being" (*Ontos* in the Greek) come to refer to the same Reality. For God has *aseity*, or being, in and from Himself alone. These are clues to what these theologians mean when they speak the word *God*.[8]

---

[7] By permission. From Paul Tillich, *Systematic Theology*, The University of Chicago Press, Chicago, 1951, vol. I, p. 237.

[8] See John Hick, *op. cit.*, pp. 6–7.

13

ROBERT L. CALHOUN | *The Language of Religion**

Religion is not primarily talk, nor symbolic behavior of any kind. It is not primarily ceremony, nor preaching and listening, not even reflective meditation, though all these have their due places in it. First of all, religion is response, deeper and more inclusive than speech or thought, to revelation—to the impact of reality apprehended as divine. In the broadest sense of the term, such reality is numinous, "a mystery full of terror and fascination." In simpler religious communities, the mystery may be found in natural objects, animals, persons, in particular places, times, or events, even in man-made implements hallowed by antiquity and tradition or by dramatic association with a crisis in human living. The gods of unsophisticated peoples are indefinite in number and often transitory in divine status. But in more discriminating religion, the divine is identified sooner or later with the ultimate in man's universe. Mystery and numinous quality are not left behind, but they are apprehended now as characters not of serpents or stars or sorcerers, but of the abiding ground of all particular existence and worth—God beyond all finite things and events, apprehended as overwhelmingly great and good. Our central concern here is with religion of this latter sort.

The primary response of one who finds himself at grips with what he takes to be ultimate reality is an all-inclusive response like the turning of a plant toward the light. It involves thought, feeling, and action, and the still deeper impulses—below the threshold of conscious experience—from which decision and action arise. Religion involves the whole self, in a commitment at once inescapable and spontaneously affirmative, like the commitment of a free mind to evident truth or of a perceptive heart to a beloved person, community, or cause. Such commitment is not calculating,

* By permission. From Robert L. Calhoun, "The Language of Religion," *The Unity of Knowledge,* ed. Lewis Leary, Doubleday & Co., Inc., New York, 1955, pp. 252–262. Reprinted by permission of The Trustees of Columbia University in the City of New York.

arbitrary, or avoidable, given the situation that evokes it. But neither is it coerced, involuntary, or enslaving. It is the affirmation of one who can do no other, yet who in such affirmation is enhanced and emancipated. Such response to the presence of God is worship that continually seeks expression in devoted work. Both are integral and inseparable components in primary religion.

This primary response finds characteristic if not inevitable elaboration in the life of religious communities whose members have been drawn into such commitment and seek then to reaffirm, to interpret, and to communicate their experience. First in this social or corporate elaboration of religion is the development of cultus or liturgy, a system of ceremonial acts in which renewal of worship is sought or sensibly embodied. Here sacraments are central—enacted means of communication between worshipers and God, and among members of the community both past and present. In a broad sense the whole liturgy is sacramental: a blending of speech and action, light and shadow, color, tone, rhythm, fragrance into a complex act (*leitourgia*) of affirmation and reception of meaning, in the presence of reality beyond the fabric of symbols. Secondly, there is a more or less elaborate system of verbalization—evangelism in the usual restricted sense of spoken and written conveyance of "the gospel" of God's living presence and acts: proclamation, reflective interpretation, and systematic teaching. In the terminology of the early Christian Church, these interrelated phases of evangelism were called *kērygma* (preaching, testimony, announcement as by a herald), spontaneous, declaratory, and particularized rather than general, critical, or systematic; *theologia* (more reflective, critical, reasoned discourse about God and man), seeking to classify, order, interpret, and defend the substance of the *kērygma* as coherent and relevant doctrine (*doctrina, dogma*) suitable, as the name suggests, for systematic study and teaching; and *catechēsis* (instruction) in which both the gist of the first-hand, eyewitness proclamation (*kērygma*) and some part of the growing system of interpretation (*theologia, doctrina*) are carefully expounded for learners. This is the area with which the major part of this paper is chiefly concerned. Thirdly, there is in every religious community more or less elaborate maintenance of organization and discipline: allocation of office, function, and authority; moral rules or norms embodied in individual and corporate living. Finally, there is active concern for the welfare of neighbors within and outside the organized community, normally expressed in practical service (*diakonia*), the everyday acts of devoted living.

If something like this account be accepted, the place of language in religion is most obvious in the first two of these elaborated phases: liturgy and evangelism. Man's primary response in worship to the impact of God's presence is concrete and immediate rather than reflective and articulate, *erleben* rather than *erkennen*. This is not to say it is irrational, nor that symbolism and language have no place in it. If neither of these statements were true, it is hard to see how theology could get a foothold as an integral component in religious life at all. If the primary response of man to God were as simply immediate and ineffable as toothache or salt taste, theology would be as external to the experience as the effort to verbalize a sensation is to the simple intuition itself. But since the religious response involves the whole person, it has an internal structure that lends itself to reflection and symbolic communication as a simple sensation does not. At the same time, like a concrete experience of love or loyalty, a concrete moment of worship is not *eo ipso* reflective, critical, even articulate. These are characteristics rather of the elaborated moments of religion, in which the implicit meanings of the primary moment are spelled out in growing detail—but never completely.

This situation is sometimes obscured by ambiguous use of the term revelation. This term refers properly to the primary moment of religion, in which God is said to reveal or disclose his presence to the worshiper and thereby to evoke the primary religious response. Sometimes this revelation is understood as consisting of propositions given as guaranteed truth. In that event, verbalization would of course be conspicuous from the very start. "The word of the Lord" to Amos or Isaiah would consist of information, instructions, and commands in verbal form. But in common with a substantial body of interpreters, this paper takes revelation to consist not in dictated propositions but in arresting events—impacts, confrontations—whose meaning is partly verbalized in further reflection.

The modes and functions of language in religion can now be examined a bit more directly, though very briefly. It seems convenient to look first at liturgy and especially at sacrament as a very inclusive and characteristic form of the language of religion, whose nature, presuppositions, and intent can help to illuminate the more precisely verbal and conceptual language of theology. It goes without saying that the latter is needed likewise for illumination of the former. The two are not separable without serious damage to both.

An essential presupposition of all genuine liturgy, as distinct from the "vain repetitions" of rote memory and habit, is the real communion or participation (*koinōnia*) of men with one another and with reality beyond themselves; and the possibility of heightening, clarifying, renewing, and extending this communion both for present worshipers and for other men. Liturgy is a complex of symbolic acts intended to express the communion that is already real, and by communication to help extend and to enhance it. *Koinōnia* is neither identity nor uniformity. It is a mutual involvement of beings that are radically other, yet profoundly interrelated. Thus, each man is radically other than his neighbor, incapable of occupying his neighbor's perspective instead of his own. Yet each is so bound up with his neighbors that without them he could not be himself, and he is able to recognize this bond. Thus also man is radically other than God, the ultimate ground of his existence, the perfect truth and right by which he is judged. Yet in moments of arresting confrontation he is able to recognize and acknowledge his dependence on the radically Other, and to find himself in his wrongness not only condemned but forgiven and accepted, reconciled, reaffirmed. This paradoxical conquest of alienation, this profound communion in radical otherness—of man from man, and of man from God—is what liturgy seeks to affirm, to mediate, and to articulate in symbolic action.

The symbols, as already noted, are of many sorts. But to fulfill their function they must be sacramental. That is to say, among other things, they must be not mere external pointers but concrete media embodying or exemplifying the communion they seek to convey. They must be like friendly handclasps or like gifts offered and received, not like calling cards or polite salutations. They must be saturated in memory, individual and corporate, so that they can call up in vivid presence the long past and enable those who share in them to share in the life of a community enduring through time. They must be rooted in the hungers and hopes of our common humanity, speaking in their many-dimensional gestures not a local dialect only but a universal language. At the same time, like any concrete living tongue as against an artificially abstracted Esperanto, they are sure to manifest the peculiarities of particular traditions and to be susceptible of incalculably various understanding. Their virtue as sacramental symbols would not be enhanced if they could be reduced to simple freedom from ambiguity. To convey a living sense of participation in the whole fabric of human life and in a specific community diversified in time and space and modes of existence, they must point in many directions at once, like a musical theme amid variations, and be themselves actual segments or foci of the communal experience they signify. Finally, they must point beyond human life to reality that transcends it yet effectively enters into it: the producing and sustaining source of our life, the goal and norm by which we are judged, the transforming influence—the divine grace—by which we are corrected, renewed, and led into unforeseen dimensions of shared living.

Sacraments are signs and symbols, and in that sense components in the language of religion. A sacrament is at once an affirmation and a reminder of the reality from which the affirmation has its meaning. *Sacramentum* is the soldier's oath of loyalty, and the legionary standard—marked SPQR—by which he swears. It is "the outward, visible sign of an inward, spiritual grace," a "means (*medium*) of grace," a "symbol and occasion of the working of the Holy Spirit." As such it is also to be called *mysterion,* as in the Greek Church, at once sign and vehicle of the presence of God. Whether God's grace is mediated exclusively, or at least in exceptional and indispensable ways by particular liturgical acts, such as ceremonial washing or common meal, or whether such acts are peculiarly effective reminders of the working of grace through all sorts of channels— the spoken word in prayer and in preaching, the everyday acts of faithful service—is a question long and widely debated among religious people. It need not detain us here, but it may serve to direct our thought from liturgy as enacted language to the more specifically verbal expressions of theology and doctrine.

Here again we meet, from the early generations in Christian history, the term *symbolon,* as a name for concise theological formula: a *credo* or formula for confession of faith in token of commitment and of membership in a committed community. The confessional formulae called symbols or creeds speedily found place in the liturgy—first for each new convert in the ceremony of baptism by which he was inducted into the Church, and thereafter as an integral part of each regular service of worship. This is a simple instance of the way in which cultus has been affected by reflective thought, by theology. The meaning of the whole liturgy is thus reoriented and further defined by the systematic effort toward verbalization. On the other hand, theological effort has proceeded in its own terms, mostly nonliturgical. Creeds and confessions have multiplied and expanded into sizable theological treatises approved by the community, related to its liturgy, but not included in it. Yet the initial intent of the whole dogmatic enterprise is clearly preserved in the use of the name symbolics for the study of all these creeds and confessions. They too, like liturgical acts of worship, intend to signify and in some sense to serve as media for the presence of God. The words they employ and the ordering of the words are never the carefully sterilized terms and propositions of algebra, of theoretical physics, or of clinical medicine. Their function as affirmations of active commitment requires a vocabulary and a snytax that have something of the urgency, ambivalence, and particularity of momentous action. They are not simple, exact results of exact reasoning—though much arduous, closely reasoned effort to attain exactitude enters into their formation. Rather they are what Plato called "articles of faith," hammered out in the midst of hard thinking yet grounded at bottom not in reasoning as such, but in rational conviction of the sort exemplified by Socrates, and serving as touchstones for genuine reasoning about God.

Such reasoning is theology, always inseparable from and pervaded by faith, never able to dispense with language in which a subjective or confessional moment is essential. At the same time, the task of theology is very largely an objective task as well. This means not merely that it is communicative as well as expressive, semantic and not simply emotive. Liturgy also, as we have urged, is communicative. Beyond that, theology is analytic, critical, interpretative, argumentative, and systematic. It seeks far more extensively than liturgy to distinguish and point out explicitly the factors involved in the primary confrontation of God and man—in revelation and religious response. It seeks to clarify and test by the familiar tests of internal coherence and empirical relevance the affirmations of religious conviction, recognizing that no more than those of love or intense loyalty, or of artistic or musical discernment can such affirmations be translated into alien terms or subordinated to alien requirements. It seeks to illuminate from various angles their characteristic structure and implications, their interconnections with other modes of human experience, and their actual sources and modifications in the course of history. It seeks, finally, to exhibit them as at once an ordered whole of which every component involves every other, and an effort to speak of mystery that is never reducible to the dimensions of any human experience or discourse.

In theology, therefore, both language and methods are employed that find place also in many sciences, in history, in philosophy, in the study of poetry and other literature, and especially in everyday personal relations. Excepting a comparatively few technical terms, indeed, there is no vocabulary peculiar to theology. What is peculiar is the perspective in which familiar words are used. That perspective, as already affirmed more than once, is determined by the impact of divine revelation and the distinctive response of faith. From this situation arise the most difficult problems for theological discourse, and the most characteristic efforts to solve them without dissolving them away.

THREE PROBLEMS FOR LANGUAGE IN RELIGION

The root of these difficulties is familiar. The ordinary use of language is to direct attention to some objectively perceptible component of the speaker's world—an "it" to which one can point by a verbal gesture.

Whether it is a sensible object (chair, planet, galaxy) or an intelligible object (Euclidean line, equality, sovereignty), words can be found or made that can indicate it with fair precision. The words are not *like* it, but in the context of human observation and converse, they come to have a conventionally accepted congruence with it. And this can come about the more easily because the words are at least of the same experiential order as the objects to which they point: the words also are objects, and as such can serve most readily as labels or finger posts for other objects. The attention of an observer ordinarily moves with least difficulty from one objective "it" to another.

When we seek to call attention to a subject, an "I," the task is notoriously much harder. David Hume even declared it impossible to point out a subject *qua* subject at all. Immanuel Kant agreed with him, but went on to explore in the immense, painstaking argument of the first two *Critiques* both reasons and methods for dealing concretely, actively, and significantly with subjects, even though they cannot be observed and described as if they were objects. Here also verbal signs provide a usable medium, since each of us is himself a subject, comes to know himself as such in active, responsible relations with others, and so can recognize and acknowledge others in the common matrix of social, historical existence.

But God is neither an observable "It" nor a finite "I." At least this is the conviction to which reflective religion sooner or later has come, in all the great traditions known to me. And only for such religion does the special problem of language arise. For such religion, God is not merely numinous but radically transcendent—incommensurable with finite things and persons, as Creator with creatures, Perfect with imperfect, Infinite with finite, and so on. Moreover, if it be true, as many religious thinkers have held, that God is the ground of rational order, the presupposition of all discourse, then trying to talk or to think articulately *about* him is a little like trying to see oneself as observing subject, the presupposed ground of all one's seeing. This last difficulty might perhaps be outflanked, in Kant's way or some other; indeed, to be able to see and state the problem seems to imply that in some sense one is already beyond it— if only the right forms of speech could be found to express what the situation implies.

But all our language is relative to the objective phenomena we observe and to the finite existence we share. More than that, all of it is culturally conditioned, like our own minds, so that any words we can use have special reference not even to the whole of human experience or of finite existence, but only to some part of it. How can such constricted language be used in valid reference to God?

One familiar answer is often associated with mysticism; recourse to some *via negativa* or *via remotionis*. Since God is incommensurable with the finite things from which our languages derive and to which they properly refer, the only true assertions about God are negative assertions, denying of him all predicates drawn from our experience of things in time and space, or of persons in human history. But such negation has at least one tremendous affirmation as its base: that God is transcendent, incommensurable with all that is finite. Hence, unless one is to keep wholly silent, avoiding even negative assertions, it seems necessary to probe further after some ground for affirmation. Three such efforts to undergird affirmations about God may be noticed briefly here: the ways of mythology, of analogy, and of paradox.

The earliest, simplest, most concrete form of religious discourse was myth. Indeed, one major theory holds that language itself arises in the matrix of mythical experience, and achieves independent status and conceptual form only after a long maturing within the context of myth. In the mythical perspective, "all things are full of gods," in Thales' well-known words. Earth and heaven interpenetrate freely, because the gods are beings in space and time, gifted with powers beyond those of men, appearing and disappearing at will, but very far from radically transcendent. This is the stage of mythical experience and discourse that Paul Tillich calls "unbroken myth." It is precritical and untroubled by misgivings about the direct applicability of mythical picture-language to divine beings, who are man's near neighbors and kinsmen in a finite world.

But with progress in critical thought concerning gods and men, this early confidence is shattered. Whenever the many gods are subordinated to one god, and the one at length absorbs or displaces the rest, the crucial step is not far off. That step is taken when the one god is declared to be the Ultimate, radically other than man, uncontainable in space and to me, incommensurable with any finite existence. Then the question is posed sharply whether mythical experience and discourse concerning God must not be abandoned. Tillich says no. Any discourse concerning God is inevitably mythical, in the sense that predicates derived from experiences with finite beings in space and time are affirmed of God, in the context of such apprehension of a numinous transcendent as Otto has described and we have noticed above. But myth as now used, says Tillich, is "broken myth," no longer naively assumed to be an actual description of divine reality but recognized as usable *faute de mieux* to signalize the presence of a transcendent other that cannot be described at all. To substitute nonmythical language (that is, a carefully desiccated technical vocabulary of some sort) would serve no good purpose. No technical vocabulary is more adequate for symbolizing the Ultimate Being, and it would have for religious discourse the great disadvantage of failing to convey effectively even the human side of the religious situation: man's awe in the presence of God.

A second way of trying to cope with the problem is the familiar scholastic theory of analogy. From one point of view, this may be taken as an effort to find a theoretic basis for such discourse as "broken myth" provides. The term *analogia,* in the sense of proportion, was not unfamiliar in Greek mathematics, and Plato used it in that sense. Aristotle extended its range into the vocabulary of logic and the theory of knowledge, as a *via media* between univocal predication that applies a term to more than one subject, with essentially identical meaning, and equivocal predication that applies a term to more than one subject, with essentially different meanings. Analogical predication applies a term to more than one subject, with meanings that are not essentially identical but that bear a certain proportion to one another, and signalize a corresponding proportionality between the subjects themselves.

When this conception was first applied to the problem of religious discourse I do not know. The second-century Platonist (?) and hostile critic of Christianity named Celsus, whom we know only through Origen's polemic against him, included "the method of analogy" among philosophic methods suited for discourse about God. Origen himself follows suit, subordinating analogy along with all other philosophic methods to revelation and the "rule of faith." Augustine gives the method and its underlying principle a central place in his work *On the Trinity,* arguing that since man is created *ad imaginem dei,* it is not improper to seek in the personal existence of man analogies that may help to illustrate, not to prove, the Church's doctrine of the true Being of God. Substantially this same line is developed in the two *Summae* of Thomas Aquinas. He too sets out from the relation between Creator and creature, being careful to warn against saying, "God is like man"—as if man were the standard— whereas the truth is that man is in some sense like God. God is the Origin, man the derivative being. The Being of God—self-existent, perfect—is not the being of man—dependent, imperfect. Yet between them is such *analogia entis* that some predicates, such as rational, just, and merciful, can be affirmed *analogice* of man and of God.

To most Roman Catholic thought today, this doctrine seems valid and essential. But there are competent theologians who reject it, because it narrows too much the gulf between Creator and creatures. Some of them, like Karl Barth, are quite willing to talk of analogy in a different context, provided not by creation as such but by incarnation, and apprehended not by natural reason but by faith—an *analogia fidei* instead of an *analogia entis*. On this view, the self-disclosure of God in Jesus Christ as God-man, the Word of God incarnate, is the indispensable break-through from God's side that makes theological discourse possible. Analogies now can be found between various aspects of life in the Church and the life of the incarnate Word, though not directly between creatures as such as their Creator. One may question whether this account as it stands is self-complete. Its stress on the need for divine initiative in revelation to make theological discourse feasible may be welcomed. But such revelation is not provided *in vacuo*. It is provided in and through created being. That is what incarnation means, in one essential perspec-tive. And whether the existing relation between created being and Creator be called *analogia entis* or not, it seems a requisite component in the situation in which *analogia fidei* can be realized.

There is a third way in which this problem has been dealt with: the way of paradoxical or dialectical affirmation. These terms are among the hallmarks of Sören Kierkegaard's thought, with leaders in the Protestant Reformation and Kant preceding him, and the dialectical theology of our day, often strongly tinged with such theistic existentialism as that of Buber, following and transforming some of his suggestions. Although most dialectical theologians, like Martin Luther and John Calvin, are wary of mysticism, their treatment of this problem of theological affirmation has strong bonds, both negative and positive, to the great mystics' thought on the same problem. The rejection of mysticism centers mainly on denial of any basic identification of man and God, and insistence on the primacy of faith—personal commitment in response to revelation—rather than immediate intuition. But there is also clear reaffirmation of a characteris-tic doctrine of the mystics: that any attempt to speak of the inexpressible Fullness of God must take the form of joint affirmation and denial, the sort of dialectical affirmation which, unlike Hegel's, can never pass smoothly to a synthesis in which antitheses are wholly combined. The Being of God is and remains Mystery.

Our affirmations then must have the paradoxical character of state-ments in which contraries are declared to be inseparable and equally necessary. This is not contradiction. A self-contradictory term or proposi-tion tries verbally to combine strictly incompatible elements each of which is intelligible in isolation from the other. Square circles and un-created creatures are of that sort. But finding life by losing it, mercy that judges more searchingly than condemnation, God everywhere present and nowhere included, at once immanent and radically transcendent—these are terms whose components cannot have in isolation the meanings they have when combined. The incarnate Word, the God-man is the supreme instance, for Kierkegaard, "The Paradox" that enables corrupted man as no teacher can do—not even Socrates, the very model of genuine teachers—to apprehend truth and reality that is radically *other* than he, of a different order of magnitude, incommensurable with his weakness and distortion of mind. The light he requires is not in him, and no Socrates can bring it into view. The light must be *given* to him, and that means he must be transformed. When the light comes, he still cannot talk simply of what he sees. He must speak in paradoxes, for the truth is not simple, objective, formulable, and never his to possess.

Implicit in all three of these proffered answers, and explicit in most of their variant forms, is the presupposition of divine self-disclosure and human faith. Faith as total personal response is much more than cognitive belief, and differently related to reasoning, knowledge, and speech. It is not a substitute for any of these, nor a first or a final leap beginning or completing a process of thought. If one may venture a concluding paradox, it is the personal context, climate, active disposition in which thought and discourse of God must go on, subject at every step to their testing yet never subordinate to them and never exhausted in what they may find to say.

Chapter 9 | On Proving that God Exists

There are two contrasting ways of grounding belief in the being of God.[1] Whenever folk argue for or against the conviction that God exists, they take very seriously either one or the other. One way says to a man to look "inside" his own conscious experience and find "something" within him that is identical with himself and yet reaches infinitely beyond himself. It is something from which he often feels estranged but from which he can never separate himself. For it is a reality that is always behind, in and through everything he thinks, does and is. This is the Augustinian way of approaching God. It consists in reaching through to what is within a man all the time even in his denials that estrange him from it. The Franciscans expressed this perspective. It is the point of view of Anselm (1033–1109) and the basis of his so-called ontological argument, rooted as it is in the Augustinian affirmation, "I believe in order to go on to understanding."

But there are others to whom this appeal to inner experience seems soft and sentimental. Such a man claims that he knows only what confronts him empirically in the world outside himself. If God exists, he must infer His existence from the things and events he actually observes in the world of nature. This is said to be the proper task of reason in theology. It interprets and infers from causal and contingent processes and relations in the natural order to a necessary Mover that is Itself unmoved, a First Cause of everything that is. This is the method of Thomas Aquinas (1225–1274), and it goes for its clues back to Aristotle. It is the basis of Aquinas's cosmological and teleological arguments.

Reason and the Living Tradition

From Augustine (354–430) to Aquinas lies a stretch of some 800 years. During the twelfth century, Greek and Arabic works in mathematics and astronomy were translated. Then in the thirteenth century the complete writings of Aristotle became accessible to the West. (In earlier times only

[1] Paul Tillich, *A History of Christian Thought*, lectures recorded and edited by Peter H. John, 2d ed., 1956. (Duplicated and distributed privately.)

portions of Aristotle's logic had been known.) Christian scholars began translating these works for their own use. The Scholastics lived in two worlds, Greco-Roman and Hebraic Christian. They examined critically original Greek source materials and related these to their own Christian convictions.

What then is Scholasticism? In general, it is precisely this task of reconciling Greek ideas, as well as Arabic science and philosophy, with tenets of the Christian faith.

Another way of stating this task is to say that it is the problem of the relation between authority and reason. We moderns associate "authority" with externally imposed power. This kind of authority did develop in the late medieval period (1300–1450), but in the earlier (1000–1200) and high (1200–1300) Middle Ages authority stood for what is sometimes called "the living tradition."

This living tradition, like the air we breathe, is not pumped up; it is given. Men live in it and participate in it. For medieval man, the faith is presupposed. But he sought also, through Scholastic methods of reasoning, to understand this given, living tradition. This tradition was made up of many elements: the Scriptures, the interpretations of earlier Church Fathers, creedal decisions of the church councils. How are these to be combined, harmonized and applied to current isues? As difficult as it is, this for them is reason's work. For the living faith is given, and reason interprets the content of this faith. Out of this situation came the basic principle for an Anselm, standing in the Augustinian tradition: "I believe in order to go on to understanding." Here, then, in the earlier and high Middle Ages, authority does not mean, as it does later, an externally imposed authority. What it means is the given, living faith.

But with Aquinas a further development took place, especially with Aristotle's works now more fully available. For Aquinas, rational men may establish by argument the existence of God. Reason's work is valid as far as it takes the thinker, but its task must be completed by authority, that which is given by divine grace and revelation. But there is no conflict, for faith can never destroy reason nor reason abolish faith. This is Thomism even today.

The Ontological Argument

The classic statement of the ontological argument is that of Anselm.[2] Anselm took his stance within the living tradition and built his theology on this foundation. He lived in, participated in, this given "truth" con-

---

[2] See Anselm, *Proslogion*. Various versions in paperback, e.g., the Open Court edition (La Salle, Ill., 1961), are available.

tained in the Bible and interpreted by the Church Fathers. This is not the truth of science asserting facts about the world of nature. It is truth of a different order and has to do with man's relation to the Ultimate. Anselm does not refer to what we call technical intellect that claims to know specific truths but 'rather to wisdom (*sapientia*), or knowledge of the principles of truth itself. For every time we make any assertions at all, we *presuppose* some standard by which we judge the truth or falsity of the claims we make.

Anselm, as did Augustine before him, held to this principle or standard of truth which even the skeptic must acknowledge in order to say anything significant at all. But now a "leap" in his thought takes place. Here modern man, devoted to empirical knowledge based on experiment and observation, has difficulty in following him. For Anselm, this basic principle of truth is rooted in God. By definition, God is Truth. Anselm pointed, within human thinking itself, to something which is not itself an object of thought but which you and I must presuppose if we are to have any objects of thought at all. If we do not assume this ground of all truth, then no knowledge is possible. This ultimate Truth, by definition, is God.

But Anselm wanted more than the given tradition, more than the "truth" that is God. He proceeded to work out this given faith into a system. He wanted to understand this faith. But understanding itself can never be separated from its source in truth—the truth given by God in His disclosure of Himself.

One further aspect of Anselm's thought is essential. We referred to this at the end of Chapter 8. God is not *a* being beside others. God is Being Itself. God does not "exist" in the sense that rocks do. For Anselm shared the Platonic conviction that all things, qualities, relations and values in our world simply are instances of universal classes or forms. The "twenty-questions" game illustrates this view. You try to find out what object I have in mind. You do so by relating class to class until you discover, for instance, that I am thinking of a specific living American male, who resides on the Pacific Coast, is a teacher, is in a certain field, is at a specific college, etc. But for an Anselm, these classes are not dead abstractions. They receive their very being from the one all-embracing Reality which includes and gives "power of being" to all the rest. Just so, for him, God is not only Truth but Being Itself. This is the ultimate Reality which is not discovered at the end of a long process of observing many things and processes in the world. Rather it is that with which I begin before I can know anything at all, that which I presuppose, the first in truth and being, the infinite and perfect, whose name is God.

Anselm's ontological argument may be viewed in two perspectives, with regard to its form or its content. We shall discuss the content of this approach in a moment. But, first, as a *formal* argument, the ontological argument states that God is by definition that than which no greater can be conceived. That something, call it X, exists not only in the mind but in reality also. But that of which nothing greater (or more perfect) can be conceived surely cannot exist in the intellect only. For this would involve the contradiction that it is possible to conceive of a yet more perfect being existing both in reality and in the mind. Therefore, something than which nothing greater can be thought exists in the intellect as well as in reality, ". . . and this art Thou, O Lord," adds Anselm.[3]

Yet God not only exists but, for Anselm, has uniquely *necessary* existence.[4] This emphasis points to what we have called God's *aseity*. God is conceived as a necessary, self-existent reality, defined in such a way that it is impossible to conceive of Him as not existing.

Descartes (1596–1650) used an externalized form of the ontological argument by drawing an analogy between the properties which belong by definition to a triangle and those which belong to a perfect God. For example, in Euclidean geometry the sum of the angles of a triangle equals two right angles. In the same fashion, existence itself is a property which belongs by definition to that perfect Being, God.

We still have under discussion here the sheer logical form of this argument rather than its content as religious expression.[5] In Anselm's time, a monk named Gaunilon took the part of the fool who has no knowledge of Divine Being and says, "There is no God," thus denying God's existence. A man might picture in his mind a perfect island, but this would not prove its existence. Thus Anselm's conception of a perfect God does not establish His existence. Anselm answered that his argument applied not to a material object like an island but to this one unique Being, God.

Kant claimed that "existence" is not a logical predicate at all. We cannot say that "God is existence," because the *is* is a copula, or connective, which links a subject to a predicate. Only sense experience can tell us whether or not an object has existence. For 100 actual dollars contain no more cents than an imaginary 100 dollars, and we can know which is actual only through sense experience.

Twentieth-century criticism is more explicit.[6] Bertrand Russell states that *exists* may be grammatically a predicate but that logically it per-

[3] *Proslogion*, Chap. 2.
[4] *Ibid.*, Chap. 3.
[5] *Ibid.*
[6] By permission. From John Hick, *Philosophy of Religion*, Prentice-Hall, Inc., Englewood Cliffs, N.J., 1963, p. 19.

forms a different function. For instance, "Dogs exist" is translated "There are x's such that 'x is a dog' is true." This is not to attribute a quality (existence) to dogs but to claim that there are actual objects in the world to which a certain description summarized in the word *dog* applies. Suppose you say negatively, "Mermaids do not exist." This is equivalent to "There are no x's such that 'x is a mermaid' is true." For centuries, men worried about the status of that "something" which does *not* exist. It is clear, according to Russell, that "Mermaids do not exist" is equivalent to the assertion that this particular concept or description has no instances.

How does this apply to the logical *form* of the ontological argument? John Hick expresses it briefly:

> If existence is, as Anselm and Descartes assumed, an attribute or predicate which can be included in a definition and which, as a desirable attribute, must be included in the definition of God, then the ontological argument is valid. It would be self-contradictory to say that the most perfect conceivable being lacks the attribute of existence. But, if existence, while it appears grammatically in the role of a predicate, has the quite different logical function of asserting that a description applies to something in reality, then the ontological argument, considered as a proof of God's existence, fails. For if existence is not a predicate it cannot be a defining predicate of God, and the question of whether anything in reality corresponds to the concept of the most perfect conceivable being remains open to inquiry. A definition of God describes one's concept of God, but cannot prove the actual existence of any such being.[7]

The basic difference then is whether existence is an attribute included by definition in the concept of God or whether existence performs the logical function of asserting that this concept has instances. In the one case, the ontological "argument" is not a proof at all but a way of unfolding man's understanding of His aseity. In the other case, it is a purported proof of God's existence.

But the ontological argument, considered as a proof of God's existence, remains in doubt. But what, second, of its *content?* Karl Barth, for example, views Anselm's argument not as an attempt to prove God's existence at all. It is rather a statement leading one who already believes into fuller understanding of the nature of the God who discloses Himself.[8] From this perspective, Anselm himself was not attempting to convert the atheist but to unfold the meaning of the God of Christian faith and of

---

[7] *Ibid.*, pp. 19–20.

[8] See Karl Barth, *Anselm: Fides Quaerens Intellectum,* The Student Christian Movement Press, London; The John Knox Press, Richmond, Va., 1960.

the given, living tradition. The roots of this tradition are found in the biblical portrayal of God's revelation in human history. In the words of John Hutchison,

> It is this view of deity which is formulated in the ontological argument, and the significance of the argument is that it communicates to the philosophic consciousness of the Western world the impact of this understanding of God. . . . the ontological argument is not an argument but a formulation of man's apprehension of the transcendent-immanent God; it is a statement in the language of philosophy of the particular kind of apprehension of finitude and infinity which characterizes the Hebrew-Christian tradition.[9]

In terms of form, then, the ontological argument is not a proof of the existence of God but a statement of definition. It expresses a faithful man's conception of the God in whom he already believes on other grounds. This is the religious content to which the argument points, and these are the religious and theological uses of language which give it expression. God does not exist as an object exists. He is rather the first, the presupposition, of all thought whatever. He is both Truth and Being in Itself, the Ground and Source of all beings, including man's own. He is that Reality from which man may be estranged but never separated. This God is the One whose being is affirmed even in doubt. As Paul Tillich express it, the very

> . . . question of God is possible because an awareness of God is present in the question of God. This awareness precedes the question. It is not the result of the argument but its presupposition. This certainly means that the "argument" is no argument at all. The so-called ontological argument points to the ontological awareness of finitude. It shows that an awareness of the infinite is included in man's awareness of finitude. Man knows that he is finite, that he is excluded from an infinity which nevertheless belong to him.[10]

The Cosmological Argument

We turn to the "five ways" of Aquinas.[11] The first four are generally regarded as statement of the cosmological argument, while the fifth states a version of the teleological argument. We shall comment on the second,

[9] By permission. From John Hutchison, *Faith Reason, and Existence*, Oxford University Press, Fair Lawn, N.J., 1956, p. 153.

[10] Paul Tillich, *Systematic Theology*, The University of Chicago Press, Chicago, 1951, vol. I, p. 206.

[11] See *Summa Theologica, Basic Writings of St. Thomas Aquinas*, ed. by Anton C. Pegis, Random House, Inc., New York, 1945.

the First Cause argument, and the third, from the contingency of the world to a necessary Being. In each case, Aquinas tells us to look first not within but outside us, to actual phenomena of nature, and then to infer from these to God as First Mover, First Cause, necessary Being, perfect Being. *Something in the world exists, therefore God, the Source and Ground of all things, exists.* This is the simple form of the argument.

Aquinas's second proof points to efficient causation in the natural order as evidence for a First Cause. Everything has a cause, and this cause has a cause which precedes it in time. The cause of this cause has a cause, and so on. But an infinite regress of causes is intolerable. For to keep on pushing causal explanation back and back is never really to explain. It is this exclusion of endless regress which presents difficulties.

Attempts have been made to reinterpret Aquinas so as to avoid this problem. Those who stress this reinterpretation remind us that Aquinas conceived of motion not as mechanical shifting of things like billiard balls from one place to another but as development. This is Aristotle's view. Each organism "moves" from what it is potentially to the actualization of its proper end. Acorns become oaks. Embryos become organisms, each in its own kind. Thus what is last in order of time is first in order of being and value. For it is the end, the goal, which determines the essential nature of each organism or person. The end or goal then coexists with what it is now.

In the same way, the First Cause, God, is not just the first of a whole series of events in order of time. He is not like the first movement of the billiard ball that moves all the others. God is not a member of the series of natural causes at all. He is, as it were by analogy, "outside" the entire series. He is the Explanation, the Ground, the Source of all processes of nature whatsoever, whether past, present or future. God is timeless, pure actuality but the condition of everything that occurs in time. As stressed in discussion of the logic of analogy, Aquinas assumes that analogies can be drawn between the world and God. For example, is it more appropriate to say "The sun is hot like the world" or "The world is hot like the sun"? The latter is correct usage because there is a causal connection between the heat of the sun and that of the world. So, it is presupposed that God is related to the world as creative Cause to effect. But to speak of this, we must use analogical terms.

But, even so, the First Cause argument still has difficulties. How do we know that the whole universe is not ". . . a mere unintelligible brute fact"?[12] The skeptic or agnostic has grave doubts about this. The world simply *is*. And to assert any more is to beg the question. "The argument

[12] Hick, *op. cit.*, p. 21.

in effect presents the dilemma: either there is a First Cause or the universe is ultimately unintelligible; but it does not impel us to accept one horn of the dilemma rather than the other."[13]

Moreover, Aquinas's notion of cause is subject to serious criticism. As for Aristotle also, an efficient cause is an actual productive force which makes things happen throughout the universe. David Hume (1711–1776) initiated for moderns a different view. Causal connections between events are just observed sequences that happen again and again. Or, as held more recently, causal laws may be statements of statistical probabilities. If so, then the notion of necessary productive power is no longer a useful concept in scientific investigation. Many present-day followers of Aquinas assert that the Aristotelian-Thomist view of cause is not to be interpreted as science but as philosophy. But even so, as a compelling formal argument, the Thomist appeal to First Cause is not convincing.

Consider now the third way, from contingent events to necessary Being. It is conceivable that any particular thing in the world around us might not have existed at all. For instance, why do you exist? You could mention your parents and then go back and back. But you would only arrive at something which itself might not have existed. Thus, to reach a satisfactory explanation, we must grasp something of which we cannot say that it might not have existed. This is the first stage of the argument. It reduces to these terms: *if anything exists, an absolutely necessary Being must exist. Something exists. Therefore an absolutely necessary Being must exist.*

There is a second part of the argument, namely, to prove that a necessarily existing Being must be an infinitely perfect Being, that is, God. Kant holds that this second stage of the argument is simply the ontological argument all over again, and thus the same criticisms apply as before.[14]

But it is with the first stage of the argument to necessary Being that we must deal. This makes the claim that the existence of a necessary Being can be established. Smart reminds us that by a necessary Being is usually meant "a *logically* necessary being," i.e., ". . . a being whose nonexistence is inconceivable just as it is inconceivable that a triangle should have four sides and still be a triangle." Contemporary philosophers point out that the concept of a necessary Being or Existence is itself contradictory. For "necessity" applies logically not to things but to propositions.

13 *Ibid.*

14 See J. J. C. Smart, "The Existence of God," Antony Flew and Alasdair MacIntyre (eds.), *New Essays in Philosophical Theology,* The Macmillan Company, New York; The Student Christian Movement Press, London, 1955, p. 36. Compare Reading 14, pp. 264–279.

Propositions are necessary only by virtue of their form and do not assert the existence or nonexistence of anything; for example, "Either it is raining, or it is not raining"; "All bachelors are unmarried males"; "A thing cannot be red and green all over." These formal propositions are guaranteed solely by virtue of the rules of language they exhibit. By contrast the following propositions are factual and refer to the actual world of sense: "It is raining now"; "John Jones is a bachelor"; "That sweater is red." Factual propositions like these may be warranted only by appeal to empirical evidence, that is, by observation. But they cannot be said to be necessary; for all statements about existences are only probable and not logically necessary. Thus formal propositions are necessary and true by virtue of their form but assert nothing about existence. Factual propositions may report probable truths about existence but are contingent only and not necessary.

In this perspective, "God is a necessary Being" is logically contradictory and can only be translated into "The proposition 'God exists' is logically necessary." But this is the principle of the ontological argument once more. This, we recall, is valid formally only as a definition of the concept of God; it does not assert that the concept refers to actual existence. In the case of the cosmological argument also, God cannot be said to be a logically necessary Being.

But if we cannot say that God is a logically necessary Being, is there some other meaning of the term "necessary" appropriate to religious and theological utterance? Neither the ontological nor the cosmological arguments are valid as formal logical proofs of God's existence. But they both point, as we have indicated, to God's *aseity*. This is the theological use of this term "necessary Being." It points beyond logical form to religious content. God is understood as self-existent, eternal, not dependent for His being upon anything else but Source and Ground of all that is.

How then is God discovered? We suggested in our discussion of Jesus Christ that we do not simply *find* God out there in the orders of nature. God is not one more datum alongside all the phenomena of nature. If God is *seen* in the existent world of nature, it is because He is the kind of God who is encountered first within the personal and historical. The myth of creation, for example, does not provide us with some additional knowledge about actual phenomena designed to supplement that of the sciences. Rather it is religious affirmation of man's own utter dependence upon God and his conviction that all that is in the universe also has its ground in God. Thus the cosmological argument especially is the translation into the language of philosophy and theology of the creation myth of the biblical tradition. Its affirmations are not conclusions from the world but presuppositions and focused imagic symbols in terms of which the world is believed to make sense and man's own existence rendered significant.

Smart asks what sort of necessity then can "theological necessity" be if not *logical* necessity. He writes:

> Let me give an analogy from physics. It is not a *logical* necessity that the velocity of light in a vacuum should be constant. It would, however, upset physical theory considerably if we denied it. Similarly it is not a logical necessity that God exists. But it would clearly upset the structure of our religious attitudes in the most violent way if we denied it or even entertained the possibility of its falsehood. So if we say that it is a *physical* necessity that the velocity of light *in vacuo* should be constant—(deny it and prevailing physical theory would have to be scrapped or at any rate drastically modified)—similarly we can say that it is a *religious* necessity that God exists. That is, we believe in the necessity of God's existence because we are Christians; we are not Christians because we believe in the necessity of God's existence. There are no short cuts to God. I draw your attention to the language of religion itself, where we talk of *conversion*, not of *proof*. In my opinion religion can stand on its own feet, but to found it on metaphysical argument *a priori* is to found it on absurdity born of ignorance of the logic of our language.[15]

The Teleological Argument

People in moments of awe often say: "Look about you at the beauty, order and design in all of nature. Surely an intelligent Designer must have brought this universe into existence." This is the most direct form of argument for God. Perhaps it is the most widely accepted. Plato gave it philosophical expression in his *Timaeus*. For Thomas Aquinas it is the last of his five ways. At the turn of the eighteenth into the nineteenth century, William Paley (1743–1805) set down one of the most famous expressions of the argument from design in his *Natural Theology: or Evidences of the Existence and Attributes of the Deity Collected from the Appearances of Nature* (1802).[16] The most devastating critique of the design argument is that of David Hume in his *Dialogues concerning Natural Religion*.

The teleological argument in all its expressions takes its start from the

---

[15] *Ibid.*, p. 41.
[16] See Frederick Ferré's edition of this work in the Liberal Arts Library edition, New York, 1962.

processes of nature, proceeds to noting how all these seem to be designed for some goal, end, *telos*, and then infers the existence of a divine Designer. The fifth way of Thomas Aquinas notes how "natural bodies" lack intelligence and yet ". . . act for an end." These cannot move toward an end ". . . unless directed by some being endowed with knowledge and intelligence. . . . Therefore some intelligent being exists by whom all natural things are directed to their end; and this being we call God."[17]

Certain assumptions, common to Greek and medieval thinking, are embedded in this statement. Inorganic processes move toward given ends even though they are not themselves conscious. They are directed, then, by an Intelligence external to themselves.

Why do natural objects in the world exist? This approach seems to say that their reason for being is to serve man's own well-being: air to sustain life, meat to eat, beautiful mountains and valleys to stir the human soul. The modern student needs to ask: does contemporary science, with its impersonal world view, cast doubt on this naïve teleological explanation? Or are the scientific models used in any specific age or culture irrelevant to man's religious response to his world order? Or may the very models which are used as religious utterance be taken over from the sciences?

For example, nineteenth-century thinkers used models or analogies taken from the adaptive processes of organisms in relation to their environments. In fact, many were impressed by a purposive direction which seems to run through all evolutionary development from simpler to more complex forms. Here men stand in awe not of detailed factual data but of the signs of progressive upward movement. The first living creatures emerged from the inorganic. And from these elemental forms there developed the most intricate of specialized organs and functions as living beings adapted themselves to an ever-shifting environment: invertebrates, fishes, amphibians, reptiles, birds, mammals and man. From this "pageant of living forms," scholars like Lloyd Morgan infer purposiveness, continuity and yet emergence of the distinctively new and different at every crucial stage of development. Morgan points to a "principle of organization," "directive factor" or "Nisus" surging up through the successive levels of matter, life and mind.

Is the final cause of all of this material or mechanical? Or is it akin to a directive Intelligence? Here again the teleological argument is convincing to many thoughtful people. They believe the evidence points to God, the intelligent Designer, gathering all the long, intricate processes of evolution into the fulfillment of universal goals and purposes.

---

[17] The "fifth way" of Aquinas.

It is instructive to move back in time to the eighteenth century. Here the models employed are not the organic but the mechanical. For the universe is viewed as a great machine. Eighteenth-century men take their cue from Newton's mechanistic account of the motion of the planets. Thus throughout this machinelike universe every part fits with every other part in harmonious cosmic operation.

If we take this analogy seriously, what is the next step? The logic of the argument is precisely the same as in the case of nineteenth-century preoccupation with organic processes. William Paley uses an analogy which is still simpler, that of a watch. What does the existence of a watch suggest? Suppose you walk through a deserted area, says Paley, and stumble over a stone and ask how the stone came to be there. You might answer that it had always been there. But if you suddenly saw a watch lying on the ground and asked how it came to be there, it would not do to say it had always been there. Why is this so? Paley asks. "For this reason, and for no other, viz. that, when we come to inspect the watch, we perceive (what we could not discover in the stone) that its several parts are framed and put together for a purpose. . . ." Indeed, these parts are formed and shaped in order to mark the hours of the day. In fact, if the springs and wheels had been shaped any differently, the watch would not accomplish its purpose. Paley writes: ". . . the inference, we think, is inevitable; that the watch must have had a maker; that there must have existed, at sometime, and at some place or other, an artificer or artificers, who formed it for the purpose which we find it actually to answer; who comprehended its construction, and designed its use."

The next step is obvious: that of drawing a direct parallel between a watch and the world, each the product of an intelligent mind. But Paley reminds us that his inference from watch to watchmaker would not be weakened if we had never seen a watch made (for we have never seen a world different from the one in which we live) and hence did not know from experience that watches are produced by intelligent human beings. Nor would our inference from watch to watchmaker be undercut if we discovered that the mechanism sometimes went wrong, for it is not necessary that a machine be perfect in order to show the purpose for which it was made. Nor would our argument be invalidated if we discovered parts of the machine whose contribution to the whole was uncertain.

From these preliminary comments, Paley proceeds, with painstaking attention to detail, to trace his argument concerning this richly complex natural order. For the argument he holds to be cumulative from the working parts of animal organisms to the human frame, muscles, blood vessels, digestive system, the eye with its self-adjusting lenses and sensitivity to light and color, the regular rotation of the planets and the order of the seasons. All this leads Paley to conclude, ". . . one mind hath planned, or at least hath prescribed, a general plan for all these productions. One Being has been concerned in all."

It is strange that David Hume's critique of the argument from design (1779) was published twenty-three years before Paley's statement, and yet Paley paid no attention to Hume's devastating criticisms. Hume is the critic, although some scholars regard him as an outright atheist. However, it is important to note that all his life Hume was concerned about religion. He could not let it alone. His attacks on organized religion and facile uncritical beliefs are devastating. Yet he is careful to say that he is not attempting to destroy religion as such. His view, all through his philosophical writings, stresses points made in this chapter concerning "necessary existence." It is that no rational, a priori demonstration of the necessary existence of anything is possible. Necessity applies only to the structure of mathematical and logical systems which make no reference to existences. Contrariwise, no existence is necessary. It just happens. Thus, with any attempt to prove the necessary existence of God, only disillusionment can result. In fact, Hume is saying, to be cautiously skeptical about the whole rational attempt in theology is a first, essential step toward sound Christian faith.

But equally important is Hume's rejection of any empirical arguments for God, following the methods of so-called natural religion. For advocates of natural or rational religion claimed to base their convictions not on revelation but on man's unaided cognitive powers. Reason therefore takes the materials of experience and draws them into conclusions by employing the same laws of logic and evidence as do any of the sciences.

All the difficulties of argument by analogy come to focus in Hume's dialogue. Is the universe like a machine, and is there any direct parallel between the maker of a machine and an intelligent Designer of the world? Hume underscores the weakness of argument by analogy. It is easy to infer from a human artifact like a house to an architect. But the whole universe may be more like an organism than a human artifact. For Hume presupposes that from similar causes there follow similar effects. Further, we do not have any warrant for reasoning from parts of the world, which we can observe, to conclusions about the whole.

Thus from a finite world we cannot infer an infinite Creator. Are we caught then in anthropomorphism from which we can never escape? The world is diverse, full of many conflicting elements, good and evil. We are not then justified in affirming one God instead of many, a good God or an all-powerful God. Most important, even if we were entitled to infer an infinite Designer of the whole universe, we would not be justified in calling that being the Creator-Father God of the Christian tradition.

In effect, Hume's criticisms of the teleological argument merge with the conclusions we advanced concerning the cosmological argument. Both arguments, at best, are translations into the language of philosophy of the creation myth of the biblical tradition. Hume and Kant admit that the teleological argument especially holds a distinctive attraction for men of every age. Yet many a person does not realize the nature of the arguments he holds in such respect. He affirms not conclusions drawn from the facts but presupposed frameworks of those images and symbols which define his life orientation. In terms of these, the world is "seen" to make sense and man's relation to the whole scheme of things is rendered significant. As a formal argument, therefore, the teleological, like the cosmological argument, is not convincing. Yet again, as a way of expressing the *content* of religious conviction, if employed with caution, it has value.

The Moral Argument

The moral argument for God's being is rooted, just as are the other three arguments, in a distinctive area of human experience. It asks us to take seriously the fact that we all have within us some sense of moral obligation and then to infer from this to God, the Sustainer of man's moral life. To be sure, the specific content of moral values and patterns of action may vary from age to age and culture to culture. But all through these variations runs a common theme, the sense of obligation itself. Moral duty may lead one group of men to a particular mode of action and another group to the opposite, but no matter what specifically each one claims he ought to do, he shares with all the others the primacy of moral imperative or awareness of a command to oneself.

It is from this universality of moral obligation that Immanuel Kant (1724–1804) moved in his argument for God. "Two things," he affirmed, "fill the mind with ever new and increasing admiration and awe, the oftener and more steadily we reflect on them: the starry heavens above and the moral law within." All of us, he is saying, live as inhabitants of two worlds, the world of what *is* and the world of what *ought to be*. The sciences and common sense give us knowledge of the "is" world, the order of natural phenomena. This is reason's work, providing us with legitimate knowledge as far as it goes. But although reason may master the natural realm of space and time and events linked in cause-and-effect relationships, this same reason cannot penetrate "reality," or things as they are in themselves. Ultimate questions of God, freedom and immortality of the soul cannot be answered by "pure" or scientific understanding. Pure reason cannot prove these tenets, but Kant's "practical reason" can establish these same tenets as what must be presupposed if the moral life is to be sustained.

Even here, then, Kant's method is that of asking the following kind of question. If the moral life is one of the primacy of obligation to the moral law as a universal demand among men, what must we assume or postulate as the Ground of that moral experience? Further, if we recognize the *summum bonum*, the highest good which is perfect happiness, how are we to sustain the necessary relation between the moral law and that *summum bonum?* It becomes necessary to postulate the existence of God, he claims. Also Kant asserts that it is necessary to presuppose immortality of the soul in order to provide man with unlimited time in which to realize his true end. But basic to all these concerns is the postulate of freedom. For unless men assume their ability to choose, to impose the moral law upon themselves without the tyranny of external compulsion of societies or governments, then they are not autonomous moral agents but only cogs in the physical scientist's machinelike world along with other mass particles moving in space.

As in the case of the other arguments, the moral argument moves on two levels: first, in the *form* of a logical argument; second, not as a logical argument at all but as an expression of the *content* of religious conviction implicit in moral conviction. The first takes the form of a logical inference from objective systems of moral law to a divine Lawgiver. Sometmes men infer from the objectivity of values to a Ground of all values or from the speaking of conscience to a God whose "voice" is its ultimate source. In all these versions of the moral argument, the form is the same: that of pointing to the fact of men's sense of values and obligation and then claiming that it is logically dependent on a transcendent Ground. Basically the assumption here is that we cannot explain moral values naturalistically, that is, without appeal to the Supernatural. It is not enough, these advocates claim, to say the values are part of the natural order, the product of human impulses, needs and interests or of the structures of the social order. But as an argument in this logical form, is the following convincing?

Moral values are objective in the sense that they are essential qualities of human nature; they are, therefore, real parts of the world-order; now man cannot but hold . . . that he and his values are real: the world-order must consequently be in some sense a moral order, in the sense, namely, that there is room in it for man and the ideal of goodness which is basal to his nature; and this could not be unless the world-order is directed by a conscious, rational Being who wills the final triumph of goodness; God exists, therefore, as the necessary implication of the objectivity of moral values.[18]

To assume that values cannot be explained naturalistically but only by appeal to the Supernatural is logically to beg the question at issue. For it is this inference itself which is in dispute. Therefore the conclusion has not been established. The naturalist or skeptic is thus still firmly supported in his position that values are altogether grounded in the natural and the human. John Hick writes:

> The second kind of moral argument is not open to the same objection, for it is not strictly an argument at all. It consists of the claim that anyone seriously committed to respect moral values as exercising a sovereign claim upon his life, must thereby implicitly believe in the reality of a transhuman source and basis for these values, which religion calls God.[19]

John Baillie, for example, finds both strength and weakness in Kant's contribution. He holds that Kant aided the recovery of Descartes's conviction that God is ". . . a Reality who more directly confronts us than do the things of sense" and our certainty of Him is ". . . prior to the certainties of science. . . ." Kant stressed the primacy of the moral over the scientific as the key to the Ultimate. "Ultimate reality meets us, not in the form of an object that invites our speculation, but in the form of a demand that is made upon our obedience." But, says Baillie, here Kant made his mistake; for ". . . his eighteenth-century education was too much for him." He analyzed ". . . this experience into mere *respect for a law.*" The spiritual life of man turns out to be ". . . mere respectful acceptance of a formula," and this ". . . was, in fact, the last absurdity of the eighteenth century." Again Baillie claims that ". . . Kant's religion remained to the end a mere legalistic moralism *plus* a syllogism that allowed him to conceive of an eighteenth-cenutry Legislator behind his eighteenth-century law."[20]

---

[18] By permission. From G. W. Cunningham, *Problems of Philosophy*, Holt, Rinehart and Winston, Inc., New York, 1924, p. 418.

[19] Hick, *op. cit.*, p. 27.

[20] John Baillie, *Our Knowledge of God*, Oxford University Press, London, 1939, pp. 157–159.

Further, Baillie cites Kant's statement that ". . . the purpose of prayer can only be to induce in us a moral disposition. . . . To wish to converse with God is absurd: we cannot talk to one we cannot intuit; and as we cannot intuit God, but can only believe in him, we cannot converse with him." And then Baillie comments, "Now it seems to me that it is precisely such a sense of *converse* with the Living God as Kant thus clearly saw to be excluded by his own system that lies at the root of all our spiritual life."[21]

This perspective, represented by John Baillie and also by his brother D. M. Baillie, holds that the so-called moral consciousness is an abstraction. Rather the moral life and faith in God are bound together. "Either our moral values tell us something about the nature and purpose of reality (i.e., give us the germ of religious belief) or they are subjective and therefore meaningless."[22]

The Moral Involves the Personal

When you and I make value judgments, we say, "This is good" or "I ought to do thus and so." Some contemporary writers insist that such value statements have two aspects. One is declarative, for it states that the speaker either prefers or does not prefer a given object in a particular way. The second is a nondeclarative element which takes the form of a command. This bids someone else to share his approval or disapproval. Philip Wheelwright holds that this nondeclarative element is not a command to someone else. It is basically a command to oneself. He writes:

Let each reader test this for himself by introspective reflection. Think of some *discovery* of value and consequent obligation—e.g., when one recognizes what one owes to a friend in need and accepts the obligation to help him. In a practical situation like this the value at issue is perhaps never formulated in words. Whether it is or not, it involves more than factual discovery. "I *want* to help my friend." Of course there is this too. But there may be an even stronger contrary pull—"It is so inconvenient to give him the help he needs!" The question is not the factual one of which motive is the stronger. The reasoner does not reduce the question to the simple factual form. "Which do I actually want to do more?" Even if he uses that form of words, there is surplus of meaning which they do not express. That additional element of meaning comes not as a discovery of fact, but as a

[21] *Ibid.*, p. 159.
[22] D. M. Baillie, *Faith in God and Its Christian Consummation*, T. & T. Clark, Edinburgh, 1927, pp. 172–173.

discovery of command; and not a command issued by one individual to another, but a command issuing somehow out of the situation, or it may be from beyond the situation, and which the reasoner beholds as an obligation to be fulfilled—or better, as a vocation, *a being called*. A real value judgment is always in part an answer to the command, a "So be it!"[23]

The man of Christian conviction would move one step further, and this is a big step, perhaps a leap of faith. The Christian holds that the source of moral imperative is the God of justice and love is disclosed in human history through Jesus, the Christ. This tenet. does not deny the obvious fact of wide variety among the standards and patterns of moral practice of different times and cultures. The Judeo-Christian tradition does not consist of legalistic codes which prescribe in detail what men must or must not do no matter what the circumstances. If this were so, its adherents would be caught in a legalism in which a specific rule is applicable to each particular kind of moral situation. But our neighbors find themselves in varying circumstances of need. What specifically ought we to do for our neighbor? Is it a loaf of bread or an extended hand to steady him when he slips and falls? In reaching out to him, we respond to a command from beyond ourselves. Implicit in this obligation itself is belief in the God who is Source and Ground of the values of justice and love. Then what we are led specifically to do in response to His demand upon our lives will disclose itself in the situation at hand. This requires sensitivity, persistence and intelligent judgment.

Is this skill given somehow automatically out of the blue? No! It is learned. God's "presence" and awareness of His demand upon men do not simply flash into human consciousness. For the single individual the disclosure may be immediate but not apart from the world of nature and the presence of the community. God's self-disclosure is always, says John Baillie, a ". . . mediated immediacy." ". . . the consciousness of God is never given save in conjunction with the consciousness of things. We do not know God through the world, but we know Him with the world; and in knowing Him with the world, we know Him as its ground. Nature is not an argument for God, but it is a sacrament of Him."[24] Baillie also adds:

. . . that all our knowledge of God is given us "in, with and under" our knowledge of one another. This means, first, that the knowledge of God is withholden from those who keep themselves aloof from the *service* of their

---

[23] By permission. From Philip Wheelwright, *The Way of Philosophy*, The Odyssey Press, Inc., New York, 1960, pp. 425–426.

[24] John Baillie, *op. cit.*, p. 178.

fellows. . . . It means, second, that only when I am in *fellowship* with my fellow men does the knowledge of God come to me individually. It means the necessity of the Church and the rejection of religious individualism.[25]

What It Means to Say: "God Exists"

Clearly one who speaks of himself as standing within a historic community, in the way Baillie describes, is not advancing a strict proof of God's existence. He is expressing what for him is a total orientation of his own existence. He is stabbed awake to an immediate demand, *mediated* through that historic community and tradition. It is an imperative placed upon him in view of what God has done and is doing in His world. To believe this is to act in a certain way and to pursue a distinctive style of life.

If this is so, we begin to discern what it means for such a person to say, "God exists." It does not mean that some sort of "objective entity exists out there." We point rather to God's *aseity*. For He does not "exist" as contingent, finite things and events exist. He is that Reality which the man of faith postulates as prior to all else, all thinking and being. To say "God exists" is to affirm that without God as Ultimate in his life man's existence and universe would be different. To spell out the precise character of this difference is difficult. But John Hick puts it affirmatively:

> To say that X exists or is real, or it is a fact that there is an X, is to claim that the character of the universe differs in some specific way from the character that an X-less universe would have. The nature of this difference will naturally depend on the X in question. And the meaning of "God exists" will be indicated by spelling out the past, present and future difference which God's existence is alleged to make within human experience.[26]

In short, "God exists" is not a statement of some static state of affairs simply to be uttered in cool detachment. Its language is rather that of intention and resolve to act in a certain way toward the future. To say "God exists" is to be aware of a self-imposed demand to become part of the difference God's purpose makes in the world. This is to be possessed not of certainty but of a warrant for imaginative and constructive living in a universe still in the making.

[25] *Ibid.*, p. 179.
[26] Hick, *op. cit.*, p. 106.

14

J. J. C. SMART | *The Existence of God**

This lecture is not to discuss whether God exists. It is to discuss reasons which philosophers have given for saying that God exists. That is, to discuss certain arguments.

First of all it may be as well to say what we may hope to get out of this. Of course, if we found that any of the traditional arguments for the existence of God were sound, we should get out of our one hour this Sunday afternoon something of inestimable value, such as one never got out of any hour's work in our lives before. For we should have got out of one hour's work the answer to that question about which, above all, we want to know the answer. (This is assuming for the moment that the question "Does God exist?" is a proper question. The fact that a question is all right as far as the rules of ordinary grammar are concerned does not ensure that it has a sense. For example, "Does virtue run faster than length?" is certainly all right as far as ordinary grammar is concerned, but it is obviously not a meaningful question. Again, "How fast does time flow?" is all right as far as ordinary grammar is concerned, but it has no clear meaning. Now some philosophers would ask whether the question "Does God exist?" is a proper question. The greatest danger to theism at the present moment does not come from people who deny the validity of the arguments for the existence of God, for many Christian theologians do not believe that the existence of God can be proved, and certainly nowhere in the Old or New Testaments do we find any evidence of people's religion having a metaphysical basis. The main danger to theism today comes from people who want to say that "God exists" and "God does not exist" are equally absurd. The concept of God, they would say, is a nonsensical one. Now I myself shall later give grounds for thinking

* By permission. From J. J. C. Smart, a public lecture given at the University of Adelaide, 1951, in Antony Flew and Alasdair MacIntyre (eds.), *New Essays in Philosophical Theology*, The Student Christian Movement Press, London, 1955, pp. 28–46.

that the question "Does God exist?" is not, in the full sense, a proper question, but I shall also give grounds for believing that to admit this is not necessarily to endanger theology.)

However, let us assume for the moment that the question "Does God exist?" is a proper question. We now ask: Can a study of the traditional proofs of the existence of God enable us to give an affirmative answer to this question? I contend that it can not. I shall point out what seem to me to be fallacies in the main traditional arguments for the existence of God. Does proving that the arguments are invalid prove that God does not exist? Not at all. For to say that an argument is invalid is by no means the same thing as to say that its conclusion is false. Still, if we do find that the arguments we consider are all fallacious, what do we *gain* out of our investigation? Well, one thing we gain is a juster (if more austere) view of what philosophical argument can do for us. But, more important, we get a deeper insight into the logical nature of certain concepts, in particular, of course, the concepts of deity and existence. Furthermore we shall get some hints as to whether philosophy can be of any service to theologians, and if it can be of service, some hints as to how it can be of service. I think that it can be, but I must warn you that many, indeed perhaps the majority, of philosophers today would not entirely agree with me here [see Ch. II above (in *New Essays in Philosophical Theology*)].

One very noteworthy feature which must strike anyone who first looks at the usual arguments for the existence of God is the extreme brevity of these arguments. They range from a few lines to a few pages. St. Thomas Aquinas presents five arguments in three pages! Would it not be rather extraordinary if such a great conclusion should be got so easily? Before going on to discuss any of the traditonal arguments in detail I want to give general grounds for suspecting anyone who claims to settle a controversial question by means of a short snappy argument.

My reason for doubting whether a short snappy argument can ever settle any controversial question is as follows: *any argument can be reversed*. Let me explain this. A question of elementary logic is involved. Let us consider an argument from two premisses, p, q, to a conclusion r:

$$p$$
$$\frac{q}{r}$$

If the argument is valid, that is, if r really does follow from p and q, the argument will lead to agreement about r provided that there already is agreement about p and q. For example, if we have the premisses *p*   All A, B and C grade cricketers are entitled to a free pass to the Adelaide Oval for Test matches, Sheffield Shield matches, etc. (quite uncontroversial, it can be got from the rules of the South Australian Cricket Association).

q   John Wilkin is an A, B or C grade cricketer. (Quite uncontroversial, everyone knows it.)

we may conclude

r   John Wilkin is entitled to a free pass to the Adelaide Oval for Test matches, Sheffield Shield matches, etc.

But we now consider this argument:[1]

p   Nothing can come into existence except through the activity of some previously existing thing or being.

q   The world had a beginning in time.

therefore

r   The world came into existence through the activity of some previously existing thing or being.

If this argument is valid (as it certainly is) then it is equally the case that

(not-*r*)   The world did not come into existence through the activity of some previously existing thing or being

implies that either

(not-*p*)   Something *can* come into existence otherwise than through the activity of a previously existing thing or being

or

(not-*q*)   The world had no beginning in time.

---

[1] I owe this illustration, and the whole application to the idea of "reversing the argument", to Prof. D. A. T. Gasking of Melbourne.

$$\text{That is, if } \frac{p}{q} \text{ is valid } \frac{\text{not-}r}{\text{not-}p} \text{ and } \frac{\text{not-}r}{\text{not-}q} \text{ must be equally valid.}$$

Now it is possible that a person might think that we have *fewer* reasons for believing r than we have for believing (not-p) or (not-q). In which case the argument $\frac{p}{q}$ though perfectly valid will not convince him. For he will be inclined to argue in the opposite direction, that is, from the falsity of r to the falsity of either p or q.

This last example is perhaps itself a—not very good—argument for the existence of God, but I have given it purely as an example to show *one* of the things to look out for when criticizing more serious arguments. The other thing to look out for, of course, is whether the argument is *valid*. It is my belief that in the case of any metaphysical argument it will be found that if the premisses are uncontroversial the argument is unfortunately not valid, and that if the argument is valid the premisses will unfortunately be just as doubtful as the conclusion they are meant to support.

With these warnings in mind let us proceed to the discussion of the three most famous arguments for the existence of God. These are:

(1)   The Ontological Argument.
(2)   The Cosmoslogical Argument.
(3)   The Teleological Argument.

The first argument—the ontological argument—really has no premisses at all. It tries to show that there would be a contradiction in denying that God exists. It was first formulated by St. Anselm and was later used by Descartes. It is not a convincing argument to modern ears, and St. Thomas Aquinas gave essentially the right reasons for rejecting it. However, it is important to discuss it, as an understanding of what is wrong with it is necessary for evaluating the second argument, that is, the cosmological argument. This argument does have a premiss, but not at all a controversial one. It is that something exists. We should all, I think, agree to that. The teleological argument is less austere in manner than the other two. It tries to argue to the existence of God not purely *a priori* and not from the mere fact of *something* existing, but from the actual features we observe in nature, namely those which seem to be evidence of design or purpose.

We shall discuss these three arguments in order. I do not say that they are the only arguments which have been propounded for the existence of God, but they are, I think, the most important ones. For example, of St. Thomas Aquinas' celebrated 'Five Ways' the first three are variants of the cosmological argument, and the fifth is a form of the teleological argument.

The Ontological Argument. This, as I remarked, contains no factual premiss. It is a *reductio-ad-absurdum* of the supposition that God does not exist. Now *reductio-ad-absurdum* proofs are to be suspected whenever there is doubt as to whether the statement to be proved is *significant.* For example, it is quite easy, as anyone who is familiar with the so-called Logical Paradoxes will know, to produce a not *obviously* nonsensical statement, such that both it *and* its denial imply a contradiction. So unless we are sure of the significance of a statement we cannot regard a *reductio-ad-absurdum* of its contradictory as proving its truth. This point of view is well known to those versed in the philosophy of mathematics; there is a well-known school of mathematicians, led by Brouwer, who refuse to employ *reductio-ad-absurdum* proofs. However, I shall not press this criticism of the ontological argument, for this criticism is somewhat abstruse (though it has been foreshadowed by Catholic philosophers, who object to the ontological argument by saying that it does not first show that the concept of an infinitely perfect being is a *possible* one). We are at present assuming that "Does God exist?" is a proper question, and if it is a proper question there is no objection so far to answering it by means of a *reductio-ad-absurdum* proof. We shall content ourselves with the more usual criticisms of the ontological argument.

The ontological argument was made famous by Descartes. It is to be found at the beginning of his Fifth Meditation. As I remarked earlier it was originally put forward by Anselm, though I am sorry to say that to read Descartes you would never suspect that fact! Descartes points out that in mathematics we can deduce various things purely *a priori*, "as for example", he says, "when I imagine a triangle, although there is not and perhaps never was in any place . . . one such figure, it remains true nevertheless that this figure possesses a certain determinate nature, form, or essence, which is . . . not framed by me, nor in any degree dependent on my thought; as appears from the circumstance, that diverse properties of the triangle may be demonstrated, for example that its three angles are equal to two right, that its greatest side is subtended by its greatest angle, and the like". Descartes now goes on to suggest that just as having the sum of its angles equal to two right angles is involved in the idea of a triangle, so *existence* is involved in the very idea of an infinitely perfect being, and that it would therefore be as much of a contradiction to assert that an infinitely perfect being does not exist as it is to assert that the three angles of a triangle do not add up to two right angles or that two of its sides are not together greater than the third side. We may then, says Descartes, assert that an infinitely perfect being *necessarily* exists, just as we may say that two sides of a triangle are together *necessarily* greater than the third side.

This argument is highly fallacious. To say that a so-and-so exists is not in the least like saying that a so-and-so has such-and-such a property. It is not to amplify a concept but to say that a concept applies to something can not be seen from an examination of the concept itself. Existence is not a property. "Growling" is a property of tigers, and to say that "tame tigers growl" is to say something about tame tigers, but to say "tame tigers exists" is not to say something about tame tigers but to say that there are tame tigers. Prof. G. E. Moore once brought out the difference between existence and a property such as that of being tame, or being a tiger, or being a growler, by reminding us that though the sentence "some tame tigers do not *growl*" makes perfect sense, the sentence "some tame tigers do not *exist*" has no clear meaning. The fundamental mistake in the ontological argument, then, is that it treats "exists" in "an infinitely perfect being exists" as if it ascribed a property existence to an infinitely perfect being, just as "is loving" in "an infinitely perfect being is loving" ascribes a property, or as "growl" in "tame tigers growl" ascribes a property: the verb "to exist" in "an infinitely perfect being exists" does not ascribe a property to something already conceived of as existing but says that the concept of an infinitely perfect being applies to something. The verb "to exist" here takes us right out of the purely conceptual world. This being so, there can never be any *logical contradiction* in denying that God exists. It is worth mentioning that we are less likely to make the sort of mistake that the ontological argument makes if we use the expression "there is a so-and-so" instead of the more misleading form of words "a so-and-so exists".

I should like to mention another interesting, though less crucial, objection to Descartes' argument. He talks as though you can deduce further properties of, say, a triangle, by considering its definition. It is worth pointing out that from the definition of a triangle as a figure bounded by three straight lines you can only deduce trivialities, such as that it is bounded by more than one straight line, for example. It is not at all a contradiction to say that the two sides of a triangle are together less then the third side, or that its angles do not add up to two right angles. To get a contradiction you have to bring in the specific axioms of

Euclidean geometry. (Remember school geometry, how you used to prove that the angles of a triangle add up to two right angles. Through the vertex C of the triangle ABC you drew a line parallel to BA, and so you assumed the axiom of parallels for a start.) Definitions, by themselves, are not deductively potent. Descartes, though a very great mathematician himself, was profoundly mistaken as to the nature of mathematics. However, we can interpret him as saying that from the definition of a triangle, *together with the axioms of Euclidean geometry*, you can deduce various things, such as that the angles of a triangle add up to two right angles. But this just shows how pure mathematics is a sort of game with symbols; you start with a set of axioms, and operate on them in accordance with certain rules of inference. All the mathematician requires is that the axiom set should be *consistent*. Whether or not it has application to reality lies outside pure mathematics. Geometry is no fit model for a proof of real existence.

We now turn to the *Cosmological Argument*. This argument does at least seem more promising than the ontological argument. It does start with a factual premiss, namely that something exists. The premiss that something exists is indeed a very abstract one, but nevertheless it *is* factual, it does give us a foothold in the real world of things, it does go beyond the consideration of mere concepts. The argument has been put forward in various forms, but for present purposes it may be put as follows:

Everything in the world around us is *contingent*. That is, with regard to any particular thing, it is quite conceivable that it might not have existed. For example, if you were asked why you existed, you could say that it was because of your parents, and if asked why they existed you could go still further back, but however far you go back you have not, so it is argued, made the fact of your existence really intelligible. For however far back you go in such a series you only get back to something which itself might not have existed. For a really satisfying explanation of why anything contingent (such as you or me or this table) exists you must eventually begin with something which is not itself contingent, that is, with something of which we cannot say that it might not have existed, that is we must begin with a necessary being. So the first part of the argument boils down to this. *If anything exists an absolutely necessary being must exist. Something exists. Therefore an absolutely necessary being must exist.*

The second part of the argument is to prove that a necessarily existing being must be an infinitely perfect being, that is, God. Kant[2] contended

[2] *Critique of Pure Reason*, A 603.

that this second stage of the argument is just the ontological argument over again, and of course if this were so the cosmological argument would plainly be a fraud; it begins happily enough with an existential premiss ("something exists") but this would only be a cover for the subsequent employment of the ontological argument. This criticism of Kant's has been generally accepted but I think that certain Thomist philosophers have been right in attributing to Kant's own criticism a mistake in elementary logic. Let us look at Kant's criticism. Kant says, correctly enough, that the conclusion of the second stage of the cosmological argument is "All necessarily existing beings are infinitely perfect beings". This, he says, implies that "Some infinitely perfect beings are necessarily existing beings". Since, however, there could be only one infinitely perfect, unlimited being, we may replace the proposition "Some infinitely perfect beings are necessarily existing beings" by the proposition "All infinitely perfect beings are necessarily existing beings". (To make this last point clearer let me take an analogous example. If it is true that some men who are Prime Minister of Australia are Liberals and if it is also true that there is only one Prime Minister of Australia, then we can equally well say that all men who are Prime Minister of Australia are Liberals. For "some" means "at least one", and if there is only one Prime Minister, then "at least one" is equivalent to "one", which in this case is "all".) So the conclusion of the second stage of the cosmological argument is that "all infinitely perfect beings are necessarily existing beings". This, however, is the principle of the ontological argument, which we have already criticized, and which, for that matter, proponents of the cosmological argument like Thomas Aquinas themselves reject.

Kant has, however, made a very simple mistake. He has forgotten that the existence of a necessary being has already been proved (or thought to have been proved) in the first part of the argument. He changes "All necessary beings are infinitely perfect beings" round to "Some infinitely perfect beings are necessary beings". If this change round is to be valid the existence of a necessary being is already presupposed. Kant has been misled by an ambiguity in "all". "All X's are Y's" may take it for granted that there are some X's or it may not. For example if I say, "All the people in this room are interested in Philosophy", it is already agreed that there are some people in this room. So we can infer that "Some of the people interested in Philosophy are people in this room". So "All the people in this room are interested in Philosophy" says more than "If anyone were in this room he would be interested in Philosophy", for this would be true even if there were in fact no people in this room. (As I wrote this lecture I was quite sure that *if* anyone came he would be interested in Philosophy, and I could have been quite sure of this even if I had doubted whether anyone would come.) Now sometimes "All X's are Y's" does mean only "If anything is an X it is a Y". Take the sentence "All trespassers will be prosecuted". This does not imply that some prosecuted people will be trespassers, for it does not imply that there are or will be any trespassers. Indeed the object of putting it on a notice is to make it more likely that there won't be any trespassers. All that "All trespassers will be prosecuted" says is, "If anyone is a trespasser then he will be prosecuted". So Kant's criticism won't do. He has taken himself and other people in by using "all" sometimes in the one way and sometimes in the other.

While agreeing thus far with Thomist critics of Kant[3] I still want to assert that the cosmological argument is radically unsound. The trouble comes much earlier than where Kant locates it. The trouble comes in the *first* stage of the argument. For the first stage of the argument purports to argue to the existence of a necessary being. And by "a necessary being" the cosmological argument means "a *logically* necessary being", i.e. "a being whose non-existence is inconceivable in the sort of way that a triangle's having four sides is inconceivable". The trouble is, however, that the concept of a logically necessary being is a self-contradictory concept, like the concept of a round square. For in the first place "necessary" is a predicate of *propositions*, not of things. That is, we can contrast *necessary* propositions such as "3 + 2 = 5", "a thing cannot be red and green all over", "either it is raining or it is not raining", with *contingent* propositions, such as "Mr. Menzies is Prime Minister of Australia", "the earth is slightly flattened at the poles", and "sugar is soluble in water". The propositions in the first class are guaranteed solely by the rules for the use of the symbols they contain. In the case of the propositions of the second class a genuine possibility of agreeing or not agreeing with reality is left open; whether they are true or false depends not on the conventions of our language but on reality. (Compare the contrast between "the equator is 90 degrees from the pole", which tells us nothing about geography but only about our map-making conventions, and "Adelaide is 55 degrees from the pole", which does tell us a geographical fact.) So no informative proposition can be logically necessary. Now since "necessary" is a word which applies primarily to propositions, we shall have to interpret "God is a necessary being" as "The proposi-

---

[3] See, for example, Fr. T. A. Johnston, *Australasian Journal of Philosophy*, Vol. XXI, pp. 14–15, or D. F. B. Hawkins, *Essentials of Theism*, pp. 67–70, and the review of Fr. Hawkins' book by A. Donagan, *Australasian Journal of Philosophy*, Vol. XXVIII, especially p. 129.

tion 'God exists' is logically necessary." But this *is* the principle of the ontological argument, and there is no way of getting round it this time in the way that we got out of Kant's criticism. No existential proposition can be logically necessary, for we saw that the truth of a logically necessary proposition depends only on our symbolism, or to put the same thing in another way, on the relationship of concepts. We saw, however, in discussing the ontological argument, that an existential proposition does not say that one concept is involved in another, but that a concept applies to something. An existential proposition must be very different from any logically necessary one, such as a mathematical one, for example, for the conventions of our symbolism clearly leave it open for us either to affirm or deny an existential proposition; it is not our symbolism but reality which decides whether or not we must affirm it or deny it.

The demand that the existence of God should be *logically* necessary is thus a self-contradictory one. When we see this and go back to look at the first stage of the cosmological argument it no longer seems compelling, indeed it now seems to contain an absurdity. If we cast our minds back, we recall that the argument was as follows: that if we explain why something exists and is what it is, we must explain it by reference to something else, and we must explain that thing's being what it is by reference to yet another thing, and so on, back and back. It is then suggested that unless we can go back to a logically necessary first cause we shall remain intellectually unsatisfied. We should otherwise only get back to something which might have been otherwise, and with reference to which the same questions can again be asked. This is the argument, but we now see that in asking for a logically necessary first cause we are doing something worse than asking for the moon. It is only *physically* impossible for us to get the moon; if I were a few million times bigger I could reach out for it and give it to you. That is, I know what it would be *like* to give you the moon, though I can not *in fact* do it. A logically necessary first cause, however, is not impossible in the way that giving you the moon is impossible; no, it is *logically* impossible. "Logically necessary being" is a self-contradictory expression like "round square". It is not any good saying that we would only be intellectually satisfied with a logically necessary cause, that nothing else would do. We can easily have an absurd wish. We should all like to be able to eat our cake and have it, but that does not alter the fact that our wish is an absurd and self-contradictory one. We reject the cosmological argument, then, because it rests on a thorough absurdity.

Having reached this conclusion I should like to make one or two remarks about the necessity of God. First of all, I think that it is undeniable that if worship is to be what religion takes it to be, then God must be a necessary being in some sense or other of "necessary". He must not be just one of the things in the word, however big. To concede that he was just one of the things in the world, even a big one, would reduce religion to something near idolatry. All I wish to point out is that God can not be a *logically* necessary being, for the very supposition that he is self-contradictory. (Hence, of course, to say that God is not logically necessary is not to place any limitations on him. It is not a limitation on your walking ability that you cannot go out of the room and not go out. To say that someone cannot do something self-contradictory is not to say that he is in any way impotent, it is to say that the sentence "he did such and such and did not do it" is not a possible description of anything.) Theological necessity cannot be logical necessity. In the second place, I think I can see roughly what sort of necessity theological necessity might be. Let me give an analogy from physics. It is not a *logical* necessity that the velocity of light in a vacuum should be constant. It would, however, upset physical theory considerably if we denied it. Similarly it is not a logical necessity that God exists. But it would clearly upset the structure of our religious attitudes in the most violent way if we denied it or even entertained the possibility of its falsehood. So if we say that it is a *physical* necessity that the velocity of light *in vacuo* should be constant—(deny it and prevailing physical theory would have to be scrapped or at any rate drastically modified)—similarly we can say that it is a *religious* necessity that God exists. That is, we believe in the necessity of God's existence because we are Christians; we are not Christians because we believe in the necessity of God's existence. There are no short cuts to God. I draw your attention to the language of religion itself, where we talk of *conversion*, not of *proof*. In my opinion religion can stand on its own feet, but to found it on a metaphysical argument *a priori* is to found it on absurdity born of ignorance of the logic of our language. I am reminded of what was said about the Boyle lectures in the eighteenth century: that no one doubted that God existed until the Boyle lecturers started to prove it.

Perhaps now is the time to say why I suggested at the beginning of the lecture that "Does God exist?" is not a proper question. Once again I make use of an analogy from science. "Do electrons exist?" (asked just like that) is not a proper question. In order to acquire the concept of an electron we must find out about experiments with cathode ray tubes, the Wilson cloud chamber, about spectra and so on. We then find the concept of the electron a useful one, one which plays a part in a mass of physical theory. When we reach this stage the question "Do electrons exist?" no longer arises. Before we reached this stage the question "Do electrons exist?" had no clear meaning. Similarly, I suggest, the question "Does God exist?" has no clear meaning for the unconverted. But for the converted the question no longer arises. The word "God" gets its meaning from the part it plays in religious speech and literature, and in religious speech and literature the question of existence does not arise. A theological professor at Glasgow once said to me: "Religion is 'O God, if you exist, save my soul if it exists!' " This of course was a joke. It clearly is just *not* what religion is. So within religion the question "Does God exist?" does not arise, any more than the question "Do electrons exist?" arises within physics. Outside religion the question "Does God exist?" has as little meaning as the question "Do electrons exist?" as asked by the scientifically ignorant. Thus I suggest that it is possible to hold that the question "Does God exist?" is not a proper question without necessarily also holding that religion and theology are nonsensical.

The cosmological argument, we saw, failed because it made use of the absurd conception of a *logically* necessary being. We now pass to the third argument which I propose to consider. This is the *Teleological Argument*. It is also called "the Argument from Design". It would be better called the argument *to* design, as Kemp Smith does call it, for clearly that the universe has been designed by a great architect is to assume a great part of the conclusion to be proved. Or we could call it "the argument from apparent design". The argument is very fully discussed in Hume's *Dialogues concerning Natural Religion,* to which I should like to draw your attention. In these dialogues the argument is presented as follows: "Look round the world: Contemplate the whole and every part of it: You will find it to be nothing but one great machine, subdivided into an infinite number of lesser machines. . . . The curious adapting of means to ends, throughout all nature, resembles exactly, though it much exceeds, the productions of human contrivance. . . . Since therefore the effects resemble each other, we are led to infer, by all the rules of analogy, that the causes also resemble; and that the Author of nature is somewhat similar to the mind of man; though possessed of much larger faculties, proportioned to the grandeur of the work which he has executed."

This argument may at once be criticized in two ways: (1) We may question whether the analogy between the universe and artificial things like houses, ships, furniture, and machines (which admittedly are designed) is very close. Now in any ordinary sense of language, it is true to say that plants and animals have *not* been designed. If we press the analogy of the universe to a plant, instead of to a machine, we get to a very different conclusion. And why should the one analogy be regarded as any better or worse than the other? (2) Even if the analogy were close, it would only go to suggest that the universe was designed by a *very great* (not infinite) architect, and note, an *architect,* not a *creator.* For if we take the analogy seriously we must notice that we do not create the materials from which we make houses, machines and so on, but only *arrange* the materials.

This, in bare outline, is the general objection to the argument from design, and will apply to any form of it. In the form in which the argument was put forward by such theologians as Paley, the argument is, of course, still more open to objection. For Paley laid special stress on such things as the eye of an animal, which he thought must have been contrived by a wise Creator for the special benefit of the animal. It seemed to him inconceivable how otherwise such a complex organ, so well suited to the needs of the animal, should have arisen. Or listen to Henry More: "For why have we three joints in our legs and arms, as also in our fingers, but that it was much better than having two or four? And why are our fore-teeth sharp like chisels to cut, but our inward teeth broad to grind, [instead of] the fore-teeth broad and the other sharp? But we might have made a hard shift to have lived through in that worser condition. Again, why are the teeth so luckily placed, or rather, why are there not teeth in other bones as well as in the jaw-bones? for they might have been as capable as these. But the reason is, nothing is done foolishly or in vain; that is, there is a divine Providence that orders all things." This type of argument has lost its persuasiveness, for the theory of Evolution explains why our teeth are so luckily placed in our jaw-bones, why we have the most convenient number of joints in our fingers, and so on. Species which did not possess advantageous features would not survive in competition with those which did.

The sort of argument Paley and Henry More used is thus quite unconvincing. Let us return to the broader conception, that of the universe as a whole, which seems to show the mark of a benevolent and intelligent Designer. Bacon expressed this belief forcibly: "I had rather beleave all the Fables in the Legend and the Talmud and the Alcoran than that this Universal Frame is without a Minde." So, in some moods, does the universe strike us. But sometimes, when we are in other moods, we see it very differently. To quote Hume's dialogues again: "Look around this Universe. What an immense profusion of beings, animated and organized, sensible and active! You admire this prodigious variety and fecundity. But inspect a little more narrowly these living existences, the only beings worth regarding. How hostile and destructive to each other! How insufficient all of them for their own happiness! . . . the whole presents nothing but the idea of a blind Nature, impregnated by a great vivifying principle, and pouring forth from her lap, without discernment or parental care, her maimed and abortive children!" There is indeed a great deal of suffering, some part of which is no doubt attributable to the moral choices of men, and to save us from which would conflict with what many people would regard as the greater good of moral freedom, but there is still an immense residue of apparently needless suffering, that is, needless in the sense that it could be prevented by an omnipotent being. The difficulty is that of reconciling the presence of evil and suffering with the assertion that God is both omnipotent and benevolent. If we *already* believe in an omnipotent and benevolent God, then some attempt may be made to solve the problem of evil by arguing that the values in the world form a sort of organic unity, and that making any *part* of the world better would perhaps nevertheless reduce the value of the whole. Paradoxical thought this thesis may appear at first sight, it is perhaps not theoretically absurd. If, however, evil presents a *difficulty* to the believing mind, it presents as *insuperable* difficulty to one who wishes to argue rationally from the world as we find it to the existence of an omnipotent and benevolent God. As Hume puts it: "Is the world considered in general, and as it appears to us in this life, different from what a man . . . would *beforehand* expect from a very powerful, wise and benevolent Deity? It must be a strange prejudice to assert the contrary. And from thence I conclude, that, however consistent the world may be, allowing certain suppositions and conjectures, with the idea of such a Deity, it can never afford us an inference concerning his existence."

The teleological argument is thus extremely shaky, and in any case, even if it were sound, it would only go to prove the existence of a very great architect, not of an omnipotent and benevolent Creator.

Nevertheless, the argument has a fascination for us that reason can not easily dispel. Hume, in his twelfth dialogue, and after pulling the argument from design to pieces in the previous eleven dialogues, nevertheless speaks as follows: "A purpose, an intention, a design strikes everywhere the most careless, the most stupid thinker; and no man can be so hardened in absurd systems as at all times to reject it . . . all the sciences almost lead us insensibly to acknowledge a first Author." Similarly Kant, before going on to exhibit the fallaciousness of the argument, nevertheless says of it: "This proof always deserves to be mentioned with respect. It is the oldest, the clearest and the most accordant with the common reason of mankind. It enlivens the study of nature, just as it itself derives its existence and gains ever new vigour from that source. It suggests ends and purposes, where our observation would not have detected them by itself, and extends our knowledge of nature by means of the guiding-concept of a special unity, the principle of which is outside nature. This knowledge . . . so strengthens the belief in a supreme Author of nature that the belief acquires the force of an irresistible conviction." It is somewhat of a paradox that an invalid argument should command so much respect even from those who have demonstrated its invalidity. The solution of the paradox is perhaps somewhat as follows[4]: The arguments from design is no good as an argument. But in those who have the seeds of a genuinely religious attitude already within them the facts to which the argument from design draws attention, facts showing the grandeur and majesty of the universe, facts that are evident to anyone who looks upwards on a starry night, and which are enormously multiplied for us by the advance of theoretical science, these facts have a powerful effect. But they only have this effect on the already religious mind, on the mind which has the capability of feeling the religious type of awe. That is, the argument from design is in reality no argument, or if it is regarded as an argument it is feeble, but it is a potent instrument in heightening religious emotions.

Something similar might even be said of the cosmological argument. As an argument it cannot pass muster at all; indeed it is completely absurd, as employing the notion of a logically necessary being. Nevertheless it does appeal to something deep seated in our natures. It takes its stand on the fact that the existence of you or me or this table is not logically necessary. Logic tells us that this fact is not a fact at all, but is a truism, like the "fact" that a circle is not a square. Again, the cosmological argument tries to base the existence of you or me or this table on the existence of a logically necessary being, and hence commits a rank absurdity, the notion of a logically necessary being being self-contradictory. So the only rational thing to say if someone asks "Why does this table exist?" is some such thing as that such and such a carpenter made it. We can go back and back in such a series, but we must not entertain the absurd idea of getting back to something logically necessary. However, now let us ask, "Why should anything exist at all?" Logic seems to tell us that the only answer which is not absurd is to say, "Why shouldn't it?" Nevertheless, though I know how any answer on the lines of the cosmological argument can be pulled to pieces by a correct logic, I still feel I want to go on asking the question. Indeed, though logic has taught me to look at such a question with the gravest suspicion, my mind often seems to reel under

---

[4] See also N. Kemp Smith's Henrietta Hertz Lecture, "Is Divine Existence Credible?", *Proceedings of the British Academy*, 1931.

the immense significance it seems to have for me. That anything should exist at all does seem to me a matter for the deepest awe. But whether other people feel this sort of awe, and whether they or I ought to is another question. I think we ought to. If so, the question arises: If "Why should anything exist at all?" cannot be interpreted after the manner of the cosmological argument, that is, as an absurd request for the non-sensical postulation of a logically necessary being, what sort of question is it? What sort of question is this question "Why should anything exist at all?" All I can say is, that I do not yet know.

15

JOHN BAILLIE | *The Order of Knowing and the Order of Being**

The position I am maintaining is that there is no reality by which we are more directly confronted than we are by the Living God. It has often been taught that it is not really necessary in the interests of personal religion to occupy such high ground. It has been thought sufficient to maintain that God is the ground of all being without going on to maintain also that He is the ground of all knowledge. It has been thought sufficient to say that He comes first in the *ordo essendi* but not in the *ordo cognoscendi;* that He is therefore *notior per se* but not *notior nobis;* or again that He is *prior simpliciter* but not *prior quoad nos*—which is of course but a translation of the Aristotelian distinction between what is πρότερον ἁπλῶς and what is πρότερον πρός ἡμᾶς. It has been justly pointed out that the attempt made in the various theistic proofs to deduce God's reality from the reality of other things does not make God's being derivative, but only makes our knowledge of Him derivative; and it has been held that to this latter derivation no proper exception can be taken, but that, on the contrary, it is in accordance with the facts of the spiritual life. God, it is said, is the first reality to exist but the last to be known.

This is the distinction which is relied on by Kant and by all Kantians— including, at least as regards one often quoted passage,[1] Albrecht Ritschl; and under the influence of the Ritschlian Wilhelm Hermann I was myself inclined to rely upon it at an earlier stage in my theological reflections. But, as the scholastic forms of its expression are themselves sufficient to indicate, it was equally relied upon, long before the days of Kantianism, by those natural theologians of the Middle Ages whom Kant so much dis-

---

* Reprinted with the permission of Charles Scribner's Sons from *Our Knowledge of God*, 1939, pages 166–189, by John Baillie. Reprinted from *Our Knowledge of God* by John Baillie published by the Oxford University Press.

[1] *Justification and Reconciliation*, vol. iii, English translation, p. 226 and footnote.

liked, and above all by St. Thomas Aquinas;[2] and it is now regarded as a necessary part of Roman orthodoxy.

Now I am not myself so anti-Roman in sentiment that it can ever be an entirely easy thing for me to find myself at variance with an important tenet of medieval orthodoxy. Yet it sometimes happens that, if only I am able to discover what were the influences leading to the adoption of such a tenet, the measure of its authority seems to be very palpably lessened. In the last chapter [of *Our Knowledge of God*] I set out very fully St. Thomas's view that in this life we have no direct knowledge of God but know Him only by causal and analogical inference from the things of which we do have direct knowledge. But we may now ask ourselves *why* St. Thomas thought it necessary to adopt such a position. The answer seems to be twofold. The first determining factor is clearly his Aristotelian epistemology, which precludes him from believing that we can have direct knowledge of any existence that is not corporeal in nature so as to be capable of being perceived by one or more of the five senses. "Aquinas", says Wicksteed, "holds firmly to the anti-mystic psychology of Aristotle as far as the natural and earthly life is concerned," so that it is only after death, when our psychical natures are miraculously changed, that ". . . we may hope to gain some powers of direct perception of spiritual beings".[3] It is very important to notice that the same psychological principles which thus preclude St. Thomas from allowing the possibility of a direct knowledge of God, preclude him also from allowing the possibility of a direct knowledge of our fellow men, or even of ourselves. Of our fellow men also it is true that we do not know at all what they are in themselves, but only know their *effects* on the material world. Their essence is no less completely hidden from us than is the essence of God. And so also is our own essence. Hereafter we may, acquiring new powers, become self-conscious, just as we shall become conscious of God; but meanwhile—so Wicksteed expounds St. Thomas—". . . it is a mistake to call the mind or soul of man 'self-conscious' . . . We are conscious of the *operations* of our souls, for these we can observe and classify just as we can the operations of anything else. But the soul itself, as a being, out of whose nature all these operations follow, so that we could predict them because we know their source and cause—what do we know of that? Here on earth, then, we do not so much as know our own souls."[4] The second determining factor in St. Thomas's view derives, however, not from Aristotelianism but from that other ancient

[2] *Summa contra Gentiles*, i. II.
[3] Op. cit., pp. 651, xxii.
[4] Op. cit., pp. 366-7.

tradition by which he was only less profoundly influenced, namely, Neo-platonism. It is well known that there is in all Neoplatonism, whether pagan or Christian, a strongly agnostic strain. It teaches us that God is to be reached not so much by a progressive enrichment of our experience as by a process of abstraction, a progressive removal of limitations, a continual subtraction rather than addition, so that in the end we can discover much that He is not, but nothing that He positively is. Here, then, is the source of that theology of the *via negativa* which so dominated the Christian thought of the Middle Ages. "By reason of His pre-eminence," wrote John Scotus Erigena in the ninth century, "God may not unjustly be spoken of as Nothing."[5] The greatest transmitter of this Neoplatonism to the Middle Ages was undoubtedly the so-called Dionysius the Areopagite, whose Greek works, dating probably from the fifth century, Erigena translated into Latin. The influence of Dionysius partly reached St. Thomas through the treatises of the eighth-century systematizer John of Damascus, whom he is constantly quoting; but of its determinative nature there can be no doubt.

But now, if we share neither St. Thomas's Aristotelian epistemology nor his Neoplatonic absolutism, there would appear to be no particular reason why we should accept his view that our only knowledge of God is of an inferential and analogical character.

Furthermore, it must be remembered not only that for all the Christian Neoplatonists the *ideal* knowledge of God is precisely such a direct vision of Him as their agnosticism makes them believe to be normally denied to us, but also that by no means all of them agree with St. Thomas that for the enjoyment of such knowledge we must necessarily wait for a future life. Erigena, it is true, goes even farther than St. Thomas in a negative direction, holding that no created being, not even the angels, can ever in any state of life, present or future, know God in His essential being. But there is in Medieval Platonism another strain, represented by St. Bernard, by Richard and Hugh of St. Victor, and above all by St. Bonaventure—while it had also been represented in an earlier century by St. Anselm—which teaches that some vision of God may be enjoyed even in this life, at the summit of the mystical ascent, and without miracle. It is indeed characteristic of the mind of St. Thomas that, standing midway between these two positions, he should draw an entirely hard and fast line between what is possible *in via* and *in patria*, holding that in this life there can (apart from miracle) be no vision at all, while it is the normal mode of knowledge among the blessed in the hereafter.

[5] *Deus per excellentiam non imnerito nihilum vacatur:* quoted by W. R. Inge, *The Philosophy of Plotinus*, vol. ii, p. 112.

Moreover, as we already had occasion to note in the last chapter, St. Bonaventure goes farther still, thereby exposing himself to the criticism of St. Thomas. For he holds not only that the ecstatic experience of God is the crown of the religious life on earth, but also that some direct knowledge of God is native to every human soul prior to the construction of all arguments to prove His existence. Such arguments, he explains, may indeed be constructed, but they are never the real point of departure. God is indeed knowable to us through the things which He has made (*per creaturas*), but He is still more clearly known to us through His presence (*per praesentiam*) and in Himself (*quantum est de se*).[6] He is ". . . most truly present to the very soul of man and is in that fact already knowable".[7] He is indeed far enough removed from us in the order of being, yet He is directly present to us in the order of knowledge. Hence he expresses His agreement with St. Anselm's contention that it is impossible for a man to conceive of God as non-existent. But what then, it will be asked, of the difference between such knowledge of God as we have on earth, and the vision of Him that is reserved for the blessed in heaven? That difference is in the last resort as present to the mind of St. Bonaventure as to that of St. Thomas, yet it is noteworthy that the former is less troubled than is the latter by the scripural use of the language of vision in respect of certain experiences that have been enjoyed by men on earth. His pilgrim spirit never forgets that ". . . now we see through a glass darkly (*per speculum in aenigmate*), but then face to face"; but, remembering also the second half of the same Pauline verse, that ". . . now we know in part (*ex parte*)",[8] he appears much less concerned than is Aquinas to draw the line sharply as between two diverse *kinds* of seeing. Even in our earthly communion with God there is something of the substance of beatitude. It can never indeed be more than an earnest, a fragmentary foretaste of that which is to come, yet it too is in its measure an enjoyment of the real presence of God. *In patria*, we shall know Him perfectly through His presence, but even *in statu viatoris* we can know Him through His presence *semiplene*—"half-fully".[9] In all this St. Bonaventure may be said to be representing the Franciscan tradition as against the Dominican tradition which is represented by St. Thomas.

As has been said, however, it is St. Thomas rather than St. Bonaventure who has ever since determined the direction taken by Roman orthodoxy.

---

[6] *Sententiae*, Dist. III, Pars I, Art. I, Quaest. I.

[7] *Quaest. disp. de Mysterio Trinitatis*, ix. I. *Deus praesentissimus est ipsi animae et eo ipso cognoscibilis.*

[8] I Corinthians xiii. 12; cf. Vulgate.

[9] *Sententiae*, Dist. III, Pars I, Art. I, Quaest. III.

The view that in this life we can know God directly, or otherwise than inferentially, has come to be spoken of within that Church as *ontologism* and as such has always been condemned. Ontologism is not the same thing as acceptance of the Ontological Argument, but there is a natural connexion between the two, and St. Thomas condemned them both alike.[10]

Twice during the nineteenth century the Holy Office thought it necessary to repeat its condemnation of ". . . the errors of the ontologists". This was mainly in connexion with the views of the two Italian philosophers, each of them in other respects a good catholic and Thomist, namely Vincenzo Gioberti (1801–52), all of whose works were finally placed on the Index, and Antonio Rosmini-Serbati (1797–1855), founder of the order of the Brethren of Charity (known in Italy as the Rosminians), and forty of whose opinions were condemned by Leo XIII in 1887. Since the promulgation of these decrees the lovers of St. Bonaventure have sought to maintain that the Seraphic Doctor was not guilty of the errors of ontologism,[11] yet Rosmini and his followers had always been in the habit of appealing to his deliverances. It is perhaps worth while to set down here the seven ontologist propositions condemned by Pius IX in the decree of the Holy Office dated 18th December 1861.

"1. The immediate knowledge of God, at least so far as it is habitual, is essential to the human intellect, so that without it nothing can be known, since it is itself the intellectual light.

"2. That being which we apprehend in all things and without which we apprehend nothing is the Divine Being.

"3. Universals, objectively considered, are not objectively distinct from God.

"4. The innate notion of God, as Being without qualification, involves every other knowledge *eminenti modo*, so that by means of it we implicitly know every living being in whatsoever respect it is knowable.

"5. All other ideas are but modifications of the idea by which God is apprehended as Being without qualification.

"6. Created things are in God as a part within a whole, not indeed in a formal whole, but in an infinite and uncompounded whole, in that He sets what are, as it were, His parts outside Himself without in any way dividing or diminishing Himself.

---

[10] *Summa contra Gentiles,* i. 10–11.
[11] e.g. *The Franciscan Vision,* by Father James (1937), pp. viii, 7.

"7. Creation is to be explained as follows: By that same special act by which God apprehends and wills Himself as distinct from a determinate creature such as man, He produces that creature."[12]

There are, indeed, in these seven propositions, as in the systems of philosophy from which they are extracted, many things that merit emphatic rejection—which, however, is something different from pontifical condemnation. Yet, I believe, there is also in them an element of truth, which we shall do right to defend against the Thomist doctrine of the priority of the things of sense. When the Holy Office condemns ontologism, it is really intending to condemn the view that the knowledge of God is *innate*, part of a fixed and given constitution with which the human species was initially endowed; and that indeed is a view to be rejected. But what ought to be affirmed in opposition to it is not the inferential nature of our knowledge of God, but rather the *continual invasion* of our life by His holy Presence.

In opposing ontologism Dr. Hubert Box thus states what he believes to be the true as well as the orthodox position: "An act of divine faith is an act by which one believes whatever God has revealed on God's authority. It is, therefore, obvious that we cannot make an act of divine faith before we have been convinced by reason that God exists and that He has spoken. . . . The conviction that there is a God can only be reached by reasoning which, when fully thought out, is tantamount to a metaphysic. . . . The ultimate basis of religious conviction is reasoning, whether it take the rough and ready form known as common sense, or appear as an elaborate argumentation which not only is metaphysical, but is recognized as such."[13] As against such an analysis I believe that ontologism has something true to contribute; and as against it I have myself already maintained that revelation essentially consists not in the communication of truths about God but in the self-revelation of the divine Personality, the truths about Him being abstracted by ourselves from the concrete reality with which we thus become acquainted, and our knowledge of His existence being given in and with the revelation rather than guessed at in advance of it.

It is not enough, then, to acknowledge God as the most real of all

---

[12] See Denzinger-Bannwart, *Enchiridion Symbolorum*, 21st edition (1937), p. 465 f. For a defence of Rosmini against the charge of ontologism see T. Davidson, *Compendium of the Philosophical System of Antonio Rosmini-Serbati* (London, 1891), p. 338 f.

[13] *The World and God; The Scholastic Approach to Theism*, by Hubert S. Box, with a preface by the Rev. M. C. D'Arcy, S.J. (London, 1934), p. 32 f.

realities. We must acknowledge Him also to be, of all realities, that by which we are most directly and intimately confronted. There is, indeed, a sense in which God's reality is a question which I, as one of His creatures standing in His holy presence, am not *allowed* to discuss. How could the thinking concerned in such discussion be really "existential" in character? How can I, who in this very moment that I write am conscious of a demand being made *now* upon my life by God and His Christ, stand aside from the situation of responsibility thus created in order coldly to debate the question whether the God who thus claims me so much as exists? Even if the demand made of me were conceived as no more than a human demand; if, for example, as I now write, some fellow men were to rush into my study, inconveniently disturbing the train of my thought by the announcement that I was needed outside to help a passer-by who had fallen among thieves; would it be permitted me to reply, "Your demand is very tiresome. But I am not yet sure that you exist. The solipsists *may* be right. Before acceding to your request, let me first see whether I can demonstrate your existence to my own satisfaction"? The comic absurdity of such a response is not greater than would be its wickedness if it should lead to even the least delay in my readiness to do what was demanded. It seems, then, that I am not allowed to take the solipsist hypothesis seriously—in spite of its having been solemnly discussed by many philosophers. And neither, I am convinced, am I allowed to take the atheistic hypothesis seriously, though that also has been the object of much discussion in the schools. Just as the unreality and impropriety of all arguments for the existence of other minds lie in the fact that they all start from a possible solipsism, so the unreality and impropriety of the theistic arguments lie in the fact that they all start from a possible atheism. They start from a situation in which God is not yet. But there is no such situation, if it be true that in every moment I am called upon to obey His holy will—and that I have been so called upon from the beginning. Atheism is not a prior situation which theism must presuppose, but a situation which itself presupposes the theism of a world already challenged by the revelation of God in Christ.

More and more, then, the thought of our time seems to be converging towards such a view as that expressed by Professor Tillich when he writes: "Arguments for the existence of God presuppose the loss of the certainty of God. That which I have to prove by argument has no immediate reality for me. Its reality is mediated for me by some other reality about which I cannot be in doubt, so that this other reality is nearer to me than the reality of God. For the more closely things are connected with our interior existence, the less are they open to doubt.

And nothing can be nearer to us than that which is at times farthest away from us, namely God. A God who has been proved is neither near enough to us nor far enough away from us. He is not far enough, because of the very attempt we have made to prove Him. He is not near enough, because nearer things are presupposed by which the knowledge of Him is mediated. Hence this ostensibly demonstrated subject is not really God."[14]

Yet, though we are more directly and intimately confronted with the presence of God than with any other presence, it does not follow that He is ever present to us *apart* from all other presences. And, in fact, it is the witness of experience that only "in, with and under" other presences is the divine presence ever vouchsafed to us. This aspect of the matter was referred to at the beginning of this chapter, but must now be more fully investigated.

I believe the view to be capable of defence that no one of the four subjects of our knowledge—ourselves, our fellows, the corporeal world, and God—is ever presented to us except in conjunction with all three of the others. Here, however, we need only concern ourselves with the fact that God does not present Himself to us except in conjunction with the presence of our fellows and of the corporeal world.

Taking the second point first, it seems plain that the consciousness of God is never given save in conjunction with the consciousness of things. We do not know God through the world, but we know Him with the world; and in knowing Him with the world we know Him as its ground. Nature is not an argument for God, but it is a sacrament of Him. Just as in the sacrament of Holy Communion the Real Presence of Christ is given (if the Lutheran phrase may here be used without prejudice) "in, with and under" the bread and wine, so in a wider sense the whole corporeal world may become sacramental to us of the presence of the Triune God. The conception of a sacramental universe thus expresses the truth that lay behind St. Thomas's natural theology, while being free from the errors in which the latter became involved. No writer has done more to clarify our thought on this matter than Baron von Hügel. "Necessity of the Thing-element in Religion" is not only the title of a section in his greatest work,[15] but a constant theme in all his works. "Spirit", he tells us, "is awakened on occasion of Sense."[16] The knowledge of God, he insists, is not during this life given to us in its isolated

---

[14] From an article on "The Religious Situation in Germany To-day", in *Religion in Life*, vol. iii, no. 2 (New York, 1934), p. 167.

[15] *The Mystical Element in Religion*, 2nd edition, vol. ii, pp. 372 ff.

[16] *Essays and Addresses*, 2nd series, p. 246.

purity, but only through ". . . the humiliations of the material order".[17] The knowledge of God which we have on earth is of a kind that we cannot conceive to exist apart from some knowledge of things.

But it is equally certain that all our knowledge of God is given us "in, with and under" our knowledge of one another. This means, first, that the knowledge of God is withholden from those who keep themselves aloof from the *service* of their fellows. It means that "He that loveth not knoweth not God",[18] whereas "If we love one another, God dwelleth in us".[19] And this is indeed a blessed provision by which God makes my knowledge of Himself pass through my brother's need. It means, second, that only when I am in *fellowship* with my fellow men does the knowledge of God come to me individually. It means the necessity of the Church and the rejection of religious individualism. It gives the true sense of the Cyprianic formula, *extra ecclesiam nulla salus.* "For where two or three are gathered together in my name, there am I in the midst of them."[20] Such was the promise; and its fulfillment came when the disciples ". . . were *all* with one accord in one place" and the Spirit ". . . sat upon *each* of them".[21] It means, third, the necessity of history. There is a necessary historical element in all religion, for we know of no religion that is not dependent on tradition; but Christianity is plainly an historical religion in the fullest possible sense. The Christian knowledge of God is not given to any man save in conjunction with the telling of an "old, old story". Therefore it means, lastly, the necessity of Christ, God incarnate in the flesh. "For there is one God, and one mediator between God and men, the man Christ Jesus; who gave himself a ransom for all, to be testified in due time."[22] The service of others, the fellowship with others, and the historical tradition in which I stand are all media that lead me to the Mediator, and the Mediator leads me to God. And all this mediation is part of God's gracious purpose in refusing to unite me to Himself without at the same time uniting me to my fellow men—in making it impossible for me to obey either of the two great commandments without at the same time obeying the other. This understanding of the relation of faith to history is one which has been greatly clarified for us by Dr. Gogarten and other writers of his school.[23] It is finely summarized

---

[17] See the chapter on "The Natural Order" in M. Nédoncelle's *Baron Friedrich von Hügel.*

[18] I John iv. 8.

[19] I John iv. 12.

[20] Matthew xviii. 20.

[21] Acts ii. 1–3.

[22] I Timothy ii. 5–6.

[23] See especially F. Gogarten, *Ich Glaube an den Dreieinigen Gott: eine Untersuchung über Glauben und Geschichte* (1926) ; *Glaube und Wirklichkeit* (1928).

by Dr. Brunner: "However inconceivable for us the miracle of the Incarnation may be, yet God lets us in some measure learn why his revelation happens precisely thus and in no other way. It is the wisdom and the goodness of the ruler of the world that he has revealed himself once for all at a particular place, at a particular time. Inasuch as God, so to speak, deposits his gift of salvation at this one historical place, he compels at the same time all men who wish to share in this gift to betake themselves to this one place, and there to meet each other. . . . It is as if God had used a stratagem by so revealing himself that he can only be found when we find our brother along with him, that in order to find him we must let ourselves be bound to our brother. Only in the bond which unites me to the historical fellowship of my fellow believers—to be more exact, in the fellowship of those who believed before me—is my faith possible. . . . I must, so to speak, submit to becoming myself a member of the fellowship, if I wish to enter into the relation with God. God will not bind me to himself on any other terms than these, that he binds me at the same time to my brother."[24]

Clearly, then, the immediacy of God's presence to our souls is a mediated immediacy. But I must now do what I can to resolve the apparent self-contradictoriness of this phrase.

What I must do is to ask myself how the knowledge of God first came to me. And here I can only repeat what was said in the opening pages of this book: unless my analysis of my memory is altogether at fault, the knowledge of God first came to me in the form of an awareness that I was "not my own" but one under authority, one who "owed" something, one who "ought" to be something which he was not. But whence did this awareness come to me? Certainly it did not come "out of the blue". I heard no voice from the skies. No, it came, without a doubt, from what I may call the spiritual climate of the home into which I was born. It came from my parents' walk and conversation. At the beginning it may have been merely the consciousness of a conflict between my mother's will and my own, between what I desired and what she desired of me. Yet I cannot profess to remember a time when it was merely that. I cannot remember a time when I did not already dimly know that what opposed my own wilfulness was something much more than mere wilfulness on my mother's part. I knew she had a right to ask of me what she did; which is the same as to say that I knew that what she asked of me was right and that my contrary desire was wrong. I knew, therefore, that my mother's will was not the ultimate source of the authority which she exercised over me. For it was plain that she herself was under that same authority. Indeed, it

[24] *God and Man*, English translation, p. 126 f.

was not only from my parents' specific demands on me that this sense of authority came to me but from the way they themselves lived. Clearly they, too, were under orders, and under essentially the same orders. I cannot remember a time when I did not already know that what my parents demanded of me and what they knew to be demanded of themselves were in the last resort one and the same demand, however different might be its detailed application to our different situations. I cannot remember a time when I did not know that my parents and their household were part of a wider community which was under the same single authority. Nor, again, can I recall a time when I did not know that this authority was closely bound up with, and indeed seemed to emanate from, *a certain story*. As far back as I can remember anything, my parents and my nurses were already speaking to me of Abraham and Isaac and Jacob, of Moses and David, of God's covenant with the Israelites and of their journey through the wilderness, of the culmination of the story in the coming of Jesus Christ, God's only Son, whom He sent to earth to suffer and die for our salvation; and then of the apostles and martyrs and saints and "Scots worthies" whose golden deeds brought the story down to very recent days. And I knew that that story was somehow the source of the authority with which I was confronted. I could not hear a Bible story read without being aware that in it I was somehow being confronted with a solemn presence that had in it both sweetness and rebuke. Nor do I remember a day when I did not already dimly know that this presence was God.

It was, then, through the media of my boyhood's home, the Christian community of which it formed a part, and the "old, old story" from which that community drew its life, that God first revealed Himself to me. This is simple matter of fact. But what I take to be matter of fact in it is not only that God used these media but that in using them He actually did reveal Himself to *my* soul.

For what I seemed to know was not merely that God had declared His will to my parents and that they in their turn had declared their will to me, but also that through my parents God had declared His will to me. The story told me how God had spoken to Abraham and Moses and the prophets and apostles, but what gave the story its power over my mind and imagination and conscience was the knowledge that "in, with and under" this speaking to these others of long ago He was also now speaking to myself. That God should have revealed Himself to certain men of long ago could not in itself be of concern to me now; first, because, not being myself privy to this revelation, I could never know for sure whether it were a real or only an imagined one; second, because mere hearsay could never be a sufficient foundation for such a thing as religion, though it might be well enough as a foundation for certain other kinds of knowledge; and third, because the revelation would necessarily lack the particular authorization and relevance to my case which alone could give it power over my recalcitrant will. What is it to me that God should have commanded David to do this or that, or called Paul to such and such a task? It is nothing at all, unless it should happen that, as I read of His calling and commanding them, I at the same time found Him calling and commanding me. If the word of God is to concern me, it must be a word addressed to me individually and to the particular concrete situation in which I am standing now. This insight into what we may perhaps venture to call the necessary "here-and-nowness"—the *hic et nunc*—of revelation is one which has emerged very strikingly from recent theological discussions. Kierkegaard's doctrine of the "existential moment"[25] has been a potent influence on many writers; but I need perhaps mention only Dr. Eberhard Grisebach's elaborate demonstration in his book called *Gegenwart*[26] that our sole touch with reality is in the present, the past and the future being alike unreal except so far as they are contained in the present moment.

In a letter to M. de Beaumont, Rousseau once asked, "Is it simple, is it natural, that God should have gone and found Moses in order to speak to Jean Jacques Rousseau?" No, it is far from simple; but what right have we to assume that truth is simple? And as to whether it is natural, have we any knowledge of what would be natural in such a region of experience apart from the witness of the experience itself? We have to take experience as we find it—though that apparently was what Rousseau was refusing to do. And especially we have to face the fact that we have here to do with an experience of an entirely unique kind, its uniqueness lying precisely in this conjunction of immediacy with mediacy—that is, in the fact that God reveals Himself to me only through others who went before, yet in so doing reveals Himself to me now.

This is, indeed, a mysterious ordering of things. Yet I would not be understood as trying to surround it with any spurious air of mystery. Mysterious though it be, it is a mystery with which all men have some degree of acquaintance. It was not *only* in the Bible stories that I was met in my youth with this peculiar conjugation of past and present. Other tales of later days were told me, and in them the same Presence seemed to be speaking to me something of the same word. Were this Presence and this word in *every* tale I was told? I think not. There were, for instance, fairy stories; and they, though they absorbed my interest and

<hr/>

[25] See especially his book *Der Augenblick* (1855).
[26] *Gegenwart, eine Kritische Ethik* (1928).

caught my imagination, seemed to have nothing to say to me, nothing to do with me. And of some other stories the same thing was true. The stories that had Presence in them for me, though they were by no means always Bible stories, were somehow of a piece with the Bible stories. Usually, indeed, they were Christian stories, and as such were definitely derivative from the Bible history. But even when that was not the case, if they had Presence in them at all, it was the same Presence as met me in the Bible. And to this day all the history that has Presence in it for me, all of the past through which I am addressed in the present, is centered in the story of the Incarnation and the Cross. All that history has to say to me is somehow related to that; and no story that was entirely out of relation to that could have any present reality in it for me at all. Every story is either B.C. or else A.D.; and that not in mere date but in its very essence; logically as well as chronologically. Indeed, the same story may be chronologically A.D. yet logically B.C., such as stories of noble deeds done within the Christian era by men of other lands whom the knowledge of Christ has not yet reached. Such deeds seem to me to look forward to the Incarnation and the Cross rather than back to them, so that the doers of them are still living as it were under the Old Dispensation. Perhaps these truths of experience on which I have been dwelling have never received better intellectual formulation than in Professor Tillich's doctrine of *die Mitte der Geschichte*, where it is taught that history can have meaning only if it have a centre, and that for the Christian that centre is necessarily Christ. "In dealing with the philosophy of history", he writes, "it is impossible to avoid the Christological problem. History and christology belong to one another as do question and answer." "Instead of the beginning and end of history determining its centre, it is its centre that determines its beginning and end. But the centre of history can only be the place where is revealed the principle that gives it meaning. History is constituted when its centre is constituted, or rather—since this is no mere subjective act—when such a centre reveals its centrality."[27]

The question may now be raised whether a story that has no Presence in it and no word to speak to us really partakes of the true nature of history at all; that is, whether anything can be history for the Christian which does not stand in relation to Christ as its centre. When Dr. Barth insists, as he does so often, that in history in general there is no revelation, since revelation interrupts history at a single point rather than informs it throughout, he is obviously thinking of history as something past

---

[27] *Religiöse Verwirklichung* (1930), pp. 111, 116. The essay from which I quote is translated in *The Interpretation of History* (1936), pp. 242 ff., but I have not followed this somewhat unsatisfactory translation.

and done with. Christ, he says, comes vertically into history and He *alone* reveals God; the history into which He comes does not reveal God *at all.* Thinking of history in this way, the Barthian theologians always oppose "the Christ of Faith" to "the Christ of History". History, they say, cannot give you the truth about Christ; only faith can do that. I believe this dichotomy to be radically mistaken. I believe that a historiographer who writes without faith produces *bad history.* I believe that faith is quite essential to sound historiography. And I believe Professor Tillich's doctrine of Christ as the centre round which all history arranges itself to be altogether profounder than the Barthian attempt to set the rest of history in contrast with Christ. To Professor Tillich history is nothing dead and desiccated, "the presence of the past in the present" being essential to its very nature, so that he can say that in ancient Greek thought ". . . there is no conception of the world as history, even though history as a report on the complex of human movements and as a pattern for politicians be not lacking to it."[28] A similar view is eloquently defended by Dr. Gogarten, to whose treatment of this whole matter I have already acknowledged my debt. "However one may try to solve it", he writes, "and however one may alter its form in so doing, the problem of history is fundamentally the problem of the presentness of the past. Were the past merely past, as it is in the case of all natural events, there would be no such thing as history but only an unhistorical present—and indeed not even that. For there can be a real present only where there is something past that becomes present." "History is something that happens in the present."[29] Such, surely, is the right way of it. *It is only in the conception of history as something that happens in the present that the apparent contradiction in our doctrine of a mediated immediacy can be reasonably resolved.*

[28] Op. cit., p. 112.
[29] *Ich Glaube an den Dreieinigen Gott,* pp. 71 f., 83.

Part III | Challenges to Contemporary Man

Chapter 10 | Faith and Verification

But the question still remains: *Is* there *really* a God? The agnostic and the atheist join forces at this point also. They would not deny that people have certain experiences which they describe as religious. These experiences lead the believer to the conviction that God is real, but the disbeliever, the skeptic, counters with the assertion that the same experiences need not lead to postulating a transcendent God. Rather they point to religion as an altogether natural phenomenon.

In Chapter 3, "The Nature of Man," we discussed certain live options among the various interpretations of man's relation to himself and to the universe. Forms of Greek philosophical thought and Oriental mysticism attempt to escape from this world into union with a transcendent Reality. The opposite trend is noted in naturalism, which posits this world of space and time as the only sphere of man's life and influence. Truth is discoverable through scientific procedures, in the broadest sense of that term. Reality is equivalent to nature, the temporal and spatial order of cause-and-effect relations with which man is capable of dealing. Humanistic naturalism places its main emphasis on the development of man's capacities for intelligent control of the world and himself. For man is a child of nature and yet is not reducible to animal or thing or chemical or physical process. Through evolutionary development, man now exhibits new and unique capacities. He is free from the limitations of nature because he can choose and utilize nature's resources for deliberately chosen ends. For the chief goal for man is the full development of his human capacities: intelligence, scientific acumen, appreciation, aspiration, the building of human character and societies based on justice and equity. Man has brought his problems of war, disease, poverty and class prejudice on himself. Let him then solve these problems himself. His chief obstacle is ignorance. The cure is knowledge. There is no transcendent "force" or "God" to assist him, or at least we do not have any way of *knowing* that there is. Man might better roll up his sleeves and go to work instead of groveling before a "god" who in any case is just a projection of his own wishes and desires.

In more specific terms, this general point of view finds expression in a sociological theory of religion and in the Freudian interpretation of religion as illusion and religious beliefs as desire for security against the world's threats. Rejection of religion as harmful has been expressed through the ages in varying forms. The Hellenistic Epicureans, for example, held that belief in the gods' relations with human existence ought to be eliminated. The "prying" gods only fill man with the pain of fear and insecurity which rob him of freedom in this life and cause uncertainty concerning the life to come. Both the efficacy of the gods and belief in immortality ought therefore to be thrust out of men's thoughts. How is this to be done? Adoption of an atomistic view of the universe will assure man that the gods have no effect on his life and that there is no life to come. For everything that *is* is the product of atoms moving in empty space.

There are, however, those who do not reject religion as utterly false and harmful. Even though God is simply a projection of man's wishes for security and religion is based on an illusion, still religion has positive value in the economy of man's individual life and the social order. Among those who take this position are Ludwig Feuerbach (1804–1872) in his *Essence of Christianity* and Julian Huxley in "The New Divinity."[1]

Huxley recommends that we adopt a religion without God. Modern man, recognizing himself as ". . . the latest dominant type in the evolution of this earth," could not ". . . transform himself as a whole species into something new." The Christian God, now rejected, need not be replaced by a "savage god." For evolutionary humanism, ". . . gods are creations of man, not vice versa." Gods are ". . . hypotheses serving to account for certain phenomena of outer nature and inner experience." Their role is to explain and make comprehensible. Gods will now disappear. But yet, says Huxley, there are some events and phenomena which transcend ordinary explanation and ordinary experience. "These inspire awe and seem mysterious, explicable only in terms of something beyond or above ordinary nature—'super-natural' power, a 'superhuman' element at work in the universe. Now we can no longer designate this as '*super*natural but *trans*natural.' " It emerges from nature itself. Yet this is the sense of the divine, emancipated from superstitious beliefs, which ". . . man finds worthy of adoration."

This religion without God is a live option for today. Some say that we still use religion as an instrument to conserve and promote human values. But can man thus master his life and destiny? This is a serious question. If belief in God cannot be "proved" by argument, can *disbelief* in God

---

[1] Julian Huxley, "The New Divinity," *Twentieth Century*, vol. CLXX, no. 1011, pp. 9–18, Autumn, 1961.

be established on provable grounds? This writer takes the position which parallels the conclusions of the chapter "On Proving that God Exists." We cannot by rational or empirical argument *prove* that God exists. By the same token, we cannot *disprove* that He exists.

A Further Word on Revelation and Faith

We have made reference to the distinction between propositional and nonpropositional views of revelation and faith. Our discussion, both of the biblical accounts and of issues in religious thought, has presupposed the latter perspective. John Hick has brought this contrast to summary in succinct form.[2]

The propositional view holds that revelation ". . . is a body of truths expressed in statements or propositions. Revelation is the imparting to man of divinely authenticated truths." If this is so, then faith is ". . . intellectual assent to the content of revelation as true because of the witnessing authority of God the Revealer."[3] In this case also then, the Bible is ". . . the place where those truths were authoritatively written down." Theology is conceived by the propositional view in a distinctive way. "Natural theology was held to consist of all those theological truths which can be worked out by the unaided human intellect. . . . Revealed theology, on the other hand, was held to consist of those further truths which are not accessible to human reason and which can be known to us only if they are specially revealed by God."[4]

The propositional view of revelation and faith is adopted not only by those who would defend specific "truths" as absolute and authoritative. Critics of religion also assume that religious persons who appeal to revelation mean absolute propositions which God is supposed to have stated to mankind and which His people are bound to defend. Philosophical critiques of religion often take this form.[5] If revelation consists of truths to be accepted, then obviously also some of the claims of science are bound to clash with these "religious" propositions. As we have pointed out, if science and religion thus face each other in open arena, then science is bound to win.

[2] John Hick, *Philosophy of Religion*, © 1963, pp. 61–64 and pp. 70–77. Reprinted by permission of Prentice-Hall, Inc., Englewood Cliffs, New Jersey.

[3] *Ibid.*, p. 62. See *The Catholic Encyclopedia*, Robert Appleton Co., New York, 1912, vol. XIII, p. 1.

[4] *Ibid.*, pp. 62–63.

[5] See Walter Kaufmann, *Critique of Religion and Philosophy*, Harper & Row, Publishers, Incorporated, New York, 1958.

A Nonpropositional View

But there is another view to which we have made various references. This is the nonpropositional conception of both faith and revelation. Here the ". . . content of revelation is not any body of truths about God, but God himself coming within the orbit of man's experience by acting in human history. From this point of view, theological propositions, as such, are not revealed, but represent human attempts to understand the significance of relevatory events."[6]

Events as seen from "the inside" rather than from "the outside" now become the medium of God's self-disclosure. The Bible is the record of these events, in which men seek to convey what they have seen and where they have been. God is personal in the sense that He confronts men with His presence and demands response. This personal response is faith. It is the first-order religious dimension of human existence. Man comes thus in freedom into a new relationship with God and fellowmen. To be aware of Him comes in, with and through awareness of other finite persons. Sometimes other persons "leave us cold." It is a matter of indifference whether we relate to them or not. But creative human relations cannot be a matter of indifference. Just so, by analogy, man may relate himself to God.

> In love, the existence of the beloved, far from being a matter of indifference, affects one's whole being. God, the object of the religious consciousness, is such that it is impossible for a finite creature to be aware of him and yet remain unaffected by this awareness. God, according to the Judaic-Christian tradition, is the source and ground of our being. It is by his will that we exist. His purpose for us is so indelibly written into our nature that the fulfillment of this purpose is the basic condition of our own personal self-fulfillment and happiness.[7]

Even though we are dependent upon God, according to this view, still our freedom and autonomy are not destroyed but rather enhanced. God has created us to live as men in this order of nature and history, but we men try to become God ourselves and put our interests and very lives at the center of existence. We seek to make absolutes out of our little relativities. But within this created order,

> . . . God reveals himself in ways which allow man the fateful freedom to recognize or fail to recognize his presence. His actions always leave room for that uncompelled response which theology calls faith. It is this element

[6] Hick, *op. cit.*, p. 70.
[7] *Ibid.*, pp. 70–71.

in the awareness of God that preserves man's cognitive freedom in relation to an infinitely greater and superior reality.[8]

Faith, then, means this voluntary response to God's action in and through specific interpreted events in human history. For all events are interpreted events, and faith involves ". . . seeing, apperceiving, or interpreting events in a special way."

Hick reminds us that there is something in ordinary nonreligious experience which is similar to what occurs in religious response. Ludwig Wittgenstein (1889–1951), who is influential in contemporary philosophical analysis, speaks of the familiar phenomenon of "seeing as."[9] For example, think of what happens when we look at a puzzle picture. Here is a page covered with seemingly random lines and dots. But if we stare at it long enough, these suddenly take the form of a picture of a man. Now the whole field of lines and dots is *seen as* bearing a particular meaning and is no longer just a formless group of marks.

Hick develops this suggestion further. Besides "seeing as," which is a purely visual type of interpreting, we are involved in the more complex phenomenon of "experiencing as." In these cases, an entire situation is experienced as having a certain significance. An illustration which Hick uses is apt. Suppose you are driving an automobile along the highway:

> To be conscious of being in this particular kind of situation is to be aware that certain reactions (and dispositions to react) are appropriate and others inappropriate; and an important part of our consciousness of the situation as having the particular character that it has consists in our readiness to act appropriately within it. Any individual would react in characteristically different ways in the midst of a battle and on a quiet Sunday afternoon stroll; he would do so in recognition of the differing character of these two types of situation. Such awareness is a matter of "experiencing as." The significance of a given situation for a given observer consists primarily in its bearing upon his behavioral dispositions. Being an interpretive act, "experiencing as" can be mistaken, as—to mention an extreme case—when a lunatic feels that everyone is threatening him and acts accordingly.[10]

It follows, as in the case of the interpretive context of biblical accounts, that the same events may be experienced on different levels at one and the same time. An event may have one significance (for instance, the

[8] *Ibid.*, p. 71.

[9] Ludwig Wittgenstein, *Philosophical Investigations*, Basil Blackwell & Mott, Ltd., Oxford, 1953, part II, sec. xi.

[10] Hick, *op. cit.*, p. 72.

Israelites' flight from Egypt) simply as an occurrence within human history and, at the same time, be a sacred, revelatory sign of God's saving activity. Thus sacred history is history experienced as bearing special, holy significance (*Heilsgeschichte*).

These events, for both Old and New Testament records, disclose the same pattern of knowledge. They may be experienced as, seen as, aspects of the human order and also as acts of God. In other words, it is possible to construe these events either naturalistically or religiously. The same is true in our modern world. The meaning which such occurrences bear will depend on where a man takes his stance (within the circle of what faith) and what he sees. Furthermore, these events become warrant for action, for behaving in a certain way, showing forth a particular style of life, committing oneself to specific values.

Besides this distinctive view of the Bible and way of interpreting events in our own day, the nonpropositional perspective of revelation and faith entails a specific view of theology. It stands against the claims of both natural and revealed theology as consisting of a set of authoritative truths to which assent is given. Revealed theology becomes *kerygmatic* theology with emphasis on God's self-disclosure. Nor is there any such thing as natural theology's grasp of divine truths through man's unaided powers apart from faith. Rather all theology, as stressed in a previous chapter, takes its starting points in first-order religious faith. This does not mean the abrogation of reason's work. Reason can deal with any faith (humanistic or theistic), offer criticism, draw out the implications, see and state its relevance to all the rest of human existence. Theological affirmations are of the second order. Therefore they must not be confused with first-order religious utterances. Theological theories cannot claim final authority beyond the reach of criticism and correction, for they are only human attempts to explicate the faith, the creed, the practice, the sacred signs and acts of a given religious community. Hence, these must be held under constant check by reference to the ways in which what is happening in human history *is seen, is experienced.*

The Noncognitive View

The issue becomes more complex when certain recent writers move one step beyond the basic view of the nonpropositional nature of revelation and faith. Now religious utterances are said to be noncognitive. Their purposes are to vent feelings, to command, to perform, to evoke emotions, to strengthen commitments, to bind communities together, to express wonder at the beauty of the world. Professors J. H. Randall, Jr., and R. B. Braithwaite might be cited in this connection. We discuss here the position of Randall. For Randall, to speak of "God" is to refer not to a reality independent of the human mind but to a religious dimension within men's experience. The products of human imagination, however rich and varied, are not eternal; they have no existence apart from man. Just so, the Divine is a temporary mental construction and a projection on the part of this strange animal, man, who has lately come to inhabit one of the satellites of a minor star.[11] The consequences of this position involve what I take to be a central concern of contemporary discussion. Modern men have substituted the term "religion" for "God."

John Hick expresses this trend in this way:

In contexts in which in former generations questions were raised and debated concerning God, his existence, attributes, purposes, and deeds, the corresponding questions today typically concern Religion, its nature, function, forms, and pragmatic value. A shift has taken place from the term "God" as head of a certain group of words and locutions to the term "Religion" as the new head of the same linguistic family. . . .

This displacement of "God" by "Religion" as the focus of a wide realm of discourse, has brought with it a change in the character of the questions that are most persistently asked in this area. Concerning God, the traditional question has naturally been whether he exists or is real. But this is not a question which arises with regard to Religion. It is obvious that Religion exists; the important queries concern the purposes which it serves in human life, whether it ought to be cultivated, and if so, in what directions it may most profitably be developed. Under the pressure of these concerns, the question of the truth of religious beliefs has fallen into the background and the issue of their practical usefulness has come forward instead to occupy the center of attention.[12]

But Still, Is It True or Not?

Traditional Judeo-Christian faith stands opposed to this noncognitive view of religion. It agrees with our commonsense impulse in insisting on the sheer factuality of man's religious assertions. It is granted that theo-

[11] See J. H. Randall, Jr., *The Role of Knowledge in Western Religion*, Beacon Press, Boston, 1958, p. 119.
[12] Hick, *op. cit.*, p. 72.

logical statements are unique and refer to matters entirely different from those of science, politics, art or any other specialized concern. But still historic faith seems to assert that it is a *fact* that the transcendent God exists. It is *true* that He acts in human history. Surely this is *not poetry*. It is *so!*

In recent years philosophy's interests have coincided, it so happens, with this concern of theology about the traditional use of the language of fact. How do we distinguish the factual from the nonfactual in any case? What are the criteria? As we have seen, the logical empiricists developed the verification theory of meaning. They were, to be sure, interested not simply in the test for true factual propositions: verifiability by appeal to observation and experiment. But behind this test for *truth* is the test to determine whether or not a proposition is *meaningful*. An informative assertion is meaningful if the conditions under which it could be verified as factually true or false can be shown. The application of this criterion to all sorts of assertions makes havoc with assertions of religious conviction and theological belief. What tests of experimental procedure and observation can be applied to such a claim? If its truth or falsity makes no observable difference, then the proposition asserted cannot establish its claim as cognitively meaningful or certifiedly factual.

More recently, philosophers, especially interested in the problem of theological claims, have adopted a modified version of the logical empiricists' verifiability principle of meaning. We are now to ask concerning theological propositions: What experienceable differences do such claims make? An example of this new approach is found in the selected reading from John Wisdom's "Gods" and those by Antony Flew, R. M. Hare, Basil Mitchell and John Hick.

In each of these papers the writer depicts a striking parable to illustrate his main contention. Wisdom uses the parable of the garden and the gardener to suggest that the believer and the unbeliever do not disagree about the facts of the situation. Both experience the same facts. Nor do they disagree about any observations they may make in the future, but they do part company over the differing ways of responding to the same set of facts. Their conflicting assertions are not mutually contradictory. We cannot claim that one is right and the other wrong. Rather they are expressing different feelings, and their words are expressive of these feelings. Such expressive statements are not assertions about the empirical situation. If this is the case, Wisdom is saying, then neither of the rival assertions is verifiable, actually or in principle.

With Flew's variation on the same theme, a shift is made from concern about verifiability to interest in falsifiability. Is there any conceivable event or state of affars which, if it were to take place, would refute the theistic claim? Not simply the existence of God but the love of God is at stake here. "Just what would have to happen not merely (morally and wrongly) to tempt but also (logically and rightly) to entitle us to say 'God does not love us' or even 'God does not exist'?"

Flew's challenge concerning falsification has elicited response from the other parties in the so-called *University* discussion. R. M. Hare agrees with Flew that nothing could ever count decisively against religious beliefs and that they cannot be classified as assertions which might be true or false. What are they? Here Hare coined the word *blik*. A *blik* is an unverifiable and unfalsifiable interpretation of one's experience. Hare illustrates his point with the parable of the lunatic who is convinced that the professors in a certain college are out to murder him. No evidence to the contrary will convince him, for his belief is not open to confirmation or refutation by experience. But Hare distinguishes between an insane and a sane *blik*. Presumably, we all have some *bliks* about the reliability of the world, etc. But with regard to *bliks* that comprise religious beliefs, does Hare answer Flew? He does not profess to, for he simply abandons the traditional view that religious statements are assertions which are true or false. But by the same token, how can *bliks* be counted even as sane or insane, appropriate or inappropriate, relevant or irrelevant? For these distinctions themselves make no sense unless reference is made to tests, evidence, verification, the sort of confirmation which Flew has demanded for religious beliefs. Thus Hare does not meet the challenge directly. His attempted avoidance of the issue becomes an evasion.

Basil Mitchell states that religious assertions are relevant to falsification but never conclusively falsifiable. For beliefs are genuinely factual even though they are not verifiable or falsifiable in a straightforward way. Mitchell develops his own parable, that of the member of the resistance movment in an occupied country. He meets a stranger who impresses him deeply and who urges him to believe that he (the stranger) is really the leader of the resistance movement and he is to trust him no matter what happens. But sometimes the stranger is seen helping the resisters and at others he seems to be collaborating with the enemy. Yet in the face of conflict, the member of the movement continues to believe that the stranger's conduct can be satisfactorily explained. Mitchell writes:

> It is here that my parable differs from Hare's. The partisan admits that many things may and do count against his belief; whereas Hare's lunatic

who has a *blik* about dons doesn't admit that anything counts against his *blik*. Nothing *can* count against *bliks*. Also the partisan has a reason for having in the first instance committed himself, viz. the character of the Stranger; whereas the lunatic has no reason for his *blik* about dons—because, of course, you can't have reasons for *bliks*.[13]

Mitchell's parable puts him on Flew's side in asserting that theological utterances must be assertions. Is the partisan's belief an explanation? Mitchell says that it is in the sense that it ". . . explains and makes sense of the Stranger's behaviour: it helps to explain also the resistance movement in the context in which it appears. In each case it differs from the interpretation which the others put upon the same facts." For Mitchell "God loves men" is similar to "the Stranger is on our side." This may be treated as a hypothesis to be discarded if experience tells against it, as a significant article of faith, or as a vacuous formula to which experience makes no difference and which makes no difference to life. The Christian cannot, once he has committed himself, adopt the first. He is in constant danger of slipping into the third.

Eschatological Verification

John Hick has developed a series of parables to support what he calls "eschatological verification." The reading entitled "Theology and Verification" presents these and deserves special attention on the part of the reader.

Hick states that the verification of a factual assertion is different from a logical demonstration of it. Verification means the ". . . removal of grounds for rational doubt." The exclusion of such grounds will vary with the subject matter. But whenever grounds for rational doubt have been removed, ". . . we rightly speak of verification having taken place." Although "verifiable" normally means "publicly verifiable," it does not follow that a given verifiable proposition has, in fact, been or will, in fact, ever be verified by everyone.

It is possible for a proposition to be, in principle, verifiable but not, in principle, falsifiable. Such a proposition may one day be verified if it is true but can never be falsified if it is false. This is so of the hypothesis of continued existence after bodily death. It is a prediction which will be

[13] Basil Mitchell, "Theology and Falsification," in Antony Flew and Alasdair MacIntyre (eds.), *New Essays in Philosophical Theology,* The Student Christian Movement Press, London, 1955, p. 105.

verified in one's own experience if it is true but which cannot be falsified if it is false. The survival hypothesis is meaningful; for if its prediction is true, it will be known to be true.

Hick then illustrates eschatological verification by means of the parable of the two men traveling along a road.

This parable has one point: that Judeo-Christian theism ". . . postulates an ultimate unambiguous existence *in patria* as well as our present ambiguous existence *in via.*" The presumed future experience cannot count as evidence for theism as a present interpretation of experience. But Hick holds that it does render the ". . . choice between theism and atheism a real and not merely an empty or verbal choice." The theist envisages the universe as a totality in a different way from that in which the atheist envisages it. This does not mean that the objective content of each and every moment is different. The atheist and the theist do not expect different events to occur in detail, nor do they entertain different expectations of the course of history as viewed from within. "But the theist does and the atheist does not expect that when history is completed it will be seen to have led to a particular end-state and to have fulfilled a specific purpose, namely, that of creating 'Children of God.' "

Within the Christian circle of faith, Hick concludes, God is defined as the Being whom Jesus taught, in relation to whom He lived, whose agape toward men was seen on earth in the life of Jesus. Put briefly, God is

. . . the transcendent Creator who is held to have revealed himself in Christ. Jesus' teaching about the Father is accordingly accepted as part of that self-disclosure, and it is from this teaching (together with that of the prophets who preceded him) that Christianity professes to derive its knowledge of God's transcendent being.

Further, says Hick:

Only God himself can know his own infinite nature; and our human belief about that nature is based, according to Christianity, upon his self-revelation to men in Christ. Such beliefs about God's infinite being are not capable of observational verification, being beyond the scope of human experience, but they *may be susceptible to indirect verification by exclusion of rational doubt concerning the authority of Christ* [italics mine]. An experience of the reign of the Son in the Kingdom of the Father would confirm that authority, and therewith, by extension, the validity of Jesus' teaching concerning the character of God in his infinite transcendent nature.[14]

[14] John Hick, "Theology and Verification," *The Existence of God*, The Macmillan Company, New York, 1964, p. 271.

Weight of Evidence?

Is this conclusive proof? No matters of fact are susceptible to a priori proof. The most that Hick can claim is that there is available such weight of evidence as leaves ". . . no room for rational doubt." Within Christianity, eschatological verification, implied in Christian theology, would constitute such evidence. Does God *exist?* Is it a *fact?* Is the transcendent God *real?* "Exist," "fact," "real" are terms which have no significance in general. In the end it seems to come to this: that their meaning depends on the use to which they are put within given contexts. It comes finally to "making a difference." Is the universe different with the existence of *X?* In the case of God, these differences must be spelled out in detail in terms of past, present and future human experience.

16

JOHN WISDOM | *Gods**

1. *The existence of God is not an experimental issue in the way it was.*
An atheist or agnostic might say to a theist "You still think there are
spirits in the trees, nymphs in the streams, a God of the world." He might
say this because he noticed the theist in time of drought pray for rain and
make a sacrifice and in the morning look for rain. But disagreement
about whether there are gods is now less of this experimental or betting
sort than it used to be. This is due in part, if not wholly, to our better
knowledge of why things happen as they do.

It is true that even in these days it is seldom that one who believes in
God has no hopes or fears which an atheist has not. Few believers now
expect prayer to still the waves, but some think it makes a difference to
people and not merely in ways the atheist would admit. Of course with
people, as opposed to waves and machines, one never knows what they
won't do next, so that expecting prayer to make a difference to them is
not so definite a thing as believing in its mechanical efficacy. Still, just as
primitive people pray in a business-like way for rain so some people still
pray for others with a real feeling of doing something to help. However,
in spite of this persistence of an experimental element in some theistic
belief, it remains true that Elijah's method on Mount Carmel of settling
the matter of what god or gods exist would be far less appropriate today
than it was then.

2. *Belief in gods is not merely a matter of expectation of a world to
come.* Someone may say "The fact that a theist no more than an atheist
expects prayer to bring down fire from heaven or cure the sick does not
mean that there is no difference between them as to the facts, it does not
mean that the theist has no expectations different from the atheist's. For

* *Proceedings of the Aristotelian Society*, new ser., vol. 45, 1944–1945, pp. 185–206.
This paper is reprinted in John Wisdom, *Philosophy and Psycho-analysis*, Basil Blackwell
& Mott, Ltd., Oxford, 1953, pp. 149–159.

very often those who believe in God believe in another world and believe that God is there and that we shall go to that world when we die."

This is true, but I do not want to consider here expectations as to what one will see and feel after death nor what sort of reasons these logically unique expectations could have. So I want to consider those theists who do not believe in a future life, or rather, I want to consider the differences between atheists and theists in so far as these differences are not a matter of belief in a future life.

3. *What are these differences? And is it that theists are superstitious or that atheists are blind?* A child may wish to sit a while with his father and he may, when he has done what his father dislikes, fear punishment and feel distress at causing vexation, and while his father is alive he may feel sure of help when danger threatens and feel that there is sympathy for him when disaster has come. When his father is dead he will no longer expect punishment or help. Maybe for a moment an old fear will come or a cry for help escape him, but he will at once remember that this is no good now. He may feel that his father is no more until perhaps someone says to him that his father is still alive though he lives now in another world and one so far away that there is no hope of seeing him or hearing his voice again. The child may be told that nevertheless his father can see him and hear all he says. When he has been told this the child will still fear no punishment nor expect any sign of his father, but now, even more than he did when his father was alive, he will feel that his father sees him all the time and will dread distressing him and when he has done something wrong he will feel separated from his father until he has felt sorry for what he has done. Maybe when he himself comes to die he will be like a man who expects to find a friend in the strange country where he is going, but even when this is so, it is by no means all of what makes the difference between a child who believes that his father lives still in another world and one who does not.

Likewise one who believes in God may face death differently from one who does not, but there is another difference between them besides this. This other difference may still be described as belief in another world, only this belief is not a matter of expecting one thing rather than another here or hereafter, it is not a matter of a world to come but of a world that now is, though beyond our senses.

We are at once reminded of those other unseen worlds which some philosophers "believe in" and others "deny", while non-philosophers unconsciously "accept" them by using them as models with which to "get the hang of" the patterns in the flux of experience. We recall the timeless entities whose changeless connections we seek to represent in symbols, and the values which stand firm[1] amidst our flickering satisfaction and remorse, and the physical things which, though not beyond the corruption of moth and rust, are yet more permanent than the shadows they throw upon the screen before our minds. We recall, too, our talk of souls and of what lies in their depths and is manifested to us partially and intermittently in our own feelings and the behaviour of others. The hypothesis of mind, of other human minds and of animal minds, is reasonable because it explains for each of us why certain things behave so cunningly all by themselves unlike even the most ingenious machines. Is the hypothesis of minds in flowers and trees reasonable for like reasons? Is the hypothesis of a world mind reasonable for like reasons—someone who adjusts the blossom to the bees, someone whose presence may at times be felt—in a garden in high summer, in the hills when clouds are gathering, but not, perhaps, in a cholera epidemic?

4. *The question "Is belief in gods reasonable?" has more than one source.* It is clear now that in order to grasp fully the logic of belief in divine minds we need to examine the logic of belief in animal and human minds. But we cannot do that here and so for the purposes of this discussion about divine minds let us acknowledge the reasonableness of our belief in human minds without troubling ourselves about its logic. The question of the reasonableness of belief in divine minds then becomes a matter of whether there are facts in nature which support claims about divine minds in the way facts in nature support our claims about human minds.

In this way we resolve the force behind the problem of the existence of gods into two components, one metaphysical and the same which prompts the question "Is there *ever any* behaviour which gives reason to believe in *any* sort of mind?" and one which finds expression in "Are there other mind-patterns in nature beside the human and animal patterns which we can easily detect, and are these other mind-patterns superhuman?"

Such over-determination of a question syndrome is common. Thus, the puzzling questions "Do dogs think?", "Do animals feel?" are partly metaphysical puzzles and partly scientific questions. They are not purely metaphysical; for the reports of scientists about the poor performances of cats in cages and old ladies' stories about the remarkable performances of their pets are not irrelevant. But nor are these questions purely scien-

[1] In another world, Dr. Joad says in the *New Statesman* recently.

tific; for the stories never settle them and therefore they have other sources. One other source is the metaphysical source we have already noticed, namely, the difficulty about getting behind an animal's behaviour to its mind, whether it is a non-human animal or a human one.

But there's a third component in the force behind these questions, these disputes have a third source, and it is one which is important in the dispute which finds expression in the words "I believe in God", "I do not". This source comes out well if we consider the question "Do flowers feel?" Like the questions about dogs and animals this question about flowers comes partly from the difficulty we sometimes feel over inference from *any* behaviour to thought or feeling and partly from ignorance as to what behaviour is to be found. But these questions, as opposed to a like question about human beings, come also from hesitation as to whether the behaviour in question is *enough* mind-like, that is, is it enough similar to or superior to human behaviour to be called "mind-proving"? Likewise, even when we are satisfied that human behaviour shows mind and even when we have learned whatever mind-suggesting things there are in nature which are not explained by human and animal minds, we may still ask "But are these things sufficiently striking to be called a mind-pattern? Can we fairly call them manifestations of a divine being?"

"The question," someone may say, "has then become merely a matter of the application of a name. And 'What's in a name?' "

5. *But the line between a question of fact and a question of decision as to the application of a name is not so simple as this way of putting things suggests.* The question "What's in a name?" is engaging because we are inclined to answer both "Nothing" and "Very much". And this "Very much" has more than one source. We might have tried to comfort Heloise by saying "It isn't that Abelard no longer loves you, for this man isn't Abelard"; we might have said to poor Mr. Tebrick in Mr. Garnett's *Lady into Fox* "But this is no longer Silvia." But if Mr. Tebrick replied "Ah, but it is!" this might come not at all from observing facts about the fox which we have not observed, but from noticing facts about the fox which we had missed, although we had in a sense observed all that Mr. Tebrick had observed. It is possible to have before one's eyes all the items of a pattern and still to miss the pattern. Consider the following conversation:

"And I think Kay and I are pretty happy. We've always been happy."
Bill lifted up his glass and put it down without drinking.

"Would you mind saying that again," he asked.

"I don't see what's so queer about it. Taken all in all, Kay and I have really been happy."

"All right," Bill said gently, "Just tell me how you and Kay have been happy."

Bill had a way of being amused by things which I could not understand.

"It's a little hard to explain," I said. "It's like taking a lot of numbers that don't look alike and that don't mean anything until you add them all together."

I stopped, because I hadn't meant to talk to him about Kay and me.

"Go ahead," Bill said. "What about the numbers?" And he began to smile.

"I don't know why you think it's so funny," I said. "All the things that two people do together, two people like Kay and me, add up to something. There are the kids and the house and the dog and all the people we have known and all the times we've been out to dinner. Of course, Kay and I do quarrel sometimes but when you add it all together, all of it isn't as bad as the parts of it seem. I mean, maybe that's all there is to anybody's life."

Bill poured himself another drink. He seemed about to say something and checked himself. He kept looking at me.[2]

Or again, suppose two people are speaking of two characters in a story which both have read[3] or of two friends which both have known, and one says "Really she hated him," and the other says "She didn't, she loved him." Then the first may have noticed what the other has not although he knows no incident in the lives of the people they are talking about which the other doesn't know too, and the second speaker may say "She didn't, she loved him" because he hasn't noticed what the first noticed, although he can remember every incident the first can remember. But then again he may say "She didn't, she loved him" not because he hasn't noticed the patterns in time which the first has noticed but because though he has noticed them he doesn't feel he still needs to emphasize them with "Really she hated him." The line between using a name because of how we feel and because of what we have noticed isn't sharp. "A difference as to the facts," "a discovery," "a relevation" these phrases cover many things. Discoveries have been made not only by Christopher Columbus and Pasteur, but also by Tolstoy and Dostoievsky and Freud. Things are revealed to us not only by the scientists with the microscopes, but also by the poets, the prophets, and the painters. What is so isn't merely a matter

---

[2] *H. M. Pulham, Esq.*, p. 320, by John P. Marquand.

[3] E.g. Havelock Ellis's autobiography.

of "the facts." For sometimes when there is agreement as to the facts there is still argument as to whether defendant did or did not "exercise reasonable care," was or was not "negligent."

And though we shall need to emphasize how much "There is a God" evinces an attitude to the familiar[4] we shall find in the end that it also evinces some recognition of patterns in time easily missed and that, therefore, difference as to there being any gods is in part a difference as to what is so and therefore as to the facts, though not in the simple ways which first occurred to us.

6. *Let us now approach these same points by a different road.*

6.1. *How it is that an explanatory hypothesis, such as the existence of God, may start by being experimental and gradually become something quite different can be seen from the following story:*

Two people return to their long neglected garden and find among the weeds a few of the old plants surprisingly vigorous. One says to the other "It must be that a gardener has been coming and doing something about these plants." Upon inquiry they find that no neighbour has ever seen anyone at work in their garden. The first man says to the other "He must have worked while people slept." The other says "No, someone would have heard him and besides, anybody who cared about the plants would have kept down these weeds." The first man says "Look at the way these are arranged. There is purpose and a feeling for beauty here. I believe that someone comes, someone invisible to mortal eyes. I believe that the more carefully we look the more we shall find confirmation of this." They examine the garden ever so carefully and sometimes they come on new things suggesting that a gardener comes and sometimes they come on new things suggesting the contrary and even that a malicious person has been at work. Besides examining the garden carefully they also study what happens to gardens left without attention. Each learns all the other learns about this and about the garden. Consequently, when after all this, one says, "I still believe a gardener comes" while the other says "I don't" their different words now reflect no difference as to what they have found in the garden, no difference as to what they would find in the garden if they looked further and no difference about how fast untended gardens fall into disorder. At this stage, in this context, the gardener hypothesis has ceased to be experimental, the difference between one who accepts and one who rejects it is now not a matter of the one

---

[4] "Persuasive Definitions," *Mind*, July, 1938, by Charles Leslie Stevenson, should be read here. It is very good. [Also in his *Ethics and Language*, Yale, 1945.—Editor.]

expecting something the other does not expect. What is the difference between them? The one says "A gardener comes unseen and unheard. He is manifested only in his works with which we are all familiar", the other says "There is no gardener" and with this difference in what they say about the gardener goes a difference in how they feel towards the garden, in spite of the fact that neither expects anything of it which the other does not expect.[5]

But is this the whole difference between them—that the one calls the garden by one name and feels one way towards it, while the other calls it by another name and feels in another way towards it? And if this is what the difference has become then is it any longer appropriate to ask "Which is right?" or "Which is reasonable?"

And yet surely such questions *are* appropriate when one person says to another "You still think the world's a garden and not a wilderness, and that the gardener has not forsaken it" or "You still think there are nymphs of the streams, a presence in the hills, a spirit of the world." Perhaps when a man sings "God's in His heaven" we need not take this as more than an expression of how he feels. But when Bishop Gore or Dr. Joad writes about belief in God and young men read them in order to settle their religious doubts the impression is not simply that of persons choosing exclamations with which to face nature and the "changes and chances of this mortal life". The disputants speak as if they are concerned with a matter of scientific fact, or of trans-sensual, trans-scientific and metaphysical fact, but still of fact and still a matter about which reasons for and against may be offered, although no scientific reasons in the sense of field surveys for fossils or experiments on delinquents are to the point.

6.2. *Now can an interjection have a logic?* Can the manifestation of an attitude in the utterance of a word, in the application of a name, have a logic? When all the facts are known how can there still be a question of fact? How can there still be a question? Surely as Hume says ". . . after every circumstance, every relation is known, the understanding has no further room to operate"?[6]

6.3 When the madness of these questions leaves us for a moment *we can all easily recollect disputes which though they cannot be settled by experiment are yet disputes in which one party may be right and the other*

[5] [For a discussion of the implications of this story see "The *University* Discussion" in *New Essays in Philosophical Theology*, eds. Antony Flew and Alasdair MacIntyre (New York: The Macmillan Company, 1955), pp. 96f., Ed.]

[6] Hume, *An Enquiry concerning the Principles of Morals*. Appendix I.

wrong and in which both parties may offer reasons and the one better reasons than the other. *This may happen in pure and applied mathematics and logic.* Two accountants or two engineers provided with the same data may reach different results and this difference is resolved not by collecting further data but by going over the calculations again. Such differences indeed share with differences as to what will win a race, the honour of being among the most "settlable" disputes in the language.

6.4. *But it won't do to describe the theistic issue as one settlable by such calculation,* or as one about what can be deduced in this *vertical* fashion from the facts we know. No doubt dispute about God has sometimes, perhaps especially in mediaeval times, been carried on in this fashion. But nowadays it is not and we must look for some other analogy, some other case in which a dispute is settled but not by experiment.

6.5. *In courts of law* it sometimes happens that opposing counsel are agreed as to the facts and are not trying to settle a question of further fact, are not trying to settle whether the man who admittedly had quarrelled with the deceased did or did not murder him, but are concerned with whether Mr. A who admittedly handed his long-trusted clerk signed blank cheques did or did not exercise reasonable care, whether a ledger is or is not a document,[7] whether a certain body was or was not a public authority.

In such cases we notice that the process of argument is not a *chain* of demonstrative reasoning. It is a presenting and representing of those features of the case which *severally co-operate* in favour of the conclusion, in favour of saying what the reasoner wishes said, in favour of calling the situation by the name by which he wishes to call it. The reasons are like the legs of a chair, not the links of a chain. Consequently although the discussion is *a priori* and the steps are not a matter of experience, the procedure resembles scientific argument in that the reasoning is not *vertically* extensive but *horizontally* extensive—it is a matter of the cumulative effect of several independent premises, not of the repeated transformation of one or two. And because the premises are severally inconclusive the process of deciding the issue becomes a matter of weighing

---

[7] *The Times*, March 2nd, 1945. Also in *The Times* of June 13th, 1945, contrast the case of Hannah V. Peel with that of the cruiser cut in two by a liner. In the latter case there is not agreement as to the facts. See also the excellent articles by Dr. Glanville L. Williams in the *Law Quarterly Review*, "Language and the Law," January, and April 1945, and "The Doctrine of Repugnancy," October, 1943, January, 1944, and April, 1944. The author, having set out how arbitrary are many legal decisions, needs now to set out how far from arbitrary they are—if his readers are ready for the next phase in the dialectic process.

the cumulative effect of one group of severally inconclusive items against the cumulative effect of another group of severally inconclusive items, and thus lends itself to description in terms of conflicting "probabilities". This encourages the feeling that the issue is one of fact—that it is a matter of guessing from the premises at a further fact, at what is to come. But this is a muddle. *The dispute does not cease to be* a priori *because it is a matter of the cumulative effect of severally inconclusive premises.* The logic of the dispute is not that of a chain of deductive reasoning as in a mathematic calculation. But nor is it a matter of collecting from several inconclusive items of information an expectation as to something further, as when a doctor from a patient's symptoms guesses at what is wrong, or a detective from many clues guesses the criminal. It has its own sort of logic and its own sort of end—the solution of the question at issue is a decision, a ruling by the judge. But it is not an arbitrary decision though the rational connections are neither quite like those in vertical deductions nor like those in inductions in which from many signs we guess at what is to come; and though the decision manifests itself in the application of a name it is no more merely the application of a name than is the pinning on of a medal merely the pinning on of a bit of metal. Whether a lion with stripes is a tiger or a lion is, if you like, merely a matter of the application of a name. Whether Mr. So-and-So of whose conduct we have so complete a record did or did not exercise reasonable care is not merely a matter of the application of a name or, if we choose to say it is, then we must remember that with this name a game is lost and won and a game with very heavy stakes. With the judges' choice of a name for the facts goes an attitude, and the declaration, the ruling, is an exclamation evincing that attitude. But *it is an exclamation which not only has a purpose but also has a logic*, a logic surprisingly like that of "futile", "deplorable", "graceful", "grand", "divine".

6.6. *Suppose two people are looking at a picture or natural scene.* One says "Excellent" or "Beautiful" or "Divine"; the other says "I don't see it". He means he doesn't see the beauty. And this reminds us of how we felt the theist accuse the atheist of blindness and the atheist accuse the theist of seeing what isn't there. And yet surely each sees what the other sees. It isn't that one can see part of the picture which the other can't see. So the difference is in a sense not one as to the facts. And so it cannot be removed by the one disputant discovering to the other what so far he hasn't seen. It isn't that the one sees the picture in a different light and so, as we might say, sees a different picture. Consequently the difference between them cannot be resolved by putting the picture in a different light. And yet surely this is just what can be done in such a case—not by moving the picture but by talk perhaps. To settle a dispute as to whether a piece of music is good or better than another we listen again, with a picture we look again. Someone perhaps points to emphasize certain features and we see it in a different light. Shall we call this "field work" and "the last of observation" or shall we call it "reviewing the premises" and "the beginning of deduction (horizontal)"?

If in spite of all this we choose to say that a difference as to whether a thing is beautiful is not a factual difference, we must be careful to remember that there is a procedure for settling these differences and that this consists not only in reasoning and redescription as in the legal case, but also in a more literal resetting-before with re-looking or re-listening.

6.7. *And if we say as we did at the beginning that when a difference as to the existence of a God is not one as to future happenings then it is not experimental and therefore not as to the facts, we must not forthwith assume that there is no right and wrong about it,* no rationality or irrationality, no appropriateness or inappropriateness, no procedure which tends to settle it, *nor even that this procedure is in no sense a discovery of new facts.* After all even in science this is not so. Our two gardeners, even when they had reached the stage when neither expected any experimental result which the other did not, might yet have continued the dispute, each presenting and representing the features of the garden favouring his hypothesis, that is, fitting his model for describing the accepted fact; each emphasizing the pattern he wishes to emphasize. True, in science, there is seldom or never a pure instance of this sort of dispute, for nearly always with difference of hypothesis goes some difference of expectation as to the facts. But scientists argue about rival hypotheses with a vigour which is not exactly proportioned to difference in expectations of experimental results.

The difference as to whether a God exists involves our feelings more than most scientific disputes and in this respect is more like a difference as to whether there is beauty in a thing.

7. *The Connecting Technique.* Let us consider again the technique used in revealing or proving beauty, in removing a blindness, including an attitude which is lacking, in reducing a reaction that is inappropriate. Besides running over in a special way the features of the picture, tracing the rhythms, making sure that this and that are not only seen but noticed, and their relation to each other—besides all this—there are other things we can do to justify our attitude and alter that of the man who cannot see. For features of the picture may be brought out by setting beside it other pictures; just as the merits of an argument may be brought out, proved, by setting beside it other arguments, in which striking but irrelevant features of the original are changed and relevant features emphasized; just as the merits and demerits of a line of action may be brought out by setting beside it other actions. To use Susan Stebbing's example: Nathan brought out for David certain features of what David had done in the matter of Uriah the Hittite by telling him a story about two sheep owners. This is the kind of thing we very often do when someone is "inconsistent" or unreasonable. This is what we do in referring to other cases in law. The paths we need to trace from other cases to the case in question are often numerous and difficult to detect and the person with whom we are discussing the matter may well draw attention to connexions which, while not incompatible with those we have tried to emphasize, are of an opposite inclination. A may have noticed in B subtle and hidden likenesses to an angel and reveal these to C, while C has noticed in B subtle and hidden likenesses to a devil which he reveals to A.

Imagine that man picks up some flowers that lie half withered on a table and gently puts them in water. Another man says to him "You believe flowers feel." He says this although he knows that the man who helps the flowers doesn't expect anything of them which he himself doesn't expect; for he himself expects the flowers to be "refreshed" and to be easily hurt, injured, I mean, by rough handling, while the man who puts them in water does not expect them to whisper "Thank you." The Sceptic says "You believe flowers feel" because something about the way the other man lifts the flowers and puts them in water suggests an attitude to the flowers which he feels inappropriate although perhaps he would not feel it inappropriate to butterflies. He feels that this attitude to flowers is somewhat crazy *just as it is sometimes felt that a lover's attitude is somewhat crazy even when this is not a matter of his having false hopes about how the person he is in love with will act.* It is often said in such cases that reasoning is useless. But the very person who says this feels that the lover's attitude is crazy, is inappropriate like some dreads and hatreds, such as some horrors of enclosed places. And often one who says "It is useless to reason" proceeds at once to reason with the lover, nor is this reasoning always quite without effect. We may draw the lover's attention to certain things done by her he is in love with and trace for him a path to these from things done by others at other times[8] which have disgusted and infuriated him. And by this means we may weaken his admiration

---

[8] Thus, like the scientist, the critic is concerned to show up the irrelevance of time and space.

and confidence, make him feel it unjustified and arouse his suspicion and contempt and make him feel our suspicion and contempt reasonable. It is possible, of course, that he has already noticed the analogies, the connexions, we point out and that he has accepted them—that is, he has not denied them nor passed them off. He has recognised them and they have altered his attitude, altered his love but he still loves. We then feel that perhaps it is we who are blind and cannot see what he can see.

8. *Connecting and Disconnecting*. But before we confess ourselves thus inadequate there are other fires his admiration must pass through. For when a man has an attitude which it seems to us he should not have or lacks one which it seems to us he should have then, not only do we suspect that he is not influenced by connexions which we feel should influence him and draw his attention to these, but also we suspect he is influenced by connexions which should not influence him and draw his attention to these. It may, for a moment, seem strange that we should draw his attention to connexions which we feel should not influence him, and which, since they do influence him, he has in a sense already noticed. But we do—such is our confidence in "the light of reason."

Sometimes the power of these connexions comes mainly from a man's mismanagement of the language he is using. This is what happens in the Monte Carlo fallacy, where by mismanaging the laws of chance a man passes from noticing that a certain colour or number has not turned up for a long while to an improper confidence that now it soon will turn up. In such cases our showing up of the false connexions is a process we call "explaining a fallacy in reasoning." To remove fallacies in reasoning we urge a man to call a spade a spade, ask him what he means by "the State" and having pointed out ambiguities and vaguenesses ask him to reconsider the steps in his argument.

9. *Unspoken Connexions. Usually, however, wrongheadedness or wrongheartedness in a situation, blindness to what is there or seeing what is not, does not arise merely from mismanagement of language but is more due to connexions which are not mishandled in language, for the reason that they are not put into language at all.* And often these misconnexions, too, weaken in the light of reason, if only we can guess where they lie and turn it on them. In so far as these connexions are not presented in language the process of removing their power is not a process of correcting the mismanagement of language. But it is still akin to such a process; for though it is not a process of setting out fairly what has been set out unfairly, it is a process of setting out fairly what has not been set out at all. And we must remember that the line between connexions ill-presented or half-presented in language and connexions operative but not presented in language, or only hinted at, is not a sharp one.

Whether or not we call the process of showing up these connexions "reasoning to remove bad unconscious reasoning" or not, it is certain that in order to settle in ourselves what weight we shall attach to someone's confidence or attitude we not only ask him for his reasons but also look for unconscious reasons both good and bad; that is, for reasons which he can't put into words, isn't explicitly aware of, is hardly aware of, isn't aware of at all—perhaps it's long experience which he *doesn't* recall which lets him know a squall is coming, perhaps it's old experience which he *can't* recall which makes the cake in the tea mean so much and makes Odette so fascinating.[9]

I am well aware of the distinction between the question "What reasons are there for the belief that S is P?" and the question "What are the sources of beliefs that S is P?" There are cases where investigation of the rationality of a claim which certain persons make is done with very little enquiry into why they say what they do, into the causes of their beliefs. This is so when we have very definite ideas about what is really logically relevant to their claim and what is not. Offered a mathematical theorem we ask for the proof; offered the generalization that parental discord causes crime we ask for the correlation co-efficients. But even in this last case, if we fancy that only the figures are reasons we underestimate the complexity of the logic of our conclusion; and yet it is difficult to describe the other features of the evidence which have weight and there is apt to be disagreement about the weight they should have. In criticizing other conclusions and especially conclusions which are largely the expression of an attitude, we have not only to ascertain what reasons there are for them but also to decide what things are reasons and how much. This latter process of sifting reasons from causes is part of the critical process for every belief, but in some spheres it has been done pretty fully already. In these spheres we don't need to examine the actual processes to belief and distil from them a logic. But in other spheres this remains to be done. Even in science or on the stock exchange or in ordinary life we sometimes hesitate to condemn a belief or a hunch[10] merely because those who believe it cannot offer the sort of reasons we had hoped for. And

[9] Proust. *Swann's Way*, Vol. 1, p. 58, Vol. 2. Phoenix Edition.
[10] Here I think of Mr. Staces' interesting reflexions in *Mind*, January, 1945, *The Problems of Unreasoned Beliefs*.

now suppose Miss Gertrude Stein finds excellent the work of a new artist while we see nothing in it. We nervously recall, perhaps, how pictures by Picasso which Miss Stein admired and others rejected, later came to be admired by many who gave attention to them, and we wonder whether the case is not a new instance of her perspicacity and our blindness. But if, upon giving all our attention to the work in question, we still do not respond to it, and we notice that the subject matter of the new pictures is perhaps birds in wild places and learn that Miss Stein is a bird-watcher, then we begin to trouble ourselves less about her admiration.

It must not be forgotten that our attempt to show up misconnexions in Miss Stein may have an opposite result and reveal to us connexions we had missed. Thinking to remove the spell exercised upon his patient by the old stories of the Greeks the psychoanalyst may himself fall under that spell and find in them what his patient has found and, incidentally, what made the Greeks tell those tales.

10. *Now what happens, what should happen, when we enquire in this way into the reasonableness, the propriety of belief in gods?* The answer is: A double and opposite-phased change. Wordsworth writes:

> . . . And I have felt
> A presence that disturbs me with the joy
> Of elevated thoughts, a sense sublime
> Of something far more deeply interfused,
> Whose dwelling is the light of setting suns,
> And the round ocean and the living air,
> And the blue sky, and in the mind of man
> A motion and a spirit, that impels
> All thinking things, all objects of all thoughts,
> And rolls through all things. . . .[11]

We most of us know this feeling. But is it well placed like the feeling that here is first-rate work, which we sometimes rightly have even before we have fully grasped the picture we are looking at or the book we are reading? Or is it misplaced like the feeling in a house that has long been empty that someone secretly lives there still. Wordsworth's feeling *is* the feeling that the world is haunted, that something watches in the hills and manages the stars. The child feels that the stone tripped him when he stumbled, that the bough struck him when it flew back in his face. He has to learn that the wind isn't buffeting him, that there is not a devil in it,

---

[11] *Tintern Abbey.*

that he was wrong, that his attitude was inappropriate. And as he learns that the wind wasn't hindering him so he also learns it wasn't helping him. But we know how, though he learns, his attitude lingers. It is plain that Wordsworth's feeling is of this family.

Belief in gods, it is true, is often very different from belief that stones are spiteful, the sun kindly. For the gods appear in human form and from the waves and control these things and by so doing reward and punish us. But varied as are the stories of the gods they have a family likeness and we have only to recall them to feel sure of the other main sources which co-operate with animism to produce them.

What are the stories of the gods? What are our feelings when we believe in God? They are feelings of awe before power, dread of the thunderbolts of Zeus, confidence in the everlasting arms, unease beneath the all-seeing eye. They are feelings of guilt and inescapable vengeance, of smothered hate and of a security we can hardly do without. We have only to remind ourselves of these feelings and the stories of the gods and goddesses and heroes in which these feelings find expression, to be reminded of how we felt as children to our parents and the big people of our childhood. Writing of a first telephone call from his grandmother Proust says: ". . . it was rather that this isolation of the voice was like a symbol, a presentation, a direct consequence of another isolation, that of my grandmother, separated for the first time in my life, from myself. The orders or prohibitions which she addressed to me at every moment in the ordinary course of my life, the tedium of obedience or the fire of rebellion which neutralized the affection that I felt for her were at this moment eliminated. . . . 'Granny!' I cried to her . . . but I had beside me only that voice, a phantom, as unpalpable as that which would come to revisit me when my grandmother was dead. 'Speak to me!' but then it happened that, left more solitary still, I ceased to catch the sound of her voice. My grandmother could no longer hear me. . . . I continued to call her, sounding the empty night, in which I felt that her appeals also must be straying. I was shaken by the same anguish which, in the distant past, I had felt once before, one day when, a little child, in a crowd, I had lost her."

Giorgio de Chirico, writing of Courbet, says: "The word yesterday envelopes us with its yearning echo, just as, on waking, when the sense of time and the logic of things remain a while confused, the memory of a happy hour we spent the day before may sometimes linger reverberating within us. At times we think of Courbet and his work as we do of our own father's youth."

When a man's father fails him by death or weakness how much he needs another father, one in the heavens with whom is "no variableness nor shadow of turning."

We understand Mr. Kenneth Graham when he wrote of the Golden Age we feel we have lived in under the Olymypians. Freud says: "The ordinary man cannot imagine this Providence in any other form but that of a greatly exalted father, for only such a one could understand the needs of the sons of men, or be softened by their prayers and be placated by the signs of their remorse. The whole thing is so patently infantile, so incongruous with reality. . . ." "So incongruous with reality"! It cannot be denied.

But here a new aspect of the matter may strike us.[12] For the very facts which make us feel that now we can recognize systems of superhuman, sub-human, elusive beings for what they are—the persistent projections of infantile phantasies—include facts which make these systems less fantastic. What are these facts? They are patterns in human reactions which are well described by saying that we are as if there were hidden within us powers, persons, not ourselves and stronger than ourselves. That this is so may perhaps be said to have been common knowledge yielded by ordinary observation of people,[13] but we did not know the degree in which this is so until recent study of extraordinary cases in extraordinary conditions had revealed it. I refer, of course, to the study of multiple personalities and the wider studies of psycho-analysts. Even when the results of this work are reported to us, that is not the same as tracing the patterns in the details of the cases on which the results are based; and even that is not the same as taking part in the studies oneself. One thing not sufficiently realized is that some of the things shut within us are not bad but good.

Now the gods, good and evil and mixed, have always been mysterious powers outside us rather than within. But they have also been within. It is not a modern theory but an old saying that in each of us a devil sleeps. Eve said: "The serpent beguiled me." Helen says to Menelaus:

> . . . And yet how strange it is!
> I ask not thee; I ask my own sad thought,
> What was there in my heart, that I forgot
> My home and land and all I loved, to fly

---

[12] This different aspect of the matter and the connexion between God, the heavenly Father, and "the good father" of the psycho-analysts was put into my head by some remarks of Dr. Susan Isaacs.

[13] Consider Tolstoy and Dostoievsky—I do not mean, of course, that their observation was ordinary.

With a strange man? Surely it was not I,
But Cypris there![14]

Elijah found that God was not in the wind, nor in the thunder, but in a still small voice. The kingdom of Heaven is within us, Christ insisted, though usually about the size of a grain of mustard seed, and he prayed that we should become one with the Father in Heaven.

New knowledge made it necessary either to give up saying "The sun is sinking" or to give the words a new meaning. In many contexts we preferred to stick to the old words and give them a new meaning which was not entirely new but, on the contrary, *practically* the same as the old. The Greeks did not speak of the dangers of repressing instincts but they did speak of the dangers of thwarting Dionysos, of neglecting Cypris for Diana, of forgetting Poseidon for Athena. We have eaten of the fruit of a garden we can't forget though were were never there, a garden we still look for though we can never find it. Maybe we look for too simple a likeness to what we dreamed. Maybe we are not as free as we fancy from the old idea that Heaven is a happy hunting ground, or a city with streets of gold. Lately Mr. Aldous Huxley has recommended our seeking not somewhere beyond the sky or late in time but a timeless state not made of the stuff of this world, which he rejects, picking it into worthless pieces. But this sounds to me still too much a looking for another place, not indeed one filled with sweets but instead so empty that some of us would rather remain in the Lamb or the Elephant, where, as we know, they stop whimpering with another bitter and so far from sneering at all things, hang pictures of winners at Kempton and stars of the 'nineties. Something good we have for each other is freed there, and in some degree and for a while the miasma of time is rolled back without obliging us to deny the present.

The artists who do most for us don't tell us only of fairylands. Proust, Manet, Breughel, even Botticelli and Vermeer show us reality. And yet

---

[14] Euripides. *The Trojan Women*, Gilbert Murray's Translation. Roger Hinks in *Myth and Allegory in Ancient Art* writes (p. 108): "Personifications made their appearance very early in Greek poetry. . . . It is out of the question to call these terrible beings 'abstractions'. . . . They are real daemons to be worshipped and propitiated. . . . These beings we observe correspond to states of mind. The experience of man teaches him that from time to time his composure is invaded and overturned by some power from outside: panic, intoxication, sexual desire."

> What use to shoot off guns at unicorns?
> Where one horn's hit another fierce horn grows.
> These beasts are fabulous, and none were born
> Of woman who could lay a fable low.
> —*The Glass Tower*. Nicholas Moore, p. 100.

they give us for a moment exhilaration without anxiety, peace without boredom. And those who, like Freud, work in a different way against that which too often comes over us and forces us into deadness or despair,[15] also deserve critical, patient and courageous attention. For they, too, work to release us from human bondage into human freedom.

Many have tried to find ways of salvation. The reports they bring back are always incomplete and apt to mislead even when they are not in words but in music or paint. But they are by no means useless; and not the worst of them are those which speak of oneness with God. But in so far as we become one with him he becomes one with us. St. John says he is in us as we love one another.

This love, I suppose, is not benevolence but something that comes of the oneness with one another of which Christ spoke.[16] Sometimes it momentarily gains strength.[17] Hate and the Devil do too. And what is oneness without otherness?

[15] Matthew Arnold. *Summer Night.*
[16] St. John xvi, 21.
[17] *The Harvesters* in *The Golden Age,* Kenneth Graham.

ANTONY FLEW, R. M. HARE, BASIL MITCHELL | *Theology and Falsification**

(i) From the University Discussion

A

ANTONY FLEW

Let us begin with a parable. It is a parable from a tale told by John Wisdom in his haunting and revelatory article "Gods". Once upon a time two explorers came upon a clearing in the jungle. In the clearing were growing many flowers and many weeds. One explorer says, "Some gardener must tend this plot". The other disagrees, "There is no gardener". So they pitch their tents and set a watch. No gardener is ever seen. "But perhaps he is an invisible gardener". So they set up a barbed-wire fence. They electrify it. They patrol with bloodhounds. (For they remember how H. G. Wells's *The Invisible Man* could be both smelt and touched though he could not be seen.) But no shrieks ever suggest that some intruder has received a shock. No movements of the wire ever betray an invisible climber. The bloodhounds never give cry. Yet still the Believer is not convinced. "But there is a gardener, invisible, intangible, insensible to electric shocks, a gardener who has no scent and makes no sound, a gardener who comes secretly to look after the garden which he loves". At last the Sceptic despairs, "But what remains of your original assertion? Just how does what you call an invisible, intangible, eternally elusive gardener differ from an imaginary gardener or even from no gardener at all?"

In this parable we can see how what starts as an assertion, that something exists or that there is some analogy between certain complexes of phenomena, may be reduced step by step to an altogether different status,

* Reprinted with permission of The Macmillan Co. from *New Essays in Philosophical Theology* by Antony Flew and Alasdair MacIntyre, eds., first printed in 1955 by The S.C.M. Press, pp. 96–108. (Footnotes omitted.)

to an expression perhaps of a "picture preference". The Sceptic says there is no gardener. The Believer says there is a gardener (but invisible, etc.). One man talks about sexual behaviour. Another man prefers to talk of Aphrodite (but knows that there is not really a superhuman person additional to, and somehow responsible for, all sexual phenomena). The process of qualification may be checked at any point before the original assertion is completely withdrawn and something of that first assertion will remain (Tautology). Mr. Wells's invisible man could not, admittedly, be seen, but in all other respects he was a man like the rest of us. But though the process of qualification may be, and of course usually is, checked in time, it is not always judiciously so halted. Someone may dissipate his assertion completely without noticing that he has done so. A fine brash hypothesis may thus be killed by inches, the death by a thousand qualifications.

And in this, it seems to me, lies the peculiar danger, the endemic evil, of theological uterance. Take such utterances as "God has a plan", "God created the world", "God loves us as a father loves his children". They look at first sight very much like assertions, vast cosmological assertions. Of course, this is no sure sign that they either are, or are intended to be, assertions. But let us confine ourselves to the cases where those who utter such sentences intend them to express assertions. (Merely remarking parenthetically that those who intend or interpret such utterances as crypto-commands, expressions of wishes, disguised ejaculations, concealed ethics, or as anything else but assertions, are unlikely to succeed in making them either properly orthodox or practically effective.)

Now to assert that such and such is the case is necessarily equivalent to denying that such and such is not the case. Suppose then that we are in doubt as to what someone who gives vent to an utterance is asserting, or suppose that, more radically, we are sceptical as to whether he is really asserting anything at all, one way of trying to understand (or perhaps it will be to expose) his utterance is to attempt to find what he would regard as counting against, or as being incompatible with, its truth. For if the utterance is indeed an assertion, it will necessarily be equivalent to a denial of the negation of that assertion. And anything which would count against the assertion, or which would induce the speaker to withdraw it and to admit that it had been mistaken, must be part of (or the whole of) the meaning of the negation of that assertion. And to know the meaning of the negation of an assertion, is as near as makes no matter, to know the meaning of that assertion. And if there is nothing which a putative assertion denies then there is nothing which it asserts either: and so it is not really an assertion. When the Sceptic in the parable asked the

Believer, "Just how does what you call an invisible, intangible, eternally elusive gardener differ from an imaginary gardener or even from no gardener at all?" he was suggesting that the Believer's earlier statement had been so eroded by qualification that it was no longer an assertion at all.

Now it often seems to people who are not religious as if there was no conceivable event or series of events the occurrence of which would be admitted by sophisticated religious people to be a sufficient reason for conceding "There wasn't a God after all" or "God does not really love us then". Someone tells us that God loves us as a father loves his children. We are reassured. But then we see a child dying of inoperable cancer of the throat. His earthly father is driven frantic in his efforts to help, but his Heavenly Father reveals no obvious sign of concern. Some qualification is made—God's love is "not a merely human love" or it is "an inscrutable love", perhaps—and we realize that such sufferings are quite compatible with the truth of the assertion that "God loves us as a father (but, of course, . . .)". We are reassured again. But then perhaps we ask: what is this assurance of God's (appropriately qualified) love worth, what is this apparent guarantee really a guarantee against? Just what would have to happen not merely (morally and wrongly) to tempt but also (logically and rightly) to entitle us to say "God does not love us" or even "God does not exist"? I therefore put to the succeeding symposiasts the simple central questions, "What would have to occur or to have occurred to constitute for you a disproof of the love of, or of the existence of, God?"

University College of North Staffordshire
England

B
R. M. HARE

I wish to make it clear that I shall not try to defend Christianity in particular, but religion in general—not because I do not believe in Christianity, but because you cannot understand what Christianity is, until you have understood what religion is.

I must begin by confessing that, on the ground marked out by Flew, he seems to me to be completely victorious. I therefore shift my ground by relating another parable. A certain lunatic is convinced that all dons want to murder him. His friends introduce him to all the mildest and most respectable dons that they can find, and after each of them has retired, they say, "You see, he doesn't really want to murder you; he spoke to you in a most cordial manner; surely you are convinced now?" But the lunatic replies "Yes, but that was only his diabolical cunning; he's really plotting against me the whole time, like the rest of them; I know it I tell you". However many kindly dons are produced, the reaction is still the same.

Now we say that such a person is deluded. But what is he deluded about? About the truth or falsity of an assertion? Let us apply Flew's test to him. There is no behaviour of dons that can be enacted which he will accept as counting against his theory; and therefore his theory, on this test, asserts nothing. But it does not follow that there is no difference between what he thinks about dons and what most of us think about them—otherwise we should not call him a lunatic and ourselves sane, and dons would have no reason to feel uneasy about his presence in Oxford.

Let us call that in which we differ from this lunatic, our respective *bliks*. He has an insane *blik* about dons; we have a sane one. It is important to realize that we have a sane one, not no *blik* at all; for there must be two sides to any argument—if he has a wrong *blik*, then those who are right about dons must have a right one. Flew has shown that a *blik* does not consist in an assertion or system of them; but nevertheless it is very important to have the right *blik*.

Let us try to imagine what it would be like to have different *bliks* about other things than dons. When I am driving my car, it sometimes occurs to me to wonder whether my movements of the steering-wheel will always continue to be followed by corresponding alterations in the directions of the car. I have never had a steering failure, though I have had skids, which must be similar. Moreover, I know enough about how the steering of my car is made, to know the sort of thing that would have to go wrong for the steering to fail—steel joints would have to part, or steel rods break, or something—but how do I know that this won't happen? The truth is, I don't know; I just have a *blik* about steel and its properties, so that normally I trust the steering of my car; but I find it not at all difficult to imagine what it would be like to lose this *blik* and acquire the opposite one. People would say I was silly about steel; but there would be no mistaking the reality of the difference between our respective *bliks*—for example, I should never go in a motor-car. Yet I should hesitate to say that the difference between us was the difference between contradictory assertions. No amount of safe arivals or bench-tests will remove my *blik* and restore the normal one; for my *blik* is compatible with any finite number of such tests.

It was Hume who taught us that our whole commerce with the world depends upon our *blik* about the world; and that differences between *bliks* about the world cannot be settled by observation of what happens in the world. That was why, having performed the interesting experiment of doubting the ordinary man's *blik* about the world, and showing that no proof could be given to make us adopt one *blik* rather than another, he turned to backgammon to take his mind off the problem. It seems, indeed, to be impossible even to formulate as an assertion the normal *blik* about the world which makes me put my confidence in the future reliability of steel joints, in the continued ability of the road to support my car, and not gape beneath it revealing nothing below; in the general non-homicidal tendencies of dons; in my own continued well-being (in some sense of that word that I may not now fully understand) if I continue to do what is right according to my lights; in the general likelihood of people like Hitler coming to a bad end. But perhaps a formulation less inadequate than most is to be found in the Pslams: "The earth is weak and all the inhabiters thereof: I bear up the pillars of it".

The mistake of the position which Flew selects for attack is to regard this kind of talk as some sort of *explanation*, as scientists are accustomed to use the word. As such, it would obviously be ludicrous. We no longer believe in God as an Atlas—*nous n'avons pas besoin de cette hypothèse.* But it is nevertheless true to say that, as Hume saw, without a *blik* there can be no explanation; for it is by our *bliks* that we decide what is and what is not an explanation. Suppose we believed that everything that happened, happened by pure chance. This would not of course be an assertion; for it is compatible with anything happening or not happening, and so, incidentally, is its contradictory. But if we had this belief, we should not be able to explain or predict or plan anything. Thus, although we should not be *asserting* anything different from those of a more normal belief, there would be a great difference between us; and this is the sort of difference that there is between those who really believe in God and those who really disbelieve in him.

The word "really" is important, and may excite suspicion. I put it in, because when people have had a good Christian upbringing, as have most of those who now profess not to believe in any sort of religion, it is very hard to discover what they really believe. The reason why they find it so easy to think that they are not religious, is that they have never got into the frame of mind of one who suffers from the doubts to which religion is the answer. Not for them the terrors of the primitive jungle. Having abandoned some of the more picturesque fringes of religion, they think that they have abandoned the whole thing—whereas in fact they still have got, and could not live without, a religion of a comfortably substantial, albeit highly sophisticated, kind, which differs from that of many "religious people" in little more than this, that "religious people" like to sing

Psalms about theirs—a very natural and proper thing to do. But nevertheless there may be a big difference lying behind—the difference between two people who, though side by side, are walking in different directions. I do not know in what direction Flew is walking; perhaps he does not know either. But we have had some examples recently of various ways in which one can walk away from Christianity, and there are any number of possibilities. After all, man has not changed biologically since primitive times; it is his religion that has changed, and it can easily change again. And if you do not think that such changes make a difference, get acquainted with some Sikhs and some Mussulmans of the same Punjabi stock; you will find them quite different sorts of people.

There is an important difference between Flew's parable and my own which we have not yet noticed. The explorers do not *mind* about their garden; they discuss it with interest, but not with concern. But my lunatic, poor fellow, minds about dons; and I mind about the steering of my car; it often has people in it that I care for. It is because I mind very much about what goes on in the garden in which I find myself, that I am unable to share the explorers' detachment.

Balliol College
Oxford

C
BASIL MITCHELL

Flew's article is searching and perceptive, but there is, I think, something odd about his conduct of the theologian's case. The theologian surely would not deny that the fact of pain counts against the assertion that God loves men. This very incompatibility generates the most intractable of theological problems—the problem of evil. So the theologian *does* recognize the fact of pain as counting against Christian doctrine. But it is true that he will not allow it—or anything—to count decisively against it; for he is committed by his faith to trust in God. His attitude is not that of the detached observer, but of the believer.

Perhaps this can be brought out by yet another parable. In time of war in an occupied country, a member of the resistance meets one night a stranger who deeply impresses him. They spend that night together in conversation. The Stranger tells the partisan that he himself is on the side of the resistance—indeed that he is in command of it, and urges the partisan to have faith in him no matter what happens. The partisan is utterly convinced at that meeting of the Stranger's sincerity and constancy and undertakes to trust him.

They never meet in conditions of intimacy again. But sometimes the Stranger is seen helping members of the resistance, and the partisan is grateful and says to his friends, "He is on our side".

Sometimes he is seen in the uniform of the police handing over patriots to the occupying power. On these occasions his friends murmur against him: but the partisan still says, "He is on our side". He still believes that, in spite of appearances, the Stranger did not deceive him. Sometimes he asks the Stranger for help and receives it. He is then thankful. Sometimes he asks and does not receive it. Then he says, "The Stranger knows best". Sometimes his friends, in exasperation, say "Well, what *would* he have to do for you to admit that you were wrong and that he is not on our side?" But the partisan refuses to answer. He will not consent to put the Stranger to the test. And sometimes his friends complain, "Well, if *that's* what you mean by his being on our side, the sooner he goes over to the other side the better".

The partisan of the parable does not allow anything to count decisively against the proposition "The Stranger is on our side". This is because he has committed himself to trust the Stranger. But he of course recognizes' that the Stanger's ambiguous behaviour *does* count against what he believes about him. It is precisely this situation which constitutes the trial of his faith.

When the partisan asks for help and doesn't get it, what can he do? He can (*a*) conclude that the Stranger is not on our side or; (*b*) maintain that he is on our side, but that he has reasons for withholding help.

The first he will refuse to do. How long can he uphold the second position without its becoming just silly?

I don't think one can say in advance. It will depend on the nature of the impression created by the Stranger in the first place. It will depend, too, on the manner in which he takes the Stranger's behaviour. If he blandly dismisses it as of no consequence, as having no bearing upon his belief, it will be assumed that he is thoughtless or insane. And it quite obviously won't do for him to say easily, "Oh, when used of the Stranger the phrase 'is on our side' *means* ambiguous behaviour of this sort". In that case he would be like the religious man who says blandly of a terrible disaster "It is God's will". No, he will only be regarded as sane and reasonable in his belief, if he experiences in himself the full force of the conflict.

It is here that my parable differs from Hare's. The partisan admits that many things may and do count against his belief; whereas Hare's lunatic who has a *blik* about dons doesn't admit that anything counts against his *blik*. Nothing *can* count against *bliks*. Also the partisan has a reason for having in the first instance committed himself, viz. the character of the Stranger; whereas the lunatic has no reason for his *blik* about dons—because, of course, you can't have reasons for *bliks*.

This means that I agree with Flew that theological utterances must be assertions. The partisan is making an assertion when he says, "The Stranger is on our side".

Do I want to say that the partisan's belief about the Stranger is, in any sense, an explanation? I think I do. It explains and makes sense of the Stranger's behaviour: it helps to explain also the resistance movement in the context of which it appears. In each case it differs from the interpretation which the others put upon the same facts.

"God loves men" resembles "the Stranger is on our side" (and many other significant statements, e.g. historical ones) in not being conclusively falsifiable. They can both be treated in at least three different ways: (1) As provisional hypotheses to be discarded if experience tells against them; (2) As significant articles of faith; (3) As vacuous formulae (expressing, perhaps, a desire for reassurance) to which experience makes no difference and which make no differences to life.

The Christian, once he has committed himself, is precluded by his faith from taking up the first attitude: "Thou shalt not tempt the Lord thy God". He is in constant danger, as Flew has observed, of slipping into the third. But he need not; and, if he does, it is a failure in faith as well as in logic.

Keble College
Oxford

D
ANTONY FLEW

It has been a good discussion: and I am glad to have helped to provoke it. But now—at least in *University*—it must come to an end: and the Editors of *University* have asked me to make some concluding remarks. Since it is impossible to deal with all the issues raised or to comment separately upon each contribution, I will concentrate on Mitchell and Hare, as representative of two very different kinds of response to the challenge made in "Theology and Falsification".

The challenge, it will be remembered, ran like this. Some theological utterances seem to, and are intended to, provide explanations or express assertions. Now an assertion, to be an assertion at all, must claim that things stand thus and thus; *and not otherwise*. Similarly an explanation, to be an explanation at all, must explain why this particular thing occurs;

and not something else. Those last clauses are crucial. And yet sophisticated religious people—or so it seemed to me—are apt to overlook this, and tend to refuse to allow, not merely that anything actually does occur, but that anything conceivably could occur, which would count against their theological assertions and explanations. But in so far as they do this their supposed explanations are actually bogus, and their seeming assertions are really vacuous.

Mitchell's response to this challenge is admirably direct, straightforward, and understanding. He agrees ". . . that theological utterances must be assertions". He agrees that if they are to be assertions, there must be somthing that would count against their truth. He agrees, too, that believers are in constant danger of transforming their would-be assertions into "vacuous formulae". But he takes me to task for an oddity in my ". . . conduct of the theologian's case. The theologian surely would not deny that the fact of pain counts against the assertion that God loves men. This very incompatibility generates the most intractable of theological problems, the problem of evil". I think he is right. I should have made a distinction between two very different ways of dealing with what looks like evidence against the love of God: the way I stressed was the expedient of qualifying the original assertion; the way the theologian usually takes, at first, is to admit that it looks bad but to insist that there is—there must be—some explanation which will show that, in spite of appearances, there really is a God who loves us. His difficulty, it seems to me, is that he has given God attributes which rule out all possible saving explanations. In Mitchell's parable of the Stranger it is easy for the believer to find plausible excuses for ambiguous behaviour: for the Stranger is a man. But suppose the Stranger is God. We cannot say that he would like to help but cannot: God is omnipotent. We cannot say that he would help if he only knew: God is omniscient. We cannot say that he is not responsible for the wickedness of others: God creates those others. Indeed an omnipotent, omniscient God must be an accessory before (and during) the fact to every human misdeed; as well as being responsible for every non-moral defect in the universe. So, though I entirely concede that Mitchell was absolutely right to insist against me that the theologian's first move is to look for an *explanation,* I still thing that in the end, if relentlessly pursued, he will have to resort to the avoiding action of *qualification.* And there lies the danger of that death by a thousand qualifications, which would, I agree, constitute ". . . a failure in faith as well as in logic".

Hare's approach is fresh and bold. He confesses that ". . . on the ground marked out by Flew, he seems to me to be completely victorious".

He therefore introduces the concept of *blik*. But while I think that there is room for some such concept in philosophy, and that philosophers should be grateful to Hare for his invention, I nevertheless want to insist that any attempt to analyse Christian religious utterances as expressions or affirmations of a *blik* rather than as (at least would-be) assertions about the cosmos is fundamentally misguided. *First*, because thus interpreted they would be entirely unorthodox. If Hare's religion really is a *blik*, involving no cosmological assertions about the nature and activities of a supposed personal creator, then surely he is not a Christian at all? *Second*, because thus interpreted, they could scarcely do the job they do. If they were not even intended as assertions then many religious activities would become fraudulent, or merely silly. If "You ought *because* it is God's will" asserts no more than "You ought", then the person who prefers the former phraseology is not really giving a reason, but a fraudulent substitute for one, a dialectical dud cheque. If "My soul must be immortal *because* God loves his children, etc." asserts no more than "My soul must be immortal", then the man who reassures himself with theological arguments for immortality is being as silly as the man who tries to clear his overdraft by writing his bank a cheque on the same account. (Of course neither of these utterances would be distinctively Christian: but this discussion never pretended to be so confined.) Religious utterances may indeed express false or even bogus assertions: but I simply do not believe that they are not both intended and interpreted to be or at any rate to presuppose assertions, at least in the context of religious practice; whatever shifts may be demanded, in another context, by the exigencies of theological apologetic.

One final suggestion. The philosophers of religion might well draw upon George Orwell's last appalling nightmare *1984* for the concept of *doublethink*. "*Doublethink* means the power of holding two contradictory beliefs simultaneously, and accepting both of them. The party intellectual knows that he is playing tricks with reality, but by the exercise of *doublethink* he also satisfies himself that reality is not violated" (*1984*, p. 220). Perhaps religious intellectuals too are sometimes driven to doublethink in order to retain their faith in a loving God in face of the reality of a heartless and indifferent world. But of this more another time, perhaps.

University College of North Staffordshire
England

JOHN HICK | *Theology and Verification**

To ask "Is the existence of God verifiable?" is to pose a question which is too imprecise to be capable of being answered. There are many different concepts of God, and it may be that statements employing some of them are open to verification or falsification while statements employing others of them are not. Again, the notion of verifying is itself by no means perfectly clear and fixed; and it may be that on some views of the nature of verification the existence of God is verifiable, whereas on other views it is not.

Instead of seeking to compile a list of the various different concepts of God and the various possible senses of "verify," I wish to argue with regard to one particular concept of deity, namely the Christian concept, that divine existence is in principle verifiable; and as the first stage of this argument I must indicate what I mean by "verifiable."

I

The central core of the concept of verification, I suggest, is the removal of ignorance or uncertainty concerning the truth of some proposition. That p is verified (whether p embodies a theory, hypothesis, prediction, or straightforward assertion) means that something happens which makes it clear that p is true. A question is settled so that there is no longer room for rational doubt concerning it. The way in which grounds for rational doubt are excluded varies, of course, with the subject matter. But the general feature common to all cases of verification is the ascertaining of truth by the removal of grounds for rational doubt. Where such grounds are removed, we rightly speak of verification having taken place.

To characterize verification in this way is to raise the question whether

* By permission. From John Hick, "Theology and Verification," *Theology Today*, April, 1960, pp. 12–31. (Footnotes omitted.)

the notion of verification is purely logical or is both logical and psychological. Is the statement that p is verified simply the statement that a certain state of affairs exists (or has existed), or is it the statement also that someone is aware that this state of affairs exists (or has existed) and notes that its existence established the truth of p? A geologist predicts that the earth's surface will be covered with ice in 15 million years time. Suppose that in 15 million years time the earth's surface *is* covered with ice, but that in the meantime the human race has perished, so that no one is left to observe the event or to draw any conclusion concerning the accuracy of the geologist's prediction. Do we now wish to say that his prediction has been verified, or shall we deny that it has been verified, on the ground that there is no one left to do the verifying?

The range of "verify" and its cognates is sufficiently wide to permit us to speak in either way. But the only sort of verification of theological propositions which is likely to interest us is one in which human beings participate. We may therefore, for our present purpose, treat verification as a logico-psychological rather than as a purely logical concept. I suggest, then, that "verify" be construed as a verb which has its primary uses in the active voice: I verify, you verify, we verify, they verify, or have verified. The impersonal passive, it is verified, now becomes logically secondary. To say that p has been verified is to say that (at least) someone has verified it, often with the implication that his or their report to this effect is generally accepted. But it is impossible, on this usage, for p to have been verified without someone having verified it. "Verification" is thus primarily the name for an event which takes place in human consciousness. It refers to an experience, the experience of ascertaining that a given proposition or set of propositions is true. To this extent verification is a psychological notion. But of course it is also a logical notion. For needless to say, not *any* experience is rightly called an experience of verifying p. Both logical and psychological conditions must be fulfilled in order for verification to have taken place. In this respect, "verify" is like "know." Knowing is an experience which someone has or undergoes, or perhaps a dispositional state in which someone is, and it cannot take place wthout someone having or undergoing it or being in it; but not by any means every experience which people have, or every dispositional state in which they are, is rightly called knowing.

With regard to this logico-psychological concept of verification, such questions as the following arise. When A, but nobody else, has ascertained that p is true, can p be said to have been verified; or is it required that others also have undergone the same ascertainment? How public, in other words, must verification be? Is it necessary that p could in principle be verified by anyone, without restriction, even though perhaps only A has in fact verified it? If so, what is meant here by "in principle"; does it signify, for example, that p must be verifiable by anyone who performs a certain operation; and does it imply that to do this is within everyone's power?

These questions cannot, I believe, be given any general answer applicable to all instances of the exclusion of rational doubt. The answers must be derived in each case from an investigation of the particular subject matter. It will be the object of subsequent sections of this article to undertake such an investigation concerning the Christian concept of God.

Verification is often construed as the verification of a prediction. However, verification, as the exclusion of grounds for rational doubt, does not necessarily consist in the proving correct of a prediction; a verifying experience does not always need to have been predicted in order to have the effect of excluding rational doubt. But when we are interested in the verifiability of propositions as the criterion for their having factual meaning, the notion of prediction becomes central. If a propositon contains or entails predictions which can be verified or falsified, its character as an assertion (though not of course its character as a true assertion) is thereby guaranteed.

Such predictions may be and often are conditional. For example, statements about the features of the dark side of the moon are rendered meaningful by the conditional predictions which they entail to the effect that if an observer comes to be in such a position in space, he will make such-and-such observations. It would in fact be more accurate to say that the prediction is always conditional, but that sometimes the conditions are so obvious and so likely to be fulfilled in any case that they require no special mention, while sometimes they require for their fulfillment some unusual expedition or operation. A prediction, for example, that the sun will rise within twenty-four hours is intended unconditionally, at least as concerns conditions to be fulfilled by the observer; he is not required by the terms of the prediction to perform any special operation. Even in this case, however, there is an implied negative condition that he shall not put himself in a situation (such as immuring himself in the depths of a coal mine) from which a sunrise would not be perceptible. Other predictions, however, are explicitly conditional. In these cases it is true for any particular individual that in order to verify the statement in question he must go through some specified course of action. The prediction is to the effect that if you conduct such an experiment you will obtain such a result; for example, if you go into the next room you will have such-and-such visual experiences, and if you then touch the table which you see you will have such-and-such tactual experiences, and so on. The content of the "if" clause is of course always determined by the particular subject matter. The logic of "table" determines what you must do to verify statements about tables; the logic of "molecule" determines what you must do to verify statements about molecules; and the logic of "God" determines what you must do to verify statements about God.

In those cases in which the individual who is to verify a proposition must himself first perform some operation, it clearly cannot follow from the circumstances that the proposition is true that everybody has in fact verified it, or that everybody will at some future time verify it. For whether or not any particular person performs the requisite operation is a contingent matter.

II

What is the relation between verification and falsification? We are all familiar today with the phrase, "theology and falsification." A. G. N. Flew and others, taking their cue from John Wisdom, have raised instead of the question, "What possible experiences would verify 'God exists'?" the matching question, "What possible experiences would falsify 'God exists'? What conceivable state of affairs would be incompatible with the existence of God?" In posing the question in this way it was apparently assumed that verification and falsification are symmetrically related, and that the latter is apt to be the more accessible of the two.

In the most common cases, certainly, verification and falsification are symmetrically related. The logically simplest case of verification is provided by the crucial instance. Here it is integral to a given hypothesis that if, in specified circumstances, A occurs, the hypothesis is thereby shown to be true, whereas if B occurs the hypothesis is thereby shown to be false. Verification and falsification are also symmetrically related in the testing of such a proposition as "There is a table in the next room." The verifying experiences in this case are experiences of seeing and touching, predictions of which are entailed by the proposition in question, under the proviso that one goes into the next room; and the absence of such experiences in those circumstances serves to falsify the proposition.

But it would be rash to assume, on this basis, that verification and falsification must always be related in this symmetrical fashion. They do not necessarily stand to one another as do the two sides of a coin, so that once the coin is spun it must fall on one side or the other. There are cases in which verification and falsification each correspond to a side on a different coin, so that one can fail to verify without this failure constituting falsification.

Consider, for example, the proposition that "there are three successive sevens in the decimal determination of π." So far as the value of π has been worked out, it does not contain a series of three sevens, but it will always be true that such a series may occur at a point not yet reached in anyone's calculations. Accordingly, the proposition may one day be verified, if it is true, but can never be falsified, if it is false.

The hypothesis of continued conscious existence after bodily death provides an instance of a different kind of such asymmetry, and one which has a direct bearing upon the theistic problem. This hypothesis has built into it a prediction that one will after the date of one's bodily death have conscious experiences, including the experience of remembering that death. This is a prediction which will be verified in one's own experience if it is true, but which cannot be falsified if it is false. That is to say, it can be false, but *that* it is false can never be a fact which anyone has experientially verified. But this circumstance does not undermine the meaningfulness of the hypothesis, since it is also such that if it be true, it will be known to be true.

It is important to remember that we do not speak of verifying logically necessary truths, but only propositions concerning matters of fact. Accordingly verification is not to be identified with the concept of logical certification or proof. The exclusion of rational doubt concerning some matter of fact is not equivalent to the exclusion of the logical possibility of error or illusion. For truths concerning fact are not logically necessary. Their contrary is never self-contradictory. But at the same time the bare logical possibility of error does not constitute ground for rational doubt as to the veracity of our experience. If it did, no empirical proposition could ever be verified, and indeed the notion of empirical verification would be without use and therefore without sense. What we rightly seek, when we desire the verification of a factual proposition, is not a demonstration of the logical impossibility of the proposition being false (for this would be a self-contradictory demand), but such weight of evidence as suffices, in the type of case in question, to exclude rational doubt.

III

These features of the concept of verification—that verification consists in the exclusion of grounds for rational doubt concerning the truth of some proposition; that this means its exclusion from particular minds;

that the nature of the experience which serves to exclude grounds for rational doubt depends upon the particular subject matter; that verification is often related to predictions and that such predictions are often conditional; that verification and falsification may be asymmetrically related; and finally, that the verification of a factual proposition is not equivalent to logical certification—are all relevant to the verification of the central religious claim, "God exists." I wish now to apply these discriminations to the notion of eschatological verification, which has been briefly employed by Ian Crombie in his contribution to *New Essays in Philosophical Theology*, and by myself in *Faith and Knowledge*. This suggestion has on each occasion been greeted with disapproval by both philosophers and theologians. I am, however, still of the opinion that the notion of eschatological verification is sound; and further, that no viable alternative to it has been offered to establish the factual character of theism.

The strength of the notion of eschatological verification is that it is not an *ad hoc* invention but is based upon an actually operative religious concept of God. In the language of Christian faith, the word "God" stands at the center of a system of terms, such as Spirit, grace, Logos, incarnation, Kingdom of God, and many more; and the distinctly Christian conception of God can only be fully grasped in its connection with these related terms. It belongs to a complex of notions which together constitute a picture of the universe in which we live, of man's place therein, of a comprehensive divine purpose interacting with human purposes, and of the general nature of the eventual fulfillment of that divine purpose. This Christian picture of the universe, entailing as it does certain distinctive expectations concerning the future, is a very different picture from any that can be accepted by one who does not believe that the God of the New Testament exists. Further, these differences are such as to show themselves in human experience. The possibility of experiential confirmation is thus built into the Christian concept of God; and the notion of eschatological verification seeks to relate this fact to the logical problem of meaning.

Let me first give a general indication of this suggestion, by repeating a parable which I have related elsewhere, and then try to make it more precise and eligible for discussion. Here, first, is the parable.

Two men are travelling together along a road. One of them believes that it leads to a Celestial City, the other that it leads nowhere; but since this is the only road there is, both must travel it. Neither has been this way before, and therefore neither is able to say what they will find around each next corner. During their journey they meet both with moments of refreshment and delight, and with moments of hardship and danger. All the time one of them thinks of his journey as a pilgrimage to the Celestial City and interprets the pleasant parts as encouragements and the obstacles as trials of his purpose and lessons in endurance, prepared by the king of that city and designed to make of him a worthy citizen of the place when at last he arrives there. The other, however, believes none of this and sees their journey as an unavoidable and aimless ramble. Since he has no choice in the matter, he enjoys the good and endures the bad. But for him there is no Celestial City to be reached, no all-encompassing purpose ordaining their journey; only the road itself and the luck of the road in good weather and in bad.

During the course of the journey the issue between them is not an experimental one. They do not entertain different expectations about the coming details of the road, but only about its ultimate destination. And yet when they do turn the last corner it will be apparent that one of them has been right all the time and the other wrong. Thus although the issue between them has not been experimental, it has nevertheless from the start been a real issue. They have not merely felt differently about the road; for one was feeling appropriately and the other inappropriately in relation to the actual state of affairs. Their opposed interpretations of the road constituted genuinely rival assertions, though assertions whose assertion-status has the peculiar characteristic of being guaranteed retrospectively by a future crux.

This parable has of course (like all parables) strict limitations. It is designed to make only one point: that Christian doctrine postulates an ultimate unambiguous state of existence *in patria* as well as our present ambiguous existence *in via*. There is a state of having arrived as well as a state of journeying, an eternal heavenly life as well as an earthly pilgrimage. The alleged future experience of this state cannot, of course, be appealed to as evidence for theism as a present interpretation of our experience; but it does suffice to render the choice between theism and atheism a real and not a merely empty or verbal choice. And although this does not affect the logic of the situation, it should be added that the alternative interpretations are more than theoretical, for they render different practical plans and policies appropriate now.

The universe as envisaged by the theist, then, differs as a totality from the universe as envisaged by the atheist. This difference does not, however, from our present standpoint within the universe, involve a difference in the objective content of each or even any of its passing moments. The theist and the atheist do not (or need not) expect different events to occur in the successive details of the temporal process. They do not (or need not) entertain divergent expectations of the course of history viewed from within. But the theist does and the atheist does not expect that when history is completed it will be seen to have led to a particular end-state and to have fulfilled a specific purpose, namely, that of creating "children of God."

IV

The idea of an eschatological verification of theism can make sense, however, only if the logically prior idea of continued personal existence after death is intelligible. A desultory debate on this topic has been going on for several years in some of the philosophical periodicals. C. I. Lewis has contended that the hypothesis of immortality ". . . is an hypothesis about our own future experience. And our understanding of what would verify it has no lack of clarity." And Morris Schlick agreed, adding, "We must conclude that immortality, in the sense defined [i.e. 'survival after death,' rather than 'never-ending life'], should not be regarded as a 'metaphysical problem,' but is an empirical hypothesis, because it possesses logical verifiability. It could be verified by following the prescription: 'Wait until you die!' " However, others have challenged this conclusion, either on the ground that the phrase "surviving death" is self-contradictory in ordinary language or, more substantially, on the ground that the traditional distinction between soul and body cannot be sustained. I should like to address myself to this latter view. The only self of which we know, it is said, is the empirical self, the walking, talking, acting, sleeping individual who lives, it may be, for some sixty to eighty years and then dies. Mental events and mental characteristics are analyzed into the modes of behavior and behavioral dispositions of this empirical self. The human being is described as an organism capable of acting in the "high-level" ways which we characterize as intelligent, thoughtful, humorous, calculating, and the like. The concept of mind or soul is thus not the concept of a "ghost in the machine" (to use Gilbert Ryle's loaded phrase), but of the more flexible and sophisticated ways in which human beings behave and have it in them to behave. On this view there is no room for the notion of soul in distinction from body; and if there is no soul in distinction from body, there can be no question of the soul surviving the death of the body. Against this philosophical background the specifically Christian (and also Jewish) belief in the resurrection of the flesh, or body, in contrast to the Hellenic notion of the survival of a disembodied soul, might be expected to have attracted more attention than it has. For it is consonant with the conception of man as an indissoluble psycho-physical unity, and yet it also offers the possibility of an empirical meaning for the idea of "life after death."

Paul is the chief Biblical expositor of the idea of the resurrection of the body. His view, as I understand it, is this. When someone has died he is, apart from any special divine action, extinct. A human being is by nature mortal and subject to annihilation by death. But in fact God, by an act of sovereign power, either sometimes or always resurrects or (better) reconstitutes or recreates him—not, however, as the identical physical organism that he was before death, but as a *soma pneumatikon* ("spiritual body") embodying the dispositional characteristics and memory traces of the deceased physical organism, and inhabiting an environment with which the *soma pneumatikon* is continuous as the *ante-mortem* body was continuous with our present world. In discussing this notion we may well abandon the word "spiritual," as lacking today any precise established usage, and speak of "resurrection bodies" and of "the resurrection world." The principal questions to be asked concern the relation between the physical world and the resurrection world, and the criteria of personal identity which are operating when it is alleged that a certain inhabitant of the resurrection world is the same person as an individual who once inhabited this world. The first of these questions turns out on investigation to be the more difficult of the two, and I shall take the easier one first.

Let me sketch a very odd possibility (concerning which, however, I wish to emphasize not so much its oddness as its possibility!), and then see how far it can be stretched in the direction of the notion of the resurrection body. In the process of stretching it will become even more odd than it was before; but my aim will be to show that, however odd, it remains within the bounds of the logically possible. This progression will be presented in three pictures, arranged in a self-explanatory order.

First picture: Suppose that at some learned gathering in this country one of the company were suddenly and inexplicably to disappear, and that at the same moment an exact replica of him were suddenly and inexplicably to appear at some comparable meeting in Australia. The person who appears in Australia is exactly similar, as to both bodily and mental characteristics, with the person who disappears in America. There is continuity of memory, complete similarity of bodily features, including even fingerprints, hair and eye coloration and stomach contents, and also of beliefs, habits, and mental propensities. In fact there is everything that would lead us to identify the one who appeared with the one who disappeared, except continuity of occupancy of space. We may suppose, for example, that a deputation of the colleagues of the man who disappeared fly to Australia to interview the replica of him which is reported there, and find that he is in all respects but one exactly as though he had travelled from say, Princeton to Melbourne, by conventional means. The only difference is that he describes how, as he was sitting listening to Dr. Z reading a paper, on blinking his eyes he suddenly found himself sitting in a different room listening to a different paper by an Australian scholar. He asks his colleagues how the meeting had gone after he ceased to be there, and what they had made of his disappearance, and so on. He clearly thinks of himself as the one who was present with them at their meeting in the United States. I suggest that faced with all these circumstances his colleagues would soon, if not immediately, find themselves thinking of him and treating him as the individual who had so inexplicably disappeared from their midst. We should be extending our normal use of "same person" in a way which the postulated facts would both demand and justify if we said that the one who appears in Australia is the same person as the one who disappears in America. The factors inclining us to identify them would far outweigh the factors disinclining us to do this. We should have no reasonable alternative but to extend our usage of "the same person" to cover the strange new case.

Second picture: Now let us suppose that the event in America is not a sudden and inexplicable disappearance, and indeed not a disappearance at all, but a sudden death. Only, at the moment when the individual dies, a replica of him as he was at the moment before his death, complete with memory up to that instant, appears in Australia. Even with the corpse on our hands, it would still, I suggest, be an extension of "same person" required and warranted by the postulated facts, to say that the same person who died has been miraculously recreated in Australia. The case would be considerably odder than in the previous picture, because of the existence of the corpse in America contemporaneously with the existence of the living person in Australia. But I admit that, although the oddness of this circumstance may be stated as strongly as you please, and can indeed hardly be overstated, yet it does not exceed the bounds of the logically possible. Once again we must imagine some of the deceased's colleagues going to Australia to interview the person who has suddenly appeared there. He would perfectly remember them and their meeting, be interested in what had happened, and be as amazed and dumbfounded about it as anyone else; and he would perhaps be worried about the possible legal complications if he should return to America to claim his property; and so on. Once again, I believe, they would soon find themselves thinking of him and treating him as the same person as the dead Princetonian. Once again the factors inclining us to say that the one who died and the one who appeared are the same person would outweigh the factors inclining us to say that they are different people. Once again we should have to extend our usage of "the same person" to cover this new case.

Third picture: My third supposal is that the replica, complete with memory, etc. appears, not in Australia, but as a resurrection replica in a different world altogether, a resurrection world inhabited by resurrected persons. This world occupies its own space, distinct from the space with which we are now familiar. That is to say, an object in the resurrection world is not situated at any distance or in any direction from an object in our present world, although each object in either world is spatially related to each other object in the same world.

Mr. X, then, dies. A Mr. X replica, complete with the set of memory traces which Mr. X had at the last moment before his death, comes into existence. It is composed of other material than physical matter, and is located in a resurrection world which does not stand in any spatial relationship with the physical world. Let us leave out of consideration St. Paul's hint that the resurrection body may be as unlike the physical body as is a full grain of wheat from the wheat seed, and consider the simpler picture in which the resurrection body has the same shape as the physical body.

In these circumstances, how does Mr. X know that he has been resurrected or recreated? He remembers dying; or rather he remembers being on what he took to be his death-bed, and becoming progressively weaker until, presumably, he lost consciousness. But how does he know that (to put it Irishly) his "dying" proved fatal; and that he did not, after losing consciousness, begin to recover strength, and has now simply waked up?

The picture is readily enough elaborated to answer this question. Mr. X meets and recognizes a number of relatives and friends and historical personages whom he knows to have died; and from the fact of their presence, and also from their testimony that he has only just now appeared in their world, he is convinced that he has died. Evidence of this kind could mount up to the point at which they are quite as strong as the evidence which, in pictures one and two, convince the individual in question that he has been miraculously translated to Australia. Resurrected persons would be individually no more in doubt about their own identity than we are now, and would be able to identify one another in the same kinds of ways, and with a like degree of assurance, as we do now.

If it be granted that resurrected persons might be able to arrive at a rationally founded conviction that their existence is *post-mortem*, how could they know that the world in which they find themselves is in a different space from that in which their physical bodies were? How could such a one know that he is not in a like situation with the person in picture number two, who dies in America and appears as a full-blooded replica in Australia, leaving his corpse in the U.S.A.—except that now the replica is situated, not in Australia, but on a planet of some other star?

It is of course conceivable that the space of the resurrection world should have properties which are manifestly incompatible with its being a region of physical space. But on the other hand, it is not of the essence of the notion of a resurrection world that its space should have properties different from those of physical space. And supposing it not to have different properties, it is not evident that a resurrected individual could learn from any direct observations that he was not on a planet of some sun which is at so great a distance from our own sun that the stellar scenery visible from it is quite unlike that which we can now see. The grounds that a resurrected person would have for believing that he is in a different space from physical space (supposing there to be no discernible difference in spatial properties) would be the same as the grounds that any of us may have now for believing this concerning resurrected individuals. These grounds are indirect and consist in all those considerations (e.g., Luke 16:26) which lead most of those who consider the question to reject as absurd the possibility of, for example, radio communication or rocket travel between earth and heaven.

V

In the present context my only concern is to claim that this doctrine of the divine creation of bodies, composed of a material other than that of physical matter, which bodies are endowed with sufficient correspondence of characteristics with our present bodies, and sufficient continuity of memory with our present consciousness, for us to speak of the same person being raised up again to life in a new environment, is not self-contradictory. If, then, it cannot be ruled out *ab initio* as meaningless, we may go on to consider whether and how it is related to the possible verification of Christian theism.

So far I have argued that a survival prediction such as is contained in the *corpus* of Christian belief is in principle subject to future verification. But this does not take the argument by any means as far as it must go if it is to succeed. For survival, simply as such, would not serve to verify theism. It would not necessarily be a state of affairs which is manifestly incompatible with the non-existence of God. It might be taken just as a surprising natural fact. The atheist, in his resurrection body, and able to remember his life on earth, might say that the universe has turned out to be more complex, and perhaps more to be approved of, than he had realized. But the mere fact of survival, with a new body in a new environment, would not demonstrate to him that there is a God. It is fully compatible with the notion of survival that the life to come be, so far as the theistic problem is concerned, essentially a continuation of the present life, and religiously no less ambiguous. And in this event, survival after bodily death would not in the least constitute a final verification of theistic faith.

I shall not spend time in trying to draw a picture of a resurrection existence which would merely prolong the religious ambiguity of our present life. The important question, for our purpose, is not whether one can conceive of after-life experiences which would *not* verify theism (and in point of fact one can fairly easily conceive them), but whether one can conceive of after-life experiences which *would* serve to verify theism.

I think that we can. In trying to do so I shall not appeal to the traditional doctrine, which figures especially in Catholic and mystical theology, of the Beatific Vision of God. The difficulty presented by this doctrine is not so much that of deciding whether there are grounds for believing it, as of deciding what it means. I shall not, however, elaborate this difficulty, but pass directly to the investigation of a different and, as it seems to me, more intelligible possibility. This is the possibility not of a direct vision of God, whatever that might mean, but of a *situation* which points unambiguously to the existence of a loving God. This would be a situation which, so far as its religious significance is concerned, contrasts in a certain important respect with our present situation. Our present situation is one which in some ways seems to confirm and in other ways to contradict the truth of theism. Some events around us suggest the presence of an unseen benevolent intelligence and others suggest that no such intelligence is at work. Our situation is religiously ambiguous. But in order for us to be aware of this fact we must already have some idea, however vague, of what it would be for our situation to be not ambiguous, but on the contrary wholly evidential of God. I therefore want to try to make clearer this presupposed concept of a religiously unambiguous situation.

There are, I suggest, two possible developments of our experience such that, if they occurred in conjunction with one another (whether in this life or in another life to come), they would assure us beyond rational doubt of the reality of God, as conceived in the Christian faith. These are, *first*, an experience of the fulfillment of God's purpose for ourselves, as this has been disclosed in the Christian revelation; in conjunction, *second*, with an experience of communion with God as he has revealed himself in the person of Christ.

The divine purpose for human life, as this is depicted in the New Testament documents, is the bringing of the human person, in society with his fellows, to enjoy a certain valuable quality of personal life, the content of which is given in the character of Christ—which quality of life (i.e. life in relationship with God, described in the Fourth Gospel as eternal life) is said to be the proper destiny of human nature and the source of man's final self-fulfillment and happiness. The verification situation with regard to such a fulfillment is asymmetrical. On the one hand, so long as the divine purpose remains unfulfilled, we cannot know that it never will be fulfilled in the future; hence no final falsification is possible of the claim that this fulfillment will occur—unless, of course, the prediction contains a specific time clause which, in Christian teaching, it does not. But on the other hand, if and when the divine purpose *is* fulfilled in our own experience, we must be able to recognize and rejoice in that fulfillment. For the fulfillment would not be for us the promised fulfillment without our own conscious participation in it.

It is important to note that one can say this much without being cognizant in advance of the concrete form which such fulfillment will take. The before-and-after situation is analogous to that of a small child looking forward to adult life and then, having grown to adulthood, looking back upon childhood. The child possesses and can use correctly in various contexts the concept of "being grown-up," although he does not know, concretely, what it is like to be grown-up. But when he reaches adulthood he is nevertheless able to know that he has reached it; he is able to recognize the experience of living a grown-up life even though he did not know in advance just what to expect. For his understanding of adult maturity grows as he himself matures. Something similar may be supposed to happen in the case of the fulfillment of the divine purpose for human life. That fulfillment may be as far removed from our present condition as is mature adulthood from the mind of a little child; nevertheless, we possess already a comparatively vague notion of this final fulfillment, and as we move towards it our concept will itself become more adequate; and if and when we finally reach that fulfillment, the problem of recognizing it will have disappeared in the process.

The other feature that must, I suggest, be present in a state of affairs that would verify theism, is that the fulfillment of God's purpose be apprehended as the fulfillment of God's purpose and not simply as a natural state of affairs. To this end it must be accompanied by an experience of communion with God as he has made himself known to men in Christ.

The specifically Christian clause, "as he has made himself known to men in Christ," is essential, for it provides a solution to the problem of recognition in the awareness of God. Several writers have pointed out the logical difficulty involved in any claim to have encountered God. How could one know that it was *God* whom one had encountered? God is described in Christian theology in terms of various absolute qualities, such as omnipotence, omnipresence, perfect goodness, infinite love, etc., which cannot as such be observed by us, as can their finite analogues, limited power, local presence, finite goodness, and human love. One can recognize that a being whom one "encounters" has a given finite degree of power, but how does one recognize that he has *un*limited power? How does one observe that an encountered being is *omni*present? How does one perceive that his goodness and love, which one can perhaps see to exceed any human goodness and love, are actually infinite? Such qualities cannot be given in human experience. One might claim, then, to have encountered a Being whom one presumes, or trusts, or hopes to be God; but one cannot claim to have encountered a Being whom one recognized to be the infinite, almighty, eternal Creator.

This difficulty is met in Christianity by the doctrine of the Incarnation—although this was not among the considerations which led to the formulation of that doctrine. The idea of incarnation provides answers to the two related questions: "How do we know that God has certain absolute qualities which, by their very nature, transcend human experience?" and "How can there be an eschatological verification of theism which is based upon a recognition of the presence of God in his Kingdom?"

In Christianity God is known as "the God and Father of our Lord Jesus Christ." God is the Being about whom Jesus taught; the Being in relation to whom Jesus lived, and into a relationship with whom he brought his disciples; the Being whose *agape* toward men was seen on earth in the life of Jesus. In short, God is the transcendent Creator who has revealed himself in Christ. Now Jesus' teaching about the Father is a part of that self-disclosure, and it is from this teaching (together with that of the prophets who preceded him) that the Christian knowledge of God's transcendent being is derived. Only God himself knows his own infinite nature; and our human belief about that nature is based upon his self-revelation to men in Christ. As Karl Barth expresses it, "Jesus Christ is the knowability of God." Our beliefs about God's infinite being are not capable of observational verification, being beyond the scope of human experience, but they are susceptible of indirect verification by the removal of rational doubt concerning the authority of Christ. An experience of the reign of the Son in the Kingdom of the Father would confirm that authority, and therewith, indirectly, the validity of Jesus' teaching concerning the character of God in his infinite transcendent nature.

The further question as to how an eschatological experience of the

Kingdom of God could be known to be such has already been answered by implication. It is God's union with man in Christ that makes possible man's recognition of the fulfillment of God's purpose for man as being indeed the fulfillment of *God's* purpose for him. The presence of Christ in his Kingdom marks this as being beyond doubt the Kingdom of the God and Father of the Lord Jesus Christ.

It is true that even the experience of the realization of the promised Kingdom of God, with Christ reigning as Lord of the New Aeon, would not constitute a logical certification of his claims nor, accordingly, of the reality of God. But this will not seem remarkable to any philosopher in the empiricist tradition, who knows that it is only a confusion to demand that a factual proposition be an analytic truth. A set of expectations based upon faith in the historic Jesus as the incarnation of God, and in his teaching as being divinely authoritative, could be so fully confirmed in *post-mortem* experience as to leave no grounds for rational doubt as to the validity of that faith.

VI

There remains of course the problem (which falls to the New Testament scholar rather than to the philosopher) whether Christian tradition, and in particular the New Testament, provides a sufficiently authentic "picture" of the mind and character of Christ to make such recognition possible. I cannot here attempt to enter into the vast field of Biblical criticism, and shall confine myself to the logical point, which only emphasizes the importance of the historical question, that a verification of theism made possible by the Incarnation is dependent upon the Christian's having a genuine contact with the person of Christ, even though this is mediated through the life and tradition of the Church.

One further point remains to be considered. When we ask the question, "To *whom* is theism verified?" one is initially inclined to assume that the answer must be, "To everyone." We are inclined to assume that, as in my parable of the journey, the believer must be confirmed in his belief, and the unbeliever converted from his unbelief. But this assumption is neither demanded by the nature of verification nor by any means unequivocably supported by our Christian sources.

We have already noted that a verifiable prediction may be conditional. "There is a table in the next room" entails conditional predictions of the form: if someone goes into the next room he will see, etc. But no one is compelled to go into the next room. Now it may be that the predictions concerning human experience which are entailed by the proposition that

God exists are conditional predictions and that no one is compelled to fulfill those conditions. Indeed we stress in much of our theology that the manner of the divine self-disclosure to men is such that our human status as free and responsible beings is respected, and an awareness of God never is forced upon us. It may then be a condition of *post-mortem* verification that we be already in some degree conscious of God by an uncompelled response to his modes of revelation in this world. It may be that such a voluntary consciousness of God is an essential element in the fulfillment of the divine purpose for human nature, so that the verification of theism which consists in an experience of the final fulfillment of that purpose can only be experienced by those who have already entered upon an awarenes of God by the religious mode of apperception which we call faith.

If this be so, it has the consequence that only the theistic believer can find the vindication of his belief. This circumstance would not of course set any restriction upon who can become a believer, but it would involve that while theistic faith can be verified—found by one who holds it to be beyond rational doubt—yet it cannot be proved to the nonbeliever. Such an asymmetry would connect with that strain of New Testament teaching which speaks of a division of mankind even in the world to come.

Having noted this possibility I will only express my personal opinion that the logic of the New Testament as a whole, though admittedly not always its explicit content, leads to a belief in ultimate universal salvation. However, my concern here is not to seek to establish the religious facts, but rather to establish that there are such things as religious facts, and in particular that the existence or nonexistence of the God of the New Testament is a matter of fact, and claims as such eventual experiential verification.

Chapter 11 | Philosophies of Existence

If God's existence can neither be proved nor disproved, then why not a religion without God? In fact, some now seem to be echoing the themes of naturalistic humanism but with a difference. For a group who call themselves "radical theologians" are now saying Christianity itself cannot flourish unless followers of Jesus Christ affirm God's *nonexistence.* It looks like but a short step from saying "God does not exist as an entity 'out there'" to affirming "God is dead." But the recent "God is dead" or radical theologians (to be discussed in the final chapter and readings) did not arrive at their conclusions suddenly nor without honest reflection on some 100 years or so of theological, philosophical and cultural development. Like many other movements, this contemporary radical theology has been distorted by popularizing journalists into a meaningless slogan. Whether, therefore, we agree or disagree with what the radical theologians have to say, it is important at least to understand their claims and to grasp the seriousness of the challenge they pose to cherished beliefs.

Anticipations of Current Movements

Contemporary theologians were not the first to say "God is dead." Nietzsche said it nearly a century ago, and Hegel had spoken of it before that; and Hegel is no atheist. Yet it is Nietzsche's word which speaks to our current condition. There is one essential difference between Nietzsche's view and that of Altizer and Hamilton, two of the current radical theologians. These twentieth-century thinkers claim they are not reporting a cultural fact about men's loss of belief in God. Rather they explicitly say that they are making a theological and ontological statement not about men's beliefs but about God Himself: "God is dead."

Nietzsche fashions a parable about the drift of our Western culture toward nihilism. "We have destroyed our own faith in God. There remains only the void. We are falling. Our dignity is gone. Our values are lost. Who is to say what is up and what is down? It has become colder and night is closing in."[1]

How can modern man escape the nihilism which Nietzsche pictures in rich, imagic language?

The Madman. Have you not heard of that madman who lit a lantern in the bright morning hours, ran to the market place, and cried incessantly, "I seek God! I seek God!" As many of those who do not believe in God were standing around just then, he provoked much laughter. Why, did he get lost? said one. Did he lose his way like a child? said another. Or is he hiding? Is he afraid of us? Has he gone on a voyage? or emigrated? Thus they yelled and laughed. The madman jumped into their midst and pierced them with his glances.

"Whither is God" he cried. "I shall tell you. *We have killed him*—you and I. All of us are his murderers. But how have we done this? How were we able to drink up the sea? Who gave us the sponge to wipe away the entire horizon? What did we do when we unchained this earth from its sun? Whither is it moving now? Whither are we moving now? Away from all suns? Are we not plunging continually? Backward, sideward, forward, in all directions? Is there any up or down left? Are we not straying as through an infinite nothing? Do we not feel the breath of empty space? Has it not become colder? Is not night and more night coming on all the while? Must not lanterns be lit in the morning? Do we not hear anything yet of the noise of the gravediggers who are burying God? Do we not smell anything yet of God's decomposition? Gods too decompose. God is dead. God remains dead. And we have killed him. How shall we, the murderers of all murderers, comfort ourselves? What was holiest and most powerful of all that the world has yet owned has bled to death under our knives. Who will wipe this blood off us? What water is there for us to clean ourselves? What festivals of atonement, what sacred games shall we have to invent? Is not the greatness of this deed too great for us? Must not we ourselves become gods simply to seem worthy of it? There has never been a greater deed; and whoever will be born after us—for the sake of this deed he will be part of a higher history than all history hitherto."

Here the madman fell silent and looked again at his listeners; and they too were silent and stared at him in astonishment. At last he threw his lantern on the ground, and it broke and went out. "I come too early," he said then; "my time has not come yet. This tremendous event is still on its way, still wandering—it has not yet reached the ears of man. Lightning and thunder require time, the light of the stars requires time, deeds require time even after they are done, before they can be seen and heard. This deed

---

[1] Walter Kaufmann, *Nietzsche*, Meridian Books, Inc., New York, 1956, p. 82.

is still more distant from them than the most distant stars—*and yet they have done it themselves.*"

It has been related further that on that same day the madman entered divers churches and there sang his *requiem aeternam deo*. Led out and called to account, he is said to have replied each time, "What are these churches now if they are not the tombs and sepulchers of God?"[2]

This seems to be Nietzsche's dilemma with respect to God's relation to human existence. On the one hand, if there is a God, then man is robbed of autonomy, dignity and worth. For if God is all, then man is nothing and his values have no significance. On the other hand, if God is not, then indeed human life teeters perilously close to the abyss of meaninglessness, for man has lost direction and sure grasp of values. If God is or if God is not, man is nothing. Are these our only alternatives? To affirm the human, it appears we must declare the death of God. However, it is possible also to conceive of a God who does not "suck the lifeblood out of man" but accords human persons freedom, autonomy and dignity. The God of the Judeo-Christian tradition is that kind of God. This, as we shall see, stands as the basic criticism of the "God is dead" theoolgians.

Kierkegaard and Sartre

Jean-Paul Sartre, a twentieth-century Existentialist, poses the dilemma of God's relation to men in much the same way. Man's freedom must be preserved at all costs. Man decides who he is and what he is, for himself individually and for humanity. No preexistent "nature of things" determines man's "nature." No primordial "God" has brought man into existence or stamped him with an indelible character. Sartre's is thus an atheistic Existentialism.

Philosophies of existence all in one way or another keep pressing men to ask seriously "existential" or personal questions: What am I as a man? What is humanity? These are not the theoretical questions: What is truth? What is good? What is God? For the questions of human *existenz* can only be answered by men making decisions. What responsible choices are mine to make if truth is to be embodied in the world or good come alive or God be related to me?

Again, philosophies of existence are concerned about persons in rela-

---

[2] From *The Portable Nietzsche*, translated and edited by Walter Kaufmann, pp. 95–96. Copyright 1954 by The Viking Press, Inc. Reprinted by permission of The Viking Press, Inc.

tion to society: how individuals have come to be lost in the crowd, alone and in despair. Words like *separation, disruption, alienation, anxiety* comprise Existentialists' vocabulary. They dramatize the splitting apart of that which belongs together. Man is alienated from a universe in which he no longer feels at home. Man is alienated from the immediate world of nature, cut off from the root of things by the very technology through which he had hoped to control nature. Man is alienated from his fellow-man in a society torn apart by hatred and struggles for power. Man is alienated from the orders of justice and equity by which he had hoped to win a society of peace and security. But, more basically still, man is alienated from himself, from the roots of his own being, and tries futilely to conceal this loss from himself by living falsely on the seeming surface of things a kind of unauthentic existence. Finally, man is alienated from the Source and Ground of all existence, and now ultimate meanings are gone and there are blankness and faceless anonymity where once there were security and hope.

How shall alienation be characterized? Alienation, loss of authentic *existenz,* means *angst,* or anxiety. As we shall see, anxiety is not a mood or emotion. It is a state of being. How shall anxiety be overcome? Perhaps it cannot be eliminated. For the suspicion lingers that simply to *be,* to exist, involves risk. There is always the danger of *not* being, not existing, failing to achieve authentic existence. Men must choose who they are. But if this is a free choice, then to be carries with it the equal and opposite possibility of not being. Free men are those who take this peril to themselves, live with it, in a "Courage-to-be-in-spite-of-this-threat-of not-being."[3]

Are all Existentialists atheists? Some are, and some are not. Existentialism is not a single school of thought. It is a name for an exceedingly broad trend. There are family resemblances among its various advocates. Each puts stress on individual decision, personal involvement, freedom, autonomy. The differences between them are spelled out in terms of the world view, ontology, theology which each adopts.

At one extreme, Sartre finds man thrust into a godless world to make his own way. No preexistent nature is given to man. Who he is, indeed, what the whole of humanity is, each person decides in every moment of responsible choice. This heavy weight of total responsibility is the source of anxiety.

At the other extreme, Kierkegaard pictures man deciding for himself but doing so transparently before God. Kierkegaard refuses to separate

[3] This is the way Paul Tillich expresses it in his book by that name, *The Courage to Be,* Yale University Press, New Haven, Conn., 1952.

man's freedom from the gracious concern and rule of God. Indeed, freedom is perfect obedience to God, for man himself is a union of the temporal and the eternal.[4]

The true conquest of this temporal existence is achieved not by escaping from it but by being related to the Ultimate here and now in the midst of everyday existence. A man may not be able to escape his past or the many conditioning influences which have brought him to this present moment. These he did not choose or will. But he can draw them into his life as he takes responsibility for his present self.

This trend is reflected in Christian Existentialism in our century, especially in the thought of Paul Tillich. Christianity reminds us that God confronts men with an absolute demand for openness, honesty, justice. This demand leaves us finite human beings shattered. Before God we must repent continually. Yet we must link self-acceptance to repentance. "Self-acceptance" does not mean that I am perfectly right before God just as I am. It means rather that, despite my bondage to the impulse to put myself at the center of existence, to make of myself an absolute (sin), I have found forgiveness and release. The Christian says, "God accepts me. Because God accepts me, I am able to accept myself."

In summary, Sartre pictures man "condemned to be free," autonomous in his decisions and yet utterly alone and anxious. Kierkegaard and contemporary Christian Existentialists yoke freedom to dependence upon God. Freedom signifies honesty and openness. Dependence means that forgiveness is given to me, for to accept God's gracious acceptance of myself is to be free.

Avoiding Caricatures of Existentialism

Many thoughtful men and women in our day respond to the Existentialists' analysis of human existence. Within the depth of their own beings, they know lostness, aloneness, alienation from themselves, from their fellowmen, from the Ultimate. They have experienced the anxiety which results from the splitting apart of what belongs together. They confront blankness and faceless anonymity.

These are not pleasant, pollyanna themes. Yet they are the perennial themes of human existence. For the philosophy of existence is not a Johnny-come-lately fad for tired and discouraged moderns. It is not a shocking, disgusting defiance of conventional society parading in beards and leotards.

---

[4] See Chapter 3, "The Nature of Man."

In contrast to this popularized and cheapened picture, the philosophy of existence sounds ageless themes going back to the ancient Greeks. The term itself indicates a trend represented by men of varying viewpoints and backgrounds. It has its roots in a Socrates in ancient Greece and finds expression in such diverse thinkers as Augustine, Pascal, Dostoevsky, Nietzsche, Kafka, Jaspers, Heidegger, Marcel, Camus, Sartre and, of course, in the person and work of that Danish writer of the nineteenth century who would not even call himself a philosopher of existence, Søren Kierkegaard.

As we read these writings, we need to avoid a second prevalent misunderstanding. It has to do with "objectivity" in contrast to "subjectivity" or "the way of existence." Two kinds of achievement contribute to our effort to understand our world and ourselves.[5] One achievement is *objectivity*. It is represented by the stance of the scientist and of the man of reasonable commonsense in practical affairs. Without objectivity, we cannot grasp the facts because blindness or emotion may twist our judgment. Objectivity means maturity. It is a necessary condition of civilization. But, say the philosophers of existence, sometimes objectivity gets in the way of fuller understanding. For men also pursue another kind of understanding: not the objective but the personal, the unique, the inward, the unrepeatable. Here we have to do with the commitments and loyalties of individual existence involving a man's whole personal being. This deepening grasp of personal significance leads to the hunch that purely objective understanding is severely limited. Factual, rational, scientific knowledge is not the whole truth about man or man's world. Awareness of these limitations of objectivity produces the philosophy of existence through the ages and today.

The misunderstanding to be avoided here centers in this contrast between *objectivity* and *the existential*. The philosophy of existence says that we enter into some truth not by working at objectivity but by entering into the intensity of personal decision, involvement and responsibility. It is, we have said, a protest against the exclusive claim of objective methods to explain all truth about our world and ourselves. But the philosopher of existence is careful at this point. He says that objectivity is a perfectly legitimate method in those areas where science and technology are essential to man's well-being. But he goes on to claim that there are those other ethicoreligious questions of man's whole being which only personal decision and responsible choice can answer. They

[5] See Roger Shinn, *The Existentialist Posture*, Reflection Books, Association Press, New York, 1959.

are the questions of ultimate concern. Who is man? What are the roots of man's freedom?

By their very use of terms like "subjective," philosophers of existence lay themselves open to the charge that man's decisions are purely private, arbitrary, without grounds. Certainly Kierkegaard was overeager to assert that ethicoreligious decisions require a man to do his own choosing and acting. He even says in effect that our concept of God does not matter at all as long as the inward (subjective) attitude we take toward whatever we worship is one of complete sincerity and devotion. He writes that ". . . the individual is in the truth even if he should happen to be thus related to what is not true." Obviously "true" is used here in two senses. Kierkegaard comes down so strongly on decision as the pivotal center of the religious consciousness that passion and faith are set over against reason. Reason's attempts to prove God's existence are futile. Even if His existence could be proved, we would have just a bare theoretical proposition on our hands. What matters is man's relation to God. In terms of the distinction we made in a previous chapter, both revelation and faith are, for Kierkegaard, nonpropositional. For these have to do with the whole man's stance before God and his response to God's demands upon him in the immediate moment.

But, despite this danger of setting the inward and personal over against the outward, the Existentialist must not be misunderstood. He is not using the term "subjective," as we do in ordinary language today, in contrast to "objective." He does not intend to refer to the wholly "private" in the "bad" sense. Rather he is attempting to point beyond this common distinction. Kierkegaard certainly stresses the demand for the man of Christian conviction to use his understanding, just as other men do, to grasp what is comprehensible. The Christian should see and state every theological objection to Christian belief and be as alert as the atheist. If nonsense crops up, the well-developed intellect can get rid of it.

What Kierkegaard is saying here is that man cannot exist in purely abstract thought. "To exist under the guidance of pure thought is like travelling in Denmark with the help of a small map of Europe, on which Denmark shows no larger than a steel pen-point—aye, it is still more impossible." The several phases of man's total culture, the intellectual, the aesthetic, the ethical and the religious, must find their unity in the life of the existing individual. For, as the theme of "The Individual" (Reading 20) unfolds, it becomes clear that ". . . only *one* attains the goal."

"The individual" is the category through which, in a religious respect, this age, all history, the human race as a whole, must pass. . . . my task is . . . to provoke, if possible, to invite, to stir up the many to press through this defile of "the individual," through which, however, no one can pass except by becoming the individual. . . .

Summarizing, we do well, first, to avoid confusing caricatures of Existentialism with this historic movement which has found many expressions throughout Western culture. Second, we need to try to grasp the meaning of existential decision, or the subjective in contrast to the objective. In neither case is this easy to do, because the statements of various philosophers of existence are not always as unambiguous as we should wish.

A third source of misunderstanding relates to the Existentialists' use or overuse of the term "anxiety." We commonly connect anxiety with sheer emotions of fright, dread, worry or with psychotic states which can be cured only by effective psychotherapy. It is clear that anxiety frequently does express itself emotionally as fear or, in psychoneurotic forms, as tension and flight from reality. But existential anxiety, or *angst*, lies deeper than any of these. It has to do, as we have stated above, with the threat that hangs over every man, the threat of nonbeing. No man can avoid this threat no matter how much he wishes it would go away. Fear is different from existential anxiety. Fear is response to a specific object: threatening fire or wild animal. It enables us to fight or flee with heightened energy. But existential anxiety is not directed at a particular object. Anxiety involves the whole self in relation to the totality of existence. It is rooted in the threat of nonbeing, nothing, emptiness. Man projects his hopes into the future. He wishes to *be* somebody, but to be somebody involves the possibility that one might be nobody. Existence means the perilous risk of nonexistence. Perhaps the child's experience illustrates the point. He looks up into the sky and imagines what it would be like if none of this around him—grass, sky, cloud, sun, earth—had ever been at all, that he himself might never have been. Existentialists paint this picture in colors of absolute contrast. There are no shades of gray. Either a man is or he is not, being or nonbeing. The awareness of these possibilities of existence and nothing is *angst*, or anxiety. This is the risk finite human beings must take. For Paul Tillich, the answer is *the courage to be in spite of the ever-present threat of nonbeing*. In his book *The Courage to Be*, Tillich cites three forms of anxiety, each in pairs: (1) fate and death, (2) emptiness and meaninglessness, (3) guilt and self-condemnation.

1. *Death* is the iron rim of mortality that rings earthly existence. It is the absolute symbol of human limitation and finitude. Today man is some-

thing. Tomorrow he may be nothing. In general we say, "All men are mortal." But there is a different ring to the utterance, "I too must die." This is the insistent personal threat of nonbeing and is the root of one form of anxiety.

Fate is closely related to death. Fatalism is the view that human existence is contingent or purposeless. What men decide or do has no effect on the ultimate outcome of events. "What will be will be," as the phrase has it. But our choices and responsible acts make no difference, have no bearing on what will be. Fate thus becomes a source of anxiety because there seems to be no final necessity but only the dark, irrational, impenetrable mysterious march of events.

How can men and women affirm their own existence in spite of the threat of nonbeing in the face of the anxiety of fate and death? This is the existential question.

2. As for emptiness and meaninglessness, nonbeing threatens men at the roots of their *spiritual* existence. This for contemporary man is the source of deepest anxiety. He wants above all else to live a "full and meaningful life." He seeks to participate in the concerns of the community, business, literature and the arts. But within and beyond all these concerns is what we, with Paul Tillich, have called man's ultimate concern. It is man's final link to the Source and Ground of all existence, drawing all finite concerns into final singleness and devotion. But what if a man should lose this ultimate concern? To lose this is a persistent possibility that lurks within every personal existence and leaves human beings with the despair of emptiness and meaninglessness. Such a threat represents the depths of existential anxiety: the loss of authentic existence, nonbeing. How do men live in spite of this threat of nothingness?

3. There are also, says Tillich, threats to man's *moral* life. The insistent question comes to each person: What have you made of yourself? Each person asks himself this question. He is his own judge. The uneasy sense of moral failure is the anxiety of guilt. Carried further, this becomes the anxiety of self-rejection or condemnation. Thus the threat of nonbeing hangs over men's attempts to be in their moral relationships. Even in what a man considers his best deed he is obsessed with the suspicion that it is not actually "his best." An ambiguity of good and evil infects his moral striving. The awareness of this ambiguity is the anxiety of guilt. For oneself is the judge. And who can stand against oneself? In its extreme forms, such guilt drives a man toward complete self-rejection, the overwhelming despair of having lost his destiny. This too is the threat of nonbeing, which is a constant possibility, the risk one takes in every effort to be morally.

All three types of anxiety (death-fate, emptiness-meaninglessness, guilt–self-condemnation), according to Tillich, are woven into the existence of man as man. This is his existential situation. We would rather gloss over the existential situation. Frequently men and women do try to thrust existential anxiety away from them or drive it deeper. But since it has to do with full human existence, it cannot be eliminated. To seek to avoid this anxiety may take a neurotic form involving the attempt to avoid the threat of nonbeing. Here a man retreats from all existence into a shadow world. Or modern secularized men and women may attempt to thrust existential anxiety deeper by losing themselves in the frantic busyness of social or vocational life. But Existentialists insist that the human situation will not fade into oblivion simply because we wish it would go away.

What is the answer? Tillich suggests a steady realism that faces the fact of human existence and the threat of nonexistence. This requires a courage that takes the threat into itself—*the courage to be in spite of the danger of nonbeing.* For the Existentialist, this assumes a form of *courage to be oneself,* to do battle against all forces that would annihilate personal existence. This movement is protest, but it also contains an articulate content and point of view concerning the way to full and authentic human existence.

Two Forms of Existentialism

In developing this content, we find that contrasting forms of Existentialism emerge.[6] There is a basic difference between Christian and non-Christian philosophies of existence. It has to do with conflicting world views. What sort of world does man have on his hands? Is humanism enough? Or is there more for man and for his world? The other option remains some form of theism: a belief that this world has its ground in, that man has his roots in, God, who is creative Source of all that is.

Sartre calls his brand of Existentialism "a new humanism." William Barrett comments:

> Like every humanism, it teaches that the proper study of mankind is man, or, as Marx put it, that the root of mankind is man. But again like every humanism, it leaves unasked the question: What is the root of man? In this

---

[6] For purposes of this study, we have deliberately chosen to contrast Sartre with Kierkegaard and Tillich. This is of course an oversimplification, for there are other and different shades of perspective: those of Jaspers, Marcel, Heidegger, etc.

search for roots for man—a search that has, as we have seen, absorbed thinkers and caused the malaise of poets for the last hundred and fifty years—Sartre does not participate. He leaves man rootless. This may be because Sartre himself is the quintessence of the urban intellectual—perhaps the most brilliant urban intellectual of our time, but still the inevitable alienation of this type. He seems to breathe the air of the modern city, of its cafes, faubourgs, and streets, as if there were no other home for man.[7]

By contrast, Kierkegaard, while also concerned about man's freedom, does not regard that freedom as rootless. Man's being is rooted in God. But no theoretical "ism," not even theism, will relate the seeking individual to God. Kierkegaard's question is how to ". . . become a Christian in Christendom . . . when one is a Christian of a sort." [8]

In the summer of 1835, while only twenty-two, Kierkegaard raised questions about what he should do with his life. He wrote in his journal:

What I really need is to become clear in my own mind *what I must do,* not what I must know—except in so far as a knowing must precede every action. The important thing is to understand what I am destined for, to perceive what the Deity wants *me* to do; the point is to find the truth which is truth *for me,* to find *that idea for which I am ready to live and die.* What good would it do me to discover so-called objective truth, though I were to work my way through the systems of the philosophers and were able, if need be, to pass them in review? . . . What good would it do me if I were able to expound the significance of Christianity, to explain many individual phenomena, if *for me* and *for my life* it did not have really profound importance?[9]

William Barrett once again writes:

It has been remarked that Kierkegaard's statement of the religious position is so severe that it has turned many people who thought themselves religious to atheism. Analogously, Sartre's view of atheism is so stark and bleak that it seems to turn many people toward religion. This is exactly as it should be. The choice must be hard either way; for man, a problematic being to his depths, cannot lay hold of his ultimate commitments with smug and easy security.[10]

---

[7] From *Irrational Man* by William Barrett, pp. 251–252. Copyright © 1958 by William Barrett. Reprinted by permission of Doubleday and Company, Inc.

[8] See *The Point of View,* part II, chap. I, selected reading in Walter Kaufmann (ed.), *Existentialism from Dostoevsky to Sartre,* Meridian Books, Inc., New York, 1957, pp. 85–86.

[9] By permission. From Walter Lowrie, *A Short Life of Kierkegaard,* Anchor Books, Doubleday & Company, Inc., Garden City, N.Y., 1961, pp. 66–67.

[10] Barrett, *op. cit.,* pp. 262–263.

19

PAUL TILLICH | *Existence and Existentialism**

EXISTENTIALISM AGAINST ESSENTIALISM

It was in protest to Hegel's perfect essentialism that the existentialism of the nineteenth and twentieth centuries arose. It was not a special trait of his thought which was criticized by the existentialists, some of whom were his pupils. They were not interested in correcting him. They attacked the essentialist idea as such, and with it the whole modern development of man's attitude toward himself and his world. Their attack was and is a revolt against the self-interpretation of man in modern industrial society. . . .

The common point in all existentialist attacks is that man's existential situation is a state of estrangement from his essential nature. Hegel is aware of this estrangement, but he believes that it has been overcome and that man has been reconciled with his true being. According to all the existentialists, this belief is Hegel's basic error. Reconciliation is a matter of anticipation and expectaton, but not of reality. The world is not reconciled, either in the individual—as Kierkegaard shows—or in society—as Marx shows—or in life as such—as Schopenhauer and Nietzsche show. Existence is estrangement and not reconciliation; it is dehumanization and not the expression of essential humanity. It is the process in which man becomes a thing and ceases to be a person. History is not the divine self-manifestation but a series of unreconciled conflicts, threatening man with self-destruction. The existence of the individual is filled with anxiety and threatened by meaninglessness. With this description of man's predicament all existentialists agree and are therefore opposed to Hegel's essentialism. They feel that it is an attempt to hide the truth about man's actual state.

The distinction has been made between atheistic and theistic existen-

* By permission. From Paul Tillich, *Systematic Theology*, The University of Chicago Press, Chicago, 1957, vol. II, pp. 24–26, 27–28, 44–47.

tialism. Certainly there are existentialists who could be called "atheistic," at least according to their intention; and there are others who can be called "theistic." But, in reality, there is no atheistic or theistic existentialism. Existentialism gives an analysis of what it means to exist. It shows the contrast between an essentialist description and an existentialist analysis. It develops the question implied in existence, but it does not try to give the answer, either in atheistic or in theistic terms. Whenever existentialists give answers, they do so in terms of religious or quasi-religious traditions which are not derived from their exstentialist analysis. Pascal derives his answers from the Augustinian tradition, Kierkegaard from the Lutheran, Marcel from the Thomist, Dostoevski from the Greek Orthodox. Or the answers are derived from humanistic traditions, as with Marx, Sartre, Nietzsche, Heidegger, and Jaspers. None of these men was able to develop answers out of his questions. The answers of the humanists come from hidden religious sources. They are matters of ultimate concern or faith, although garbed in a secular gown. Hence the distinction between atheistic and theistic existentialism fails. Existentialism is an analysis of the human predicament. And the answers to the questions implied in man's predicament are religious, whether open or hidden.

EXISTENTIAL AND EXISTENTIALIST THINKING

For the sake of further philological clarification, it is useful to distinguish between existential and existentialist. The former refers to a human attitude, the latter to a philosophical school. The opposite of existential is detached; the opposite of existentialist is essentialist. In existential thinking, the object is involved. In non-existential thinking, the object is detached. By its very nature, theology is existential; by its very nature, science is non-existential. Philosophy unites elements of both. In intention, it is non-existential; in reality, it is an ever changing combination of elements of involvement and detachment. This makes futile all attempts to create a so-called "scientific philosophy."

Existential is not existentialist, but they are related in having a common root, namely, "existence." Generally speaking, one can describe essential structures in terms of detachment, and existential predicament in terms of involvement. But this statement needs drastic qualifications. There is an element of involvement in the construction of geometrical figures; and there is an element of detachment in the observation of one's own anxiety and estrangement. The logician and mathematician are driven by *eros*, including desire and passion. The existentialist theologian, who analyzes existence, discovers structures through cognitive detachment, even if they are structures of destruction. And between these poles there are many mixtures of detachment and involvement, as in biology, history, and psychology. Nevertheless, a cognitive attitude in which the element of involvement is dominant is called "existential." The converse is also true. Since the element of involvement is so dominant, the most striking existentialist analyses have been made by novelists, poets, and painters. But even they could escape irrelevant subjectivity only by submitting themselves to detached and objective observation. As a result, the materials brought out by the detached methods of therapeutic psychology are used in existentialist literature and art. Involvement and detachment are poles, not conflicting alternatives; there is no existentialist analysis without non-existential detachment.

EXISTENTIALISM AND CHRISTIAN THEOLOGY

. . . Existentialism has analyzed the "old eon," namely, the predicament of man and his world in the state of estrangement. In doing so, existentialism is a natural ally of Christianity. Immanuel Kant once said that mathematics is the good luck of human reason. In the same way, one could say that existentialism is the good luck of Christian theology. It has helped to rediscover the classical Christian interpretation of human existence. Any theological attempt to do this would not have had the same effect. This positive use refers not only to existentialist philosophy but also to analytic psychology, literature, poetry, drama and art. In all these realms there is an immense amount of material which the theologian can use and organize in the attempt to present Christ as the answer to the questions implied within existence. In earlier centuries a similar task was undertaken mainly by monastic theologians, who analyzed themselves and the members of their small community so penetratingly that there are few present-day insights into the human predicament which they did not anticipate. The penitential and devotional literature impressively shows this. But this tradition was lost under the impact of the philosophies and theologies of pure consciousness, represented, above all, by Cartesianism and Calvinism. Notwithstanding differences, they were allies in helping to repress the unconscious and half-conscious sides of human nature, thus preventing a full understanding of man's existential predicament (in spite of Calvin's doctrine of man's total depravity and the Augustinianism of the Cartesian school). In recovering the elements of man's nature which were suppressed by the psychology of consciousness, existentialism and contemporary theology should become allies and analyze the character of existence in all its manifestations, the unconscious as well as the conscious. . . .

ESTRANGEMENT AND SIN

The state of existence is the state of estrangement. Man is estranged from the ground of his being, from other beings, and from himself. The transition from essence to existence results in personal guilt and universal tragedy. It is now necessary to give a description of existential estrangement and its self-destructive implications. But, before doing so, we must answer the question which has already arisen: What is the relation of the concept of estrangement to the traditional concept of sin? . . .

Estrangement is not a biblical term but is implied in most of the biblical descriptions of man's predicament. It is implied in the symbols of the expulsion from paradise, in the hostility between man and nature, in the deadly hostility of brother against brother, in the estrangement of nation from nation through the confusion of language, and in the continuous complaints of the prophets against their kings and people who turn to alien gods. Estrangement is implied in Paul's statement that man perverted the image of God into that of idols, in his classical description of "man against himself," in his vision of man's hostility against man as combined with his distorted desires. In all these interpretations of man's predicament, estrangement is implicitly asserted. Therefore, it is certainly not unbiblical to use the term "estrangement" in describing man's existential situation.

Nevertheless, "estrangement" cannot replace "sin." Yet the reasons for attempts to replace the word "sin" with another word are obvious. The term has been used in a way which has little to do with its genuine biblical meaning. Paul often spoke of "Sin" in the singular and without an article. He saw it as a quasi-personal power which ruled this world. But in the Christian churches, both Catholic and Protestant, sin has been used predominantly in the plural, and "sins" are deviations from moral laws. This has little to do with "sin" as the state of estrangement from that to which one belongs—God, one's self, one's world. Therefore, the characteristics of sin are here considered under the heading of "estrangement". And the word "estrangement" itself implies a reinterpretation of sin from a religious point of view.

Nevertheless, the word "sin" cannot be overlooked. It expresses what is not implied in the term "estrangement", namely, the personal act of turning away from that to which one belongs. Sin expresses most sharply the personal character of estrangement over against its tragic side. It expresses personal freedom and guilt in contrast to tragic guilt and the universal destiny of estrangement. The word "sin" can and must be saved, not only because classical literature and liturgy continuously employ it but more particularly because the word has a sharpness which accusingly points to the element of personal responsibility in one's estrangement. Man's predicament is estrangement, but his estrangement is sin. It is not a state of things, like the laws of nature, but a matter of both personal freedom and universal destiny. For this reason the term "sin" must be used after it has been reinterpreted religiously. An important tool for this reinterpretation is the term "estrangement."

Reinterpretation is also needed for the terms "original" or "hereditary" with respect to sin. But in this case reinterpretation may demand the rejection of the terms. Both point to the universal character of estrangement, expressing the element of destiny in estrangement. But both words are so much burdened with literalistic absurdities that it is practically impossible to use them any longer.

If one speaks of "sins" and refers to special acts which are considered as sinful, one should always be conscious of the fact that "sins" are the expressions of "sin." It is not the disobedience to a law which makes an act sinful but the fact that it is an expression of man's estrangement from God, from men, from himself. Therefore, Paul calls everything sin which does not result from faith, from the unity with God. And in another context (following Jesus) all laws are summed up in the law of love by which estrangement is conquered. Love as the striving for the reunion of the separated is the opposite of estrangement. In faith and love, sin is conquered because estrangement is overcome by reunion.

20

SØREN KIERKEGAARD | *The Individual**

There is a view of life which conceives that where the crowd is, there also is the truth, and that in truth itself there is need of having the crowd on its side.[1] There is another view of life which conceives that wherever there is a crowd there is untruth, so that (to consider for a moment the extreme case), even if every individual, each for himself in private, were to be in possession of the truth, yet in case they were all to get together in a crowd—a crowd to which any sort of *decisive* significance is attributed, a voting, noisy, audible crowd—untruth would at once be in evidence.[2]

For a "crowd" is the untruth. In a godly sense it is true, eternally, Christianly, as St. Paul says, that ". . . only one attains the goal"—which is not meant in a comparative sense, for comparison takes others into account. It means that every man can be that one, God helping him therein—but only one attains the goal. And again this means that every man should be chary about having to do with "the others", and essentially should talk only with God and with himself—for only one attains the goal. And again this means that man, or to be a man, is akin to deity.— In a worldly and temporal sense, it will be said by the man of bustle,

---

* By permission. From Søren Kierkegaard, *The Point of View for My Work as an Author*, Harper & Row, Publishers, Incorporated, New York, 1962, pp. 110–119.

[1] Perhaps it may be well to note here once for all a thing that goes without saying and which I never have denied, that in relation to all temporal, earthly, worldly matters the crowd may have competency, and even decisive competency as a court of last resort. But it is not of such matters I am speaking, nor have I ever concerned myself with such things. I am speaking about the ethical, about the ethico-religious, about "the truth", and I am affirming the untruth of the crowd, ethico-religiously regarded, when it is treated as a criterion for what "truth" is.

[2] Perhaps it may be well to note here, although it seems to me almost superfluous, that it naturally could not occur to me to object to the fact, for example, that preaching is done or that the truth is proclaimed, even though it were to an assemblage of hundreds of thousands. Not at all; but if there were an assemblage even of only ten— and if they should put the truth to the ballot, that is to say, if the assemblage should be regarded as the authority, if it is the crowd which turns the scale—then there *is* untruth.

370

sociability, and amicableness, "How unreasonable that only one attains the goal; for it is far more likely that many by the strength of united effort, should attain the goal; and when we are many success is more certain and it is easier for each man severally." True enough, it is far more *likely*; and it is true also with respect to all earthly and material goods. If it is allowed to have its way, this becomes the only true point of view, for it does away with God and eternity and with man's kinship with deity. It does away with it or transforms it into a fable, and puts in its place the modern (or, we might rather say, the old pagan) notion that to be a man is to belong to a race endowed with reason, to belong to it as a specimen, so that the race or species is higher than the individual, which is to say that there are no more individuals but only specimens. But eternity which arches over and high above the temporal, tranquil as the starry vault at night, and God in heaven who in the bliss of that sublime tranquillity holds in survey, without the least sense of dizziness at such a height, these countless multitudes of men and knows each single individual by name—He, the great Examiner, says that only one attains the goal. That means, every one can and every one should be this *one*— but only one attains the goal. Hence where there is a multitude, a crowd, or where decisive significance is attached to the fact that there is a multitude, *there* it is sure that no one is working, living, striving for the highest aim, but only for one or another earthly aim; since to work for the eternal decisive aim is possible only where there is one, and to be this one which all can be is to let God be the helper—the "crowd" is the untruth.

A crowd—not this crowd or that, the crowd now living or the crowd long deceased, a crowd of humble people or of superior people, of rich or of poor, &c.—a crowd in its very concept[3] is the untruth, by reason of the fact that it renders the individual completely impenitent and irresponsible, or at least weakens his sense of responsibility by reducing it to a fraction. Observe that there was not one single soldier that dared lay hands upon Caius Marius—this was an instance of truth. But given merely three or four women with the consciousness or the impression that they were a crowd, and with hope of a sort in the possibility that no one could say definitely who was doing it or who began it—then they

---

[3] The reader will also remember that here the word "crowd" is understood in a purely formal sense, not in the sense one commonly attaches to "the crowd" when it is meant as an invidious qualification, the distinction which human selfishness irreligiously erects between "the crowd" and superior persons, &c. Good God! How could a religious man hit upon such an inhuman equality! No, "crowd" stands for number, the numerical, a number of noblemen, millionaires, high dignitaries, &c.—as soon as the numerical is involved it is "crowd", "the crowd".

had courage for it. What a falsehood! The falsehood first of all is the
notion that the crowd does what in fact only the *individual* in the crowd
does, though it be every *individual*. For "crowd" is an abstraction and
has no hands: but each individual has ordinarily two hands, and so when
an individual lays his two hands upon Caius Marius they are the two
hands of the individual, certainly not those of his neighbour, and still less
those of the . . . crowd which has no hands. In the next place, the
falsehood is that the crowd had the "courage" for it, for no one of the
individuals was ever so cowardly as the crowd always is. For every individual who flees for refuge into the crowd, and so flees in cowardice
from being an individual (who had not the courage to lay his hands
upon Caius Marius, nor even to admit that he had it not), such a man
contributes his share of cowardliness to the cowardliness which we know
as the "crowd".—Take the highest example, think of Christ—and the
whole human race, all the men that ever were born or are to be born. But
let the situation be one that challenges the individual, requiring each one
for himself to be alone with Him in a solitary place and as an individual
to step up to Him and spit upon Him—the man never was born and never
will be born with courage or insolence enough to do such a thing. This is
untruth.

The crowd is untruth. Hence none has more contempt for what it
is to be a man than they who make it their profession to lead the crowd.
Let some one approach a person of this sort, some individual—that is
an affair far too small for his attention, and he proudly repels him. There
must be hundreds at the least. And when there are thousands, he defers
to the crowd, bowing and scraping to them. What untruth! No, when it
is a question of a single individual man, then is the time to give expression to the truth by showing one's respect for what it is to be a man; and
if perhaps it was, as it is cruelly said, a poor wretch of a man, then the
thing to do is to invite him into the best room, and one who possesses
several voices should use the kindest and most friendly. That is truth. If
on the other hand there were an assemblage of thousands or more and
the truth was to be decided by ballot, then this is what one should do
(unless one were to prefer to utter silently the petition of the Lord's
Prayer, "Deliver us from evil"): one should in godly fear give expression to the fact that the crowd, regarded as a judge over ethical and
religious matter, is untruth, whereas it is eternally true that every man
can be the *one*. This is truth.

The crowd is untruth. Therefore was Christ crucified, because, although
He addressed himself to all, He would have no dealings with the crowd,
because He would not permit the crowd to aid him in any way, because

in this regard He repelled people absolutely, would not found a party, did not permit balloting, but would be what He is, the Truth, which relates itself to the individual.—And hence every one who truly would serve the truth is *eo ipso*, in one way or another, a martyr. If it were possible for a person in his mother's womb to make the decision to will to serve the truth truly, then whatever his martyrdom turns out to be, he is *eo ipso* from his mother's womb a martyr. For it is not so great a trick to win the crowd. All that is needed is some talent, a certain dose of falsehood, and a little acquaintance with human passions. But no witness for the truth (ah! and that is what every man should be, including you and me)—no witness for the truth dare become engaged with the crowd. The witness for the truth—who naturally has nothing to do with politics and must above everything else be most vigilantly on the watch not to be confounded with the politician—the God-fearing work of the witness to the truth is to engage himself if possible with all, but always individually, talking to every one severally on the streets and lanes . . . in order to disintegrate the crowd, or to talk even to the crowd, though not with the intent of forming a crowd, but rather with the hope that one or another individual might return from this assemblage and become a single individual. On the other hand the "crowd", when it is treated as an authority and its judgement regarded as the final judgement, is detested by the witness for the truth more heartily than a maiden of good morals detests the public dance-floor; and he who addresses the crowd as the supreme authority as regarded by him as the tool of the untruth. For (to repeat what I have said) that which in politics or in similar fields may be justifiable, wholly or in part, becomes untruth when it is transferred to the intellectual, the spiritual, the religious fields. And one thing more I would say, perhaps with a cautiousness which is exaggerated. By "truth" I mean always "eternal truth". But politics, &c., have nothing to do with "eternal truth". A policy which in the proper sense of "eternal truth" were to make serious work of introducing "eternal truth" into real life would show itself in that very same second to be in the most eminent degree the most "impolitic" thing that can be imagined.

A crowd is untruth. And I could weep, or at least I could learn to long for eternity, at thinking of the misery of our age, in comparison even with the greatest misery of bygone ages, owing to the fact that the daily press with its anonymity makes the situation madder still with the help of the public, this abstraction which claims to be the judge in matters of "truth". For in reality assemblies which make this claim do not now take place. The fact that an anonymous author by the help of the press can day by day find occasion to say (even about intellectual, moral, and religious matters) whatever he pleases to say, and what perhaps he would be very far from having the courage to say as an individual; that every time he opens his mouth (or shall we say his abysmal gullet?) he at once is addressing thousands of thousands; that he can get ten thousand times ten thousand to repeat after him what he has said—and with all this nobody has any responsibility, so that it is not as in ancient times the relatively unrepentant crowd which possesses omnipotence, but the absolutely unrepentant thing, a nobody, an anonymity, who is the producer (*auctor*), and another anonymity, the public, sometimes even anonymous subscribers, and with all this, nobody, nobody! Good God! And yet our states call themselves Christian states! Let no one say that in this case it is possible for "truth" in its turn by the help of the press to get the better of lies and errors. O thou who speakest thus, dost thou venture to maintain that men regarded as a crowd are just as quick to seize upon truth which is not always palatable as upon falsehood which always is prepared delicately to give delight?—not to mention the fact that acceptance of the truth is made the more difficult by the necessity of admitting that one has been deceived! Or dost thou venture even to maintain that "truth" can just as quickly be understood as falsehood, which requires no preliminary knowledge, no schooling, no discipline, no abstinence, no self-denial, no honest concern about oneself, no patient labour?

Nay, truth—which abhors also this untruth of aspiring after broad dissemination as the one aim—is not nimble on its feet. In the first place it cannot work by means of the fantastical means of the press, which is the untruth; the communicator of the truth can only be a single individual. And again the communication of it can only be addressed to the individual; for the truth consists precisely in that conception of life which is expressed by the individual. The truth can neither be communicated nor be received except as it were under God's eyes, not without God's help, not without God's being involved as the middle term, He himself being the Truth. It can therefore only be communicated by and received by "the individual", which as a matter of fact can be every living man. The mark which distinguishes such a man is merely that of the truth, in contrast to the abstract, the fantastical, the impersonal, the crowd—the public excludes God as the middle term (for the *personal* God cannot be a middle term in an *impersonal* relationship), and thereby excludes also the truth, for God is at once the Truth and the middle term which renders it intelligible.

And to honour every man, absolutely every man, is the truth, and this is what it is to fear God and love one's "neighbour". But from an ethicoreligious point of view, to recognize the "crowd" as the court of last resort is to deny God, and it cannot exactly mean to love the "neighbour". And the "neighbour" is the absolutely true expression for human equality. In case every one were in truth to love his neighbour as himself, complete human equality would be attained. Every one who loves his neighbour in truth, expresses unconditionally human equality. Every one who, like me, admits that his effort is weak and imperfect, yet is aware that the task is to love one's neighbour, is also aware of what human equality is. But never have I read in Holy Scripture the commandment, Thou shalt love the crowd—and still less, Thou shalt recognize, ethico-religiously, in the crowd the supreme authority in matters of "truth". But the thing is simple enough: this thing of loving one's neighbour is self-denial; that of loving the crowd, or of pretending to love it, of making it the authority in matters of truth, is the way to material power, the way to temporal and earthly advantages of all sorts—at the same time it is the untruth, for a crowd is the untruth.

But he who acknowledges the truth of this view, which is seldom presented (for it often happens that a man thinks that the crowd is the untruth, but when it—the crowd—accepts his opinion *en masse,* everything is all right again), admits for himself that he is weak and impotent; for how could it be possible for an individual to make a stand against the crowd which possesses the power! And he could not wish to get the crowd on his side for the sake of ensuring that his view would prevail, the crowd, ethico-religiously regarded, being the untruth—that would be mocking himself. But although from the first this view involves an admission of weakness and impotence, and seems therefore far from inviting, and for this reason perhaps is so seldom heard, yet it has the good feature that it is even-handed, that it offends no one, not a single person, that it is no respecter of persons, not a single one. The crowd, in fact, is composed of individuals; it must therefore be in every man's power to become what he is, an individual. From becoming an individual no one, no one at all, is excluded, except he who excludes himself by becoming a crowd. To become a crowd, to collect a crowd about one, is on the contrary to affirm the distinctions of human life. The most well-meaning person who talks about these distinctions can easily offend an individual. But then it is not the crowd which possesses power, influence, repute, and mastery over men, but it is the invidious distinctions of human life which despotically ignore the single individual as the weak and impotent, which in a temporal and worldly interest ignore the eternal truth—the single individual.

21

JEAN-PAUL SARTRE | *Existentialism**

I should like on this occasion to defend existentialism against some charges which have been brought against it.

First, it has been charged with inviting people to remain in a kind of desperate quietism because, since no solutions are possible, we should have to consider action in this world as quite impossible. We should then end up in a philosophy of contemplation; and since contemplation is a luxury, we come in the end to a bourgeois philosophy. The communists in particular have made these charges.

On the other hand, we have been charged with dwelling on human degradation, with pointing up everywhere the sordid, shady, and slimy, and neglecting the gracious and beautiful, the bright side of human nature; for example, according to Mlle. Mercier, a Catholic critic, with forgetting the smile of the child. Both sides charge us with having ignored human solidarity, with considering man as an isolated being. The communists say that the main reason for this is that we take pure subjectivity, the *Cartesian I think*, as our starting point; in other words, the moment in which man becomes fully aware of what it means to him to be an isolated being; as a result, we are unable to return to a state of solidarity with the men who are not ourselves, a state which we can never reach in the *cogito*.

From the Christian standpoint, we are charged with denying the reality and seriousness of human undertakings, since, if we reject God's commandments and the eternal verities, there no longer remains anything but pure caprice, with everyone permitted to do as he pleases and incapable, from his own point of view, of condemning the points of view and acts of others.

I shall try today to answer these different charges. Many people are going to be surprised at what is said here about humanism. We shall try

---

* By permission. From Jean-Paul Sartre, *Existentialism*, trans. by Bernard Frechtman, Philosophical Library, Inc., New York, 1947, pp. 11–61.

to see in what sense it is to be understood. In any case, what can be said from the very beginning is that by existentialism we mean a doctrine which makes human life possible and, in addition, declares that every truth and every action implies a human setting and a human subjectivity.

As is generally known, the basic charge against us is that we put the emphasis on the dark side of human life. Someone recently told me of a lady who, when she let slip a vulgar word in a moment of irritation, excused herself by saying, "I guess I'm becoming an existentialist." Consequently, existentialism is regarded as something ugly; that is why we are said to be naturalists; and if we are, it is rather surprising that in this day and age we cause so much more alarm and scandal than does naturalism, properly so called. The kind of person who can take in his stride such a novel as Zola's *The Earth* is disgusted as soon as he starts reading an existentialist novel; the kind of person who is resigned to the wisdom of the ages—which is pretty sad—finds us even sadder. Yet, what can be more disillusioning than saying "true charity begins at home" or "a scoundrel will always return evil for good"?

We know the commonplace remarks made when this subject comes up, remarks which always add up to the same thing: we shouldn't struggle against the powers-that-be; we shouldn't resist authority; we shouldn't try to rise above our station; any action which doesn't conform to authority is romantic; any effort not based on past experience is doomed to failure; experience shows that man's bent is always toward trouble, that there must be a strong hand to hold him in check, if not, there will be anarchy. There are still people who go on mumbling these melancholy old saws, the people who say, "It's only human!" whenever a more or less repugnant act is pointed out to them, the people who glut themselves on *chansons réalistes;* these are the people who accuse existentialism of being too gloomy, and to such an extent that I wonder whether they are complaining about it, not for its pessimism, but much rather its optimism. Can it be that what really scares them in the doctrine I shall try to present here is that it leaves to man a possibility of choice? To answer this question we must re-examine it on a strictly philosophical plane. What is meant by the term *existentialism?*

Most people who use the word would be rather embarrassed if they had to explain it, since, now that the word is all the rage, even the work of a musician or painter is being called existentialist. A gossip columnist in *Clartés* signs himself *The Existentialist,* so that by this time the word has been so stretched and has taken on so broad a meaning, that it no longer means anything at all. It seems that for want of an advance-guard doctrine analogous to surrealism, the kind of people who are eager for scandal and flurry turn to this philosophy which in other respects does not at all serve their purposes in this sphere.

Actually, it is the least scandalous, the most austere of doctrines. It is intended strictly for specialists and philosophers. Yet it can be defined easily. What complicates matters is that there are two kinds of existentialist; first, those who are Christian, among whom I would include Jaspers and Gabriel Marcel, both Catholic; and on the other hand the atheistic existentialists, among whom I class Heidegger, and then the French existentialists and myself. What they have in common is that they think that existence precedes essence, or, if you prefer, that subjectivity must be the starting point.

Just what does that mean? Let us consider some object that is manufactured, for example, a book or a paper-cutter: here is an object which has been made by an artisan whose inspiration came from a concept. He referred to the concept of what a paper-cutter is and likewise to a known method of production, which is part of the concept, something which is, by and large, a routine. Thus, the paper-cutter is at once an object produced in a certain way and, on the other hand, one having a specific use; and one cannot postulate a man who produces a paper-cutter but does not know what it is used for. Therefore, let us say that, for the paper-cutter, essence—that is, the ensemble of both the production routines and the properties which enable it to be both produced and defined—precedes existence. Thus, the presence of the paper-cutter or book in front of me is determined. Therefore, we have here a technical view of the world whereby it can be said that production precedes existence.

When we conceive God as the Creator, He is generally thought of as a superior sort of artisan. Whatever doctrine we may be considering, whether one like that of Descartes or that of Leibnitz, we always grant that will more or less follows understanding or, at the very least, accompanies it, and that when God creates He knows exactly what He is creating. Thus, the concept of man in the mind of God is comparable to the concept of paper-cutter in the mind of the manufacturer, and, following certain techniques and a conception, God produces man, just as the artisan, following a definition and a technique, makes a paper-cutter. Thus, the individual man is the realization of a certain concept in the divine intelligence.

In the eighteenth century, the atheism of the *philosophes* discarded the idea of God, but not so much for the notion that essence precedes existence. To a certain extent, this idea is found everywhere; we find it in Diderot, in Voltaire, and even in Kant. Man has a human nature; this human nature, which is the concept of the human, is found in all men, which means that each man is a particular example of a universal concept, man. In Kant, the result of this universality is that the wild-man, the natural man, as well as the bourgeois, are circumscribed by the same definition and have the same basic qualities. Thus, here too the essence of man precedes the historical existence that we find in nature.

Atheistic existentialism, which I represent, is more coherent. It states that if God does not exist, there is at least one being in whom existence precedes essence, a being who exists before he can be defined by any concept, and that this being is man, or, as Heidegger says, human reality. What is meant here by saying that existence precedes essence? It means that, first of all, man exists, turns up, appears on the scene, and, only afterwards, defines himself. If man, as the existentialist conceives him, is indefinable, it is because at first he is nothing. Only afterward will he be something, and he himself will have made what he will be. Thus, there is no human nature, since there is no God to conceive it. Not only is man what he conceives himself to be, but he is also only what he wills himself to be after this thrust toward existence.

Man is nothing else but what he makes of himself. Such is the first principle of existentialism. It is also what is called subjectivity, the name we are labeled with when charges are brought against us. But what do we mean by this, if not that man has a greater dignity than a stone or table? For we mean that man first exists, that is, that man first of all is the being who hurls himself toward a future and who is conscious of imagining himself as being in the future. Man is at the start a plan which is aware of itself, rather than a patch of moss, a piece of garbage, or a cauliflower; nothing exists prior to this plan; there is nothing in heaven; man will be what he will have planned to be. Not what he will want to be. Because by the word "will" we generally mean a conscious decision, which is subsequent to what we have already made of ourselves. I may want to belong to a political party, write a book, get married; but all that is only a manifestation of an earlier, more spontaneous choice that is called "will." But if existence really does precede essence, man is responsible for what he is. Thus, existentialism's first move is to make every man aware of what he is and to make the full responsibility of his existence rest on him. And when we say that a man is responsible for himself, we do not only mean that he is responsible for his own individuality, but that he is responsible for all men.

The word subjectivism has two meanings, and our opponents play on the two. Subjectivism means, on the one hand, that an individual chooses and makes himself; and, on the other, that it is impossible for man to transcend human subjectivity. The second of these is the essential meaning of existentialism. When we say that man choses his own self, we mean that every one of us does likewise; but we also mean by that that in making this choice he also chooses all men. In fact, in creating the man that we want to be, there is not a single one of our acts which does not at the same time create an image of man as we think he ought to be. To choose to be this or that is to affirm at the same time the value of what we choose, because we can never choose evil. We always choose the good, and nothing can be good for us without being good for all.

If, on the other hand, existence precedes essence, and if we grant that we exist and fashion our image at one and the same time, the image is valid for everybody and for our whole age. Thus, our responsibility is much greater than we might have supposed, because it involves all mankind. If I am a workingman and choose to join a Christian trade-union rather than be a communist, and if by being a member I want to show that the best thing for man is resignation, that the kingdom of man is not of this world, I am not only involving my own case—I want to be resigned for everyone. As a result, my action has involved all humanity. To take a more individual matter, if I want to marry, to have children; even if this marriage depends solely on my own circumstances or passion or wish, I am involving all humanity in monogamy and not merely myself. Therefore, I am responsible for myself and for everyone else. I am creating a certain image of man of my own choosing. In choosing myself, I choose man.

This helps us understand what the actual content is of such rather grandiloquent words as anguish, forlornness, despair. As you will see, it's all quite simple.

First, what is meant by anguish? The existentialists say at once that man is anguish. What that means is this: the man who involves himself and who realizes that he is not only the person he chooses to be, but also a law-maker who is, at the same time, choosing all mankind as well as himself, can not help escape the feeling of his total and deep responsibility. Of course, there are many people who are not anxious; but we claim that they are hiding their anxiety, that they are fleeing from it. Certainly, many people believe that when they do something, they themselves are the only ones involved, and when someone says to them, "What if everyone acted that way?" they shrug their shoulders and answer, "Everyone doesn't act that way." But really, one should always ask himself, "What would happen if everybody looked at things that way?" There is no escaping this disturbing thought except by a kind of double-dealing. A man who lies and makes excuses for himself by saying "not everybody does that," is someone with an uneasy conscience, because the act of lying implies that a universal value is conferred upon the lie.

Anguish is evident even when it conceals itself. This is the anguish that Kierkegaard called the anguish of Abraham. You know the story: an angel has ordered Abraham to sacrifice his son; if it really were an angel who has come and said, "You are Abraham, you shall sacrifice your son," everything would be all right. But everyone might first wonder, "Is it really an angel, and am I really Abraham? What proof do I have?"

There was a madwoman who had hallucinations; someone used to speak to her on the telephone and give her orders. Her doctor asked her, "Who is it who talks to you?" She answered, "He says it's God." What proof did she really have that it was God? If an angel comes to me, what proof is there that it's an angel? And if I hear voices, what proof is there that they come from heaven and not from hell, or from the subconscious, or a pathological condition? What proves that they are addressed to me? What proof is there that I have been appointed to impose my choice and my conception of man on humanity? I'll never find any proof or sign to convince me of that. If a voice addresses me, it is always for me to decide that this is the angel's voice; if I consider that such an act is a good one, it is I who will choose to say that it is good rather than bad.

Now, I'm not being singled out as an Abraham, and yet at every moment I'm obliged to perform exemplary acts. For every man, everything happens as if all mankind had its eyes fixed on him and were guiding itself by what he does. And every man ought to say to himself, "Am I really the kind of man who has the right to act in such a way that humanity might guide itself by my actions?" And if he does not say that to himself, he is masking his anguish.

There is no question here of the kind of anguish which would lead to quietism, to inaction. It is a matter of a simple sort of anguish that anybody who has had responsibilities is familiar with. For example, when a military officer takes the responsibility for an attack and sends a certain number of men to death, he chooses to do so, and in the main he alone makes the choice. Doubtless, orders come from above, but they are too broad; he interprets them, and on this interpretation depend the lives of ten or fourteen or twenty men. In making a decision he can not help having a certain anguish. All leaders know this anguish. That doesn't keep them from acting; on the contrary, it is the very condition of their action. For it implies that they envisage a number of possibilities, and when they choose one, they realize that it has value only because it is chosen. We shall see that this kind of anguish, which is the kind that existentialism describes, is explained, in addition, by a direct responsibility to the other men whom it involves. It is not a curtain separating us from action, but is part of action itself.

When we speak of forlornness, a term Heidegger was fond of, we mean only that God does not exist and that we have to face all the consequences of this. The existentialist is strongly opposed to a certain kind of secular ethics which would like to abolish God with the least possible expense. About 1880, some French teachers tried to set up a secular ethics which went something like this: God is a useless and costly hypothesis; we are discarding it; but, meanwhile, in order for there to be an ethics, a society, a civilization, it is essential that certain values be taken seriously and that they be considered as having an *a priori* existence. It must be obligatory, *a priori*, to be honest, not to lie, not to beat your wife, to have children, etc., etc. So we're going to try a little device which will make it possible to show that values exist all the same, inscribed in a heaven of ideas, though otherwise God does not exist. In other words—and this, I believe, is the tendency of everything called reformism in France—nothing will be changed if God does not exist. We shall find ourselves with the same norms of honesty, progress, and humanism, and we shall have made of God an outdated hypothesis which will peacefully die off by itself.

The existentialist, on the contrary, thinks it very distressing that God does not exist, because all possibility of finding values in a heaven of ideas disappears along with Him; there can no longer be an *a priori* Good, since there is no infinite and perfect consciousness to think it. Nowhere is it written that the Good exists, that we must be honest, that we must not lie; because the fact is we are on a plane where there are only men. Dostoevsky said, "If God didn't exist, everything would be possible." That is the very starting point of existentialism. Indeed, everything is permissible if God does not exist, and as a result man is forlorn, because neither within him nor without does he find anything to cling to. He can't start making excuses for himself.

If existence really does precede essence, there is no explaining things away by reference to a fixed and given human nature. In other words, there is no determinism, man is free, man is freedom. On the other hand, if God does not exist, we find no values or commands to turn to which legitimize our conduct. So, in the bright realm of values, we have no excuse behind us, nor justification before us. We are alone, with no excuses.

That is the idea I shall try to convey when I say that man is condemned to be free. Condemned, because he did not create himself, yet in other respects is free; because, once thrown into the world, he is responsible for everything he does. The existentialist does not believe in the power of passion. He will never agree that a sweeping passion is a ravaging torrent which fatally leads a man to certain acts and is therefore an excuse. He thinks that man is responsible for his passion.

The existentialist does not think that man is going to help himself by finding in the world some omen by which to orient himself. Because he thinks that man will interpret the omen to suit himself. Therefore, he thinks than man, with no support and no aid, is condemned every moment to invent man. Ponge, in a very fine article, has said, "Man is the future of man." That's exactly it. But if it is taken to mean that this future is recorded in heaven, that God sees it, then it is false, because it would really no longer be a future. If it is taken to mean that, whatever a man may be, there is a future to be forged, a virgin future before him, then this remark is sound. But then we are forlorn.

To give you an example which will enable you to understand forlornness better, I shall cite the case of one of my students who came to see me under the following circumstances: his father was on bad terms with his mother, and, moreover, was inclined to be a collaborationist; his older brother had been killed in the German offensive of 1940, and the young man, with somewhat immature but generous feelings, wanted to avenge him. His mother lived alone with him, very much upset by the half-treason of her husband and the death of her older son; the boy was her only consolation.

The boy was faced with the choice of leaving for England and joining the Free French Forces—that is, leaving his mother behind—or remaining with his mother and helping her to carry on. He was fully aware that the woman lived only for him and that his going-off—and perhaps his death—would plunge her into despair. He was also aware that every act that he did for his mother's sake was a sure thing, in the sense that it was helping her to carry on, whereas every effort he made toward going off and fighting was an uncertain move which might run aground and prove completely useless; for example, on his way to England he might, while passing through Spain, be detained indefinitely in a Spanish camp; he might reach England or Algiers and be stuck in an office at a desk job. As a result, he was faced with two very different kinds of action: one, concrete, immediate, but concerning only one individual; the other concerned an incomparably vaster group, a national collectivity, but for that very reason was dubious, and might be interrupted en route. And, at the same time, he was wavering between two kinds of ethics. On the one hand, an ethics of sympathy, of personal devotion; on the other, a broader ethics, but one whose efficacy was more dubious. He had to choose between the two.

Who could help him choose? Christian doctrine? No. Christian doctrine says, "Be charitable, love your neighbor, take the more rugged path, etc., etc." But which is the more rugged path? Whom should he love as a brother? The fighting man or his mother? Which does the greater good, the vague act of fighting in a group, or the concrete one of helping a particular human being to go on living? Who can decide *a priori?* Nobody. No book of ethics can tell him. The Kantian ethics says, "Never treat any person as a means, but as an end." Very well, if I stay with my mother, I'll treat her as an end and not as a means; but by virtue of this very fact, I'm running the risk of treating the people around me who are fighting, as means; and, conversely, if I go to join those who are fighting, I'll be treating them as an end, and, by doing that, I run the risk of treating by mother as a means.

If values are vague, and if they are always too broad for the concrete and specific case that we are considering, the only thing left for us is to trust our instincts. That's what this young man tried to do; and when I saw him, he said, "In the end, feeling is what counts. I ought to choose whichever pushes me in one direction. If I feel that I love my mother enough to sacrifice everything else for her—my desire for vengeance, for action, for adventure—then I'll stay with her. If, on the contrary, I feel that my love for my mother isn't enough, I'll leave."

But how is the value of a feeling determined? What gives his feeling for his mother value? Precisely the fact that he remained with her. I may say that I like so-and-so well enough to sacrifice a certain amount of money for him, but I may say so only if I've done it. I may say "I love my mother well enough to remain with her" if I have remained with her. The only way to determine the value of this affection is, precisely, to perform an act which confirms and defines it. But, since I require this affection to justify my act, I find myself caught in a vicious circle.

On the other hand, Gide has well said that mock feeling and a true feeling are almost indistinguishable; to decide that I love my mother and will remain with her, or to remain with her by putting on an act, amount somewhat to the same thing. In other words, the feeling is formed by the acts one performs; so, I can not refer to it in order to act upon it. Which means that I can neither seek within myself the true condition which will impel me to act, nor apply to a system of ethics for concepts which will permit me to act. You will say, "At least, he did go to a teacher for advice." But if you seek advice from a priest, for example, you have chosen this priest; you already knew, more or less, just about what advice he was going to give you. In other words, choosing your adviser is involving yourself. The proof of this is that if you are a Christian, you will say, "Consult a priest." But some priests are collaborating, some are just marking time, some are resisting. Which to choose? If the young man chooses a priest who is resisting, or collaborating, he has already decided on the kind of advice he's going to get. Therefore, in coming to see me he knew the answer I was going to give him, and I had only one answer to give: "You're free, choose, that is, invent." No general ethics can show you what is to be done; there are no omens in the world. The Catholics will reply, "But there are." Granted—but, in any case, I myself choose the meaning they have.

When I was a prisoner, I knew a rather remarkable young man who was a Jesuit. He had entered the Jesuit order in the following way: he had had a number of very bad breaks; in childhood, his father died, leaving him in poverty, and he was a scholarship student at a religious institution where he was constantly made to feel that he was being kept out of charity; then, he failed to get any of the honors and distinctions that children like; later on, at about eighteen, he bungled a love affair; finally, at twenty-two, he failed in military training, a childish enough matter, but it was the last straw.

This young fellow might well have felt that he had botched everything. It was a sign of something, but of what? He might have taken refuge in bitterness or despair. But he very wisely looked upon all this as a sign that he was not made for secular triumphs, and that only the triumphs of religion, holiness, and faith were open to him. He saw the hand of God in all this, and so he entered the order. Who can help seeing that he alone decided what the sign meant?

Some other interpretation might have been drawn from this series of setbacks; for example, that he might have done better to turn carpenter or revolutionist. Therefore, he is fully responsible for the interpretation. Forlornness implies that we ourselves choose our being. Forlornness and anguish go together.

As for despair, the term has a very simple meaning. It means that we shall confine ourselves to reckoning only with what depends upon our will, or on the ensemble of probabilities which make our action possible. When we want something, we always have to reckon with probabilities. I may be counting on the arrival of a friend. The friend is coming by rail or street-car; this supposes that the train will arrive on schedule, or that the street-car will not jump the track. I am left in the realm of possibility; but possibilities are to be reckoned with only to the point where my action comports with the ensemble of these possibilities, and no further. The moment the possibilities I am considering are not rigorously involved by my action, I ought to disengage myself from them, because no God, no scheme, can adapt the world and its possibilities to my will. When

Descartes said, "Conquer yourself rather than the world," he meant essentially the same thing.

The Marxists to whom I have spoken reply, "You can rely on the support of others in your action, which obviously has certain limits because you're not going to live forever. That means: rely on both what others are doing elsewhere to help you, in China, in Russia, and what they will do later on, after your death, to carry on the action and lead it to its fulfillment, which will be the revolution. You even *have* to rely upon that, otherwise you're immoral." I reply at once that I will always rely on fellow-fighters insofar as these comrades are involved with me in a common struggle, in the unity of a party or a group in which I can more or less make my weight felt; that is, one whose ranks I am in as a fighter and whose movements I am aware of at every moment. In such a situation, relying on the unity and will of the party is exactly like counting on the fact that the train will arrive on time or that the car won't jump the track. But, given that man is free and that there is no human nature for me to depend on, I can not count on men whom I do not know by relying on human goodness or man's concern for the good of society. I don't know what will become of the Russian revolution; I may make an example of it to the extent that at the present time it is apparent that the proletariat plays a part in Russia that it plays in no other nation. But I can't swear that this will inevitably lead to a triumph of the proletariat. I've got to limit myself to what I see.

Given that men are free and that tomorrow they will freely decide what man will be, I can not be sure that, after my death, fellow-fighters will carry on my work to bring it to its maximum perfection. Tomorrow, after my death, some men may decide to set up Fascism, and the others may be cowardly and muddled enough to let them do it. Fascism will then be the human reality, so much the worse for us.

Actually, things will be as man will have decided they are to be. Does that mean that I should abandon myself to quietism? No. First, I should involve myself; then act on the old saw, "Nothing ventured, nothing gained." Nor does it mean that I shouldn't belong to a party, but rather that I shall have no illusions and shall do what I can. For example, suppose I ask myself, "Will socialization, as such, ever come about?" I know nothing about it. All I know is that I'm going to do everything in my power to bring it about. Beyond that, I can't count on anything. Quietism is the attitude of people who say, "Let others do what I can't do." The doctrine I am presenting is the very opposite of quietism, since it declares, "There is no reality except in action." Moreover, it goes further, since it adds, "Man is nothing else than his plan; he exists only to the extent that he fulfills himself; he is therefore nothing else than the ensemble of his acts, nothing else than his life."

According to this, we can understand why our doctrine horrifies certain people. Because often the only way they can bear their wretchedness is to think, "Circumstances have been against me. What I've been and done doesn't show my true worth. To be sure, I've had no great love, no great friendship, but that's because I haven't met a man or woman who was worthy. The books I've written haven't been very good because I haven't had the proper leisure. I haven't had children to devote myself to because I didn't find a man with whom I could have spent my life. So there remains within me, unused and quite viable, a host of propensities, inclinations, possibilities, that one wouldn't guess from the mere series of things I've done."

Now, for the existentialist there is really no love other than one which manifests itself in a person's being in love. There is no genius other than one which is expressed in works of art; the genius of Proust is the sum of Proust's works; the genius of Racine is his series of tragedies. Outside of that there is nothing. Why say that Racine could have written another tragedy, when he didn't write it? A man is involved in life, leaves his impress on it, and outside of that there is nothing. To be sure, this may seem a harsh thought to someone whose life hasn't been a success. But, on the other hand, it prompts people to understand that reality alone is what counts, that dreams, expectations, and hopes warrant no more than to define a man as a disappointed dream, as miscarried hopes, as vain expectations. In other words, to define him negatively and not positively. However, when we say, "You are nothing else than your life," that does not imply that the artist will be judged solely on the basis of his works of art; a thousand other things will contribute toward summing him up. What we mean is that a man is nothing else than a series of undertakings, that he is the sum, the organization, the ensemble of the relationships which make up these undertakings.

When all is said and done, what we are accused of, at bottom, is not our pessimism, but an optimistic toughness. If people throw up to us our works of fiction in which we write about people who are soft, weak, cowardly, and sometimes even downright bad, it's not because these people are soft, weak, cowardly, or bad; because if we were to say, as Zola did, that they are that way because of heredity, the workings of environment, society, because of biological or psychological determinism, people would be reassured. They would say, "Well, that's what we're like, no one can do anything about it." But when the existentialist writes about a coward, he says that this coward is responsible for his cowardice. He's not like that because he has a cowardly heart or lung or brain; he's not like that on account of his physiological make-up; but he's like that because he has made himself a coward by his acts. There's no such thing as a cowardly constitution; there are nervous constitutions; there is poor blood, as the common people say, or strong constitutions. But the man whose blood is poor is not a coward on that account, for what makes cowardice is the act of renouncing or yielding. A constitution is not an act; the coward is defined on the basis of the acts he performs. People feel, in a vague sort of way, that this coward we're talking about is guilty of being a coward, and the thought frightens them. What people would like is that a coward or a hero be born that way.

One of the complaints most frequently made about *The Ways of Freedom*[1] can be summed up as follows: "After all, these people are so spineless, how are you going to make heroes out of them?" This objection almost makes me laugh, for it assumes that people are born heroes. That's what people really want to think. If you're born cowardly, you may set your mind perfectly at rest; there's nothing you can do about it; you'll be cowardly all your life, whatever you may do. If you're born a hero, you may set your mind just as much at rest; you'll be a hero all your life; you'll drink like a hero and eat like a hero. What the existentialist says is that the coward makes himself cowardly, that the hero makes himself heroic. There's always a possibility for the coward not to be cowardly any more and for the hero to stop being heroic. What counts is total involvement; some one particular action or set of circumstances is not total involvement.

Thus, I think we have answered a number of the charges concerning existentialism. You see that it can not be taken for a philosophy of quietism, since it defines man in terms of action; nor for a pessimistic description of man—there is no doctrine more optimistic, since man's destiny is within himself; nor for an attempt to discourage man from acting, since it tells him that the only hope is in his acting and that action is the only thing that enables a man to live. Consequently, we are dealing here with an ethics of action and involvement.

Nevertheless, on the basis of a few notions like these, we are still charged with immuring man in his private subjectivity. There again we're very much misunderstood. Subjectivity of the individual is indeed our

---

[1] *Les Chemins de la Liberté,* M. Sartre's projected trilogy of novels, two of which, *L'Age de Raison* (*The Age of Reason*) and *Le Sursis* (*The Reprieve*) have already appeared.—Translator's note. [The third novel, *La mort dans l'âme,* was published in English as *Troubled Sleep,* Bantam Books, Inc., New York, 1964. The other two novels were also published by Bantam: *The Age of Reason,* 1959, and *The Reprieve,* 1960.]

point of departure, and this for strictly philosophic reasons. Not because
we are bourgeois, but because we want a doctrine based on truth and not
a lot of fine theories, full of hope but with no real basis. There can be no
other truth to take off from than this: *I think; therefore, I exist.* There
we have the absolute truth of consciousness becoming aware of itself.
Every theory which takes man out of the moment in which he becomes
aware of himself is, at its very beginning, a theory which confounds truth,
for outside the Cartesian *cogito*, all views are only probable, and a doctrine of probability which is not bound to a truth dissolves into thin air.
In order to describe the probable, you must have a firm hold on the true.
Therefore, before there can be any truth whatsoever, there must be an
absolute truth; and this one is simple and easily arrived at; it's on everyone's doorstep; it's a matter of grasping it directly.

Secondly, this theory is the only one which gives man dignity, the
only one which does not reduce him to an object. The effect of all materialism is to treat all men, including the one philosophizing, as objects,
that is, as an ensemble of determined reactions in no way distinguished
from the ensemble of qualities and phenomena which constitute a table or
a chair or a stone. We definitely wish to establish the human realm as an
ensemble of values distinct from the material realm. But the subjectivity
that we have thus arrived at, and which we have claimed to be truth, is
not a strictly individual subjectivity, for we have demonstrated that one
discovers in the *cogito* not only himself, but others as well.

The philosophies of Descartes and Kant to the contrary, through the
I think we reach our own self in the presence of others, and the others
are just as real to us as our own self. Thus, the man who becomes aware
of himself through the *cogito* also perceives all others, and he perceives
them as the condition of his own existence. He realizes that he can not be
anything (in the sense that we say that someone is witty or nasty or
jealous) unless others recognize it as such. In order to get any truth about
myself, I must have contact with another person. The other is indispensable to my own existence, as well as to my knowledge about myself.
This being so, in discovering my inner being I discover the other person
at the same time, like a freedom placed in front of me which thinks and
wills only for or against me. Hence, let us at once announce the discovery
of a world which we shall call intersubjectivity; this is the world in
which man decides what he is and what others are.

Besides, if it is impossible to find in every man some universal essence
which would be human nature, yet there does exist a universal human
condition. It's not by chance that today's thinkers speak more readily of
man's condition than of his nature. By condition they mean, more or less

definitely, the *a priori* limits which outline man's fundamental situation in the universe. Historical situations vary; a man may be born a slave in a pagan society or a feudal lord or a proletarian. What does not vary is the necessity for him to exist in the world, to be at work there, to be there in the midst of other people, and to be mortal there. The limits are neither subjective or objective, or, rather, they have an objective and a subjective side. Objective because they are to be found everywhere and are recognizable everywhere; subjective because they are *lived* and are nothing if man does not live them, that is, freely determine his existence with reference to them. And though the configurations may differ, at least none of them are completely strange to me, because they all appear as attempts either to pass beyond these limits or recede from them or deny them or adapt to them. Consequently, every configuration, however individual it may be, has a universal value.

Every configuration, even the Chinese, the Indian, or the Negro, can be understood by a Westerner. "Can be understood" means that by virtue of a situation that he can imagine, a European of 1945 can, in like manner, push himself to his limits and reconstitute within himself the configuration of the Chinese, the Indian, or the African. Every configuration has universality in the sense that every configuration can be understood by every man. This does not at all mean that this configuration defines man forever, but that it can be met with again. There is always a way to understand the idiot, the child, the savage, the foreigner, provided one has the necessary information.

In this sense we may say that there is a universality of man; but it is not given, it is perpetually being made. I build the universal in choosing myself; I build it in understanding the configuration of every other man, whatever age he might have lived in. This absoluteness of choice does not do away with the relativeness of each epoch. At heart, what existentialism shows is the connection between the absolute character of free involvement, by virtue of which every man realizes himself in realizing a type of mankind, an involvement always comprehensible in any age whatsoever and by any person whosoever, and the relativeness of the cultural ensemble which may result from such a choice; it must be stressed that the relativity of Cartesianism and the absolute character of Cartesian involvement go together. In this sense, you may, if you like, say that each of us performs an absolute act in breathing, eating, sleeping, or behaving in any way whatever. There is no difference between being free, like a configuration, like an existence which chooses its essence, and being absolute. There is no difference between being an absolute temporarily localised, that is, localised in history, and being universally comprehensible.

This does not entirely settle the objection to subjectivism. In fact, the objection still takes several forms. First, there is the following: we are told, "So you're able to do anything, no matter what!" This is expressed in various ways. First we are accused of anarchy; then they say, "You're unable to pass judgment on others, because there's no reason to prefer one configuration to another"; finally they tell us, "Everything is arbitrary in this choosing of yours. You take something from one pocket and pretend your're putting it into the other."

These three objections aren't very serious. Take the first objection. "You're able to do anything, no matter what" is not to the point. In one sense choice is possible, but what is not possible is not to choose. I can always choose, but I ought to know that if I do not choose, I am still choosing. Though this may seem purely formal, it is highly important for keeping fantasy and caprice within bounds. If it is true that in facing a situation, for example, one in which, as a person capable of having sexual relations, of having children, I am obliged to choose an attitude, and if I in any way assume responsibility for a choice which, in involving myself, also involves all mankind, this has nothing to do with caprice, even if no *a priori* value determines my choice.

If anybody thinks that he recognizes here Gide's theory of the arbitrary act, he fails to see the enormous difference between this doctrine and Gide's. Gide does not know what a situation is. He acts out of pure caprice. For us, on the contrary, man is in an organized situation in which he himself is involved. Through his choice, he involves all mankind, and he can not avoid making a choice: either he will remain chaste, or he will marry without having children, or he will marry and have children; anyhow, whatever he may do, it is impossible for him not to take full responsibility for the way he handles this problem. Doubtless, he chooses without referring to pre-established values, but it is unfair to accuse him of caprice. Instead, let us say that moral choice is to be compared to the making of a work of art. And before going any further, let it be said at once that we are not dealing here with an aesthetic ethics, because our opponents are so dishonest that they even accuse us of that. The example I've chosen is a comparison only.

Having said that, may I ask whether anyone has ever accused an artist who has painted a picture of not having drawn his inspiration from rules set up *a priori?* Has anyone ever asked, "What painting ought he to make?" It is clearly understood that there is no definite painting to be made, that the artist is engaged in the making of his painting, and that the painting to be made is precisely the painting he will have made. It is clearly understood that there are no *a priori* aesthetic values, but that there are values which appear subsequently in the coherence of the painting, in the correspondence between what the artist intended and the result. Nobody can tell what the painting of tomorrow will be like. Painting can be judged only after it has once been made. What connection does that have with ethics? We are in the same creative situation. We never say that a work of art is arbitrary. When we speak of a canvas of Picasso, we never say that it is arbitrary; we understand quite well that he was making himself what he is at the very time he was painting, that the ensemble of his work is embodied in his life.

The same holds on the ethical plane. What art and ethics have in common is that we have creation and invention in both cases. We can not decide *a priori* what there is to be done. I think that I pointed that out quite sufficiently when I mentioned the case of the student who came to see me, and who might have applied to all the ethical systems, Kantian or otherwise, without getting any sort of guidance. He was obliged to devise his law himself. Never let it be said by us that this man—who, taking affection, individual action, and kind-heartedness toward a specific person as his ethical first principle, chooses to remain with his mother, or who, preferring to make a sacrifice, chooses to go to England—has made an arbitrary choice. Man makes himself. He isn't ready made at the start. In choosing his ethics, he makes himself, and force of circumstances is such that he can not abstain from choosing one. We define man only in relationship to involvement. It is therefore absurd to charge us with arbitrariness of choice.

In the second place, it is said that we are unable to pass judgement on others. In a way this is true, and in another way, false. It is true in this sense, that, whenever a man sanely and sincerely involves himself and chooses his configuration, it is impossible for him to prefer another configuration, regardless of what his own may be in other respects. It is true in this sense, that we do not believe in progress. Progress is betterment. Man is always the same. The situation confronting him varies. Choice always remains a choice in a situation. The problem has not changed since the time one could choose between those for and those against slavery, for example, at the time of the Civil War, and the present time, when one can side with the Maquis Resistance Party, or with the Communists.

But, nevertheless, one can still pass judgment, for, as I have said, one makes a choice in relationship to others. First, one can judge (and this is perhaps not a judgment of value, but a logical judgment) that certain choices are based on error and others on truth. If we have defined man's situation as a free choice, with no excuses and no recourse, every man who takes refuge behind the excuse of his passions, every man who sets up a determinism, is a dishonest man.

The objection may be raised, "But why mayn't he choose himself dishonestly?" I reply that I am not obliged to pass moral judgment on him, but that I do define his dishonesty as an error. One can not help considering the truth of the matter. Dishonesty is obviously a falsehood because it belies the complete freedom of involvement. On the same grounds, I maintain that there is also dishonesty if I choose to state that certain values exist prior to me; it is self-contradictory for me to want them and at the same time state that they are imposed on me. Suppose someone says to me, "What if I want to be dishonest?" I'll answer, "There's no reason for you not to be, but I'm saying that that's what you are, and that the strictly coherent attitude is that of honesty."

Besides, I can bring moral judgment to bear. When I declare that freedom in every concrete circumstance can have no other aim than to want itself, if man has once become aware that in his forlornness he imposes values, he can no longer want but one thing, and that is freedom, as the basis of all values. That doesn't mean that he wants it in the abstract. It means simply that the ultimate meaning of the acts of honest men is the quest for freedom as such. A man who belongs to a communist or revolutionary union wants concrete goals; these goals imply an abstract desire for freedom; but this freedom is wanted in something concrete. We want freedom for freedom's sake and in every particular circumstance. And in wanting freedom we discover that it depends entirely on the freedom of others, and that the freedom of others depends on ours. Of course, freedom as the definition of man does not depend on others, but as soon as there is involvement, I am obliged to want others to have freedom at the same time that I want my own freedom. I can take freedom as my goal only if I take that of others as a goal as well. Consequently, when, in all honesty, I've recognized that man is a being in whom existence precedes essence, that he is a free being who, in various circumstances, can want only his freedom, I have at the same time recognized that I can want only the freedom of others.

Therefore, in the name of this will for freedom, which freedom itself implies, I may pass judgment on those who seek to hide from themselves the complete arbitrariness and the complete freedom of their existence. Those who hide their complete freedom from themselves out of a spirit of seriousness or by means of deterministic excuses, I shall call cowards; those who try to show that their existence was necessary, when it is the very contingency of man's appearance on earth, I shall call stinkers. But cowards or stinkers can be judged only from a strictly unbiased point of view.

Therefore though the content of ethics is variable, a certain form of it is universal. Kant says that freedom desires both itself and the freedom of others. Granted. But he believes that the formal and the universal are enough to constitute an ethics. We, on the other hand, think that principles which are too abstract run aground in trying to decide action. Once again, take the case of the student. In the name of what, in the name of what great moral maxim do you think he could have decided, in perfect peace of mind, to abandon his mother or to say with her? There is no way of judging. The content is always concrete and thereby unforeseeable; there is always the element of invention. The one thing that counts is knowing whether the inventing that has been done, has been in the name of freedom.

For example, let us look at the following two cases. You will see to what extent they correspond, yet differ. Take *The Mill on the Floss*. We find a certain young girl, Maggie Tulliver, who is an embodiment of the value of passion and who is aware of it. She is in love with a young man, Stephen, who is engaged to an insignificant young girl. This Maggie Tulliver, instead of heedlessly preferring her own happiness, chooses, in the name of human solidarity, to sacrifice herself and give up the man she loves. On the other hand, Sanseverina, in *The Charterhouse of Parma*, believing that passion is man's true value, would say that a great love deserves sacrifices; that it is to be preferred to the banality of the conjugal love that would tie Stephen to the young ninny he had to marry. She would choose to sacrifice the girl and fulfill her happiness; and, as Stendhal shows, she is even ready to sacrifice herself for the sake of passion, if this life demands it. Here we are in the presence of two strictly opposed moralities. I claim that they are much the same thing; in both cases what has been set up as the goal is freedom.

You can imagine two highly similar attitudes: one girl prefers to renounce her love out of resignation; another prefers to disregard the prior attachment of the man she loves out of sexual desire. On the surface these two actions resemble those we've just described. However, they are completely different. Sanseverina's attitude is much nearer that of Maggie Tulliver, one of heedless rapacity.

Thus, you see that the second charge is true and, at the same time, false. One may choose anything if it is on the grounds of free involvement.

The third objection is the following: "You take something from one pocket and put it into the other. That is, fundamentally, values aren't serious, since you choose them." My answer to this is that I'm quite vexed that that's the way it is; but if I've discarded God the Father, there has to be someone to invent values. You've got to take things as they are. Moreover, to say that we invent values means nothing else but this: life has no meaning *a priori*. Before you come alive, life is nothing; it's up to you to give it a meaning, and value is nothing else but the meaning that you choose. In that way, you see, there is a possibility of creating a human community.

I've been reproached for asking whether existentialism is humanistic. It's been said, "But you said in *Nausea* that the humanists were all wrong. You made fun of a certain kind of humanist. Why come back to it now?" Actually, the word humanism has two very different meanings. By humanism one can mean a theory which takes man as an end and as a higher value. Humanism in this sense can be found in Cocteau's tale *Around the World in Eighty Hours* when a character, because he is flying over some mountains in an airplane, declares, "Man is simply amazing." That means that I, who did not build the airplanes, shall personally benefit from these particular inventions, and that I, as man, shall personally consider myself responsible for, and honored by, acts of a few particular men. This would imply that we ascribe a value to man on the basis of the highest deeds of certain men. This humanism is absurd, because only the dog or the horse would be able to make such an over-all judgment about man, which they are careful not to do, at least to my knowledge.

But it can not be granted that a man may make a judgment about man. Existentialism spares him from any such judgment. The existentialist will never consider man as an end because he is always in the making. Nor should we believe that there is a mankind to which we might set up a cult in the manner of Auguste Comte. The cult of mankind ends in the self-enclosed humanism of Comte, and, let it be said, of fascism. This kind of humanism we can do without.

But there is another meaning of humanism. Fundamentally it is this: man is constantly outside of himself; in projecting himself, in losing himself outside of himself, he makes for man's existing; and, on the other hand, it is by pursuing transcendent goals that he is able to exist; man, being this state of passing-beyond, and seizing upon things only as they bear upon this passing-beyond, is at the heart, at the center of this passing-beyond. There is no universe other than a human universe, the universe of human subjectivity. This connection between transcendency, as a constituent element of man—not in the sense that God is transcendent, but in the sense of passing-beyond—and subjectivity, in the sense that man is not closed in on himself but is always present in a human universe, is what we call existentialist humanism. Humanism, because we remind man that there is no law-maker other than himself, and that in his forlornness he will decide by himself; because we point out that man will fulfill himself as man, not in turning toward himself, but in seeking outside of himself a goal which is just this liberation, just this particular fulfillment.

From these few reflections it is evident that nothing is more unjust than the objections that have been raised against us. Existentialism is nothing else than an attempt to draw all the consequences of a coherent atheistic position. It isn't trying to plunge man into despair at all. But if one calls every attitude of unbelief despair, like the Christians, then the word is not being used in its original sense. Existentialism isn't so atheistic that it wears itself out showing that God doesn't exist. Rather, it declares that even if God did exist, that would change nothing. There you've got our point of view. Not that we believe that God exists, but we think that the problem of His existence is not the issue. In this sense existentialism is optimistic, a doctrine of action, and it is plain dishonesty for Christians to make no distinction between their own despair and ours and then to call us despairing.

22

PAUL TILLICH | *The Courage to Be**

The question then is this: Is there a courage which can conquer the anxiety of meaninglessness and doubt? Or in other words, can the faith which accepts acceptance resist the power of nonbeing in its most radical form? Can faith resist meaninglessness? Is there a kind of faith which can exist together with doubt and meaninglessness? These questions lead to the last aspect of the problem discussed in these lectures and the one most relevant to our time: How is the courage to be possible if all the ways to create it are barred by the experience of their ultimate insufficiency? If life is as meaningless as death, if guilt is as questionable as perfection, if being is no more meaningful than nonbeing, on what can one base the courage to be?

There is an inclination in some Existentialists to answer these questions by a leap from doubt to dogmatic certitude, from meaninglessness to a set of symbols in which the meaning of a special ecclesiastical or political group is embodied. This leap can be interpreted in different ways. It may be the expression of a desire for safety; it may be as arbitrary as, according to Existentialist principles, every decision is; it may be the feeling that the Christian message is the answer to the questions raised by an analysis of human existence; it may be a genuine conversion, independent of the theoretical situation. In any case it is not a solution of the problem of radical doubt. It gives the courage to be to those who are converted but it does not answer the question as to how such a courage is possible in itself. The answer must accept, as its precondition, the state of meaninglessness. It is not an answer if it demands the removal of this state; for that is just what cannot be done. He who is in the grip of doubt and meaninglessness cannot liberate himself from this grip; but he asks for an answer which is valid within and not outside the situation of his despair. He asks for the ultimate foundation of what we have called

* By permission. From Paul Tillich, *The Courage to Be*, Yale University Press, New Haven, Conn., 1952, pp. 174–190.

the "courage of despair." There is only one possible answer, if one does not try to escape the question: namely that the acceptance of despair is in itself faith and on the boundary line of the courage to be. In this situation the meaning of life is reduced to despair about the meaning of life. But as long as this despair is an act of life it is positive in its negativity. Cynically speaking, one could say that it is true to life to be cynical about it. Religiously speaking, one would say that one accepts oneself as accepted in spite of one's despair about the meaning of this acceptance. The paradox of every radical negativity, as long as it is an active negativity, is that it must affirm itself in order to be able to negate itself. No actual negation can be without an implicit affirmation. The hidden pleasure produced by despair witnesses to the paradoxical character of self-negation. The negative lives from the positive it negates.

The faith which makes the courage of despair possible is the acceptance of the power of being, even in the grip of nonbeing. Even in the despair about meaning being affirms itself through us. The act of accepting meaninglessness is in itself a meaningful act. It is an act of faith. We have seen that he who has the courage to affirm his being in spite of fate and guilt has not removed them. He remains threatened and hit by them. But he accepts his acceptance by the power of being-itself in which he participates and which gives him the courage to take the anxieties of fate and guilt upon himself. The same is true of doubt and meaninglessness. The faith which creates the courage to take them into itself has no special content. It is simply faith, undirected, absolute. It is undefinable, since everything defined is dissolved by doubt and meaninglessness. Nevertheless, even absolute faith is not an eruption of subjective emotions or a mood without objective foundation.

An analysis of the nature of absolute faith reveals the following elements in it. The first is the experience of the power of being which is present even in face of the most radical manifestation of nonbeing. If one says that in this experience vitality resists despair one must add that vitality in man is proportional to intentionality. The vitality that can stand the abyss of meaninglessness is aware of a hidden meaning within the destruction of meaning. The second element in absolute faith is the dependence of the experience of nonbeing on the experience of being and the dependence of the experience of meaninglessness on the experience of meaning. Even in the state of despair one has enough being to make despair possible. There is a third element in absolute faith, the acceptance of being accepted. Of course, in the state of despair there is nobody and nothing that accepts. But there is the power of acceptance itself which is experienced. Meaninglessness, as long as it is experienced, includes an experience of the "power of acceptance." To accept this power of acceptance consciously is the religious answer of absolute faith, of a faith which has been deprived by doubt of any concrete content, which nevertheless is faith and the source of the most paradoxical manifestation of the courage to be.

This faith transcends both the mystical experience and the divine-human encounter. The mystical experience seems to be nearer to absolute faith but it is not. Absolute faith includes an element of skepticism which one cannot find in the mystical experience. Certainly mysticism also transcends all specific contents, but not because it doubts them or has found them meaningless; rather it deems them to be preliminary. Mysticism uses the specific contents as grades, st_pping on them after having used them. The experience of meaninglessness, however, denies them (and everything that goes with them) without having used them. The experience of meaninglessness is more radical than mysticism. Therefore it transcends the mystical experience.

Absolute faith also transcends the divine-human encounter. In this encounter the subject-object scheme is valid: a definite subject (man) meets a definite object (God). One can reverse this statement and say that a definite subject (God) meets a definite object (man). But in both cases the attack of doubt undercuts the subject-object structure. The theologians who speak so strongly and with such self-certainty about the divine-human encounter should be aware of a situation in which this encounter is prevented by radical doubt and nothing is left but absolute faith. The acceptance of such a situation as religiously valid has, however, the consequence that the concrete contents of ordinary faith must be subjected to criticism and transformation. The courage to be in its radical form is a key to an idea of God which transcends both mysticism and the person-to-person encounter.

THE COURAGE TO BE AS THE KEY TO BEING-ITSELF

Nonbeing Opening Up Being

The courage to be in all its forms has, by itself, revelatory character. It shows the nature of being, it shows that the self-affirmation of being is an affirmation that overcomes negation. In a metaphorical statement (and every assertion about being-itself is either metaphorical or symbolic) one could say that being includes nonbeing but nonbeing does not prevail against it. "Including" is a spatial metaphor which indicates that being embraces itself and that which is opposed to it, nonbeing. Nonbeing belongs to being, it cannot be separated from it. We could not even think "being" without a double negation: being must be thought as the negation of the negation of being. This is why we describe being best by the metaphor "power of being." Power is the possibility a being has to actualize itself against the resistance of other beings. If we speak of the power of being-itself we indicate that being affirms itself against nonbeing. In our discussion of courage and life we have mentioned the dynamic understanding of reality by the philosophers of life. Such an understanding is possible only if one accepts the view that nonbeing belongs to being, that being could not be the ground of life without nonbeing. The self-affirmation of being without nonbeing would not even be self-affirmation but an immovable self-identity. Nothing would be manifest, nothing expressed, nothing revealed. But nonbeing drives being out of its seclusion, it forces it to affirm itself dynamically. Philosophy has dealt with the dynamic self-affirmation of being-itself wherever it spoke dialectically, notably in Neoplatonism, Hegel, and the philosophers of life and process. Theology has done the same whenever it took the idea of the living God seriously, most obviously in the trinitarian symbolization of the inner life of God. Spinoza, in spite of his static definition of substance (which is his name for the ultimate power of being) unites philosophical and mystical tendencies when he speaks of the love and knowledge with which God loves and knows himself through the love and knowledge of finite beings. Nonbeing (that in God which makes his self-affirmation dynamic) opens up the divine self-seclusion and reveals him as power and love. Nonbeing makes God a living God. Without the No he has to overcome in himself and in his creature, the divine Yes to himself would be lifeless. There would be no revelation of the ground of being, there would be no life.

But where there is nonbeing there is finitude and anxiety. If we say that nonbeing belongs to being-itself, we say that finitude and anxiety belong to being-itself. Wherever philosophers or theologians have spoken of the divine blessedness they have implicitly (and sometimes explicitly) spoken of the anxiety of finitude which is eternally taken into the blessedness of the divine infinity. The infinite embraces itself and the anxiety of which it is the conquest. All this is implied if one says that being includes nonbeing and that through nonbeing it reveals itself. It is a highly symbolic language which must be used at this point. But its symbolic character does not diminish its truth; on the contrary, it is a condition of its truth. To speak unsymbolically about being-itself is untrue.

The divine self-affirmation is the power that makes the self-affirmation of the finite being, the courage to be, possible. Only because being-itself has the character of self-affirmation in spite of nonbeing is courage possible. Courage participates in the self-affirmation of being-itself, it participates in the power of being which prevails against nonbeing. He who receives this power in an act of mystical or personal or absolute faith is aware of the source of his courage to be.

Man is not necessarily aware of this source. In situations of cynicism and indifference he is not aware of it. But it works in him as long as he maintains the courage to take his anxiety upon himself. In the act of the courage to be the power of being is effective in us, whether we recognize it or not. Every act of courage is a manifestation of the ground of being, however questionable the content of the act may be. The content may hide or distort true being, the courage in it reveals true being. Not arguments but the courage to be reveals the true nature of being-itself. By affirming our being we participate in the self-affirmation of being-itself. There are no valid arguments for the "existence" of God, but there are acts of courage in which we affirm the power of being, whether we know it or not. If we know it, we accept acceptance consciously. If we do not know it, we nevertheless accept it and participate in it. And in our acceptance of that which we do not know the power of being is manifest to us. Courage has revealing power, the courage to be is the key to being-itself.

Theism Transcended

The courage to take meaninglessness into itself presupposes a relation to the ground of being which we have called "absolute faith." It is without a *special* content, yet it is not without content. The content of absolute faith is the "God above God." Absolute faith and its consequence, the courage that takes the radical doubt, the doubt about God, into itself, transcends the theistic idea of God.

Theism can mean the unspecified affirmation of God. Theism in this sense does not say what it means if it uses the name of God. Because of the traditional and psychological connotations of the word God such an empty theism can produce a reverent mood if it speaks of God. Politicians, dictators, and other people who wish to use rhetoric to make an impression on their audience like to use the word God in this sense. It produces the feeling in their listeners that the speaker is serious and morally trustworthy. This is especially successful if they can brand their foes as atheistic. On a higher level people without a definite religious commitment like to call themselves theistic, not for special purposes but because they cannot stand a world without God, whatever this God may be. They need some of the connotations of the word God and they are afraid of what they call atheism. On the highest level of this kind of theism the name of God is used as a poetic or practical symbol, expressing a profound emotional state or the highest ethical idea. It is a theism which stands on the boundary line between the second type of theism and what we call "theism transcended." But it is still too indefinite to cross this boundary line. The atheistic negation of this whole type of theism is as vague as the theism itself. It may produce an irreverent mood and angry reaction of those who take their theistic affirmation seriously. It may even be felt as justified against the rhetorical-political abuse of the name God, but it is ultimately as irrelevant as the theism which it negates. It cannot reach the state of despair any more than the theism against which it fights can reach the state of faith.

Theism can have another meaning, quite contrary to the first one: it can be the name of what we have called the divine-human encounter. In this case it points to those elements in the Jewish-Christian tradition which emphasize the person-to-person relationship with God. Theism in this sense emphasizes the personalistic passages in the Bible and the Protestant creeds, the personalistic image of God, the word as the tool of creation and revelation, the ethical and social character of the kingdom of God, the personal nature of human faith and divine forgiveness, the historical vision of the universe, the idea of a divine purpose, the infinite distance between creator and creature, the absolute separation between God and the world, the conflict between holy God and sinful man, the person-to-person character of prayer and practical devotion. Theism in this sense is the nonmystical side of biblical religion and historical Christianity. Atheism from the point of view of this theism is the human attempt to escape the divine-human encounter. It is an existential—not a theoretical—problem.

Theism has a third meaning, a strictly theological one. Theological theism is, like every theology, dependent on the religious substance which it conceptualizes. It is dependent on theism in the first sense insofar as it tries to prove the necessity of affirming God in some way; it usually develops the so-called arguments for the "existence" of God. But it is more dependent on theism in the second sense insofar as it tries to establish a doctrine of God which transforms the person-to-person encounter with God into a doctrine about two persons who may or may not meet but who have a reality independent of each other.

Now theism in the first sense must be transcended because it is irrelevant, and theism in the second sense must be transcended because it is one-sided. But theism in the third sense must be transcended because it is wrong. It is bad theology. This can be shown by a more penetrating analysis. The God of theological theism is a being beside others and as such a part of the whole of reality. He certainly is considered its most important part, but as a part and therefore as subjected to the structure of the whole. He is supposed to be beyond the ontological elements and categories which constitute reality. But every statement subjects him to them. He is seen as a self which has a world, as an ego which is related to a thou, as a cause which is separated from its effect, as having a definite space and an endless time. He is a being, not being-itself. As such he is bound to the subject-object structure of reality, he is an object for us as subjects. At the same time we are objects for him as a subject. And this is decisive for the necessity of transcending theological theism. For God as a subject makes me into an object which is nothing more than an object. He deprives me of my subjectivity because he is all-powerful and all-knowing. I revolt and try to make *him* into an object, but the revolt fails and becomes desperate. God appears as the invincible tyrant, the being in contrast with whom all other beings are without freedom and subjectivity. He is equated with the recent tyrants who with the help of terror try to transform everything into a mere object, a thing among things, a cog in the machine they control. He becomes the model of everything against which Existentialism revolted. This is the God Nietzsche said had to be killed because nobody can tolerate being made into a mere object of absolute knowledge and absolute control. This is the deepest root of atheism. It is an atheism which is justified as the reaction against theological theism and its disturbing implications. It is also the deepest root of the Existentialist despair and the widespread anxiety of meaninglessness in our period.

Theism in all its forms is transcended in the experience we have called absolute faith. It is the accepting of the acceptance without somebody or something that accepts. It is the power of being-itself that accepts and gives the courage to be. This is the highest point to which our analysis has brought us. It cannot be described in the way God of all forms of theism can be described. It cannot be described in mystical terms either. It transcends both mysticism and personal encounter, as it transcends both the courage to be as a part and the courage to be as oneself.

The God above God and the Courage to Be

The ultimate source of the courage to be is the "God above God"; this is the result of our demand to transcend theism. Only if the God of theism is transcended can the anxiety of doubt and meaninglessness be taken into the courage to be. The God above God is the object of all mystical longing, but mysticism also must be transcended in order to reach him. Mysticism does not take seriously the concrete and the doubt concerning the concrete. It plunges directly into the ground of being and meaning, and leaves the concrete, the world of finite values and meanings, behind. Therefore it does not solve the problem of meaninglessness. In terms of the present religious situation this means that Eastern mysticism is not the solution of the problems of Western Existentialism, although many people attempt this solution. The God above the God of theism is not the devaluation of the meanings which doubt has thrown into the abyss of meaninglessness; he is their potential restitution. Nevertheless absolute faith agrees with the faith implied in mysticism in that both transcend the theistic objectivation of a God who is a being. For mysticism such a God is not more real than any finite being, for the courage to be such a God has disappeared in the abyss of meaninglessness with every other value and meaning.

The God above the God of theism is present, although hidden, in every divine-human encounter. Biblical religion as well as Protestant theology are aware of the paradoxical character of this encounter. They are aware that if God encounters man God is neither object nor subject and is therefore above the scheme into which theism has forced him. They are aware that personalism with respect to God is balanced by a transpersonal presence of the divine. They are aware that forgiveness can be accepted only if the power of acceptance is effective in man—biblically speaking, if the power of grace is effective in man. They are aware of the paradoxical character of every prayer, of speaking to somebody to whom you cannot speak because he is not "somebody", of asking somebody of whom you cannot ask anything because he gives or gives not before you ask, of saying "thou" to somebody who is nearer to the I than the I is to itself. Each of these paradoxes drives the religious consciousness toward a God above the God of theism.

The courage to be which is rooted in the experience of the God above the God of theism unites and transcends the courage to be as a part and the courage to be as oneself. It avoids both the loss of oneself by participation and the loss of one's world by individualization. The acceptance of the God above the God of theism makes us a part of that which is not also a part but is the ground of the whole. Therefore our self is not lost in a larger whole, which submerges it in the life of a limited group. If the self participates in the power of being-itself it receives itself back. For the power of being acts through the power of the individual selves. It does not swallow them as every limited whole, every collectivism, and every conformism does. This is why the Church, which stands for the power of being-itself or for the God who transcends the God of the religions, claims to be the mediator of the courage to be. A church which is based on the authority of the God of theism cannot make such a claim. It inescapably develops into a collectivist or semicollectivist system itself.

But a church which raises itself in its message and its devotion to the God above the God of theism without sacrificing its concrete symbols can mediate a courage which takes doubt and meaninglessness into itself. It is the Church under the Cross which alone can do this, the Church which preaches the Crucified who cried to God who remained his God after the God of confidence had left him in the darkness of doubt and meaninglessness. To be as a part in such a church is to receive a courage to be in which one cannot lose one's self and in which one receives one's world.

Absolute faith, or the state of being grasped by the God beyond God, is not a state which appears beside other states of the mind. It never is something separated and definite, an event which could be isolated and described. It is always a movement in, with, and under other states of the mind. It is the situation on the boundary of man's possibilities. It *is* this boundary. Therefore it is both the courage of despair and the courage in and above every courage. It is not a place where one can live, it is without the safety of words and concepts, it is without a name, a church, a cult, a theology. But it is moving in the depth of all of them. It is the power of being, in which they participate and of which they are fragmentary expressions.

One can become aware of it in the anxiety of fate and death when the traditional symbols, which enable men to stand the vicissitudes of fate and the horror of death, have lost their power. When "providence" has become a superstition and "immortality" something imaginary, that which once was the power in these symbols can still be present and create the courage to be in spite of the experience of a chaotic world and a finite existence. The Stoic courage returns but not as the faith in universal reason. It returns as the absolute faith which says Yes to being without seeing anything concrete which could conquer the nonbeing in fate and death.

And one can become aware of the God above the God of theism in the anxiety of guilt and condemnation when the traditional symbols that enable men to withstand the anxiety of guilt and condemnation have lost their power. When "divine judgment" is interpreted as a psychological complex and forgiveness as a remnant of the "father-image" what once was the power in those symbols can still be present and create the courage to be in spite of the experience of an infinite gap between what we are and what we ought to be. The Lutheran courage returns but not supported by the faith in a judging and forgiving God. It returns in terms of the absolute faith which says Yes although there is no special power that conquers guilt. The courage to take the anxiety of meaninglessness upon oneself is the boundary line up to which the courage to be can go. Beyond it is mere non-being. Within it all forms of courage are reestablished in the power of the God above the God of theism. *The courage to be is rooted in the God who appears when God has disappeared in the anxiety of doubt.*

Chapter 12 | Current Theological Options

Background for a Radical Theology

But contemporary secularized man makes no claim to having ultimate commitments of any sort. "Whenever anybody asks me about my 'ultimate concern,' " says a student, "I turn and run in the other direction." The same student, with considerable vehemence, expresses disgust with ". . . those whose 'ultimate concern' is that everybody should have an 'ultimate concern.' " Thus, for countless moderns, it is no longer self-evident that man must refer to some transcendent Reality to make sense of his world. In fact, many go on to say that man indeed cannot make any sense of himself and his world unless he leaves God out of account.

How then can the Christian community communicate with men living in today's culture? This is a perennial problem for the church in any age, but now it is particularly acute. The gathered congregation rises to declare its sense of unity with the past, "I believe in God, the Father Almighty," or to sing "Faith of our fathers, living still." But to "cultured" men of our day this historic Christian language is also an embarrassment because it sounds archaic and strangely irrelevant. However, the startling fact is that it is not simply folk outside the "circle of faith" who are embarrassed but many inside the church as well. For these latter count themselves members of the Christian community, and yet they remain open to the secular culture within which they live and work. And it is this openness to contemporary culture ". . . which has set the stage for the 'death of God' theology."[1]

John B. Cobb, Jr., writes:

> The new recognition of the inescapability of taking culture seriously seems relatively innocuous. The problem, however, is that the culture we are

[1] Thomas W. Ogletree, *The Death of God Controversy*, Abington Press, Nashville, Tenn., 1966, p. 18.

called to take seriously is one increasingly devoid of Christian form and substance. It is a post-Christian culture, a culture for which God is dead.

"What does it mean," he then asks, "for Christian theology to take this culture seriously?"[2] The options which apparently confront us then are either ". . . to live the death of God" or to back off from culture and seek to preserve traditional faith as much as possible from the corroding influences of the modern world.[3]

During the late 1950s and on into the 1960s this attitude of openness and sense of continuity with the secular world has been infiltrating the writings of theologians.[4] Probably Dietrich Bonhoeffer's *Letter and Papers from Prison* and his other writings have been the occasion for encouraging this new attitude. Bonhoeffer was no "death of God" theologian, but he took it as his function to call attention to what had been going on for some time in our Western world. Thus he wrote from his place of imprisonment under the Nazis:

> Man has learned to cope with all questions of importance without recourse to God as a working hypothesis. In questions concerning science, art, and even ethics, this has become an understood thing which one scarcely dares to tilt at any more. But for the last hundred years or so it has become increasingly true of religious questions also: it is becoming evident that everything gets along without "God," and just as well as before.[5]

But Bonhoeffer was simply calling attention to the abandonment of a certain false conception of God so that the God of the Bible might be affirmed. For the biblical God is not a crutch or a problem solver who magically rescues men from trouble. He is rather the God who meets man where he lives and suffers in the midst of the world. Here man, come of age, encounters that living God as he also participates in the suffering of God within the world. By means of fragments of writing and suggestions, Bonhoeffer was trying to face squarely modern man's basic dilemma of religious concern: How can men take the reality of God seriously in a world of men who no longer have need of Him?

[2] By permission. From John B. Cobb, Jr., "From Crisis Theology to the Post-modern World," *Centennial Review*, vol. 8, p. 175, Spring, 1964.

[3] *Ibid.*, p. 176. See Ogletree, *op. cit.*, p. 18.

[4] For popular writings, see Suggested Reading list.

[5] By permission. From Dietrich Bonhoeffer, *Letters and Papers from Prison*, ed. by Eberhard Bethge and trans. by Reginald H. Fuller, The Macmillan Company, New York, 1953, p. 195.

Theology of the Word

Yet the interesting point is that, for several decades previous to our own current developments, theology stressed the reality of God without reference to culture. This took place under the influence of the Continental theologian Karl Barth, especially in the thought of his earlier years. His is often called the "theology of the Word," for its main concern is what God has to say to men. The subject of theology is this Word of God. It is unique, *sui generis*, authoritative. Men must simply listen and respond. It is a kerygmatic theology that Barth seeks to express, for it is based on the kerygma, or proclamation of the saving acts of God. His is also a dialectical theology insofar as no simple formula can capture the paradoxical nature of this God who transcends our finite existence. It is sometimes called a theology of crisis because it points to the crisis or judgment of God's Word upon the world. In all this, Barth holds that the Word stands over against all philosophies, speculations and cultural achievements and judges these as well. In his later thought (e.g., *The Humanity of God*, Reading 23) Barth has modified his point of view. While in his first writings he believed it essential to stress the "wholly otherness" of God, later he recognized the "humanity" of God. But this emphasis on God's relation to man does not represent surrender of God's otherness. Rather in terms of dialectical method, it means that one statement about God needs to be balanced by a paradoxical statement of contrast. For God is both transcendent and related to humanity.

But Karl Barth's theology does not confuse the Word of God with literal "words" either of the Bible or of orthodox propositions. In this respect Barth stands opposed to the fundamentalists and doctrinaire adherents to authoritative creedal systems. For Barth the Word to which he refers is the incarnate living Word, Jesus Christ, to whom the words of the Bible bear witness but whom they cannot fully express.

Liberal Theology

If the theology of the Word stands opposed to literalistic fundamentalism, it is also a reaction against so-called liberal theology. Liberal theology has its roots in Friedrich Schleiermacher (1768–1834) and his emphasis on immediate experience of the "Infinite and Eternal" as prior in authority to creeds and dogmas. This theological perspective developed along with new critical and historical understanding of the Scriptures.

It became articulate under the stimulus of evolutionary thought, both as biological theory and as social interpretation. Liberalism owes a debt to Albrecht Ritschl (1822–1889) and his stress on moral values and the practical bearing of religious conviction. It received sharpened expression with Adolph Harnack (1851–1930) and his view that the core of Christianity is found in the person and teaching of Jesus concerning the coming of the kingdom of God, the fatherhood of God, the infinite value of human beings and the supremacy of love. Marxism developed as criticism of the socioeconomic order. But already there were stirrings within the church of a powerful movement to overthrow the uncritical identification of Christianity with the existing order. Christian Socialists such as F. D. Maurice undertook methods of social reform in England. The social gospel represents a major thrust of liberalism in America. Belonging to this vigorous insistence on the relevance of Christianity to the social order are such men as Horace Bushnell (1802–1876) and Walter Rauschenbusch (1861–1918).

For liberalism, the key term is "continuity." The theological liberal centers his conviction in the authority of "Christian experience" and the life of faith and action which grows out of that experience. Thus he wishes to maintain continuity with the living tradition rooted in Jesus Christ. But, at the same time, the liberal remains open to all the prevailing thought currents of his period, including scientific, philosophical, economic and political movements. Thus, if conflict between belief and the demands of the intellectual life arises, then adjustment in belief or in the way belief is stated is called for. The liberal spirit is one of tolerance toward other Christians. It seeks to understand other religions and cultures. The liberal spirit means humility in making one's own claims and devotion to truth wherever it may be found. For devotion to truth is rooted in the conviction that God is indeed the source of all truth and that no scientific or philosophical knowledge claim can ever finally contradict faith in Him.

It follows also, for the liberal, that there is continuity between man and the natural order, of which he is a part. Likewise there are no gaps between the natural and the supernatural nor between man and God. Thus the liberal stresses the immanence rather than the transcendence of God. God is the spirit which dwells within the world in all its breadth and depth. He is not a God who exists apart from this temporal order to act only occasionally or miraculously to effect His will for men. For all events are the expression of God's dynamic concern. As Schleiermacher wrote in his *Speeches:* "Miracle is only the religious name for event. Every event, even the most natural and common, is a miracle if it lends itself to a controllingly religious interpretation. To me all is miracle."

As for revelation, the liberal does not hold that God is disclosed equally everywhere. Rather He is known most clearly in the insights and experiences of religious men and especially in the life, example and teaching of Jesus Christ. In effect, this means emphasis on the humanity of Christ. Whatever else Jesus was, He was a man with all the limitations that manhood implies. But liberals tend to press this point of belief to its extreme. For they find it difficult to claim that Jesus Christ was anything more than a man. In any case, to say that Christ is "divine" is simply to assert that He was "godlike" or only humanity elevated to the highest point of perfection. But, positively, this liberal conviction about Jesus Christ stresses experience, decision and action rather than mere intellectual assent. Jesus Christ is our supreme example, teacher, leader, friend, source of moral inspiration, the fulfillment of all that we may hope to be as God comes to dwell within us also.

Finally, this doctrine of continuity and divine immanence leads the liberal to assert an optimistic estimate of man and human society. Man is created for dignity and not for degradation. Human society is making sure progress toward God's intended goals of justice and righteousness. Sin is due not to inherited guilt but to the drag of man's impulsive and selfish nature. The cure is to be found in man's free and decisive response to God's commandments and renewing forgiveness. This means not only man's willingness to cooperate with the divine Will in redeeming the world but also the exercise of rational intelligence in specific programs of action. For the focus of the Christian life is in this life, here and now, rather than in some indefinite future.

Options in Theology

The *theology of the Word* stands over against both *fundamentalism* and *liberalism*. As such, the theology of the Word, or neoorthodoxy, is an attempt to rethink and restate the Christian faith. But this recasting of theological understanding is not a simple attack on liberalism or a mere return to traditional views.

We must remember that these terms are convenient labels and not fixed categories. For no thinker is altogether typical, nor do the insights of one school wholly exclude those of the others. All are participants in an open dialogue.

Then, too, the recent radical, "God is dead" theologians have grown to maturity under the influence of this continuing dialogue. And what they have to say is largely a rejection of these older issues. Indeed, it is a question whether the labels of past decades are any longer adequate to represent current living issues in theology. Yet what the radical theologians do is to press these more traditional views of God, Christ, man and the world to their logical extreme.

Thus, God, the "wholly other," the transcendent, is rejected in favor of total immanence. The God who intervenes in human affairs, the God who who bails man out of his predicaments, has ceased to exist. As we shall see, God has died, has utterly emptied himself in Christ, so that now the human Jesus confronts us as final object of loyalty and commitment. Man now must act responsibily to bring about substantive changes in society. Man sins and needs forgiveness, and yet he needs to concentrate on the realization of a more just human order. This view means a new optimism. For man is at home in the world alongside his neighbors, participating in the daily life of struggle and suffering. As we study this newer radical theology more thoroughly, we raise this question: Are these theologians simply reviving liberalism, or are there essential differences?

"Who Died in Atlanta?"

The current group of radical, God-is-dead theologians includes Thomas J. J. Altizer, Emory University; William Hamilton, Colgate-Rochester Divinity School; Paul M. Van Buren, Temple University. Gabriel Vahanian, Syracuse University, whose work we have chosen as a reading, is reporting a fact about our culture but differs from the others in his theological stance. Other literature is easily available in paperback form, as the Suggested Reading list indicates.

An amusing parody, referring to Dr. Thomas J. J. Altizer of Atlanta in the form of a fictitious news dispatch to the *New York Times,* carries the headline "*God Is Dead in Georgia.*"[6] It pictures Dr. Altizer as the surgeon and God's dying ". . . during major surgery undertaken to correct a massive diminishing influence." Among the prominent men who supposedly comment for the press is Karl Barth. "I don't know who died in Atlanta," he is reported to have said, "but whoever he was he's an impostor."

Who died in Atlanta? Is this the God we have fashioned out of the stuff of human experience, an anthropomorphic God, an idol who perishes out of our imagination as rapidly as we put him there? Or is it that modern men just don't care? Representatives of the so-called death-of-God movement claim that they are not stating a fact about our culture.

---

[6] By permission. From Anthony Towne, "God is Dead in Georgia," *Motive*, February, 1966.

Altizer says it is not just an idolatrous God who has died—indeed, who must die. It is ". . . the God whom we ourselves worship insofar as we live in the past, who must die to make possible a faith that would live in the present." It is not simply our pictures of God that must perish! For what can we mean when we say that God is dead? Not that modern man is incapable of believing in God, or that modern culture is in idolatrous flight from the presence of God or even that we exist in a time in which God has chosen to be silent.

Altizer's View

Altizer is deadly serious. Yet he's possessed of a kind of exultation ". . . executing a primitive choreographic joy," says one writer, and, like Snoopy in "Peanuts," twirls around and around singing his Easter message, "God is dead! God is dead!" He means it! "No longer may we linger with the dying echoes of God's former presence; we must confess that God has truly and actually died before we can speak the Word which is present to us."[7]

A more thorough understanding of Altizer's view involves tracing his indebtedness to the nineteenth-century writers Blake, Hegel and Nietzsche as well as the influence of Oriental thought. This is a study in itself, and we can only refer briefly to this phase of his thinking. For Altizer, it is the "primordial God" of the past who is dead. The old give way to new possibilities within the forward thrust of movements in the world. Thus there is the reality of dynamic process in which men are involved here and now and in expectation of the future. The past must be negated as the precondition of these new possibilities in the present and for men's tomorrows. This annihilation of the old is symbolized as a form of "death." Altizer therefore seems to claim that the God of the beginnings of things must pass away. For this dying is the precondition of the on-moving processes of the now and the yet-to-be. But there is this "God" who has become "process." He has not died. There is also the "God for whom men wait" in the future. That God is not dead. Thus "the Word" speaks to men of present process and future, eschatological fulfillment.

As support for this view, Altizer links the Incarnation to Hegel's metaphysic of the Absolute Spirit. Spirit, or pure Being, negates Itself and becomes the actuality of the world. In like manner, God "empties" Himself utterly as Spirit (kenosis) in order to become "flesh" in Jesus Christ.

[7] By permission. From James Alvin Sanders, "The Vitality of the Old Testament: Three Theses," *Union Seminary Quarterly Bulletin*, vol. 21, no. 2, part I, p. 173, January, 1966.

God no longer is that primordial, unmoving, eternal Being to whom men look back. In Jesus Christ He has entered completely the world of flesh and transiency within which human beings live an ambiguous and impure life.

If the "God" of the past is no more and the "God" of present process lives, then there is also the "God" for whom men wait. For the world process moves toward its intended goal. That goal will be realized when flesh will be united once more with Spirit. Altizer speaks here of a "coincidence of opposites." Just as Spirit dies in the human Jesus Christ to become flesh, so will all flesh be finally united with Spirit. This is the fulfillment for which men wait.

But, once again, throughout this process of negation and fulfillment, God still remains God. Even in emptying Himself in utter sacrifice, God undergoes a kind of self-estrangement. As the Incarnation, He removes Himself from that otherness and transcendent abstractness of His primordial being. God leaves behind His celestial isolation and enters this world of changing process. He is also the same God who moves toward the eventual goal when flesh shall be negated and reunited in Spirit. This is the God who is alive. And the strange paradox is that "God is dead" in order that He might live.

The Position of Hamilton

Another writer, William Hamilton, makes the point more clearly. Does "death of God" refer to an event? If so, where did it happen? Out there, as part of some historical or ontological Reality; or within, in that part of the self that does the believing? Or perhaps in our language? Questions like these are being asked and taken seriously, Hamilton says. "I am inclined," he declares, "to avoid the idea of event altogether and to speak of 'death of God' more as a metaphor describing something that is happening to a particular group of modern Western Christians today."[8] Hamilton prefers this metaphor of death to such terms as "absence of God," "disappearance," "eclipse" or "hidden God." It is a "real" loss. No longer can we fool ourselves with the comforting thought that One who is lost will be found or that the hidden One will once again disclose Himself. God is dead!

But another theme expresses what the death-of-God theologians have in mind. It has to do with Jesus Christ. Christ now becomes the center of

[8] William Hamilton, "The Shape of a Radical Theology," *Christian Century*, Oct. 6, 1965, p. 1220.

concern, of faith, of life. ". . . The time of the death of God is also the time of obedience to Jesus." For it is Jesus Christ who remains in the midst of human existence as the One who gives His life utterly for others. What happened on the Cross? God died on the Cross! It was not just a physical death. For God literally emptied Himself in that death on the Cross. God died that man might live! Christ is now fully the Incarnation in the midst of human history. He stands beckoning to those who would follow Him. "The Christian is defined, therefore, as the man bound to Jesus, obedient to him and obedient as he was obedient."

Basic Assumptions

In summation, it is God who has really died, not just our pictures of God. God gave Himself, emptied Himself, killed Himself for man's sake, so that man might mature and come of age. There now stands before us the man, Jesus of Nazareth, who beckons us to utter obedience in the life of love. This, says one writer, is ". . . the Incarnation without a stopper."

But we need to inquire as to what these theologians are taking for granted. For beneath all this radical theology lies a basic assumption: it is that an absolute split has to be made between the sacred and the profane, between God and the world. How can we preserve this world, then, as something in its own right? We must get rid of the sacred. We must proclaim God's death. Our world is thus completely secularized, or desacralized. It is a real world—a verifiable, provable world, a world we can deal with on its own terms. No longer do we need to wrestle with the unverifiable, noncognitive "truths" of theology and mythology. For we have an empirical task here and now, where men live and history is made.

Critical Comment

This is the challenge to contemporary men's thinking in its boldest form: Can a truly contemporary person *not* be an atheist? (That is the way John A. T. Robinson puts it.) Why not reject God in favor of the world? As we have stated, Nietzsche back in the nineteenth century voiced this view: "God is dead—and we have killed Him—but this event has not yet reached the ears of man." Nietzsche is saying, as Camus and Sartre say, if God is, then human beings are robbed of dignity, worth, freedom as persons in their own right. If God is, then man is nothing, a zero. But

Nietzsche also saw the other side of the dilemma: if God is not, then man has lost his moorings; he drifts to and fro, up and down; his values have become meaningless. In this case too man's achievements add up to nothing, a zero. Man is nothing, then, if God is or if God is not! So the question of God turns out to be the question of man. Is man a zero or something?

But the modern atheist and the radical theologian grasp the first horn of the dilemma. God must die if man is to live. "If God did not exist," said Voltaire, "we should have to invent Him." The twentieth-century atheist reverses this: "If God did exist, we should have to abolish him." Why? Because God is morally intolerable, as one writer puts it. God is "the great bloodsucker," who has drained away man's very life. God as the great problem solver is dead! We must solve our own problems. We must roll up our sleeves and tend to the world's proper business and do something decisive about disease, poverty, racial discrimination and war. To push evil off onto God makes Him into a devil, and it is cowardly evasion to do this. Our concern is with humanity, then. It is an optimistic view, says Hamilton. Radical theology relates itself to a ". . . new feeling of hope and optimism in American life today." This new optimism is trying to discipline itself to say "Yes" to the world of rapid change, new technologies, automation and mass media. It is close to the spirit of the civil-rights movement and protest on behalf of world peace, singing "We shall overcome!"

But is it so? That to save man's freedom and dignity and worth in this world, we must proclaim the death of God? *Post mortem Dei?* After the death of God, what? Is faith possible out on the other side of the grave? The radical theologians say "Yes!" not just in spite of the death of God but because of it. This means not the destruction but the liberation of Christianity itself. Christianity, Paul Tillich said, was ". . . born in the grave." The Resurrection can happen only after the death of God.

What do we make of all this? Is our belief in God lip service? Or our rejection of God a flailing of a "straw god"? Perhaps it is belief in a certain kind of God that sucks the life blood out of man. These theologians challenge us to get rid of our gods, whom we can drag in, run to or blame when the going gets tough. In reply to the radical theologians we would state that there is a theism for mature men and women. It is a kind, to be sure, that will drive men and women to a certain sort of atheism: the abolition of the gods in order that God "the beyond in our midst" might live. If this God, who is Source and Ground of all existence, lives, then man lives too. The God of Judeo-Christian faith holds the world in his grasp but does not squeeze the life out of it. God ". . . uses the forces of nature to serve his purposes without making them any less natural and the actions of men without making them any less human." "He uses the conflicting desires and purposes of men to achieve his will, without destroying human freedom or converting man into a mere puppet in his hands."[9]

"In the Bible it is God alone who lives; it is man who dies."[10] For radical theology, man becomes "God" or "three billion gods." "The temptation not to accept finitude, but rather to lift one's self to the level of the Unconditioned, the Divine, runs through all history."[11] James Alvin Sanders, who cites Tillich at this point, makes comment. While admiring their honesty, he criticizes the death-of-God group:

> Only he who fancies man to be god can call his God dead, that is, has convinced himself that there is no truth which transcends man. Only he who thinks that our current honesty is the final honesty can truly believe that God is dead. Does "man come of age" not mean man fancying himself to be God? But he who knows that tomorrow's honesty will stand in judgment over today's honesty, and that the work of Truth or unveiling, and unmasking is never done, can truly believe that God is dead. "What is truth?" asked Pilate of *our* Lord. And he did not answer, for Truth is judgment, divine judgment; it is the judgment of the condemned on the accuser, of the oppressed on the oppressor, of tomorrow's discovery on today's ignorance. It is the saving judgment of the Ultimate on all our penultima: it is the silence of God's Christ in the presence of our Pilate.[12]

Critics of the radical theologians clearly reverse the latter's claim that, to preserve man's dignity and freedom, God's death must be proclaimed. For Schubert Ogden writes: "Man utterly without God is man utterly without dignity and freedom by which he can and should be something more than a dog."[13] Again Sanders, speaking as a Christian theologian, writes:

> To believe that Jesus, without God, is out in the world today doing his work, which we should seek out to share, is simply to remythologize the New Testament message in a way vaguely acceptable today. *Christology without theology is anthropology.* To those in Israel who are confident that God is dead and Jesus is his son, Elijah issues his challenge on Mt. Carmel, "How long will you go limping with two different opinions?

[9] H. H. Rowley, *The Faith of Israel*, The Westminster Press, Philadelphia, 1956, p. 34.
[10] Sanders, *op. cit.*, p. 179.
[11] Paul Tillich, "Frontiers," *Journal of Bible and Religion*, vol. 33, no. 1, pp. 17–23, January, 1965. (See p. 22.)
[12] Sanders, *op. cit.*
[13] Schubert Ogden, "The Christians and Unbelievers," *Motive*, May, 1965, pp. 21–23. (See p. 23.)

If the Lord is God, follow him; but if Baal, then follow Baal" (I Kings 18:21).

To opt for the world (Baal) as over against God is to set up a false dichotomy and then run the course of the old Liberalism far beyond anything the Liberals ever imagined. To demand immediate relevance and meaning and significance, free of the judgments of seeming irrelevance and apparent insignificance, is to make the world, as we understand it, that is, to make of empiricism the canon of truth. Are we reduced to accepting as truth things simply as they appear? Gordon Allport has recently cautioned against overbelief in Itsy-Bitsy Empiricism, accepting the immediate results of verifiable studies as truth. Luther was right to say "*Entweder Gott oder Abgott*": we do worship either the one, true God, or idols.[14]

"I believe in God the Father Almighty, Maker of heaven and earth," affirms the Apostles' Creed. It quickly moves on to the second article "and in Jesus Christ, His only Son. . . ." These two articles belong together. Affirmation about God, the Creator, cannot be separated from God's relation to man. God does not exist for Himself. There is a reality over against Him—the world; but He is alive and at work within that world. We need to beware then of a false division between the sacred and the profane between God and the world. It is a God utterly separated from His world who must die. Indeed He has never lived, except as a straw god bearing no relation to the God of the biblical tradition.

This Post-Christian Age

Gabriel Vahanian, in Reading 24, makes an important distinction. Every age is post-Christian in the *theological* sense that "every man and every situation stand under God's judgment." Thus the Christian community is always in need of reform and renewal. Our age is no exception. But this present era is also ". . . post-Christian *culturally*." This is to say that ". . . Christianity has lost its relevance." "*Theologically*," Vahanian writes, "no age, no culture, no nation, no society is Christian, just as no man *is* but *becomes* a Christian, continually. This age is post-Christian culturally in that man cannot even *become* a Christian."[15] Again the basic reason for this is that "The world-view of Christianity is transcendental, ours is immanental; the divergence is not only theological, it is also cultural."[16]

Thus the religious dilemma for this age returns in radical form: How

[14] Sanders, *op. cit.*, pp. 180–181.
[15] Gabriel Vahanian, *The Death of God*, George Braziller, Inc., New York, 1961, p. 139.
[16] *Ibid.*, p. 140.

can men take the reality of a transcendent God seriously in a culture in which men live in a world of immanence? The dean of Harvard Divinity School writes, "God is no longer responsible for the world—since he is dead. But man is." Once again, man is today ". . . not hostile to religion, or even concerned. He simply does not raise the religious question at all, not even in church."[17]

But this does raise the question of the responsibility of the Christian community itself, clergy and laity alike. In the face of secularized men of the world for whom the traditional, transcendental God is irrelevant, sentimental "religiosity," or "faith in faith," is no answer. For this too is a religion of immanence in which human sentiments and church programs, organizations, systems of doctrine and pietistic moral codes are worshiped for their own sake and become idols. God stands over against these human achievements as over against all orders of culture. But He does not simply judge or condemn. God sustains and gives meaning to existence, a meaning that man cannot give to himself. This is Christian conviction against all odds.

In the final analysis, the open-ended issue yet to be explored by thoughtful men and women in our day is the significance of transcendence. Without returning to primitive pictures of "gods" who are "existing entities out somewhere beyond the world," we moderns can grasp the dialectical polarities involved in man's existence and human history. Otherwise we live in a flattened-out world, within which no distinctions of meaning can be made.

The issue turns once more on the distinctive ways we use language to convey religious and theological meanings. Perhaps we need a new way to talk about the transcendent. Or, rather, there has been a way available to us all along, that which is the common currency of communication within the biblical tradition. The very word *transcendent* in modern usage is not a biblical term. William Hordern makes the point:

> When the Christian says that God is transcendent he is using a symbol to refer to the mystery of God. To say that God is transcendent is not to picture the universe as a spatial box with God overflowing it or standing outside it. It is to point to the mystery of God. The same is true when we speak of God as ". . . high and lifted up" (Isaiah 6:1). This does not mean that we need a telescope to see God beyond the furthest star; it means that God is the Mysterious One. When a Russian astronaut orbits in space and announces that he did not see God, it does not surprise the Christian. The astronaut forgot (or never knew) that God is mystery.[18]

[17] *Ibid.*, p. 148.

[18] By permission. From William Hordern, *Speaking of God*, The Macmillan Company, New York, 1964, pp. 113–114.

But a mystery is not a riddle or a problem to be solved by cognitive procedures. For the character of a mystery is not a matter of ignorance to be liquidated by extension of knowledge. Rather the mystery remains even after all the riddles that challenge man are resolved. The mystery confronts man as that which fills him with awe, wonder, reverence. He thus stands before the sacred, the holy, and becomes aware of his finiteness.

> This is why mystery leads to worship. We cannot worship that of which we are simply ignorant. We may fear the unknown, and we may even seek to propitiate it with various stratagems, but we can worship only when we are in the presence of that which reveals to us our finitude by revealing its own mystery.[19]

No amount of theorizing, no matter how subtle, seems capable of restoring to contemporary man this sense of mystery. Without it, the "gods" he accepts, rejects, argues for or argues against are distorted gods. They are pictured as manipulators of the universe or as explanatory hypotheses necessary to account for the existence of the universe. It may be that, having abandoned "proofs" and search for such gods as these, modern man can begin again with the mystery of things before which finally all men, theists and atheists alike, must bow in awe and reverence. It is from this sense of mystery that theological language begins as it attempts to express the inexpressible. And the starting point is worship within a community whose very existence is nourished by the signs and symbols of living faith. The late Alexander Miller of Stanford University used to say to students: "*Belonging* is much more important than *believing*." The paradox is that no man or women can completely work out his creed and then decide to join that community or movement which seems to hold most closely to it. Rather allegiance to one community or another comes first, perhaps as a leap of faith and involvement in human relationships of a special kind. This is the priority of first-order religion. It is a matter of total life orientation. Then will follow, for those who are thoughtful, the second and third orders of a coherent theology and a philosophy of religion. But as Ian Ramsey has said, "We can be sure about God; but we must be tentative in theology."[20]

[19] *Ibid.*, pp. 115–116.
[20] Ian T. Ramsey, *Christian Discourse*, Oxford University Press, London, 1965, p. 89.

23

KARL BARTH | *The Humanity of God**

Who God is and what He is in His deity He proves and reveals not in a vacuum as a divine being-for-Himself, but precisely and authentically in the fact that He exists, speaks, and acts as the *partner* of man, though of course as the absolutely superior partner. He who does *that* is the living God. And the freedom in which He does *that* is His deity. It is the deity which as such also has the character of humanity. . . . It is precisely God's *deity* which, rightly understood, includes his *humanity*.

How do we come to know that? What permits and requires this statement? It is a *Christological* statement, or rather one grounded in and to be unfolded from Christology. . . . Certainly in *Jesus Christ*, as He is attested in Holy Scripture, we are not dealing with man in the abstract: not with the man who is able with his modicum of religion and religious morality to be sufficient unto himself without God and thus himself to be God. But neither are we dealing with *God* in the abstract: not with one who in His deity exists only separated from man, distant and strange and thus a nonhuman if not indeed an inhuman God. In Jesus Christ there is no isolation of man from God or of God from man. Rather, in Him we encounter the history, the dialogue, in which God and man meet together and are together, the reality of the covenant *mutually* contracted, preserved, and fulfilled by them. Jesus Christ is in His one Person, as true *God, man's* loyal partner, and as true *man, God's*. He is the Lord humbled for communion with man and likewise the Servant exalted to communion with God. He is the Word spoken from the loftiest, most luminous transcendence and likewise the Word heard in the deepest, darkest immanence. He is both, without their being confused but also without their being divided; He is wholly the one and wholly the other. Thus in this oneness Jesus Christ is the Mediator, the Reconciler, between God and

* By permission. From Karl Barth, *The Humanity of God*, trans. by John Newton Thomas and Thomas Wieser, The John Knox Press, Richmond, Va., 1960, pp. 45–49, 51, 52–55.

man. Thus He comes forward to *man* on behalf of *God* calling for and awakening faith, love, and hope, and to *God* on behalf of *man*, representing man, making satisfaction and interceding. Thus He attests and guarantees to man God's free *grace* and at the same time attests and guarantees to God man's free *gratitude*. Thus He establishes in His Person the justice of God vis-à-vis man and also the justice of man before God. Thus He is in His Person the covenant in its fullness, the Kingdom of heaven which is at hand, in which God speaks and man hears, God gives and man receives, God commands and man obeys, God's glory shines in the heights and thence into the depths, and peace on earth comes to pass among men in whom He is well pleased. Moreover, exactly in this way Jesus Christ, as this Mediator and Reconciler between God and man, is also the *Revealer* of them both. We do not need to engage in a free-ranging investigation to seek out and construct who and what God truly is, and who and what man truly is, but only to read the truth about both where it resides, namely, in the fullness of their togetherness, their covenant which proclaims itself in Jesus Christ.

Who and what *God* is—this is what in particular we have to learn better. . . . But the question must be, who and what is God in *Jesus Christ,* if we here today would push forward to a better answer.

Beyond doubt God's deity is the first and fundamental fact that strikes us when we look at the existence of Jesus Christ as attested in the Holy Scripture. And God's deity in Jesus Christ consists in the fact that God Himself in Him is the *subject* who speaks and acts with sovereignty. *He* is the free One in whom all freedom has its ground, its meaning, its prototype. *He* is the initiator, founder, preserver, and fulfiller of the covenant. . . . In the existence of Jesus Christ, the fact that God speaks, gives, orders, comes absolutely first—that man hears, receives, obeys, can and must only follow this first act. In Jesus Christ man's freedom is wholly enclosed in the freedom of God. Without the condescension of God there would be no exaltation of man. As the Son of God and not otherwise, Jesus Christ is the Son of Man. This sequence is irreversible. . . . Thus we have here no universal deity capable of being reached conceptually, but this concrete deity—real and recognizable in the *descent* grounded in that sequence and peculiar to the existence of Jesus Christ.

But here there is something even more concrete to be seen. God's high freedom in Jesus Christ is His freedom for *love*. The divine capacity which operates and exhibits itself in that superiority and subordination is manifestly also God's capacity to bend downwards, to attach Himself to another and this other to Himself, to be together with him. This takes place in that irreversible sequence, but in it is completely real. In that sequence there arises and continues in Jesus Christ the highest communion of God with man. God's deity is thus no prison in which He can exist only in and for Himself. It is rather His freedom to be in and for Himself but also with and for us, to assert but also to sacrifice Himself, to be wholly exalted but also completely humble, not only almighty but also almighty mercy, not only Lord but also servant, not only judge but also Himself the judged, not only man's eternal king but also his brother in time. . . .

In this divinely free volition and election, in this sovereign decision (the ancients said, in His decree), God is *human*. His free affirmation of man, His free concern for him, His free substitution for him—this is God's humanity. We recognize it exactly at the point where we also first recognize His deity. Is it not true that in Jesus Christ, as He is attested in the Holy Scripture, genuine deity includes in itself genuine humanity? There is the father who cares for his lost son, the king who does the same for his insolvent debtor, the Samaritan who takes pity on the one who fell among robbers and in his thoroughgoing act of compassion cares for him in a fashion as unexpected as it is liberal. And this is the act of compassion to which all these parables as parables of the Kingdom of heaven refer. The very One who speaks in these parables takes to His heart the weakness and the perversity, the helplessness and the misery, of the human race surrounding Him. He does not despise men, but in an inconceivable manner esteems them highly just as they are, takes them into His heart and sets Himself in their place. He perceives that the superior will of God, to which He wholly subordinates Himself, requires that He sacrifice Himself for the human race, and seeks His honor in doing this. . . .

From the fact that God is human in the sense described, there follows first of all a quite definite *distinction* of *man* as such. It is a distinction of every being which bears the human countenance. This includes the whole stock of those capacities and possibilities which are in part common to man and to other creatures, and in part peculiar to him, and likewise man's work and his productions. The acknowledgement of this distinction has nothing to do with an optimistic judgment of man. It is due him because he is the being whom God willed to exalt as His covenant-partner, not otherwise. But just because God is human in this sense, it is actually *due* man and may not be denied him through any pessimistic judgment, whatever its basis. On the basis of the eternal will of God we have to think of *every human being,* even the oddest, most villainous or miserable, as one to whom Jesus Christ is Brother and God is Father; and we have to deal with him on this assumption. If the other person knows that already, then we have to strengthen him in the knowledge. If he does not know it yet or no longer knows it, our business is to transmit this knowledge to him. On the basis of the knowledge of the humanity of God no other attitude to any kind of fellow man is possible. It is identical with the practical acknowledgement of his human rights and his human dignity. To deny it to him would be for us to renounce having Jesus Christ as Brother and God as Father.

The distinction due to man as such through the humanity of God, however, extends also to everything with which man as man is endowed and equipped by God, his Creator. This gift, his humanity, is not blotted out through the fall of man, nor is its goodness diminished. Man is not elected to intercourse with God because, by virtue of his humanity, he deserved such preference. He is elected through God's grace alone. He is elected, however, as the being especially endowed by God. This is manifest in his special bodily nature, in which he of course has ever so much in common with plant and animal, and also on the fact that he is a rationally thinking, willing, and speaking being destined for responsible and spontaneous decision. Above all, however, it is shown in the fact that from the beginning he is constituted, bound, and obligated as a fellow man. God concerns Himself with, loves, and calls him as *this* being in his particular totality. In bringing into action his particular nature man, as *this* being, may and should praise Him and be submissive to His grace in thankfulness. It would not do even partially to cast suspicion upon, undervalue, or speak ill of his humanity, the gift of God, which characterizes him as this being. We can meet God only within the limits of humanity determined by Him. But in these limits we may meet Him. He does not reject the human! Quite the contrary! We must hold fast to this.

The distinction of man, however, goes still further. It extends itself indeed even to the particular human activity based on his endowment, to to what one is accustomed to call human *culture* in its higher and lower levels. . . . What is culture in itself except the attempt of man to be man and thus to hold the good gift of his humanity in honor and to put it to work? That in this attempt he ever and again runs aground and even accomplishes the opposite is a problem in itself, but one which in no way alters the fact that this attempt is inevitable. Above all, the fact remains that the *man* who, either as the creator or as the beneficiary, somehow participates in this attempt is the being who interests God. Finally, it also remains true that God, as Creator and Lord of man, is always free to produce even in human activity and its results, in spite of the problems involved, *parables* of His own eternal good will and actions. It is more than ever true, then, that with regard to these no proud abstention but only reverence, joy, and gratitude are appropriate.

24

GABRIEL VAHANIAN | *The Death of God**

Theologically speaking, every age is post-Christian. This means that every man and every situation stand under God's judgment. They constantly need to be measured against the yardstick of God's justice and must be, time and again, redeemed from their natural propensity toward corruption and sinfulness. Just as no man is holy once and for all, so also no situation exhibits the reality of God's presence once and for all. If men are in need of constant renewal, human achievements and cultural realizations need to be revised almost instantaneously. This applies to every man, to every generation, to every age. It applies particularly to Christendom and even more particularly to Christianity, especially at a time when the churches have comfortably slipped into the hedonism of religiosity.

Such a claim about the post-Christian character emerges directly from the New Testament. Quite apart from the Book of Revelation—really the first book to claim that "this age" is post-Christian—Jesus on more than one occasion during his lifetime rebuked his disciples for lacking faith, although they were full of religiosity, as Peter was when he thought that the Christ could not suffer. Jesus even observed: "When the Son of Man comes, will he find faith on earth?"

The Christian ideals of one generation invariably degenerate by the time another generation rises up. But Christendom in the past always displayed enough strength to correct this process. The parallelism between the situation of the last century and a half and that of Christendom's expansion into the barbarian provinces of Europe is pertinent. Charles Williams's assessment of the Christianization of those areas fits the predicament of modern Christianity:

> The missionaries pressed out with the Gospel precisely as the parish priests baptized babies. Christendom moved outward in space as it at-

* By permission. From Gabriel Vahanian, *The Death of God*, George Braziller, Inc., New York, 1961, pp. 137–151, 180–189.

tempted to move forward in time. There is no other institution which suffers from time so much as religion. At the moment when it is remotely possible that a whole generation might have learned something both of theory and practice, the learners and their learning are removed by death, and the Church is confronted by the necessity of beginning all over again. The whole labour of regenerating mankind has to begin again every thirty years or so.[1]

Charles Williams goes on to indicate the reason why the present situation differs from that of Christendom in the Dark Ages. The difference is that ". . . in spite of all its temptations and difficulties Christendom had really achieved a nature." It is this "nature" which is now spent or does not accord itself with the modern condition of man.

Because this age is post-Christian *culturally*, Christianity has lost its relevance. Being intrinsically bound to a decaying cultural pattern, it cannot extricate itself from the compromises it has engendered and the allegiances by which it shaped the past. To say, therefore, that this age is post-Christian culturally is a much more serious indictment of Christianity than the homiletic reminder that every age comes anew under God's judgment. The latter is meaningful only to the extent that Christianity really and positively acts as a leaven in any given cultural framework. But, today, the structures of the world have changed from top to bottom and Christianity, it seems, has been left out of them.

RETROSPECT AND PROSPECT

This age is post-Christian not only *theologically* but also *culturally*. *Theologically*, no age, no culture, no nation, no society, is Christian, just as no man *is* but *becomes* a Christian, continually. This age is post-Christian culturally in that man cannot even *become* a Christian. The fundamentals of our culture—those things that govern our self-understanding—make us impervious to the conception of Christianity.

The world-view of Christianity is transcendental, ours is immanental; the divergence is not only theological, it is also cultural. The leveling down can be seen not only in the failure of faith and the quest for consistency which accompany it; it can also be seen in the social and political realms. Western culture has evinced the masks of this leveling down; since the end of the eighteenth century, almost every historical event points to it.

Both the American and the French Revolutions not only brought social

---

[1] Charles Williams, *The Descent of the Dove* (New York: Meridian Books, 1956), p. 83.

and political changes; they also ushered in, or simply endorsed, cultural as well as theological transformations. Political liberty was and remains the most spectacular achievement of these two revolutions. But the American Revolution was also the herald of theological liberty, as shown by the subsequent First Amendment of the American Constitution. The French proclaimed the same ideal by more or less official attempts to mark the end of what might be called the ecclesiastical era of Western culture. On the American Continent, the traditional Christian concepts of ransom, redemption, and forgiveness were deprived of their ethical and social connotations and implications, and were taken over by the more democratic if not yet purely secular ideals of justice, constitutional government, and moral law.[2] Gradually, theological liberty, which at first meant freedom from dogmatic restraint or constraint, more and more imperturbably signified freedom from theology. Nor did it take long to find that concrete justice is a more relevant factor in the business of daily existence than any agreement or disagreement on a substitutionary theory about an otherworldly justice.

The French Revolution marks even more emphatically, though sometimes in a tragically ostentatious way, the repudiation of ecclesiastical authority and its exclusion from the pursuit of political emancipation and social adjustments. The decapitation of the French king not only is synonymous, as Camus suggests, with the death of God which Nietzsche was later to proclaim; it also brings to an end the ecclesiastically controlled civilization which Christianity had inspired until then. The Reformation had shaken this ecclesiastical control; but, in its beginnings at least, it had substituted the conception of a civilization reinforced by the sporadic control of various brands of theologies. In such matters the civilization built on the foundations of the Reformation was not less authoritarian, as Troeltsch points out in *Protestantism and Progress*, than the coercion exerted by Christianity in the Middle Ages. But by the beginning of the nineteenth century, both versions of Christian culture, one under ecclesiastic and the other under theological control, had officially been discarded. The ensuing expansion of Christianity in Africa and elsewhere was a posthumous tribute to the cultural significance of Christianity now superseded in its homeland. Within the provinces of Christianity a secularization of religion had meanwhile been taking place, and the secular institutions now arrogated to themselves what sacral aura they could capture from the religious ones. The Rights of Man disestablished God's redemptive covenant, democracy evicted the communion of saints,

[2] Herbert W. Schneider, *The Puritan Mind* (Ann Arbor: The University of Michigan Press, Ann Arbor Paperbacks, 1958).

and the attributes of God were now conceived as simply the highest predicates of man; but the divine and transcendental categories through which the purpose of human existence was annotated and elucidated did not expire. At the same time as God was identified with the essence of man, man himself was deified, and a general apotheosis enveloped and transfigured man no less than the tools and institutions with which he annexed the world and conquered his destiny.

In this context Ludwig Feuerbach, by the middle of the nineteenth century, could claim that "theology is anthropology"; that nothing other than the knowledge of man is divine; and that God is but a notion derived from the highest and purest predicates of man. All this Feuerbach candidly deduces from what he considers the essence of Christianity. Those that would accuse him of commiting a sacrilege he rebuffs with the expostulation that when Christianity lowered God into man, it made man into God. Feuerbach was recording the collapse of theology, just as the French Revolution had recorded the disintegration of ecclesiastical dominion over civilization as well as the eclipse of God—which became a fact as soon as God was conceived of as a clockmaker or an absentee landlord. The contemporary theologian Karl Barth argues in his essay on Feuerbach, that theology had already become anthropology, ". . . ever since Protestantism itself, and especially Luther, emphatically shifted the interest from what God is in himself to what a God is for man. Its course of development runs uninterruptedly in such a direction that man more and more renounces God and addresses himself." In Feuerbach's words: "So long as man adores a good being as his God, so long does he contemplate in God the goodness of his own nature. . . . He who makes God act humanly, declares human activity to be divine; he says: A god who is not active, and not morally or humanly active, is no god; and thus he makes the idea of the Godhead dependent on the idea of activity, that is, of human activity, for a higher he knows not."[3]

The classical dogmas have lost one of their chief functions, that of protecting man's mind by delineating the sphere of human speculation and action, even as the City of God, under the aspect of the church, no longer delimits the area of social and political activity. In neither respect can Christianity pragmatically reinforce its claim as the protector of man's body or of man's mind. To neither field does it seem to be now pertinent. Retrospectively, this accounts for the ambiguous feeling discernible in Montesquieu's ejeculation: "Chose admirable! La religion chrétienne, qui

[3] Ludwig Feuerbach, *The Essence of Christianity*, trans. from the German by George Eliot (New York: Harper Torchbooks, 1957), p. 29.

ne semble avoir d'objet que la félicité de l'autre vie, fait encore notre bonheur dans celle-ci" ("Admirable thing! The Christian religion, which seems to have no purpose other than felicity in the afterlife, still makes our happiness in this life").[4] The advantages which the establishment of Christianity had allegedly procured for the human race, and which Turgot extolled in a discourse at the Sorbonne in 1750, were no longer self-evident; excepting that, for want of a more direct suzerainty of the Christian faith and morality over the ways of this world, the idea of an afterlife was still honored with some degree of acquiescence.

CULTURAL INCAPACITY FOR GOD

The post-Christian cultural framework in which modern man lives and moves is reflected in the contrast between the Christian and the modern conception of man. According to the former, human nature is understood within a transcendental frame of reference. Saint Paul said in the Areopagus, reminiscing a line from Epimenides for apologetic purposes: "In Him we live and move and have our being" (Acts 17:28). Whatever Epimenides meant, Saint Paul's point is that man knows himself in proportion as he knows God, and that he finds himself only if he seeks God. Saint Augustine later emphatically declared: *"Deum et animam scire cupio. Nihilne plus? Nihil omnino"* (God and the soul do I desire to know. Nothing more? Nothing at all). In the sixteenth century, Calvin was even more systematically emphatic when he began the first paragraph of his major work, the *Institutes of the Christian Religion,* with these statements:

> True and substantial wisdom principally consists of two parts, the knowledge of God and the knowledge of ourselves. But, while these two branches of knowledge are so intimately connected, which of them precedes and produces the other, is not easy to discover. For in the first place, no man can take a survey of himself but he must immediately turn to the contemplation of God. . . . Nor can we really aspire toward him, till we have begun to be displeased with ourselves. . . . On the other hand, it is plain that no man can arrive at the true knowledge of himself, without having first contemplated the divine character, and then descended to the consideration of his own.[5]

[4] Montesquieu, *De l'esprit des lois*, Vol. XXIV, chap. 3, *Oeuvres complètes de Montesquieu* (Paris: Firmin Didot, 1870), p. 407.

[5] John Calvin, *Institutes of the Christian Religion*, trans. John Allen (Philadelphia: Presbyterian Board of Christian Education, 1935), Book I, chap. 1, secs. 1, 2.

Even the interpretation of the essence of Christianity in Harnack's liberal theology has two foci: "God and the soul; the soul and its God."

No doubt contemporary theologians would agree on the interdependence of the knowledge of God and self-knowledge. But they do so in a different context. This context is non-Christian in a more basic sense than Bishop Lilje depicted it when he declared: "The scenery for Christianity has changed in our time more deeply and more fundamentally than most church people realize. We do live, for all practical purposes, in a non-Christian world."[6] If only the scenery were non-Christian, the contrast between now and past epochs of Christianity would be simply one of degree; but the difference is so fundamental that it can only be depicted by pointing to the culturally post-Christian nature of this age.

This period is not even anti-Christian. If it were non-Christian or anti-Christian, one could be witness unto it, even a marytr. Any of these possibilities would appear natural. Holden Caulfield, in Salinger's *Catcher in the Rye*, reflects the true temper of the age when he remarks about ministers that ". . . they all have these Holy Joe voices when they start giving their sermons. God, I hate that. I don't see why the hell they can't talk in their natural voice." There is no correlation any longer between the Christian faith and the modern situation of man. That is why Christianity seems, in the word of a post-Christian, "unnatural."

What is taking place on the stage of Western culture is not "a struggle against God for God," to use Jasper's phrase in describing the Book of Job. In order to struggle against God for God, man needs faith. Such a struggle ceases as soon as faith dies. This faith has died from its own application. If knowledge of God is essential to self-knowledge, the traditional Christian optimism about human destiny must be relevant to the human situation. That the Christian tradition realized this is shown historically by the philosophical, artistic, and even technological reality of Christian culture. The Christian tradition understood this relevance so well that it always affirmed in one form or another, though perhaps more or less unhappily, that commitment to God implied involvement in the world and, conversely, that man's involvement in the world should be concerned with the ultimate goal of God's glorification. Man's involvement in the affairs of this world was never separated from the transcendental frame of reference in which self-understanding took place.

Today only the reality of the world, in all its immediacy and its immanence, provides man with a context for possible self-understanding.

[6] Hanns Lilje, *The New York Times*, March 11, 1960, p. 2.

This self-understanding is amputated from any necessity of a fundamental knowledge of God. It is easier to understand oneself without God than with God. Modern man lives in a world of immanence. If he is the prey of anxiety, it is not because he feels guilty before a just God. Nor is it because he fails to explain the justice and love of God in the obvious presence of evil and injustice. God is no longer responsible for the world—since he is dead. But man is. He cannot avoid assuming full responsibility for a world of immanence, in terms of which he knows and understands himself or seeks to do so. The dilemma of Christianity is that it taught man how to be responsible for his actions in this world, and for this world itself. Now man has declared God not responsible and not relevant to human self-knowledge. The existence of God, no longer questioned, has become useless to man's predicament and its resolution.

Jean Giono's position is logical: Only a human paganism can save modern man, or a deliberately post-Christian humanism like that of Camus and many others. In contrast to the Christian position which advocates, "Find God and you will find yourself," this kind of humanism proposes, as a contributor to *The Village Voice* sums it up, "Find yourself and you will not need to find God." In the words of the Dean of the Harvard Divinity school: "[The post-Christian] man is not hostile to religion, or even concerned. He simply does not raise the religious question at all, not even in church."[7] The churches themselves continue to think that Christianity remains a positive factor in the shaping of the emergent civilization. So also did the Hellenistc syncretism of the dying Roman Empire believe concerning its religions.

Admittedly, not only was there no room for primitive Christianity within the structures of the Roman society, but its very nature excluded it from them. Yet it overcame them. Christopher Dawson, believing that contemporary Christianity is in a similar situation, writes with confidence: "The same tradition [which proved victorious over the pagan world in the past] exists today, for though the Church no longer inspires and dominates the external culture of the modern world, it still remains the guardian of all the riches of its own inner life and is the bearer of a sacred tradition." He goes on to interpret rather devoutly the contemporary invalidation of Christianity as a latent ". . . movement toward Christian culture" and as a ". . . return to our own fatherland—to the sacred tradition of the Christians past which flows underneath the streets and cinemas and skyscrapers of the new Babylon as the tradition of the

[7] *The Village Voice*, February 17, 1960.

patriarchs and prophets flowed beneath the palaces and amphitheaters of Imperial Rome."[8]

There are two major differences which Mr. Dawson eloquently overlooks. The first is that this civilization of asphalt and glamor and reinforced concrete is not merely pagan, it is primarily post-Christian; it is the heir of a Christian culture and its "sacred tradition." Secondly, primitive Christianity was, comparatively speaking, in a positon of strength. It could afford to look forward, whereas twentieth century Christianity seems caught in a nostalgic whirl, and it looks backward to what is taken for a golden age. How could Christianity dissociate itself from the implications of its own cultural and technological achievements? Is it because Dawson and Maritain and Bonhoeffer think it could or should that they envision the flowering of a new Christian culture as a concrete possibility? How can they forget that all interplay of religion and culture creates bondage, and that religion is only significant to the degree that it is bound to a culture? Of course, the eventuality of commencing another interplay is plausible theoretically. But this plausibility hinges on the degree of receptivity the cardinal Christian categories will find in the structures of a given culture. How can this happen if these structures *have become* impervious to these categories?

The devaluation of the fundamental categories of the Christian faith, of those that gave birth to the Christian culture, has reached such a point that the imperviousness of our world to the ideas and values characteristic of Christianity can be observed in practice.

Medieval civilization spent itself on building churches, cathedrals, and monasteries. Today in Paris the tourist will visit Notre Dame, but he will also ride in the elevator to the top of the Eiffel Tower; or in New York, he will be attracted by the Empire State Building, or Radio City Music Hall, or Rockefeller Center at the same time as some imitation Gothic churches incongruously recreate for him a feeling of the past. Professor Sorokin claims that in the twelfth and thirteenth centuries 97 per cent of the subjects in the fine arts were devoted to religious motifs, against 3 per cent depicting secular life; and that, in the twentieth century, the ratio is almost exactly the opposite. Whatever else these figures may mean, they certainly indicate that the concern has shifted from transcendentals to immanentals.

The gap between the categories of the Christian faith and the realities and aspiration of this world grows wider and wider. This disparateness, becoming more and more accentuated, can only result in the withdrawal

---

[8] Christopher Dawson, *The Historic Reality of Christian Culture* (New York: Harper and Brothers, 1960), pp. 29–30.

of this world from the trusteeship of Christianity. A question arises that cannot be silenced by mere assent to the Christian tradition—a twofold question dealing with the permanency of the Christian religion, and the fate of Western culture. The question is this: Does the present age manifest any need for categories of faith? Or is the present stage of Western culture strongly enough mature and integrated to go it alone— after having thanked Christianity for the formative role it has played and forthwith dismissing it?

THE ETHIC OF RADICAL IMMANENTISM

The inauguration of a post-Christian universe is to be imputed to the delinquency of Christianity rather than wholly to the arrogance of science or any other movement, materalistic or ideological, that Christians would like to construe as secularistic. Even if it intended to grapple with actual and not theoretically abstract problems confronting the concrete man of the nineteenth century, Christianity had intellectually misconducted itself, and forfeited its relevance. For the sake of winning the world, it lost its soul. This constant dilemma of Christianity was never more desperately urgent than to those who faced it with the embalmed corpse of a dead body of beliefs.

Christianity had not altogether ruled out the possibility, let alone the necessity, of reconciliation between faith in God and man's not unnatural desire to find meaning in the universe and see it objectively confirmed. But, traditionally, faith in God was itself the document confirming that there is meaning in the universe. In the modern period Christianity began with a guileless but fatigued assent to the seemingly evidential confirmation of the meaningfulness of the universe and, taking this as a document, hoped to have it at least countersigned by God. God became but an appendix to the marvels and wonders of a scientific universe. The cart had been placed before the horse. And since then, those who still hold to the Christian faith have been trying to keep pace with the irresistible forces of a post-Christian era.

Every age molds man according to its own image. The mark of this post-Christian age is that it has lost the power of contemplation so necessary to the Christian world-view. Its motto seems to be: That is scientific and accordingly humanistic which, if it can be done, ought to be done, and if it ought to be done, can be done. The measure of all things, man claims for himself the privilege of being responsible for this world. But this he construes no longer in the sense in which Christianity understood man's responsible involvement in the world as a corollary to his commitment to God. His responsibility to this world is the only kind of commitment he knows and can justify. This justification follows the path of a reasoning which resembles the traditional Christian motif of a fallen universe needing God's redemptive action. But man himself is now assuming this divine prerogative. His responsibility toward the universe is to redeem it from the incoherent elements of which he claims himself innocent. This claiming of responsibility, Lacroix aptly remarks, is accompanied by a refusal to assume culpability. Contemporary atheism is largely a claiming of innocence, even as it is a vindication of humanism. It does not even bother to be antitheistic, since it does not undertake the problem of reconciling the presence of evil and suffering with the justice and the goodness of God.

The cornerstone of this post-Christian age is not an attempt to fit evil into a coherent view of the universe, but to eliminate it from the universe. How else could man's dominion over nature and its elements be concretely manifested? Man now is what Christ, according to the New Testament, was to the world. He is the new redeemer, the meaning-giving center of this post-Christian era. In Toynbee's warning, the danger today is not a reemergence of nature-worship but the creeping religiosity of man-worship. Vincent van Gogh's burning desire, though quite susceptible to loftier aims, provides a zealous if ambiguous confirmation of this tendency to attribute to man what formerly was a divine quality. "I would," he said, "paint men and women with that eternal *je ne sais quoi,* of which a halo was once the symbol." Much less ambiguously, Sartre and Camus picture man as the only one worthy of governing that which is his own kingdom anyway, especially now that God has been finally persuaded to give up his protracted regency.

Just as Sartre and Camus are aware that the solution of old problems, even pseudo problems, only raises a new series of dilemmas, science and humanism do not consider that the major questions have been answered. No doubt with a certain amount of malice, Sartre said in his short essay on existentialism that the absence of God does not make things any easier—on the contrary. One can no longer appeal to an ultimate seat of judgment and mercy to complete and correct in a heavenly realm what has been left incomplete and uncorrected on this earth. Just as it was difficult ever to be sure of precisely what the will of God entailed, so it is equally difficult to determine which image of man is going to govern man's responsibility for this world. The atomic bomb and the repression of the Hungarian uprisings are revelations of one image, even while the harnessing of the atom and the artificial satellites reflect another image. The will of man may be even more difficult to fathom than the will of God.

Modern man is in at least one respect as helpless and disoriented as Mary Magdalene, who stood weeping outside Jesus's apparently empty tomb ". . . because they have taken away my Lord." The drive toward logical consistency has not, despite the success of its logic in eliminating God, achieved consistency where it matters most. No longer in need of God, modern man still needs to find himself. He is back where he started from. Previously his quest was undertaken under theistic auspices. It is now undertaken under post-Christian and sometimes atheistic auspices. The directions are no longer the same. They are no longer transcendental but purely immanental. Their meaning does not depend on a beginning in the action of a Creator God; nor does it depend on an end fulfilled by a divine intervention. It is neither at the foot nor at the top of Sisyphus's mountain; it is in the rock's subordination to Sisyphus. In the name of the Kingdom of God, Christianity negates any self-sufficient order cozily established in a self-reliant universe. But in the name of man, post-Christian thought denies the moral and spiritual certitudes invested in a Kingdom of God, and refuses them the task of ameliorating the deficient order evolved from an unreliable universe.

This post-Christian ethic presents characteristics analogous to the Christian. Like the Christian, it is primarily an ethic of solidarity. But here this solidarity is achieved only if God is excluded, for instead of cementing it, he would betray it. Kant notwithstanding, God has become superflous as a postulate authenticating moral action. This ethic is thoroughly anthropocentric. It perhaps agrees with the Christian tradition about the universality of the law of nature; but unlike the Christian tradition, it does not regard the natural law as a prop for a theologically oriented ethic. Instead of considering the law of nature as implying the divine law, it regards that implication as a usurpation of the human order in favor of a divine order at best improbable and irrelevant.

The post-Christian ethic here diverges from the Christian to the point of opposing it radically. In the Christian view, Adam's fall simultaneously precipitated the corruption of the whole world. The solidarity of mankind, on this account, is a corollary of its common sinfulness. Responsibility surges from the realization of guilt and its forgiveness by a divine intervention. By contrast, the post-Christian ethic establishes solidarity on the basis of man's innocence of the absurdity of the world. The great difference lies in this: the Christian ethic is an ethic of forgiveness; the post-Christian is an ethic of innocence. Because in each case responsibility is the essential cornerstone, the post-Christian ethic cannot be lightly dismissed on the pretext that it is merely a secularization, an amputated and negative version of the Christian. If anything, it does not propose to be easier than the Christian ethic. Neither optimistic nor self-complacent, it constitutes a serious challenge to the Christian view and a more authentic choice in a "desacralized" universe. Jean-Paul Sartre's play, *The Flies*, describes the present post-Christian situation as providing man with the only condition relevant to an authentic apprehension of his existence and his destiny. This situation is both a result of the Christian tradition and its ultimate negation. Modern man has been so fashioned by Christianity that he can only reject it in order to be himself.

JUPITER: I am not your King, impudent worm. Who then has created you?
ORESTES: You, but you should not have created me free.
JUPITER: I gave you freedom in order to serve me.
ORESTES: This may be so, but it turned against you and neither you nor I can do anything about it. . . . Nor am I excusing myself for this.[9]

Orestes further explains his attitude by declaring that Jupiter may be the king of gods as well as the king of stones and the stars, and the king of the waves of the sea, but he is not the king of man. So far as modern man is concerned, Christianity may be the only or the best religion, but it is not his religion. He will not forsake the world in order to find the meaning of the only existence to which he is bound, as he is to this world. And by forsaking Christianity, he finds that this world contains at least one meaning—that of human existence.

The life of a religion is to be measured by the efficacy of its symbols. A symbol, though it has an authenticity of its own and therefore imposes itself, yet may die. So, also, a religion.

The symbols of Christianity are all theocentric, as were the culture and the humanism they fostered. It is difficult to make them relevant to a milieu like the present one, which is impregnated by an atheistic and anthropocentric humanism. Even where religiosity survives, there also the concern is centered on man.

But the prevalent anthropocentrism of today does not signify that men are now more egotistical than their ancestors. Selfishness has always been equally and profusely distributed to all men in all ages. A man may believe in God for purely selfish reasons, often eloquently externalized as the fear of hell. That kind of selfishness at least has lost its appeal now that hell has become a questionable reality; or, rather, now that man is his own redeemer. The clear meaning of the present anthropocentrism is this: the improbability of God is a practical fact; it is an everyday reality available to the experience of all existing beings.

This, then, is the force of the ineluctably anthropocentric categories

---

[9] Jean-Paul Sartre, "Les Mouches," *Théâtre* (Paris: Gallimard, 1947), I, 99–100.

by which this age understands its situation. The death of God is not an intellectual cry of merely iconoclastic value. Nor was God's presence ever a matter of purely intellectual assertion or demonstration. As such it meant little, unless it was translated into concrete realities and concern. But God's absence, or the death of God itself, has become what a man directly experiences. It is no longer a theoretical declaration; it is a practical awareness by which authentic existence often is measured. The classical Christian who believed in God and lived accordingly was often incapable of intellectually arguing the existence of God. And, certainly, he did not have to demonstrate it with arguments and counterarguments. But this did not invalidate the reality of God—it was no less relevant to a man's concrete situation. What today's anthropocentrism expresses is the irrelevance of God—be he real or just an idea—to concrete existence. God is dead, not in sheer intellectual scaffoldings, but in the down-to-earth give and take of the human condition.

The era of God's death may be only a transition. New social structures and cultural forces may pick up what Western culture has now deserted. Through the Pilgrim fathers, America picked up and re-enlivened the spirit of utopian and radical-Christian adventurousness when a disintegrating Christendom was torn by religious, economic, and nationalist strifes. The Pilgrims infused this spirit into a commonwealth which was all the more majestic because it implied a radical rupture with the past and a bold new beginning. Something of the sort is still theoretically conceivable; it seems, though, that such a recurrence is a matter of faith and hope rather than of an objective diagnosis, for in the present context Christianity has no strong foothold. It seems to have fulfilled its rôle and reached the point of obsolescence. Life is replete with such built-in obsolescent devices: they are discarded once they have accomplished their usefulness. And, again, the result is a radically immanentist conception of life.

If anything characterizes the modern temper, it is a radical immanentism. This immanentism is significant because scientifically and culturally as well as theologically it is impossible to identify God as prime mover or universal sustainer of the world of phenomena. Ethically, this immanentism prohibits reliance on any ready-made codes, whose enforcement depends on inquisitorial procedures or on obscurantist theologies. Consequently, it means going beyond the temporal and temporary realizations Christianity has bequeathed to the contemporary world. Irony reaches its climax when even the Christian discovers that his God really is not the foundation stone of all that he had been accustomed to regarding as an integral part of a culture he termed Christian. This same Christian is then in the position where he must at least grant validity to the counter-choices proposed by a thoroughly immanental humanism. If the contemporary human predicament is not necessarily as the humanists and atheists describe it, the Christian view is even less self-evident and, in fact, its relevance is even more hypothetical. Thus, at the present juncture, the least that a Christian can and must do is to acknowledge the dichotomy, even antinomy, between the Christian ideal and the assumptions that gird the spirit of this de-Christianized world. Such an acknowledgment, minimal though it is, warrants the assertion that the post-Christian era has dawned.

Here listed are some of the books available in the various fields of interest discussed in this volume. Wise use of tables of contents will aid in finding relevant materials concerning specific topics. Exploration beyond the reading selections included in this volume will assist class discussion as well as broaden perspectives for the individual student.

CHAPTER 1. SIGNS, EVENTS AND REVELATION
and
CHAPTER 2. GOD, CREATION AND THE WORLD

Anderson, Bernhard W. (ed.): *The Old Testament and Christian Faith: A Theological Discussion,* Harper & Row, Publishers, Incorporated, New York, 1963.

————: *Understanding the Old Testament,* Prentice Hall, Inc., Englewood Cliffs, N.J., 1957.

Eichrodt, Walter: *Theology of the Old Testament,* The Westminster Press, Philadelphia, 1961, vol. I.

Eliade, Mircea: *The Sacred and the Profane,* trans. by Willard R. Trask, Harper Torchbooks, Harper & Row, Publishers, New York, 1959.

Flanders, Henry Jackson, Jr., et al.: *People of the Covenant: An Introduction to the Old Testament,* The Ronald Press Company, New York, 1963.

Gottwald, Norman K.: *A Light to the Nations,* Harper & Row, Publishers, Incorporated, New York, 1959.

Henderson, Joseph L., and Maud Oakes (eds.): *The Wisdom of the Serpent: The Myths of Birth, Rebirth and Resurrection,* George Braziller, Inc., New York, 1963.

Jacob, Edmond: *Theology of the Old Testament,* trans. by Arthur W. Heathcote and Philip J. Allcock, Harper & Row, Publishers, Incorporated, New York, 1958.

Long, Charles H. (ed.): *Alpha: The Myths of Creation,* George Braziller, Inc., New York, 1963.

May, Rollo (ed.): *Symbolism in Religion and Literature,* George Braziller, Inc., New York, 1960.

Noth, Martin: *The History of Israel*, Harper & Row, Publishers, Incorporated, New York, 1959.

Rad, Gerhard von: *Old Testament Theology*, vol. I, *The Theology of Israel's Historical Traditions*, Harper & Row, Publishers, Incorporated, New York, 1962.

CHAPTER 3. THE NATURE OF MAN

Buber, Martin: *Between Man and Man*, Routledge & Kegan Paul, Ltd., London, 1947.

————: *I and Thou*, T. & T. Clark, Edinburgh, 1937.

Bultmann, Rudolf Karl: *Primitive Christianity in Its Contemporary Setting*, trans. by the Rev. R. H. Fuller, Meridian Books, Inc., New York, 1957.

Cassirer, Ernst: *An Essay on Man*, Yale University Press, New Haven, Conn., 1944.

Come, Arnold: *Human Spirit and Holy Spirit*, The Westminster Press, Philadelphia, 1959.

May, Rollo: *Man's Search for Himself*, W. W. Norton & Company, Inc., New York, 1953.

Miller, Alexander: *The Man in the Mirror*, Doubleday & Company, Inc., Garden City, N.Y., 1955.

————: *The Renewal of Man: A Twentieth Century Essay on Justification by Faith*, Doubleday & Company, Inc., Garden City, N.Y., 1955.

Niebuhr, Reinhold: *Man's Nature and His Communities*, Charles Scribner's Sons, New York, 1965.

————: *The Nature and Destiny of Man*, Charles Scribner's Sons, New York, 1941, vol. I.

————: *The Self and the Dramas of History*, Charles Scribner's Sons, New York, 1955.

Roberts, David E.: *The Grandeur and the Misery of Man*, Oxford University Press, Fair Lawn, N.J., 1958.

CHAPTER 4. THE PROBLEM OF THE HISTORICAL JESUS

Anderson, Bernhard W.: *Rediscovering the Bible*, Association Press, New York, 1951.

Bornkamm, G.: *Jesus of Nazareth*, trans. by Irene McLuskey and Fraser McLuskey, with James M. Robinson, Harper & Row, Publishers, Incorporated, New York, 1960.

Bultmann, Rudolf Karl: *Jesus and the Word,* Charles Scribner's Sons, New York, 1934; John M. Fontana, New York, 1958.

———: *Theology of the New Testament,* Charles Scribner's Sons, New York, 1955, vols. I and II.

——— et al.: *Kerygma and Myth,* Harper Torchbooks, Harper & Row, Publishers, New York, 1961.

Cullmann, Oscar: *The Christology of the New Testament,* rev. ed., The Westminster Press, Philadelphia, 1964.

Dibelius, Martin: *Jesus,* trans. by Charles B. Hedrick and Frederick C. Grant, The Westminster Press, Philadelphia, 1950.

Goodspeed, Edgar J.: *A Life of Jesus,* Harper & Row, Publishers, Incorporated, New York, 1950.

Grant, Frederick C.: *An Introduction to New Testament Thought,* Abingdon Press, Nashville, Tenn., 1950.

Grant, Robert M.: *The Formation of the New Testament,* Harper & Row, Publishers, Incorporated, New York, 1965.

Hunter, A. M.: *Introducing the New Testament,* The Westminster Press, Philadelphia, 1946.

———: *The Work and Words of Jesus,* The Westminster Press, Philadelphia, 1950.

Kee, H. C., and F. W. Young: *Understanding the New Testament,* Prentice-Hall, Inc., Englewood Cliffs, N.J., 1957.

Price, J. L.: *Interpreting the New Testament,* Holt, Rinehart and Winston, Inc., New York, 1961.

Robinson, James M.: *A New Quest of the Historical Jesus,* Studies in Biblical Theology, no. 25, Alec E. Allenson, Inc., Naperville, Ill., 1959.

Taylor, V.: *The Life and Ministry of Jesus,* Abingdon Press, Nashville, Tenn., 1955.

CHAPTER 5. CRUCIFIXION AND RESURRECTION

Dillistone, F. W.: *The Significance of the Cross,* The Westminster Press, Philadelphia, 1944.

Fuller, R. H.: *The New Testament in Current Study,* Charles Scribner's Sons, New York, 1962.

Grant, Frederick C.: *An Introduction to New Testament Thought,* Abingdon Press, Nashville, Tenn., 1950.

Hodgson, Leonard: *The Doctrine of the Atonement,* Charles Scribner's Sons, New York, 1951.

Ramsey, A. Michael: *The Resurrection of Christ,* The Westminster Press, Philadelphia, 1946.

Richardson, A.: *An Introduction to the Theology of the New Testament,* Harper & Row, Publishers, Incorporated, New York, 1958.

CHAPTER 6. JESUS CHRIST, BOTH MAN AND GOD

Baillie, D. M.: *God Was in Christ,* Charles Scribner's Sons, New York, 1948.

Baillie, John B.: *The Place of Christ in Modern Christianity,* Charles Scribner's Sons, New York, 1929.

Brown, William A.: *How to Think of Christ,* Charles Scribner's Sons, New York, 1945.

Cullman, Oscar: *Christ and Time,* The Westminster Press, Philadelphia, 1949.

Knox, John: *Christ the Lord,* Harper & Row, Publishers, Incorporated, New York, 1945.

————: *On the Meaning of Christ,* Charles Scribner's Sons, New York, 1947.

Manson, William: *Jesus the Messiah,* The Westminster Press, Philadelphia, 1946.

Miller, Alexander: *The Renewal of Man: A Twentieth Century Essay on Justification by Faith,* Doubleday & Company, Inc., Garden City, N.Y., 1955.

CHAPTER 7. PHILOSOPHY, RELIGION AND THEOLOGY

Brunner, Heinrich Emil: *The Philosophy of Religion,* trans. by A. J. D. Farrer and Bertram Lee Woolf, Charles Scribner's Sons, New York, 1937, especially pp. 11–21.

Chisholm, Roderick M.: *Philosophy,* Prentice-Hall, Inc., Englewood Cliffs, N.J., 1964.

Christian Scholar, vol. 43, no. 3, Fall, 1960.

Christian, William A.: "Philosophical Analysis and the Philosophy of Religion," *Journal of Religion,* vol. 29, no. 2, April, 1959.

Hick, John: *Classical and Contemporary Readings in the Philosophy of Religion,* Prentice-Hall, Inc., Englewood Cliffs, N.J., 1964.

————: *Philosophy of Religion,* Prentice-Hall, Inc., Englewood Cliffs, N.J., 1963.

Hook, Sidney (ed.): *Religious Experience and Truth,* New York University Press, New York, 1961.

Hordern, William: *Speaking of God: The Nature and Purpose of Theological Language*, The Macmillan Company, New York; Collier-Macmillan Limited, London, 1964.

Hutchison, John A.: *Faith, Reason, and Existence*, Oxford University Press, Fair Lawn, N.J., 1956.

Smith, John E.: *Reason and God*, Yale University Press, New Haven, Conn., 1961.

Temple, William: *Nature, Man and God*, The Macmillan Company, New York, 1934, especially pp. 34–39, 44–45, 51–56.

Thompson, Samuel M.: *A Modern Philosophy of Religion*, Henry Regnery Company, Chicago, 1955, especially pp. 24–40.

Tillich, Paul: "Philosophy and Theology," *The Protestant Era*, trans. by James L. Adams, abridged ed., The University of Chicago Press, Chicago, 1957.

————: *Systematic Theology*, The University of Chicago Press, Chicago, 1951, vol. I, especially pp. 18–28.

Weitz, Morris: *Twentieth Century Philosophy: The Analytic Tradition*, The Macmillan Company, New York, 1966.

CHAPTER 8. LANGUAGE AND GOD

Altizer, Thomas J. J., William A. Beardslee, and J. H. Young: *Truth, Myth and Symbol*, Spectrum Books, Prentice-Hall, Inc., Englewood Cliffs, N.J., 1962.

Austin, J. L.: *How to Do Things with Words*, ed. by J. O. Urmson, Galaxy Books, Oxford University Press, London; Harvard University Press, Cambridge, Mass., 1962.

————: *Philosophical Papers*, Oxford University Press, London, 1961.

Bevan, Edwyn Robert: *Symbolism and Belief*, The Macmillan Company, New York, 1938.

Buber, Martin: *Moses: The Revelation and the Covenant*, Harper Torchbooks, Harper & Row, Publishers, New York, 1958.

Cassirer, Ernst: *An Essay on Man*, Yale University Press, New Haven, Conn., 1944.

Caton, Charles E. (ed.): *Philosophy and Ordinary Language*, The University of Illinois Press, Urbana, Ill., 1963.

Christian Scholar, vol. 37, no. 3, September, 1955. (Entire issue on langauge, symbol, and the Gospel; see especially articles by Geddes MacGreggor, John A. Hutchison, and Paul Tillich.)

Eliade, Mircea: *The Sacred and the Profane*, trans. by Willard R. Trask, Harper Torchbooks, Harper & Row, Publishers, New York, 1961.

Ferré, Frederick: *Language, Logic and God*, Harper & Row, Publishers, Incorporated, New York, 1961.

Hordern, William: *Speaking of God: The Nature and Purpose of Theological Language*, The Macmillan Company, New York; Collier-Macmillan Limited, London, 1964.

Hutchison, John A.: *Faith, Reason, and Existence*, Oxford University Press, Fair Lawn, N.J., 1956.

————: *Language and Faith*, The Westminster Press, Philadelphia, 1963.

Langer, Susanne: *Philosophy in a New Key*, Penguin Books, Inc., Baltimore, 1948.

Mascall, E. L.: *Words and Images*, The Ronald Press Company, New York, 1957.

Ramsey, Ian T.: *Christian Discourse*, Oxford University Press, London, 1965.

————: *Religious Language*, The Student Christian Movement Press, London, 1957.

Wheelwright, Philip: *Metaphor and Reality*, Indiana University Press, Bloomington, Ind., 1962.

Wittgenstein, Ludwig: *The Blue and Brown Books*, Harper Torchbooks, Harper & Row, Publishers, New York, 1965.

————: *Philosophical Investigations*, trans. by G. E. M. Anscombe, The Macmillan Company, New York, 1953.

CHAPTER 9. ON PROVING THAT GOD EXISTS

Anselm: *Basic Writings*, trans. by S. N. Deane, 2d ed., The Open Court Publishing Company, La Salle, Ill., 1962.

————: *Proslogion*, in Eugene R. Fairweather (ed.), *A Scholastic Miscellany*, The Westminster Press, Philadelphia, 1956.

Aquinas, Thomas: *Introduction to St. Thomas Aquinas*, ed. by Anton C. Pegis, Modern Library, Inc., New York, 1948.

————: *Summa Theologica*, trans. by English Dominican Fathers, Benziger Bros. Inc., New York, 1945.

Barth, Karl: *Anselm: Fides Quaerens Intellectum*, The Student Christian Movement Press, London; The John Knox Press, Richmond, Va., 1961.

————: *The Knowledge of God and the Service of God: Gifford Lectures*, Charles Scribner's Sons, New York, 1939; Alec E. Allenson, Inc., Naperville, Ill., 1955.

Coppleston, Frederick C.: *Medieval Philosophy*, Philosophical Library, Inc., New York, 1952.

Hartshorne, Charles: *Anselm's Discovery: A Re-examination of the*

Ontological Proof for God's Existence, The Open Court Publishing Company, La Salle, Ill., 1965.

Hepburn Ronald W.: *Christianity and Paradox,* C. A. Watts & Co., Ltd., London; Humanities Press, Inc., New York, 1958.

Hick, John: *The Existence of God,* The Macmillan Company, New York, 1964.

————: *Philosophy of Religion,* Prentice-Hall, Inc., Englewood Cliffs, N.J., 1963.

Hook, Sidney (ed.): *Religious Experience and Truth,* New York University Press, New York, 1961.

Hume, David: *Dialogues concerning Natural Religion,* ed. by Henry D. Aiken, Hafner Library of Classics, no. 5, Hafner Publishing Company, Inc., New York, 1948.

Kant, Immanuel: *The Critique of Pure Reason,* trans. by Norman Kemp Smith, Macmillan & Co., Ltd., London; St Martin's Press, Inc., New York, 1929.

Kaufmann, Walter: *The Faith of a Heretic,* Doubleday & Company, Inc., Garden City, N.Y., 1962.

MacGreggor, Geddes: *Introduction to Religious Philosophy,* Houghton Mifflin Company, Boston, 1959.

———— and J. W. Robb: *Readings in Religious Philosophy,* Houghton Mifflin Company, Boston, 1962.

Martin, C. B.: *Religious Belief,* Cornell University Press, Ithaca, N.Y., 1959.

Mascall, E. L.: *He Who Is,* Longmans, Green & Co., Ltd., London, 1943.

Owen, H. P.: *The Moral Argument for Christian Theism,* George Allen & Unwin, Ltd., London, 1965; Humanities Press, Inc., New York, 1967.

Plantinga, Alvin (ed.): *The Ontological Argument: From St. Anselm to Contemporary Philosophers,* Anchor Books, Doubleday & Company, Inc., Garden City, N.Y., 1965.

Taylor, A. E.: *Does God Exist?* Macmillan & Co., Ltd., London, 1945.

CHAPTER 10. FAITH AND VERIFICATION

Ayer, A. J.: *Language, Truth and Logic,* Dover Publications, Inc., New York, 1952.

————: *The Problem of Knowledge,* Penguin Books, Inc., Balimore, 1956.

Blackstone, W. T.: *The Problem of Religious Knowledge,* Prentice-Hall, Inc., Englewood Cliffs, N.J., 1963.

Braithwaite, R. B.: *An Empiricist's View of the Nature of Religious Belief*, Cambridge University Press, New York, 1955.

Caton, Charles E. (ed.): *Philosophy and Ordinary Language*, The University of Illinois Press, Urbana Ill., 1963.

Christian, William A.: "Philosophical Analysis and the Philosophy of Religion," *Journal of Religion*, vol. 29, no. 2, April, 1959.

Christian Scholar, vol. 43, no. 3, Fall, 1960.

Ferré, Frederick: *Language, Logic, and God*, Harper & Row, Publishers, Incorporated, New York, 1961.

Flew, A. G. N.; *Logic and Language*, ser. 1 and 2, Anchor Books, Doubleday & Company, Inc., Garden City, N.Y., 1965.

Hick, John: *Faith and Knowledge*, Cornell University Press, Ithaca, N.Y., 1957.

————: *Philosophy of Religion*, Prentice-Hall, Inc., Englewood Cliffs, N.J., 1963.

Wittgenstein, Ludwig: *The Blue and Brown Books*, Harper Torchbooks, Harper & Row, Publishers, New York, 1965.

————: *Lectures and Conversations on Aesthetics, Psychology, and Religious Belief*, ed. by Cyril Barrett, S.J., University of California Press, Berkeley, Calif., 1966.

————: *Philosophical Investigations*, trans. by G. E. M. Anscombe, The Macmillan Company, New York, 1953.

Zurdeeg, W.: *An Analytical Philosophy of Religion*, Abingdon Press, Nashville, Tenn., 1958.

CHAPTER 11. PHILOSOPHIES OF EXISTENCE

Barrett, William: *Irrational Man: A Study in Existential Philosophy*, Anchor Books, Doubleday & Company, Inc., Garden City, N.Y., 1962.

Bultmann, Rudolf Karl: *Jesus and the Word*, Charles Scribner's Sons, New York, 1934; John M. Fontana, New York, 1958.

Heidegger, Martin: *Being and Time*, trans. by John Macquarrie and Edward Robinson, Harper & Row, Publishers, Incorporated, New York, 1962.

————: *Introduction to Metaphysics*, Anchor Books, Doubleday & Company, Inc., Garden City, N.Y., 1961.

Jaspers, Karl: *The Origin and Goal of History*, trans. by Michael Bullock, Yale University Press, New Haven, Conn., 1953.

————: *The Way to Wisdom: An Introduction to Philosophy*, trans. by Ralph Monheim, Yale University Press, New Haven Conn., 1960.

Kierkegaard, Søren: *Attack upon "Christendom,"* trans. by Walter Lowrie, Princeton University Press, Princeton, N.J., 1944.

————: *Either/Or*, vol. I, trans. by David F. Swenson and Lillian Swenson, vol. II, trans. by Walter Lowrie, Anchor Books, Doubleday & Company, Inc., Garden City, N.Y., 1959.

————: *Fear and Trembling and the Sickness unto Death*, trans. by Walter Lowrie, Anchor Books, Doubleday & Company, Inc., Garden City, N.Y., 1954.

————: *Selections from the Writings of Kierkegaard*, trans. with an introduction by L. M. Hollander, Anchor Books, Doubleday & Company, Inc., Garden City, N.Y., 1960.

Lowrie, Walter: *A Short Life of Kierkegaard*, Anchor Books, Doubleday & Company, Inc., Garden City, N.Y., 1961.

Marcel, Gabriel: *Being and Having: An Existential Diary*, introduction by James Collins, Harper Torchbooks, Harper & Row, Publishers, New York, 1965.

————: *The Mystery of Being: Gifford Lectures*, Gateway Editions, Henry Regnery Company, Chicago, 1951, vols. I, II.

————: *The Philosophy of Existentialism*, trans. by Manya Harari, The Citadel Press, New York, 1966.

Sartre, Jean-Paul: *Being and Nothingness: An Essay on Phenomenological Ontology*, trans. with an introduction by Hazel Barnes, Washington Square Press, Pocket Books, Inc., New York, 1966.

————: *The Emotions: Outline of a Theory*, trans. by Bernard Frechtman, Philosophical Library, Inc., New York, 1948.

————: *Existentialism*, trans. by Bernard Frechtman, Philosophical Library, Inc., New York, 1947.

Tillich, Paul: *The Courage to Be*, Yale University Press, New Haven, Conn., 1952.

————: *Dynamics of Faith*, Harper Torchbooks, Harper & Row, Publishers, 1957.

————: *Systematic Theology*, The University of Chicago Press, Chicago, vol. I, 1951, vol. II, 1957, vol. III, 1963.

————: *Theology of Culture*, ed. by Robert C. Kimball, Oxford University Press, Fair Lawn, N.J., 1959.

CHAPTER 12. CURRENT THEOLOGICAL OPTIONS

Surveys of Protestant Thought

Bainton, Roland H.: *The Reformation of the Sixteenth Century*, Beacon Press, Boston, 1952.

Brown, Robert McAfee: *The Spirit of Protestantism*, Oxford University Press, Fair Lawn, N.J., 1965.

Dillenberger, John, and Claude Welch: *Protestant Christianity*, Charles Scribner's Sons, New York, 1958.

Fosdick, Harry Emerson: *Great Voices of the Reformation: An Anthology*, Random House, Inc., New York, 1952.

Hudson, Winthrop S.: *Religion in America*, Charles Scribner's Sons, New York, 1965.

Macquarrie, John: *Principles of Christian Theology*, Charles Scribner's Sons, New York, 1966.

————: *Twentieth-century Religious Thought*, Harper & Row, Publishers, Incorporated, New York, 1963.

Pauck, Wilhelm: *The Heritage of the Reformation*, The Free Press of Glencoe, New York, 1950.

Thomas, George F.: *Religious Philosophies of the West*, Charles Scribner's Sons, New York, 1965.

Theology of the Word

Aulen, Gustof Emanuel Hildebrand: *Christus Victor*, The Macmillan Company, New York, 1937.

————: *The Faith of the Christian Church*, Muhlenberg Press, Philadelphia, 1948.

Barth, Karl: *Church Dogmatics: A Selection*, Harper Torchbooks, Harper & Row, Publishers, New York, 1962.

————: *Credo*, Charles Scribner's Sons, New York, 1936.

————: *Dogmatics in Outline*, Harper Torchbooks, Harper & Row, Publishers, New York, 1959.

————: *The Epistle to the Romans*, trans. from 6th ed. by E. C. Hoskyns, Oxford University Press, London, 1933.

————: *From Rousseau to Ritschl*, The Student Christian Movement Press, London; American ed., *Protestant Thought from Rousseau to Ritschl*, Harper & Row, Publishers, Incorporated, 1959.

————: *The Humanity of God*, The John Knox Press, Richmond, Va., 1960.

————: *The Knowledge of God and the Service of God: Gifford Lectures*, Charles Scribner's Sons, New York, 1939; Alec E. Allenson, Inc., Naperville, Ill., 1955.

————: *The Word of God and the Word of Man*, trans. by Douglas Horton, Harper Torchbooks, Harper & Row, Publishers, New York, 1957.

Bonhoeffer, Dietrich: *The Cost of Discipleship*, rev. ed., The Macmillan Company, New York, 1965.

————: *Ethics*, ed. by Eberhard Bethge, The Macmillan Company, New York, 1965.

————: *Prisoner for God: Letters and Papers from Prison*, The Macmillan Company, New York, 1962.

Brunner, Heinrich Emil: *The Divine-Human Encounter*, The Westminster Press, Philadelphia, 1943.

————: *The Divine Imperative*, The Westminster Press, Philadelphia, 1947.

————: *The Mediator*, The Westminster Press, Philadelphia, 1947.

————: *Revelation and Reason*, The Westminster Press, Philadelphia, 1946.

Cullmann, Oscar: *Christ and Time*, The Westminster Press, Philadelphia, 1949.

Nygren, Anders Theodor Samuel: *Agape and Eros*, trans. by P. S. Watson, The Westminster Press, Philadelphia, 1953.

Liberal Theology

Cauthen, Kenneth: *The Impact of American Religious Liberalism*, Harper & Row, Publishers, Incorporated, New York, 1962.

DeWolf, L. Harold: *The Theology of the Living Church*, Harper & Row, Publishers, Incorporated, New York, 1953.

Harnack, Adolf: *What Is Christianity?* G. P. Putnam's Sons, New York, 1901.

Horton, Walter Marshall: *Christian Theology: An Ecumenical Approach*, Harper & Row, Publishers, Incorporated, New York, 1955.

Niebuhr, H. Richard: *The Kingdom of God in America*, Harper & Row, Publishers, Incorporated, New York, 1937.

Rauschenbusch, W.: *A Theology for the Social Gospel*, The Macmillan Company, New York, 1919.

Ritschl, Albrecht: *The Christian Doctrine of Justification and Reconciliation*, T. & T. Clark, Edinburgh, 1902.

Schleiermacher, Friedrich: *The Christian Faith*, Charles Scribner's Sons, New York, 1948.

————: *Speeches on Religion*, Kegan Paul, Trench, Trübner & Co., Ltd., London, 1893.

Van Dusen, Henry P.: *The Vindication of Liberal Theology*, Charles Scribner's Sons, New York, 1963.

Conservative Theology

Carnell, John E.: *The Case for Orthodox Theology*, The Westminster Press, Philadelphia, 1959.

Warfield, Benjamin B.: *The Inspiration and Authority of the Bible,* 2d ed., Presbyterian & Reformed Publishing Co., Nutley, N.J., 1948.

Postliberal Theology

Baillie, D. M. *God Was in Christ,* Charles Scribner's Sons, New York, 1948.

————: *The Idea of Revelation in Recent Thought,* Columbia University Press, New York, 1964.

Baillie, John: *Our Knowledge of God,* Charles Scribner's Sons, New York, 1939.

————: *The Sense of the Presence of God: Gifford Lectures,* Charles Scribner's Sons, New York, 1962.

Niebuhr, H. Richard: *Christ and Culture,* Harper Torchbooks, Harper & Row, Publishers, New York, 1956.

————: *The Meaning of Revelation,* The Macmillan Company, New York, 1941.

Niebuhr, Reinhold: *Beyond Tragedy,* Charles Scribner's Sons, New York, 1937.

————: *Faith and History,* Charles Scribner's Sons, New York, 1949.

————: *The Nature and Destiny of Man,* Charles Scribner's Sons, New York, 1941, vols. I and II.

Roman Catholic Theology

Abbott, Walter M., S.J. (general ed.): *The Documents of Vatican II,* Guild Press, America Press, Association Press, New York, 1966.

Adam, Karl: *The Spirit of Catholicism,* Doubleday & Company, Inc., Garden City, N.Y., 1959.

Brown, Robert McAfee: *Observer in Understanding Rome: A Protestant Report on the Vatican Council,* Doubleday & Company, Inc., Garden City, N.Y., 1964.

Caponigri, A. Robert (ed.): *Modern Catholic Thinkers,* Harper Torchbooks, Harper & Row, Publishers, New York, 1965, vols. I–III.

Coppleston, Frederick C.: *Medieval Philosophy,* Harper Torchbooks, Harper & Row, Publishers, New York, 1961, vols. I and II.

Farrer, Austin M.: *Finite and Infinite,* 2d ed., Alec Allenson, Inc., Naperville, Ill., 1964.

————: *The Glass of Vision,* Alec E. Allenson, Inc., Naperville, Ill., 1948.

Gilson, Étienne: *History of Christian Philosophy,* Random House, Inc., New York, 1955.

————: *The Philosophy of Thomas Aquinas*, Random House, Inc., New York, 1956.

————: *The Spirit of Medieval Philosophy: Gifford Lectures*, Charles Scribner's Sons, New York, 1936.

Maritain, Jacques: *The Range of Reason*, Charles Scribner's Sons, New York, 1952.

Teilhard de Chardin, Pierre: *The Phenomenon of Man*, Harper Torchbooks, Harper & Row, Publishers, New York, 1959.

Radical Theology

Altizer, Thomas J. J.: *The Gospel of Christain Atheism*, The Westminster Press, Philadelphia, 1954.

————: *Mircea Eliade and the Dialectic of the Sacred*, The Westminster Press, Philadelphia, 1964.

————: "Nirvana and the Kingdom of God," in Martin E. Marty and D. G. Peerman (eds.), *New Theology I*, The Macmillan Company, New York, 1964.

———— and William Hamilton: *Radical Theology and the Death of God*, The Bobbs-Merrill Company, Inc., Indianapolis,, 1966.

Callahan, Daniel: "Comment: Is God Dead?" *Commonweal*, Nov. 5, 1965.

Cobb, John B., Jr.: "From Christian Theology to the Post-modern World," *Centennial Review*, vol. 8, Spring, 1964.

Hamilton, William: "The Death of God Theology," *Christian Scholar*, vol. 48, 1965.

Vahanian, Gabriel: *The Death of God: The Culture of Our Post-Christian Era*, George Braziller, Inc., New York, 1961.

————: *Wait without Idols*, George Braziller, Inc., New York, 1964.

Van Buren, Paul M.: *The Secular Meaning of the Gospel: An Original Inquiry*, The Macmillan Company, New York, 1963.

New Reformation Theology

Bergar, Peter: *Noise of Solemn Assemblies*, Doubleday & Company Inc., Garden City, N.Y., 1961.

Chadwick, Owen: *The Reformation*, Penguin Books, Inc., Baltimore, 1964.

Cox, Harvey: *The Secular City*, The Macmillan Company, New York, 1965.

Dewart, Leslie: *The Future of Belief: Theism in a World Come of Age*, Herder and Herder, Inc., New York, 1966.

Edwards, David L. (ed.): *Honest to God Debate*, The Westminster Press, Philadelphia, 1963.

Gibbs, Mark, and T. Ralph Morton: *God's Frozen People*, The Westminster Press, Philadelphia, 1965.

Kraemer, H.: *A Theology of the Laity*, Lutterworth Press, London, 1958.

Marty, Martin E.: *The Place of Bonhoeffer*, Association Press, New York, 1962.

Robinson, John A. T.: *Honest to God*, The Westminster Press, Philadelphia, 1963.

————: *The New Reformation*, The Westminster Press, Philadelphia, 1965.